ARCHER'S DIGEST

5th Edition

Edited by
Roger Combs

DBI BOOKS, INC.

About the Cover

A pair of Browning Compound Bows along with Easton Arrows and accessories are featured on this 5th Edition of ARCHER'S DIGEST. On the left, in red, is the Browning Pro 300 equipped with their Ultimate Overdraw system and an Easton Stabilizer. The blue bow, on the right, is Browning's Pro 300SD equipped with a Browning Target Sight and an Easton Stabilizer. Photo by John Hanusin.

Editorial Director
Jack Lewis

Art Director
Sonya Kaiser

Artists
Gary Duck
Brad Wood

Production Coordinator
Nadine Symons

Copy Editor
Kathryn Coulter

Photo Service
Lori Arsenault

Lithographic Service
Gallant Graphics

Technical Advisors:
Sam Fadala
Bob Grewell
Leroy Janulewicz
C.R. Learn
Emery Loiselle
Mark Thiffault
Russ Thurman

Publisher
Sheldon Factor

Produced by

GALLANT CHARGER

OUTDOOR GROUP

ISBN 0-87349-114-9

Library of Congress Catalog Card Number 77-148722

CONTENTS

INTRODUCTION

Much has happened to archery in the five years since we worked on the Fourth Edition of ARCHER'S DIGEST. New developments, new materials, new technology and new products by the hundreds have come along; some have gone along into obscurity.

Bowhunting continues to grow in popularity throughout North America and through many countries of Europe and Africa. Hunting is the basis of the growth of archery everywhere.

There is an increase in participation in target archery, especially field archery and all types of realistic three-dimensional target shooting. Some aspects of the sport have seen dramatic growth in popularity. Some tournaments are offering tens of thousands of dollars in cash and product prizes for competitors. These shoots have become big business.

Through it all, the traditional aspects of this ancient activity continue to draw adherents; those who prefer to shoot only longbows and make their own wooden arrows.

There is room for everyone, young or old, male or female. I hope one of them will be you. — *Roger Combs*

BEGINNING ARCHERY

To Learn This New Skill, One Needs A Stick, A String, Some Arrows — And A Coach

ARCHERY, as a sport, may be as old as the invention itself. It is certainly a popular pastime in the Twentieth Century over most of the world. Millions of adults and children shoot arrows recreationally, supporting a manufacturing industry which has flourished, particularly since the invention of the compound bow.

Archery, has found favor in the Olympic Games, where it was popular shortly after the turn of the century, later dropped, then re-admitted in 1972. Most of the gold medals have been won by the United States; the publicity surrounding it probably has added to the acceptance of the sport. The vast majority of archers, however, do not limit themselves to paper targets. They are bowhunters.

Many archers are introduced to the sport while in Scouts, 4-H, Campfire or other youth groups. Others receive beginning instruction with bows and arrows in school athletic programs. "Oh, we had that when I was in school," is a common remark. Unfortunately, most have not continued their relationship with the sport.

Many organizations have active, aggressive programs to introduce, reintroduce and extend interest in archery to young and old through schools, clubs and gatherings. Several of the larger archery manufacturers actively seek to expose thousands of persons to the sport of archery, especially to hunters who may become bowhunters. A number of individuals — trick shot artist Bob Markworth and professional archer Ann Clark are two — present aspects of the sport to school assemblies and youth group meetings around North America. Many of these programs are successful in bringing new archers to the sport.

Any gathering of archers draws crowds of onlookers who sometimes express an interest in the sport. Tournaments, especially the 3-D target contests, attract potential archers. Some of these archery contests have thousands of competitors and spectators, because of the challenge,

Target archers from many places and with many skill levels may be seen at large tournaments such as the annual Pete Shepley Desert Shoot-Out in Tucson, Arizona. Here, the pace is relaxed and all types of equipment are in evidence.

Beginners need help, encouragement in their first efforts. Equipment should be basic, uncomplicated for results.

The basic school bow is made of fiberglass, has a handle which will function for right- or left-handed shooting.

This lad needs some help on bow arm position, but his follow-through looks good. Older boys await their turn.

Southern California's high desert foothills offer plenty of shooting space, easily reached as a place to practice.

the excitement and variety of the terrain or targets and the potential for top archers to win thousands of dollars in prizes.

Large public shows such as the National Archery Show, held in Las Vegas early in each year; Pete Shepley's Desert Shoot-Out archery tournament in Tucson, Arizona, each May; the Anderson Archery International Bowhunters Clinic in Grand Ledge, Michigan, each mid-June; and dozens of other hunting or outdoor shows throughout the country offer opportunities to introduce new people to the sport.

The Anderson Clinic, for instance, regularly draws more than 20,000 persons who gladly pay an entry fee into the clinic grounds. Other outdoor hunting and fishing shows attract even more consumers, but their interests are more diverse, with only a few committed to archery.

With an interest awakened in archery, where do you go from here? How do you learn the sport? Who will teach you the basics?

As mentioned, many of us count our first interest in archery from school days. Depending on one's age, financial status, location and time constraints, possible answers

lie in school, commuity college or adult education courses. Budget shortages are placing added burdens on many school districts, but some community colleges around the country have active adult eduation classes available evenings or weekends offering archery instruction. Many of these same schools also have viable collegiate athletic programs which include archery. Student fees are usually low and instruction professional; a good place to start.

Formal courses at public schools usually are given to mixed age groups with varying degrees of skills or previous experience. Lessons are not, of course, private, and personal instruction may be limited by the number of students enrolled. But, if available, an archery class is an excellent way to learn the basics and begin to develop skills in the sport. The most important asset offered by schools is an experienced coach and teacher. The coach will be able to detect and correct early flaws in technique before they develop into habits that have to be re-learned.

A coach or teacher is essential for the beginning archer. Another observer, even one who may not know a great deal about archery, must observe beginning techniques to offer corrections and suggestions for improvements. The stu-

This group of boys is part of the National 4-H program, involved in projects such as archery, outdoor adventures.

dent will seldom, if ever, be aware of his or her own mistakes.

Another possible and common starting place is the archery pro shop; the local retailer with the skills to teach basic archery. Many archers, especially bowhunters, get their initial training from the same store where bows and arrows were purchased. The pro shop operator is interested in a successful and happy customer, and will see that the rookie gets off to a good start. Initial equipment tuning is usually done at the pro shop.

The professional archery store operator is interested in providing the best possible service, satisfying his customer — and in selling his products. To compete with the larger discount department stores and mail order houses, he has the one product the others cannot provide: complete personal service. The pro shop can provide sales, tuning and coaching on a one-on-one basis. Such services are just plain good business, as well as a benefit to local archers.

Some pro shops have small archery ranges inside or just outside the shop building. Such ranges offer potential customers a chance to try out the bows and equipment before the sale. Shooting on site makes tuning easier. Many of these ranges also are utilized by the local archery or bowhunting club for regular competition and even organizational meetings.

Club tournaments are excellent opportunities for beginning — and even experienced — archers to obtain advice and coaching. Competition is not so keen that friendly help is not available when needed. Not only does the archer have a chance to learn and improve skills, but he or she can observe others, noting their techniques and, yes, their mis-

takes. In some parts of the country, most practice can be outdoors, but in most locations, an indoor range is a necessity.

Archery clubs often are sponsored or, at least, associated with a pro shop, and the shop owner is a good source as to where to locate other club members. Usually, a contact name and number is posted at the range to accommodate prospective new members.

If the new archer is young, youth groups such as the Boy and Girl Scouts and 4-H Clubs are excellent places to learn archery basics. These organizations have professionally prepared lesson plans and guides available, so the instruction offered is complete and is presented in a logical, progressive manner. The volunteer instructors are usually persons with an interest in the sport, anxious to pass on their knowledge to youngsters.

Some youth groups and schools have their own equipment and supplies to be used by students, saving a lot of dollars. The bows usually are simple straight longbows made of fiberglass or fiberglass and wood laminate. Draw weight — the amount of force necessary to draw the arrow back across the bow a specific distance (usually twenty-eight inches) — is kept low. Draw weights often, fifteen to twenty-five pounds are common "school bow" specifications.

Low draw weights are recommended for beginners learning the sport, even though they may have plenty of strength to pull much higher poundages. Beginners need to work on the basics of good form and technique before getting into more powerful bows. Boys and young men, especially, should be taught not to give in to a macho image, shooting strong bows meant for hunting by experienced archers. Mistakes are corrected more easily, if the shooter is able to concentrate on form and technique, not struggling to bend the bow.

Inexpensive wood arrows usually accompany school bows used by youth groups or classes. The more expensive Port Orford cedar arrows, balanced and matched for stiffness, are better saved for the more advanced students.

There is nothing wrong with using aluminum arrows while learning to shoot, but it may not be possible to match shaft spine to the lightest draw bows. The Easton Aluminum target arrow shaft size selection chart — the standard

As the students improve their skills, some may advance to more sophisticated equipment. Shooting form will improve.

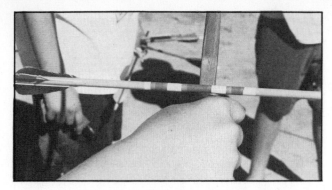

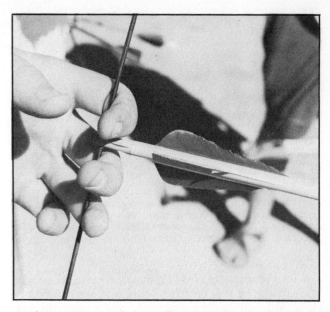

Student's hand and arm positions should be constantly monitored, especially during early shooting sessions. Archer, above, right, will shoot left-handed bow.

Young man, above, demonstrates follow-through with his release hand, important for the best shooting. Safety must be stressed at all times, including retrieval, right.

outdoor ranges, and depending upon the typcial winter weather of the area, possibly an indoor range, as well. An established archery range usually is safe and well laid out with shooting lanes, target butts, marked and unmarked targets ready for use.

Two types of archery ranges are found: Target ranges, using only bullseye paper targets set at established distances and field archery ranges with paper and 3-D animal targets in natural settings, often at unknown yardages. Formal bullseye target ranges are few, except at schools and some clubs. The number of archers who participate in this area of the sport total only a few thousands, while there are several million bowhunters in North America.

While learning and developing correct techniques, the

target archery range is a good place to start. Initially, accuracy of arrow flight is less important than good technique. Arrow accuracy will be difficult to come by later, if the new archer has developed bad shooting habits in early training.

Most avid archers have backyard set-ups for flinging a few arrows every day. Those who do not have a satisfactory natural backstop, a sandy, rock-free bank, for instance, usually will accommodate two or three hay bales as butts for everyday shooting.

reference by which all arrows are judged and selected — lists shafts to match recurve bows down to twenty pounds in draw weight. The lowest compound bow draw weight for which Easton lists shafts is twenty-three pounds. These minimum draw weights are excellent for the beginner.

Those unable to locate or qualify for formal school archery classes or who are too old to get into a youth group most likely will rely upon a local archery club for instruction. There are many clubs around the country, but they may be difficult to locate: Typically, their addresses will change each time a new club president or secretary is elected. Watch the activities section of local newspapers or archery shop bulletin boards for club meeting places, time and dates. New members or guests are always welcome at meetings and practice sessions.

Archery clubs and pro shops are the best sources of shooting ranges, as well as coaching help. Most clubs have

Archery tournaments may attract hundreds of shooters, spectators, creating interest among potential archers. Gymnasiums, tennis courts, armorys are likely ranges as Easton Aluminum sponsors outdoor range facilities in Southern California, near Olympic competition site, right.

With a bow, a set of arrows and a target range, the rookie is ready to start shooting. It is possible to learn the sport alone, with only this or another publication as a guide, but a coach or instructor of some sort is recommended. Even a person with little experience often can observe and detect mistakes of which the shooter is unaware.

Dozens of accessories and gadgets may be added to the archer's kit, but a bow and a dozen arrows are all one needs to get started. The beginner can add accessories, as skills grow.

Most school bows have a small arrow shelf on top of the bow handle. It is simply a slight protrusion above the hand grip area. To start, one may use that shelf from which to shoot arrows. School bows are built so they may be shot right- or left-handed and the beginner can try a few arrows either way, no matter which is the dominant hand or eye. The dominant eye is a more important consideration.

An easy way to determine the dominant eye is simply to point a finger at a distant object with both eyes open. Close the left eye. If the object does not appear to move, the right eye is dominant. If the object seems to jump away from the finger, the left eye may be the stronger. Open the left eye and close the right for confirmation.

The rank beginner may find that he or she is right-handed, but left-eyed. The situation is not uncommon and the first-time archer should have no problem learning the correct skills from the start, relying upon the dominant eye.

Grasp the bow in the bow hand firmly enough to control it, but there is no need to "choke" the handle. It takes some getting used to, but the archer soon will learn just how much is enough to hold the bow without dropping it, as the arrow is released. A person who never has held a bow before might not realize which is the top side of the handle and the coach or teacher should insure the student is holding the bow correctly.

The bow may have an obvious arrow rest moulded into the window or handle area above the bow hand. If the bow is a compound, there will be some sort of plastic or metal arrow rest, adjustable or not. On many school bows, a simple shelf above the handle has soft moleskin to smooth and quiet draw and release.

Inexpensive wooden arrows go along fine with bows of twenty-five or thirty pounds of draw weight. They may have plastic or dyed feather fletching and lightweight, fixed

target points. Fletching colors should be bright for maximum visibility to help identify the student's hits on the target.

At first, the beginner need not be equipped with a finger tab for the string hand. Bare fingers will hold up for the initial shooting.

Finer points will come later and the student should be encouraged to shoot a few arrows into a well-butted target from no more than ten yards away. Some youngsters will have difficulty drawing bows as light as twenty pounds and should be watched and coached to avoid developing bad shooting habits.

The teacher must stress safety procedures at all times. Point out and demonstrate to the student, especially children, that an arrow can be lethal to animals and humans. Insist that safe range procedures be followed during every practice session, whether one or a dozen persons are involved. Arrows always should be pointed only toward the target and the bow should be drawn back only when it is to be shot.

Shooters should proceed forward to retrieve arrows and obtain scores only when all shooters on the line have grounded their bows and arrows. All such equipment must be left at the line and not carried forward when approaching the target. Equipment must remain untouched until the last shooter or coach has returned to the line and the instructor informs the students to proceed with shooting. This same procedure is followed during formal target archery tournaments.

Depending upon the target butt material, arrows may be difficult or easy to extract. Student archers should be warned to never stand behind another who is pulling an arrow out of the target. A sudden release of the arrow may carry on into the eye of an onlooker as the arrow jerks backward.

If the students are children, they must be cautioned against running back to the line with arrows in their hands. Arrows should be placed in a hip quiver or carried point downward. The instructor/coach must be on the alert for stray pets or unaware humans wandering onto the archery field. Cease all shooting until the area is clear.

At first, many beginners will have difficulty in fully drawing a bow. The muscles used are unaccustomed to the required action, and usually, only arm strength is used. The coach should demonstrate and remind students that certain muscles in the back also come into play when drawing a bow.

Many archers, especially children, pick up the techniques rapidly. Progress can be quite swift. Shooters who can barely draw a bow all the way back and who were missing a ten-yard target completely, soon are getting fast arrows downrange and into relatively tight groups on the target. It can happen within the first fifteen minutes of shooting.

Now is the time for the coach to maintain close, one-on-one observation and correction of the student. Observe the student's shooting position, release and follow-through from a series of perspectives, including from each side and the rear. Watch the arrow flight, elbow position, bow hand grip, fingers and release. Follow-through of the string hand is particularly important, and often is incorrect with beginners. Watch the release hand to determine that it does not fly to either side, but pulls straight back along the shooter's face. Make corrections, if necessary.

The Police Athletic League (PAL) has an archery program. These volunteers are learning basic archery to later go on to teaching youths of Colorado Springs, Colorado area.

After a few shots using only bare fingers on the string, most will begin to feel sore finger tips or blisters forming. Left to continue in that fashion, beginners are likely to develop some incorrect habits as they shy away from the pain.

This is a good place to introduce finger tabs and forearm guards. Schools usually will have their own supply of right- and left-hand tabs, but the individual will do better to purchase them. They are not expensive, and will improve most archer's shooting dramatically.

Most instructors would agree that the first few lessons may not be the time to introduce additional accessories such as bow sights, string peep sights, mechanical release aids, overdraw devices, stabilizers and others. But many pro shop operators/retailers will outfit the beginning archer with all the gear at once. Not only do they increase their sales, but all the accessories will match the bow and the shooter and everything can be melded into a single shooting unit.

It may be better, according to this philosophy, to get all the "goodies" at once at the start, and practice with them all the time. This seems more important to the future bowhunter than for the person who will not go beyond casual paper target shooting.

As the students begin to hit their targets with more precision and consistency, their confidence rises, as does their interest. As muscles begin to tire, accuracy may suffer. It is better to restrict early practice sessions to no more than half an hour at a time. Two practice periods a day work well, if schedules permit, although some schools offer considerably more.

Incorrect shooting habits are much more difficult to eliminate than to prevent in the first place. The archery coach should observe each student closely for several shots and correct each mistake immediately. It is true that many bowhunters are never coached and manage to take their share of game animals each year, but any sport will be better appreciated if learned correctly at the start. Today's student is tomorrow's teacher, and bad habits should not be passed on in the guise of good technique.

Archery shooting muscles must be developed in most people and daily practice sessions are encouraged. However, students may develop incorrect techniques easily by shooting without supervision, especially when the teacher may not be available but once a week. The coach must get to know the beginning archer and decide how much shooting to allow between scheduled instruction periods.

Most instructors will encourage shooting bows in the low draw weight area for several weeks, working on technique improvement only. The urge to shoot heavier draw weight bows will arise early, however.

An excellent compromise is a compound bow with a fifteen-pound draw adjustment range from forty to fifty-five pounds. The heaviest setting is adequate for most bowhunting in North America and the lighter adjustment is drawn easily by the youngest beginners. The draw weight can be increased upward as the student improves.

Shooting technique errors often reveal themselves during the bow tuning phase. Attempts to obtain more accuracy with any bow and arrow combination may be frustrated more by poor shooting as much as by improper tuning and adjustments.

CHAPTER
2

YOUR FIRST BOW

A Number Of Variables And Choices Must Be Made Before You Invest In That Next Bow!

Many young people have their first try at archery through organized youth groups such as Boy Scouts. They are good places to try out several bows.

SELECTING A FIRST bow — or the second or tenth — should not be taken lightly. There are dozens of variables to be considered, including your age, build, sex, strength, arm length, type of bow, your budget and even your preference of materials. A bow is a highly personal tool and must be chosen carefully.

The short answer of how to best find a bow that fits is to visit your local professional archery shop, the same place you went to find a coach and a place to shoot. The pro shop is the best place to start looking. However, not every com-munity has a pro shop, nor one within practical traveling distance. The next choice is an archery or bowhunting club where you will obtain plenty of good advice. Good advice and basic knowledge are what the new archer/buyer needs.

For personal help, also try high schools, community colleges and, especially, private schools. Ask around for anyone with archery experience, just as you do to find a coach. If you have located a coach or teacher, that is your best source of help with the new bow. Rely on their experi-ence and avoid costly mistakes.

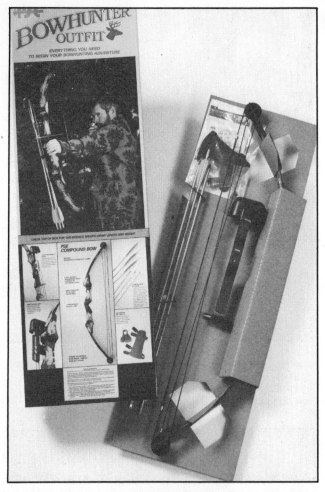

Commercially available archery outfits and kits, left, provide the new bow shooter everything to get started. Young shooters, above, especially need the right bow.

Used bows often are found at garage sales and swap meets, but purchasing one is risky business, unless you are armed with considerable experience or help. Unless you are familiar with the make and model being offered, the chances of getting a bow which fits your needs are slim to none.

Take the time to study several archery magazines and books, examine the advertisements to get an idea of what is available and the prices asked currently. As of early 1991, new compound bows start at slightly more than $100 and may be found at $500 or more, complete with accessories and options. Custom-made longbows and recurves will fall into the same range; $210 is a good starting figure for everything to suit a beginner, if it is in the chosen price range.

Children's bows and beginner archery sets are offered by mail order catalog companies and at larger discount sporting goods stores for as low as $30; many others are shown for well under $100. Youth and children's bows are quite sophisticated and well made these days and the buyer can feel confident with any of the brand-name sets. Many include the bow, some arrows, quiver, a finger tab and instructions.

Now we have a cost outlay figure in mind. We also already have determined our dominant eye and draw length as shown in the previous chapter. Will it be a longbow, recurve or compound? Fifteen to twenty-five-pound school bows are not expensive. The advantage of these bows is that most beginners may shoot them, regardless of their

individual draw length. Even long-draw, strong individuals, if careful, can learn the basics of archery shooting with such a lightweight bow. But beginners should avoid heavy draw weight bows of any type. Poor shooting habits are easy to learn and difficult to correct at a later date. Start low and work up.

Remember to measure or have measured your correct draw length. Arm length, build, body shape, weight and strength are variables different for each individual. While another's bow may seem to fit you, it may not be the best fit.

If you have no plans to try bowhunting, stay with a

Archery tournaments and club competitions offer ideal locations to see, perhaps try out bows. Often there will be used, bargain archery equipment for re-sale.

lightweight school bow and enjoy plenty of target shooting without muscle strain. If there is a chance you will want to try bowhunting within a year or two, go for an adjustable draw weight compound bow. All the manufacturers have bows that may shoot as low as forty-five pounds, which will adjust up to fifty-five or sixty pounds draw weight. Keep in mind that, with those weights, you will be holding only half or less weight, depending on the amount of let-off designed into the bow. These days, most bows have fifty or sixty-five percent let-off.

Your height and arm length, independent of draw length, also will affect the choice of the bow which will suit you best. Persons with shorter arms and draw lengths may wish to try a short overall length bow which might not be suitable for taller shooters. The shorter axle-to-axle distance will create a sharper angle at the arrow nock when fully drawn than will a longer bow. If you shoot with fingers, not using a mechanical release, your fingers may be squeezed tightly together at full draw. If a release aid is used, the string angle is not so critical, but it is important to use all the same gear you will be shooting with when trying any bow. That rule will save you money and grief later.

Shorter limbs will help you get through heavy brush easier when out hunting, but the longer limbs may be a bit more quiet on release. Some will argue that longer limbs will shoot a bit more smoothly than short limbs.

The choice of wood or metal risers is mostly a matter of personal preference. You may prefer the look, warmth and feel of wood over metal. Modern wood risers are made of laminated epoxy-wood material and are just as strong as magnesium, although the metal is more easily camouflaged the same color pattern as the limbs. Most wood risers are built to accept an overdraw today, as are most metal risers.

That is still another decision to be made: to shoot an overdraw-length arrow or not. Most hunters will opt for the

The beginning archer will spend time well by visiting field archery, above, and target tournaments, below, observing the variety of bows available. Most archers will pass on their experience and opinions, if asked.

Compound bows are built to fit all manner of physical shape, size. Various draw lengths, weights are made.

overdraw arrows and will add the overdraw shelf to the bow to shoot shorter, stiffer arrows. These options may be added later to the bow, but you should practice with whatever you choose to shoot with.

Another minor consideration is the composition of the limbs. Some manufacturers use all fiberglass limbs, others prefer laminated wood and fiberglass or carbon-graphite combinations. If the maker offers several bow models, some with different limbs, give each type a try; you may prefer the look or the feel of one or the other.

There are several other factors to consider, including the amount of let-off on a compound bow. For years, the standard amount was fifty percent. Most bows are still available with that much relaxation, but the standard has been changed to sixty-five percent let-off, especially when shooting short, carbon-graphite overdraw arrows.

Many bowhunters prefer the higher percentage, because they can draw and hold on target for much longer without having to let down from muscle fatigue. The amount may be changed from one percentage to the other on many bows and the buyer should inquire about it.

Eccentric wheels or cams? Wheels give a smoother draw and quieter release most of the time, but cams are noted for the arrow speeds they can produce. If you are dealing with a well stocked pro shop, they often can change the eccentric action by changing the wheels or the cams on an existing bow. This is not a task for beginners, however.

Modern compound bows are adjustable for draw length as well as draw weight. The bow buyer will be ahead by getting a bow with the lower adjustment to your current draw. After some practice, most of us will find draw length increasing by a half inch or so and easily will improve draw weight by ten or more pounds. Start shooting at the lower limits of the bow and adjust upward as you gain experience and strength.

A well made bow, properly maintained, will last for years, although many archers buy a new one every two or three years. This leads to a supply of used bows on the market, many only a couple of years old. The dealer may have them as trade-ins or they may be for outright sale by

Las Vegas indoor archery tournament in February each year is a wonderful place to see every type of bow made, as well as watch World and Olympic champions in action.

the owner. Most pro shops will have several such bows advertised on a bulletin board as a service to customers. If any of these bows match your measurements, be sure to give them a try.

When shooting used bows, listen carefully as they are drawn and shot for any unusual sounds or squeaks. There should be none. Look for worn strings, the first thing to wear out on any bow. Replacement strings are not expensive, and if that seems to be all that is wrong with a used bow, it can be a good buy.

Catalog sales companies offer genuine bargain prices on new bows and equipment, but you have to know exactly what you want before ordering. You must have in mind the model, draw specifications, color, style and brand you want to purchase. Most items, can be returned, but it takes time and costs money.

The most important message from all of this discussion is: Try the bow before buying. Shoot a dozen or more arrows — the same arrows you will be shooting — with the bow before making a commitment. A bow is a personal thing and there is no "perfect" or "best" bow for all individuals. The situation is similar to that of buying a new car. The best one for you is the one you are happiest with within your budget.

Above: Large archery manufacturers such as PSE, above, present dozens of bow models at consumer shows. Formal target archery meets, right, restrict types of bows, arrows.

TUNING TECHNIQUES FOR BOW AND ARROWS

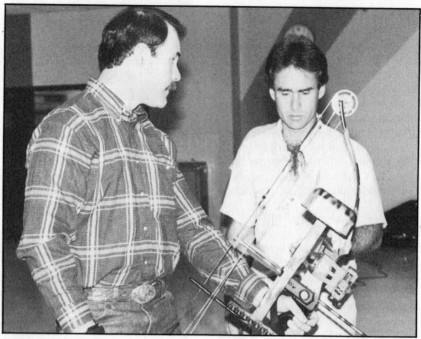

Archers shooting extremely heavy draw bows, such as this ninety-pounder, will be flinging arrows out mighty fast and flat. Professional shooter, Terry Ragsdale, right, advises on matching bow, quiver, sights, arrows.

EMERY LOISELLE is an engineer, technician and archery pro shop operator who has tuned hundreds of bows for customers and others. He has written dozens of articles on all kinds of bows. In fact, he is the author of two of the first books on compound bow tuning: *Sensabout Bow Tuning* and *Doctor your Own Compound Bow.*

Every bow, even the most basic stick-and-string longbow, must be tuned to the arrows and the archer. Every person holds and shoots differently and the bow, along with its accessories, must be adjusted to that person. Several methods of accomplishing this have evolved over the years. The results will be more accurate arrows and more enjoyable archery shooting.

TUNING for good arrow flight starts earlier than you might think. The bow and accessories must be compatible with each other and suit the archer. The arrows must be properly spined for the archer's draw length and the cast of the bow.

The archer shooting any type of bow needs a draw weight comfortable for him. If the bow will be used for target shooting with many arrows to be shot in a tournament, a light enough draw weight should be selected that the shooter will not tire unduly and the last arrow may be shot as accurately as the first. If the bow is a compound, the draw length should be accurately specified and adjusted if

necessary so the archer is shooting from the middle of the valley of the Force/Draw curve, the point of least holding weight.

You must make a wise choice concerning the arrow rest. On a longbow with little centershot cutout, you need a rest that will keep the arrow close to the window; perhaps with its own arrow plate included. You will use no cushion plunger. In the old days with no sight window cut into the longbow, we used the index finger of the bow hand as an arrow rest. With the advent of an arrow shelf, we padded the shelf and the side of the window with leather or material similar to moleskin or Bear Hair. The simple plastic finger rest or a wire finger rest, such as the Flipper, works nicely today.

The window cutout on a wood-handled recurve bow allows use of most stick-on rests and a cushion plunger. Metal-handled recurves generally have enough cut beyond center so that almost any rest setup can be used.

Compound bow risers are now available in many handle configurations and those which are overdraw-ready are cut beyond center enough in the rest areas that a broadhead can be pulled completely by the bow. This type of riser will accept rests which can be extended out from the bow such as the Centerest or springy rests, as well as most Golden Key-type rests. Some overdraw bows provide an adjustable rest carriage to allow use of a Flipper-type or plastic finger rest.

The main choice an archer must make in deciding on an

New Bow Or Old, Beginner Or Expert, Every Bow Must Be Tuned For Best Results

arrow rest is whether to use a shoot-around rest or a shoot-through type. The former category includes rests we are most familiar with, such as the Flipper rest, plastic finger rests and the springy rest. Flippers and plastic finger rests are generally used with a cushion plunger and the arrow nock is oriented so that the cock feather is horizontally positioned on the outboard side away from the bow. Shoot-through rests include types like the TM Hunter and the Hunter Supreme, which may or may not be used with a cushion plunger. On these rests, it is intended that one of the vanes will pass between the rest and the plunger, or between the support prongs on the TM Hunter.

Shooting with a release aid induces less paradox or bending of the arrow as the nock leaves pretty much straight out. An archer with good shooting technique and shooting with a release aid can use a shoot-through rest and, with proper tuning, can get the cock vane to pass between the prongs of the TM Hunter rest, or the lower hen fletch to pass between the cushion plunger and the outboard rest. It

Once nock location is established on the string, above, two NokSets are tightened to lock the position in place. Arrow rest, below right, is typical shoot-through rest.

may be beneficial to rotate the arrow nocks to better suit the type of rest used.

With fingers, bending of the shaft is radically increased and the tail end of the shaft is bent away from the bow window as it passes. With proper matching and tuning, the fletching passes to the side of a shoot-around rest without striking anything. I believe that most finger shooters using a shoot-through rest think the lower fletch is passing between the supports when actually it may be passing on the outboard side. I have seen archers tearing up fletches while tuning this setup. In my own pro shop, I suggest to finger shooters that they use a shoot-around setup. I personally like a Flipper rest and cushion plunger when shooting fingers as this combination gives a broad range of tuning capabilities, including centershot adjustment and tension or pressure adjustment of the button.

An extremely important consideration in equipment matching is the spine or stiffness of the arrow shaft. Good flight cannot be achieved if arrow spine is not properly matched to the archer's draw length and the cast of his bow. There is greater leeway when using a release aid. Finger shooters must make a closer match and spine be-

A simple way to determine actual draw length is to use a yard stick. Bow hand is placed flat-knuckles against any vertical surface as distance to anchor point is measured.

comes even more critical on bows where centershot is not fully attainable.

An understanding of the bending of an arrow as it leaves the bow should impress the target archer and the bowhunter with the importance of proper spine matching. At each annual session of The World Archery Center (TWAC) we watch a movie made by Dr. Clarence Hickman in 1938, showing, in extremely slow motion, an arrow in paradox from a moment prior to the release until it is well past the bow. The nock actually jumps to the left — a right-hand shooter — as it escapes the fingers, even before the relaxed fingers are pushed aside by the string. There is no way the archer can open his fingers fast enough — and it's a no-no to try — to have the string go straight out. You just wouldn't believe the bending of the arrow. It looks like a snake coming out of the bow. Jim Dougherty's Serpent shafts are

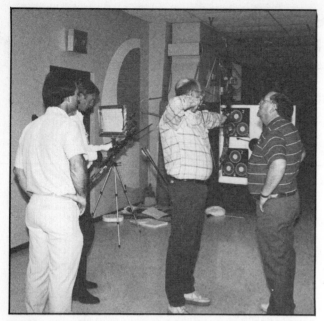

During tuning, each shot should be as nearly perfect and uniform as possible, advises coach George Chapman.

Arrows are cut to length, prepared for head installation of inserts during part of PSE Shooter's School instruction.

appropriately named. At the last TWAC session, Jim Easton showed a similar video — an arrow leaving the bow in slow motion — and that video is available to archers from Easton Aluminum.

When the finger shooter looses the string, the nock moves suddenly to the left — right-hand shooter — and the forward end of the arrow pushes into and rebounds from the arrow plate or plunger. The first bend therefore bellies the shaft in toward the bow. The second bend, if the arrow is properly spined, occurs belly out about half-way by the bow riser. The third bend, with belly in as the fletching passes the riser, provides the clearance needed with the nock end of the arrow as it moves by to the left of the rest.

An arrow shaft, when bent to one side then released, has a special frequency of vibration or oscillation; rapid if stiff

An indoor shooting area, if available, is ideal, because the conditions remain constant, with no worries about wind.

or short, slower if more limber and even slower as length and mass weight increase. These bends or vibrations are almost too fast for the eye to see, but three of these bends should occur in the time it takes the arrow to get past the riser of the bow. A long draw arrow moves farther to get by the bow, so you might think it would need a more limber shaft to bend slower than an arrow shot from a short draw bow of equal draw weight. However, the longer draw stores more energy and the longer arrow becomes weaker in effective spine. These two factors, plus the additional weight of the longer shaft, outweigh the "more limber" theory and a stiffer shaft is actually required for the long-draw bow.

THE ESSENTIAL ELEMENT IS THE TIMING OF THESE BENDS so that the three bends occur as explained. A too-stiff shaft will bend too fast and start its fourth bend before the arrow is by the bow, the tail moving in to strike the rest or window. A too-limber arrow will bend too slowly and the fletching may strike the window on the second bend before the start of the third bend has moved the arrow tail sufficiently away from the window. So there you have it. It behooves you to spine the arrow correctly to the draw length and cast of the bow, or change the draw weight of the bow to match the spine of the particular arrow.

You will note I use the term "cast" rather than draw weight in most instances. Spine charts are predicated on draw weight because cast, which is what the arrow feels, is affected by many variables. The compound bow, because of its rocket-like thrust, is more gentle on the arrow and uses a smaller or more limber shaft than does a recurve or longbow of similar draw weight. Cams store more energy and give a greater and more jarring thrust to the shaft, so spine must be stiffer even with the same draw weight.

Design of the bow, weight at the limb tips, amount of limb travel, efficiency of the bow/arrow combination; these and other factors all combine to affect cast or thrust. One

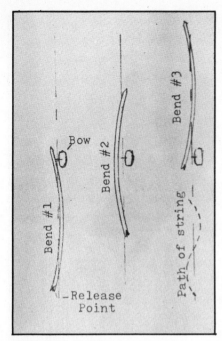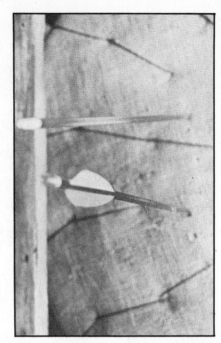

Left: Sketch demonstrates how an arrow with the proper spine clears the bow riser. Bare shaft test, center, will help determine correct arrow spine. In this illustration, the bare shaft impacting to left of fletched arrow indicates spine is too stiff for set up. For centershot, right, arrow is aligned with string, push point, slightly left of center. All are right-handed.

bow may require a different spine than another of equal draw weight. Witness that the Oneida spine chart requires for their Eagle bows much stiffer arrows than shown in the Easton chart for bows of similar draw weight. And believe me, with the Oneida Screaming Eagle, you actually do need that extra stiffness or the arrows won't fly.

When buying arrows for your bow, you should not go only by the chart. Find out what the chart covers as to type of bow, wheels or cams, point weight, et cetera, and compare with your particular setup. If you feel your bow is faster than the norm, you may be wise to go up a bit in spine. An overdraw setup will need a little thought, because the

chart will show spine for your short arrow, but not consider the extra energy cranked in by the long string travel. The foregoing information should help an archer hit upon proper arrows before spending a bundle on arrows which won't fly from his setup.

The object of tuning arrow flight is to get the arrow to fly without wobble, no porpoising or fishtailing, while striving for a condition where the arrow, line of sight and arrow flight path are in the same plane — more important to instinctive or barebow shooters — and broadheads group with field arrows, although this is not absolutely necessary. These ideals may all be achieved through fine tuning, although good arrow flight where the shooter sees nothing, but the nock of the arrow going away from him is the first and foremost requirement.

Tuning for target and field arrows is a similar procedure. The first requisite is that the bow be equipped with all the accessories which will normally be attached to the bow. This includes stabilizers and, for the bowhunter, the bowquiver loaded with the same number of arrows he expects to carry while hunting. The bowquiver especially can have a great effect on arrow flight and point of impact. As the bow jumps backward and forward at the shot, the quiver offset to one side represents a moment of inertia which tends to twist the bow in the vertical axis. A weight positioned outward from the riser on the opposite side of the quiver will help offset this. Moving the quiver out ahead of the bow can help transform it into a stabilizer.

Tuning for an archer whose bow is well suited to him as to draw weight and exact draw length can be started with certain basic adjustments. These include setting nocking

On this bow, the riser is arched outward around arrow rest to provide shoot-through and slight overdraw capabilities.

Above: A cushion plunger and hinged wire rest provide tuning capabilities. Plunger tension, centershot may be adjusted. On compound bows, limb bolts are turned, right.

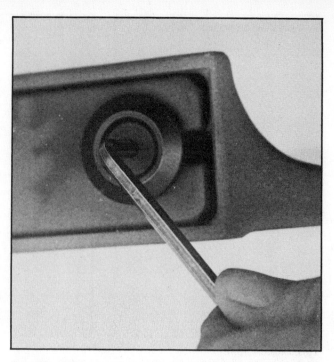

height, centershot position and button tension. On a compound bow, assuming tiller and wheel balance are good, the draw weight may be adjusted to compensate for an unsuitable shaft spine. A little tuning of the arrow itself to change its effective spine can be done by changing arrow length or point weight.

I personally set up and rough-tune each new bow in my pro shop before hanging it up. In most cases, after setting up in the manner described here and giving some thought to a matching arrow spine, the customer finds arrow flight to be up to his expectations or better. Only the more discerning archers or bowhunters want more refinement.

Here's what I do. With arrow rest installed and using a bow square, I set the nock locator five-sixteenths-inch above square on the bowstring. I use a NokSet clamped loose enough while tuning that it can be screwed up and down the string as needed. With an arrow nocked below the NokSet, this positions the arrow approximately one-eighth-inch above square. After tuning, the NokSet can be clamped tight and a second installed above it for insurance that it won't slide up the string.

The next thing I do is adjust cushion plunger tension, if the customer has decided on this kind of setup. The great majority of my customers are bowhunters shooting with fingers, because release aids are not allowed for hunting in my state. With the greater paradox induced by finger shooting, the adjustability of the hardness of the pressure point is a great aid to tuning. As a starter, I set the tension to eighteen or twenty ounces. My own feeling is that this is optimal, providing arrow spine is right. You can use a small scale like one used in a kitchen or home-type postal scale to set the tension.

The last thing is setting centershot. *Just what is centershot?* Some bow manufacturers and bow tuners and writers say the rest or cushion plunger should be adjusted so the arrow will be in the same plane as a sighting taken with the bowstring aligned to an off-center point on the limb base, measured in from the edge of the limb the same distance that the wheel is offset from that same edge. Others, the great majority I would say, consider center of the limb base or riser end to be center, even though the eccentrics are off-center at the limb tips. So who is right? Well, maybe the manufacturers, while not in agreement, are all provid-

ing effective centershot recommendations since it depends on the design of the riser, especially as pertains to the grip location.

Way back when Allen and Jennings bows were the only compounds being made, I designed and built an unusual, many-featured compound bow for experimental purposes. This big bow was dubbed The Monster Bow and is featured on the cover of my book *Doctor Your Own Compound Bow.* The wooden riser was a cage-like shoot-through design with a long central platform at the center. The swivel grip positioned below was movable forward and back, and could be adjusted from side to side. The rest carriage above the platform could likewise be positioned anywhere, from forward of the grip to well behind the grip for an overdraw effect, as well as from side to side. Whenever I moved the grip to the left, arrows would not fly until the rest

A fine-tooth, fast-turning cut-off saw will provide accurate, clean shaft cuts. Spine is changed with arrow length.

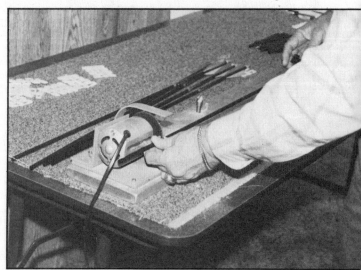

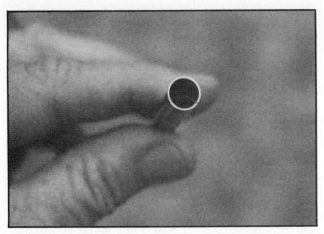

A slight metal burr or thread is left on the shaft when it is cut with a tubing cutter, rather than preferred shaft saw.

was also moved to the same side the same amount. This proved to me that the string, when released, wants to return to the grip, not to any other part of the bow.

Forget statements like "parallel with the edge of the limb" or "adjust centershot to the center of the limb base." Each manufacturer knows what constitutes centershot on his bows even though not all say the same thing. A case in point: Total Shooting Systems recommends setting centershot parallel with the limbs on the Quadraflex. A close look at the riser makes it apparent that the grip is definitely offset to the left of the riser centerline. The rest must be similarly offset.

TUNE TO THE PUSH POINT ON THE GRIP! Almost two decades ago — 1971 — I published, *Sensabout Bow Tuning.* This important information is included in that publication. I have seen only one writer pick up on this. The grip center is not necessarily the *exact* push point, but it is close. Most right-handers tend to concentrate the pushing forces slightly to the left of center. This is undoubtedly why, without saying why, most instructions state, "adjust centershot so the arrow is slightly left of center."

So now, determine push point on your grip by feeling as you draw just where the push in your case is concentrated and *adjust centershot to the push point on the grip.* With an arrow on the string, sight from behind the string, slightly below the arrow and align the string with the push point on the grip. Holding this picture, screw the cushion plunger in or out until the arrow is aligned in this plane.

As previously stated, in my own pro shop I hang the bow up at this stage until the new owner is available for final touchup. I have so much faith in these three basic settings — except maybe for touchup of nocking height — that I prefer to fine-tune by draw weight adjustments from here on.

Now we are ready to shoot arrows and fine-tune flight. Top archers each have their own favorite tuning method — bare shaft method, shoot-through-paper method, Eliason tuning method, Vic Berger's French method — to name a few. I like Ed Eliason's as presented at TWAC, which requires use of three fletched arrows and one bare shaft. The bare shaft will plane to a point in the bale separate from the arrow group and you make adjustments to NokSet and plunger to compensate.

Since this article is becoming too book-like, here is a short rundown on what can be done with the three basic settings to improve arrow flight. Stand fairly close to the butt during first adjustments, as too many straightenings of the bare shaft will change its spine characteristics and give untrue readings.

Check nock height first. If the bare shaft impacts below the arrow group — tail high — lower the nocking point. This will not be final for nock height setting, because other adjustments interact and some touchup back and forth is needed. If bare shaft impacts to the left of the group — tail right — a stiff shaft condition is indicated. If you don't wish to increase draw weight at this point, soften the plunger. Or if you don't feel comfortable with your initial centershot setting, move the plunger in to the right. If the bare shaft impacts to the right of the group — tail left — the indication is a weak, too-limber shaft. Make reverse adjustments to correct. A left-handed archer will do the opposite on the cushion plunger adjustments. Tune until at fifteen or twenty yards, the bare shaft flies true and impacts with the arrows.

I try not to deviate too much from the initial settings of the cushion plunger. I find that when the pressure point is too soft, or when centershot is positioned too much to the right, the group tends to spread in the horizontal plane. Better to adjust draw weight or get arrows of a different spine.

A compact, collapsible paper frame from Saunders is just the thing for paper tuning. Clips hold newspaper in frame, which is mounted atop camera or scope tripod.

BOW TUNING

COMPOUND & RECURVE BOWS

BARE SHAFT
PLANING TEST
Finger Release

Before you begin the tuning process, your bow must have a nocking point, cushion plunger and arrow rest that can be adjusted to correct the three possible arrow flight problems: **Porpoising, Fishtailing** and **Clearance**. Optional equipment such as a bowsight, stabilizer, peep sight, etc., must be installed on the bow before you can begin tuning.

Tuning Procedure

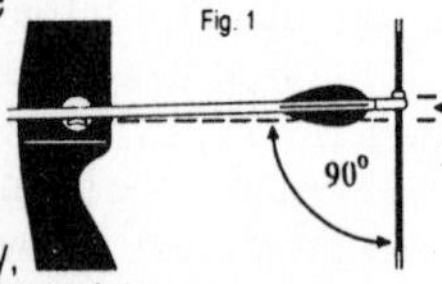

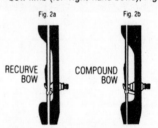

1. Install a movable nocking point on the bowstring (clamp-on types are ideal). Initially, position the nocking point on the bowstring about ¹/₂" (1.3 cm) above square, Fig. 1.

Fig. 1   90°   ¹/₂"

2. Adjust the in/out position of the cushion plunger so the centerline (axis) of the arrow point is aligned ¹/₈" to ³/₁₆" (3.2 - 4.8 mm) outside the bowstring with the bowstring correctly centered to the bow. The bowstring on the recurve is aligned with the center of the bow limbs, Fig. 2a. On compound bows, the bowstring is aligned approximately ¹/₄" (6.3 mm) to the left of the center of the bow limb (for right-hand bows), Fig. 2b.

Fig. 2a   Fig. 2b

RECURVE BOW   COMPOUND BOW

3. Initially, set the sight pin on your bow sight over the centerline of the arrow shaft.

Arrows that do not fly well or group tightly are usually affected by one or more of the following problems:
1. They may **Porpoise** in flight.
2. They may **Fishtail** in flight.
3. They may not **Clear** the arrow rest as they leave the bow.

Porpoising
If the arrow leaves the bowstring with the nock too high or too low, a motion known as Porpoising will occur. The nock end of the arrow appears to move up and down as the arrow follows its flight path, Fig. 3. ◎ Porpoising is caused by incorrect nocking point location.

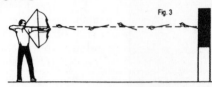

Fig. 3

To find the proper nocking point location, shoot at least three fletched shafts at a distance of 15 meters. Then shoot two identically-aimed unfletched shafts. If the unfletched shafts impact above the point where the fletched shafts impact, Fig. 4, move the nocking point up on the bowstring until both fletched and unfletched shafts strike at the same elevation. If the unfletched shafts impact below the identically-aimed fletched shafts, Fig. 5, move the nocking point down on the bowstring until the unfletched shafts hit at the same elevation as the fletched shafts.*

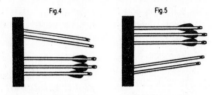

Fig.4   Fig.5

To assure you have eliminated Porpoising, repeat the test at 25 meters. ◎ **It is important to correct Porpoising first when starting the tuning process.**

Fishtailing
If the arrow leaves the bow with the nock end shifted to one side or the other, Fishtailing will occur. The nock end of the arrow appears to move from side to side as the arrow follows its flight path, Fig. 6.

Fig. 6

To correct Fishtailing, continue the Bare Shaft Test by shooting three fletched shafts at a distance of 15 meters, then shoot two identically-aimed unfletched shafts.* If the unfletched shafts impact left of the identically-aimed fletched shafts, (see Fig. 7 for a right-handed archer), decrease the spring tension on the cushion plunger. ◎ If the unfletched shafts impact right

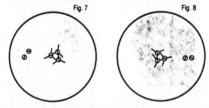

Fig. 7   Fig. 8

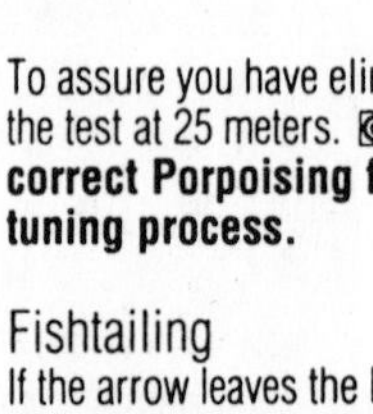

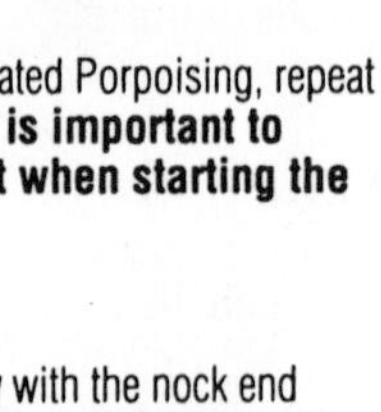

* It is sometimes desirable to have the bare shafts impact just slightly below the identically-aimed fletched shafts. However, bare shafts that impact above identically-aimed fletched shafts should be corrected.

of the identically-aimed fletched shafts, (see Fig. 8 for a right-handed archer), increase the spring tension on the cushion plunger. ◎ When correcting for Fishtailing using the **Bare Shaft Planing Test**, you may not be able to adjust the unfletched shaft to impact with the fletched shaft. Your arrows might be too weak (unfletched shafts impact to the right of the fletched shafts for right-handed archers) or too stiff (unfletched shafts impact to the left of the fletched shafts for right-handed archers). If this is the case, the following suggestions will help you obtain the best arrow flight from your bow:

1. Bow weight adjustment – Most compound bows and some recurve bows have the ability to adjust draw weight. If your arrow is too stiff, increase the draw weight. If the arrow is too weak, decrease the draw weight.
2. Bowstrings – The mass weight of the bowstring can have a tremendous effect on arrow spine. By increasing or decreasing the number of strands in the bowstring or by changing bowstring material, you can make an arrow shaft shoot as if it were one shaft size stiffer or weaker. To make the arrow shoot as if it were weaker, decrease the number of strands or use lighter bowstring material. To make the arrow shoot as if it were stiffer, increase the number of strands (or use a heavier bowstring material). If, after trying the tuning procedures listed, your arrows are still too weak or too stiff to fly properly, choose a different arrow size and retune.

Clearance
Clearance is the ability of the arrow and fletching to pass by the bow and arrow rest without contact. Good Clearance is absolutely essential for consistent grouping and optimum accuracy. ◎ To check for Clearance, spray dry powder deodorant or a similar product on the last quarter of the arrow shaft, fletching, arrow rest and surrounding area. Do not disturb the powder sprayed on the arrow and bow while preparing to shoot. ◎ The arrow should be shot into a firm target so that it will not penetrate to the fletching. ◎ By examining the areas where the dry powder spray has scraped off, the contact area and the position of the fletching as the arrow leaves the bow can be identified. If you are not achieving good arrow Clearance, and the arrow shaft makes contact with the bow or arrow rest, optimum grouping cannot be achieved. ◎ If a Clearance problem exists, the following procedures may help correct this problem:

1. Rotate the arrow nocks ¹/₁₆ turn at a time until Clearance is achieved.
2. Make sure your arrow rest support arm does not protrude past the outside of the arrow shaft.
3. Move the cushion plunger out further away from the bow to help increase Clearance.

COMPOUND BOWS

Release Aids

Listed below are additional bow tuning procedures for archers using release aids:

1. Bowstring alignment – Align the arrow down the center of the bowstring with the bowstring correctly positioned as indicated in Fig. 2b.
2. Sight alignment – Initially position the sight pin over the centerline of the arrow.
3. Clearance – Because the arrow more often bends vertically than horizontally, good clearance is essential. Nearly the full length of the arrow may contact the rest during the shot. Therefore, the vane-to-nock indexing is very important and should be adjusted to achieve maximum Clearance.
   a. Rotate the nock 1/16 turn at a time until Clearance is achieved.
   b. On "shoot through" rests, it may be necessary to adjust the width of the arrow rest support arm so the fletching will pass cleanly over it.
   c. On "shoot around" rests, make sure your arrow rest support arm does not project past the outside of the arrow shaft.

Paper Tuning Arrow Test

The paper test is the most commonly used bow tuning test for archers using compound bows with release aids.

1. Use a picture frame type rack to firmly hold a sheet of 24" x 24" paper. Position the center of the paper about shoulder height. Make sure there is a target mat about 6 feet behind the paper to stop the arrows.
2. Stand approximately 6' from the paper.
3. Shoot a fletched arrow through the center of the paper with the arrow at shoulder height (parallel to the floor).
4. Observe how the paper is torn.

 This tear indicates correct arrow flight. The point and fletching enter the same hole.

 This tear indicates a low nocking point. To correct, raise the nocking point and repeat the procedure.

 This tear indicates a high nocking point or a clearance problem. To correct, lower the nocking point and repeat the procedure. If, after moving the nocking point a few times, the problem is unchanged, the disturbance is most likely caused by lack of clearance. If the arrow fletching is hitting the arrow rest, see paragraph #3, "Clearance," under "Release Aids" above.

 This tear indicates a stiff arrow reaction for right-handed archers. Left-handed archers will have an opposite pattern.
To correct, try:
a. Moving the arrow rest in toward the bow.
b. Increasing peak weight.
c. Using a heavier arrow point.
d. Using a lighter bowstring (less strands or lighter material, like Fast Flight®).
e. Using a weaker spine arrow.
f. Decreasing cushion plunger tension or using a weaker spring on "shoot around" rests.

 This tear indicates a weak arrow spine or clearance problem for right-handed archers. Left-handed archers will have an opposite pattern. This is probably the most common disturbance problem archers will experience and can be corrected by:

a. Decreasing peak weight.
b. Decreasing arrow point weight.
c. Increasing bow string weight (more strands or heavier material).
d. Moving the arrow rest out away from the bow.
e. Using a stiffer spined arrow.
f. Increasing cushion plunger tension or using a stiffer spring on "shoot around" rests.
g. Following the steps in paragraph #3, "Clearance," under "Release Aids" at the left.

 This tear shows a combination of more than one flight disturbance. Use the procedures that apply to the tear pattern, and combine the recommendations for correction, correcting the vertical pattern first, then the horizontal.

◙ Once you have achieved a good tune, move back 6' to 10' more and continue to shoot through the paper. This ensures that the tune is correct and that the arrow was not just in a recovery position when it passed through the paper at 6'. ◙ For more detailed information on bow tuning, please send for Easton's Technical Bulletin #6.

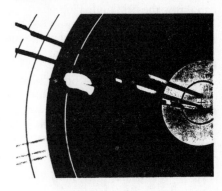

Tuning broadhead flight should come easy now if you have properly tuned for field points. The broadheads should be of similar weight to the field points and the blades should be well vented. Chances are, impact point will be different from fields points, but I attribute this mostly to the rudder syndrome as the arrow bends in paradox at the beginning of its flight. Also, the broadhead will be more sensative than the bare shaft to planing tendencies associated with incomplete tuning.

Refine the nock locator first until the broadhead hits the same height as field points, assuming weights of both are alike. Refine line, trying for similar impact points in the vertical plane, by adjusting draw weight; down slightly if broadheads impact to the right of field points, up a bit if broadheads hit to the left. They are feeling tail-left and tail-right conditions more sensitively than field points. Touch up plunger location and tension only as a last resort if you can't live with a condition where target and hunting points don't impact alike. You're going to have to make final sight adjustments anyhow.

Chuck Saunders is one of the pioneers of modern archery, having been in business for longer than most of us have been around. Saunders Archery offers hundreds of archery accessory items which have been researched and developed by experts in the field.

Saunders also offers some excellent bow-tuning tips to customers and other archers, based on his decades of experience. He advises that there are three methods used to tune bowhunting equipment — most of his customers are bowhunters, rather than simply target archers — which will work well: bare shaft, paper and the arrow angle technique. Saunders recommends the arrow angle method and offers the following points to keep in mind.

"Feather fletching is much more forgiving than plastic.

"Use arrows that have a full five-inch helical fletch.

"The weight of the field or bullet point must be the same as the broadhead you intend to use when hunting.

"The window of the bow should be cut out so the arrow at full draw lies on the same plane as the path of the string. This gives the fletching a chance to clear the bow.

"Run the tests with the bow set up as you use it for hunting. If you hunt with eight arrows in your bow quiver, have eight in the quiver during the tests. If you use kissers, peeps, string silencers and stabilizers, install them before

When paper tuning, arrows should be shot from about six or seven feet from sheet, left. Camera tripod holds paper frame. The type of fletching effects arrow flight. Feathers are recommended for long bows, above, shot off shelf. Safe backstop is essential to tuning, below.

you start the tests. If you hunt with your quiver in place on your bow, conduct testing with it on the bow.

"The bow should have a flexible shelf arrow rest which will fold against the bow window or drop down. Many shop owners immediately install a Saunders Silver Star arrow rest because it is easier to tune," declares Saunders.

"Always draw the bow the same amount," he cautions. "Many archers, when wearing a heavy hunting jacket or shooting out of a tree stand, shorten their draw length. This can throw the best tuning job off.

"Be sure your bow is set up so that you are releasing from the middle of the valley of the force-draw curve.

"Use the glove, tab or release you intend to use when hunting.

"Keep string height — brace height — constant.

"And don't overlook the obvious: your arrows should be straight and matched to your bow weight and draw length."

Saunders goes on to outline the following methods for achieving the correct tuning he recommends.

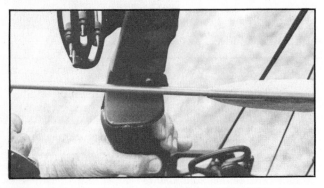

Plunger pressure may be softened or stiffened, above, in tuning procedure. Two nock positioners are used to place arrow below. Rubber spaces mechanical release.

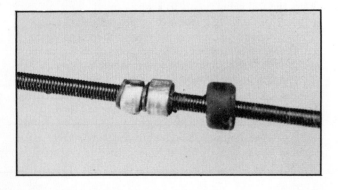

Before starting, he says, suspend the bow by setting the limbs on two cross-bars that are spaced so they will support the limbs about two inches from the limb axles or three inches from string grooves on a recurve. Nock an arrow in the proper position on the string. Move the pressure button in until it touches the arrow, then give it one-quarter turn and lock in position. After this, make any additional change in or out with great caution. The equipment is now ready to be tuned, says Saunders.

To correct for vertical flip-flopping, also known as porpoising, install a nock indicator on the string so the nock end of the shaft is about three-sixteenths-inch above the arrow shaft at a square to the string position. Always close the nock indicator — Saunders' is called a NokSet — using special nocking pliers. Several companies, including Saunders, sell them.

With field points on the shaft, shoot an arrow into the edge of a target butt from about five yards away. Remain in the position you had when the shot was made. If the nock end of the arrow is higher than the point end, lower the nocking point; if lower, raise the nock point. Continue this test from your shooting position until the fletching and nock end are the same height. At this point, disregard any right or left nock positions.

To correct the horizontal flip-flopping — also known as fishtailing — shoot an arrow into the top edge of the target. Check the arrow angle. To get the shaft square with the shooter's eye, change the pressure button pressure; make it

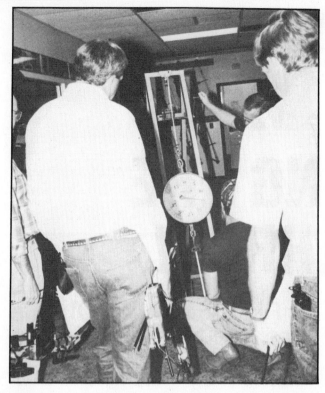

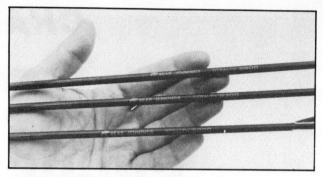

Left: Most archery pro shops will have a bow scale so each archer may determine exactly the draw and holding weight. Carbon shafts, above, give high arrow speeds, but will require additional tuning to best results.

stronger if the nock is to the left — for a right-handed shooter — weaker if it is to the right. If this fails to correct the problem, increase the draw weight of the compound bow if the nock is to the right, weaken it if to the left.

If these adjustments do not square the arrow, check for vane clearance. An arrow should clear the bow and rest if the equipment is tuned. Spray eight inches of the nock end of the arrow with some sort of spray talcum powder. Shoot and check for contact between the fletching and the rest or bow window. If there is powder on the back side of the window, get the next stiffer spine arrow. If it hits the inside of the window, try a weaker shaft.

On a compound, the peak draw weight can be changed down for a weak shaft and up if the shaft is too stiff. Point weight will also affect fishtailing; use a heavier point or a longer shaft if the contact area is on the inside of the window. Contact between the rest and the shaft is acceptable. Fletching contact should be avoided. Run the above test at a twenty-five yard distance and adjust as necessary.

With some arrow rests, says Saunders, to get fletch clearance it may be necessary to change the nocks so the string slot is positioned differently in relationship to the cock feather. If this is necessary, remove the nock from one arrow, turn it slightly and re-shoot. If there is powder on the rest, turn to a different position and re-check. Once your test arrow clears the rest, re-set the nocks on the balance of your arrows. The tension of the nocks on the string should be just enough so a nocked arrow hanging from the string will drop if the string is tapped.

Saunders goes on to urge that only one element change be made at a time when tuning a bow. For instance, if you change the pressure button tension, test *before* increasing or decreasing peak weight. All the given changes are for a right hand bow; the left-hander must reverse the instructions for horizontal flip-flop. Arrows that are not properly spined will give inconsistent results. If after making these tests, there are still problems, the best advice is to visit a local archery pro shop.

Overdraw bows have their own special problems and the pro shop is the best place to obtain help when tuning these bows.

Confidence in your tuning will bring confidence in your shooting. Handle the equipment with care so as not to bend the rest, slide the nock locator or peep up the string, bend sight pins or arrows, or dull the broadhead cutting edges. The arrows must hit where aimed and do the job intended. You owe it to the game you hunt and to yourself.

Often, archery tournaments and product shows will include arrow speed measuring chronographs. This is a good time to find out how fast your arrows are really flying.

CHAPTER 3

CHOOSING THE BEST ARROW

The Right Bow Needs The Right Selection Of Arrows — There Are Many Types And Materials To Try

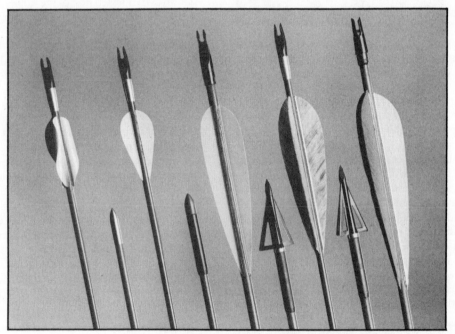

The latest material to be used for arrow shafts is carbon-graphite, a fast, lightweight substance which will break, but not bend during normal usage. This set by AFC demonstrates the versatility of heads and fletching used.

WITH A NEW BOW in hand, most of us will look to the selection and purchase of a dozen arrows and head for the target range. But hold on! Selecting the correct arrow is as important as the bow. The correct set of arrows will give consistent and accurate flight to the target with each shot, so long as the archer does his or her job properly. No amount of practice or tuning will compensate for shooting the wrong arrows.

Proper arrow selection depends on several factors. The type of bow sometimes will determine which shaft material is used, as will the kind of archery, the physical size and strength of the archer, as well as the financial resources at hand. All must be considered.

Most, but not all, longbow shooters prefer to take the traditional route and go with wood shafts, although aluminum will perform as well. The fletching should be of real feathers, though, as they are more forgiving when shot across the bow shelf than are plastic vanes. Tradition demands wood shafts.

It is possible, of course, to obtain the cedar or fir wood to make our own arrows from start to finish, but most begin-

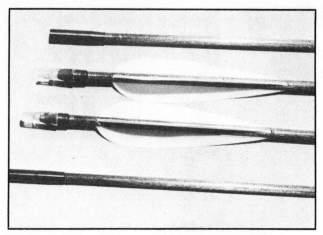

Supershafts by AFC are carbon-graphite shafts, thinner than aluminum, requiring special external head and nock attachments for target or hunting.

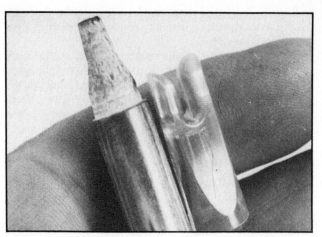

Cedar wood shafts are still available and popular with many archers. The nock taper is critical and requires a special tapering tool for correct fit.

ners will do well to buy their first set of finished arrows. The popular Port Orford cedar arrows are available through a number of mail order houses, as well as some pro shops. Feathers, plastic vanes, feather burners, nocks, glue, lacquer, fletching jigs, cresting kits and everything else needed are for sale. Some pro shops carry better wood arrows, or they can make them up for the customer as they are ordered.

Only a few years ago, good wooden arrows were the most inexpensive to buy and use. That is no longer true.

Most bow quivers are built to accept the standard diameter aluminum shafts, left. Special rubber holders or inserts are now available for carbon.

Technology, modern production methods and supply and demand have placed aluminum arrows in the least expensive category. Wood arrows are now more expensive.

Aluminum or composite arrows will fly just as well from longbows or recurve bows, although feather fletching is almost a requirement. The feathers have more give to them and compress and spring back to shape as they are shot from the shelf. Plastic vanes, while impervious to wet weather, will cause erratic flight unless the arrows are shot off arrow rests so there will be no contact with the bow shelf.

Some recurve bows are made with lightweight metal — usually aluminum or magnesium alloy — so risers and the launch area can be cut beyond center for plenty of fletching clearance. Somewhere, sometime, someone has made a longbow with a metal handle and cut past center, but it is not common and should be considered a curio or collector item. Most archers will shoot aluminum or carbon fiber arrows from recurve bows, especially when hunting.

Probably ninety-nine percent of all compound bow shooters use aluminum, carbon fiber or aluminum/carbon arrows. About ninety-seven percent of all bowhunters use arrows other than wood.

The simplest way to get the correct arrows for your bow is to visit your favorite pro shop with your bow and get the correct weight, spine and draw. However, not every community has a good archery shop, and some beginners may feel intimidated about asking for help with highly experienced archers looking on. Of course, if you bought the bow from the shop in the first place, getting the correct set of arrows should be no problem.

Good arrows, even when purchased by mail order, do not come cheap. A dozen aluminum arrows, made up with standard components and at standard lengths, will carry a price tag of from $30 to $50 per dozen. Cost of composites can be twice that. Carbon fiber can be costly and any optional additions, such as special fletching, colors, camouflage, four or more vanes and the like will bring the price up. It pays to know something about correct arrow selection before you buy.

Most archers shoot aluminum arrows and most aluminum arrows anywhere in the world are made by Easton Aluminum. Easton was the pioneer of the product and still is the leader. They set the standard by which all others are compared. A decade ago, Easton developed aluminum/carbon shafts which have become popular with target tournament shooters and in Olympic and world archery competition.

In the late 1970s, another shaft material was gaining some popularity: fiberglass and fiberglass compounds. They could be made to any length and spine — stiffness — and were rather inexpensive to manufacture. They did not take a permanent bend and were impervious to weather conditions. However, when abused, they could and did develop longitudinal splits in the material and could shatter upon release from a strong bow. They are occasionally found for sale and some archers still shoot fiberglass arrows, but they can be dangerous, and will not be discussed here.

In 1981, Easton introduced a composite arrow made of aluminum and carbon, called the A/C. The thin-walled aluminum tubing is wrapped with layers of carbon fiber. The A/C arrows are lighter than standard aluminum arrows and are used by many tournament shooters, including Olympic Archers.

In 1987, the development was carried a step further and the A/C/Hunter arrow was introduced. However, Easton was soon running into potential liability problems as the A/C/H shafts might shed strands of carbon fiber in shot game which might pose a health risk to those consuming the game meat. As a result, Easton no longer recommends the shaft for bowhunters, although it is still available for target shooters. In 1990, Easton was offering the extra lightweight A/C/Comp shaft for target archers, gaining considerable acceptance in a short time.

Aluminum's dominance of the arrow market is being challenged by the newer carbon-graphite shafts. This new material offers even lighter weight and stiffer spine per

Eric Melquiond is the operations manager for Beman's American operations for the French company in Chicago.

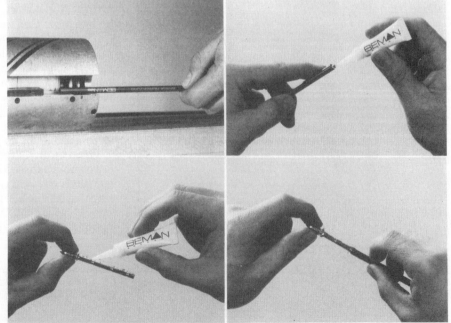

Beman recommends the use of a fast cut-off saw, using fine teeth to cut carbon-graphite shafts. It is vital, says Beman, to thoroughly coat all shaft and insert surfaces with glue.

arrow than others. It has a "memory" so that each arrow returns to its straight mode after every shot. Carbon-graphite shafts will break if stressed too far, but not as readily as other materials. They have found particular favor with archers shooting short, overdraw arrows from heavy draw weight bows. The overdraw accessory permits arrows of only twenty-five or twenty-six inches, lighter in weight, flying as well as heavier, longer arrows. The carbon-graphite

arrows are quite fast, giving a flatter trajectory to reduce range-estimating errors by bowhunters and 3-D target shooters.

Many believe the new carbon-graphite arrows are the wave of the future. They are offered in several different spine ratings, but not as many as Easton Aluminum shafts. Stiffness — spine rating — is altered by changing the outside diameter and wall thickness of the shaft, so within cer-

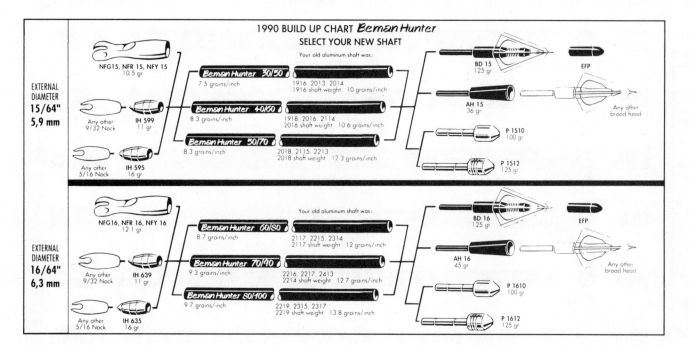

Beman Hunter CARBON GRAPHITE SHAFT SELECTION CHART

Recurve Bow Weight	Compound Bow Weight	Over Draw				Correct hunting arrow length							
		22"	23"	24"	25"	26"	27"	28"	29"	30"	31"	32"	33"
		56 cm	58 cm	61 cm	63 cm	66 cm	69 cm	71 cm	74 cm	76 cm	79 cm	81 cm	84 cm
(at your arrow length)		For your arrow length and bow you'll select a Beman - Hunter :											
25-30	30-35	30/50	30/50	30/50	30/50	30/50	30/50	30/50	40/60	40/60	50/70	50/70	60/80
30-35	35-40	30/50	30/50	30/50	30/50	30/50	30/50	30/50	40/60	40/60	50/70	50/70	60/80
35-40	40-45	30/50	30/50	30/50	30/50	30/50	40/60	40/60	50/70	50/70	60/80	60/80	60/80
40-45	45-50	30/50	30/50	30/50	30/50	30/50	40/60	40/60	50/70	50/70	60/80	60/80	60/80
45-50	50-55	30/50	30/50	30/50	30/50	30/50	40/60	40/60	50/70	50/70	60/80	60/80	70/90
50-55	55-60	30/50	30/50	30/50	30/50	30/50	40/60	50/70	50/70	60/80	60/80	70/90	
55-60	60-65	30/50	30/50	30/50	30/50	40/60	40/60	50/70	50/70	60/80	60/80	70/90	70/90
60-65	65-70	30/50	30/50	30/50	30/50	40/60	40/60	50/70	50/70	60/80	60/80	70/90	70/90
65-70	70-75	30/50	30/50	30/50	40/60	40/60	50/70	50/70	60/80	60/80	70/90	70/90	80/100
70-75	75-80	30/50	30/50	30/50	40/60	40/60	50/70	50/70	60/80	60/80	70/90	70/90	80/100
75-80	80-85	30/50	30/50	40/60	40/60	50/70	50/70	60/80	60/80	70/90	70/90	80/100	80/100
80-85	85-90	30/50	30/50	40/60	40/60	50/70	50/70	60/80	60/80	70/90	70/90	80/100	80/100
85-90	90-95	30/50	40/60	40/60	50/70	50/70	60/80	60/80	70/90	70/90	80/100	80/100	80/100
90-95	95-100	30/50	40/60	40/60	50/70	50/70	60/80	60/80	70/90	70/90	80/100	80/100	80/100

To choose exactly your BEMAN HUNTER, select your correct bow weight at the left column, follow across to your arrow length.

MAX-5™ Shafting

DRAWN AT ACTUAL SIZE

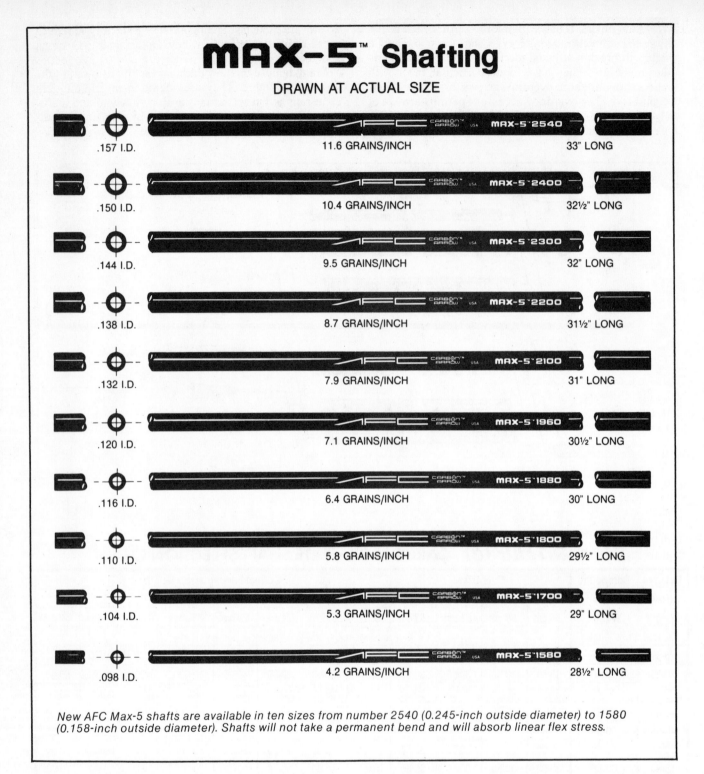

.157 I.D.   MAX-5˚2540   11.6 GRAINS/INCH   33" LONG

.150 I.D.   MAX-5˚2400   10.4 GRAINS/INCH   32½" LONG

.144 I.D.   MAX-5˚2300   9.5 GRAINS/INCH   32" LONG

.138 I.D.   MAX-5˚2200   8.7 GRAINS/INCH   31½" LONG

.132 I.D.   MAX-5˚2100   7.9 GRAINS/INCH   31" LONG

.120 I.D.   MAX-5˚1960   7.1 GRAINS/INCH   30½" LONG

.116 I.D.   MAX-5˚1880   6.4 GRAINS/INCH   30" LONG

.110 I.D.   MAX-5˚1800   5.8 GRAINS/INCH   29½" LONG

.104 I.D.   MAX-5˚1700   5.3 GRAINS/INCH   29" LONG

.098 I.D.   MAX-5˚1580   4.2 GRAINS/INCH   28½" LONG

New AFC Max-5 shafts are available in ten sizes from number 2540 (0.245-inch outside diameter) to 1580 (0.158-inch outside diameter). Shafts will not take a permanent bend and will absorb linear flex stress.

tain groupings, the head inserts and nocks must change size.

Overall, the carbon-graphite arrows are more expensive than most aluminums, although all prices may vary according to the type and number of options included. Some aluminum-carbon arrows are more expensive than either, but those who use them believe the extra cost is well worth the results.

If a bow is already set up and tuned for aluminum arrows and the archer decides to switch to carbon-graphite, certain adjustments to the bow must be made. The carbon shaft is smaller in diameter, so the arrow rest and the nock point must be altered to compensate. If one is starting from scratch, with a new bow not shot before, the adjustments will come when tuning the bow.

To select the correct arrow, the archer first must determine four basic things to better use the Easton Shaft Selection Chart. The chart is available from any Easton dealer and will be found in most archery shops. The chart, or portions of it, are printed commonly in large mail order catalogs. As mentioned, Easton is the standard by which all arrow shafts are measured. Arrow selection is further simplified,

Headquarters of the AFC operation are in Chatfield, Minnesota. Company personnel are aware of the importance of public exposure for the product and are visible at most large trade and consumer archery, sporting shows.

if the services of a pro shop are utilized.

The first thing we need to determine is the actual draw length. Draw length varies with each individual. It depends on physical size, build, arm length and shooting style. The easiest method of determining draw length is to visit a pro shop and let the dealer help. Many of them maintain a special lightweight bow for the purpose. It may have a marked full-length arrow. The bow is drawn by the archer and the actual distance from the individual's anchor point to the arrow rest is measured. This is the draw length, not the arrow length. Usually, arrow length is about an inch longer than draw length.

If such a set-up is not available, there is a secondary method which may be used. For this, the archer stands facing a wall or other solid object, makes a fist with the bow hand and places the knuckles flat against the wall. An associate then uses a yardstick or tape to measure the distance from the wall to the anchor point, usually the corner of the mouth. The bow arm must be fully extended, the knuckles flat against the wall. Head, body and hand are in a shooting position. New archers often find that, after some practice, their muscles become accustomed to the work, and draw length may increase by about a half-inch. The trial length may be rounded off to the next full inch upward.

For bowhunters, the extra arrow length allows the broadhead blades to not be drawn into the bow handle or the arrow rest. If one is making arrows from raw shafts, this extra length is doubly important before the shafts are cut and finished. Target arrows may be drawn farther back and can be slightly shorter, but if there is the possibility of using the arrows later for hunting, it is better to compensate for the extra length.

When draw and arrow length have been determined, the actual bow draw weight must be found. This determination is slightly different for recurve bows and for compound bows. Most archery shops have a bow weighing jig and the figures, at the actual draw length, are easily found as the retailer weighs the bow on the scale.

For recurve bows, the Archery Manufacturers Organization (AMO) designates the draw weight as the force required to draw the bow to twenty-eight inches measured from the front of the bow handle — away from the archer — to a point on the arrow where the string contacts the nock. If the archer's draw length matches that exactly, the draw weight marked on the bow is what to work with. The pro shop also will weigh the bow to the archer's draw length, or the archer may add or subtract three pounds from the listed weight for each inch over or under twenty-eight inches.

For instance, if the actual measured draw length is twenty-nine inches, three pounds are added to the fifty-pound draw weight. The actual draw weight becomes fifty-three pounds. This figure is used when referring to the Easton Selection Chart.

For compound bows, the simplest test is to have the bow weighed at the pro shop. The draw weight is marked on the bow, usually on the lower limb, as is the draw length and percent of draw let-off. Compound bows may be varied in draw weight and length, so the weighing machine is the most accurate method of determining actual draw weight. Most compounds are set and marked at the factory and this figure, if the bow has not been adjusted, may be used for determination of draw weight.

The Easton charts were established, using a Fast Flight string and finger release. If the bow is equipped with a Dacron string, and/or if the archer uses a mechanical release

RECURVE BOW / COMPOUND BOW Shaft Selection Chart

RECURVE BOW — Actual or Calculated Bow Weight (Pounds); Broadhead or Field Point Weight Only

COMPOUND BOW — Actual or Calculated Peak Bow Weight (Pounds); Broadhead or Field Point Weight Only

CAUTION: Carbon arrows are not recommended for hunting unless special precautions are taken. See dealer or Easton information furnished with each set of A/C/C shafts.

Arrow length column groups (Shaft Size / Shaft Model / Shaft Weight):
21½″- **22″** -22½″ | 22½″- **23″** -23½″ | 23½″- **24″** -24½″ | 24½″- **25″** -25½″

Note (printed in upper portion of chart): This shaft selection chart was set up using Fast Flite™ String, finger release and modern, efficient recurve and compound bows. The shaft size recommendations for compound bows were determined using 50-65% let-off and round wheels. If your equipment varies from the above, see the "Variables" section or the **EASTON BOWHUNTING** brochure to determine your **Calculated Bow Weight** or **Calculated Peak Bow Weight** before using this chart.

Rec 75 (65-85)	Rec 100 (90-110)	Rec 125 (115-135)	Rec 150 (140-160)	Rec 175 (165-185)	Comp 75 (65-85)	Comp 100 (90-110)	Comp 125 (115-135)	Comp 150 (140-160)	Comp 175 (165-185)	22″ Size	22″ Model	22″ Wt	23″ Size	23″ Model	23″ Wt	24″ Size	24″ Model	24″ Wt	25″ Size	25″ Model	25″ Wt
30-34	27-31	24-28	21-25	18-22	35-40	32-37	29-34	26-31	23-28										1813	XX75	197 A
35-39	32-36	29-33	26-30	23-27	41-46	38-43	35-40	32-37	29-34							1813	XX75	189 A	1913 1816 3L-04	XX75 XX75,E A/C/C	209 A 232 A 173
40-44	37-41	34-38	31-35	28-32	47-52	44-49	41-46	38-43	35-40				1813	XX75	181 A	1913 1816 3L-04	XX75 XX75,E A/C/C	200 A 223 A 167	1913 1816 1818 3-04	XX75 XX75,E XX75 A/C/C	209 B 232 B 268 A 180
45-49	42-46	39-43	36-40	33-37	53-58	50-55	47-52	44-49	41-46	1813	XX75	173 A	1913 1816 3L-04	XX75 XX75,E A/C/C	192 A 213 A 160	1913 1816 1818 3-04	XX75 XX75,E XX75 A/C/C	200 B 223 B 257 A 173	2013 1916 1818 3L-18	XX75 XX75,E XX75 A/C/C	225 A 251 A 268 B 186
50-54	47-51	44-48	41-45	38-42	59-64	56-61	53-58	50-55	47-52	1913 1816 3L-04	XX75 XX75,E A/C/C	184 A 204 A 153	1913 1816 1818 3-04	XX75 XX75,E XX75 A/C/C	192 B 213 B 246 A 166	2013 1916 1818 3L-18	XX75 XX75,E XX75 A/C/C	216 A 241 A 257 B 179	2013 1916 1918 3L-18 3-18	XX75 XX75,E XX75 A/C/C A/C/C	225 B 251 B 290 A 186 195
55-59	52-56	49-53	46-50	43-47	65-70	62-67	59-64	56-61	53-58	1913 1816 1818 3-04	XX75 XX75,E XX75 A/C/C	184 B 204 B 235 A 158	2013 1916 1818 3L-18	XX75 XX75,E XX75 A/C/C	207 A 231 A 246 B 172	2013 1916 1918 3L-18 3-18	XX75 XX75,E XX75 A/C/C A/C/C	216 B 241 B 278 A 179 187	2113 2016 1918 3-18	XX75 XX75 XX75 A/C/C	233 A 264 B 290 B 195
60-64	57-61	54-58	51-55	48-52	71-76	68-73	65-70	62-67	59-64	2013 1916 1818 3L-18	XX75 XX75,E XX75 A/C/C	198 A 221 A 235 B 164	2013 1916 1918 3L-18 3-18	XX75 XX75,E XX75 A/C/C A/C/C	207 B 231 B 266 A 172 180	2113 2016 1918 3-18	XX75 XX75 XX75 A/C/C	223 A 253 A 278 B 187	2113 2114 2016 2115 2018 3-28	XX75 XX75 XX75 XX75 XX75,E A/C/C	233 C 247 B 264 C 269 A 307 A 203
65-69	62-66	59-63	56-60	53-57	77-82	74-79	71-76	68-73	65-70	2013 1916 1918 3L-18 3-18	XX75 XX75,E XX75 A/C/C A/C/C	198 B 221 A 255 A 164 172	2113 2016 1918 3-18	XX75 XX75 XX75 A/C/C	214 A 243 A 266 B 180	2113 2114 2016 2115 2018 3-28	XX75 XX75 XX75 XX75 XX75,E A/C/C	223 C 237 B 253 C 259 A 295 A 194	2213 2114 2115 2018 2020 3-28	XX75 XX75 XX75 XX75,E XX75 A/C/C	246 A 247 C 269 B 307 B 337 A 203
70-74	67-71	64-68	61-65	58-62	83-88	80-85	77-82	74-79	71-76	2113 2016 1918 3-18	XX75 XX75 XX75 A/C/C	205 A 232 A 255 B 172	2113 2114 2016 2115 2018 3-28	XX75 XX75 XX75 XX75 XX75,E A/C/C	214 C 227 B 243 C 248 B 282 A 186	2213 2114 2115 2018 2020 3-28	XX75 XX75 XX75 XX75,E XX75 A/C/C	236 A 237 C 259 B 295 B 324 A 194	2312 2213 2215 2117 2020 3-39	XX75 XX75 XX75 XX75,E XX75 A/C/C	235 A 246 B 267 A 301 A 337 B 210
75-79	72-76	69-73	66-70	63-67	89-94	86-91	83-88	80-85	77-82	2113 2114 2016 2115 2018 3-28	XX75 XX75 XX75 XX75 XX75,E A/C/C	205 C 217 B 232 C 237 A 270 A 178	2213 2114 2115 2018 2020 3-28	XX75 XX75 XX75 XX75,E XX75 A/C/C	226 A 227 C 248 B 282 B 310 A 186	2312 2213 2215 2117 2020 3-39	XX75 XX75 XX75 XX75,E XX75 A/C/C	225 A 236 B 256 A 289 A 324 B 202	2312 2314 2215 2117 2216 3-49	XX75 XX75 XX75 XX75,E XX75 A/C/C	235 B 266 A 267 B 301 B 301 A 217
80-84	77-81	74-78	71-75	68-72	95-100	92-97	89-94	86-91	83-88	2213 2114 2115 2018 2020 3-28	XX75 XX75 XX75 XX75,E XX75 A/C/C	216 A 217 C 237 B 270 B 297 A 178	2312 2213 2215 2117 2020 3-39	XX75 XX75 XX75 XX75,E XX75 A/C/C	216 A 226 B 245 A 277 A 310 A 193	2312 2314 2215 2117 2216 3-49	XX75 XX75 XX75 XX75,E XX75 A/C/C	225 B 255 A 256 B 289 B 289 A 208	2413 2314 2315 2216 2219 3-49	XX75 XX75 XX75 XX75 XX75,E A/C/C	260 A 266 B 292 A 301 B 344 A 217

The chart indicates that more than one shaft size may shoot well from your bow. **Shaft sizes in bold type are the most widely used**, but you may decide to shoot a lighter shaft for speed, or a heavier shaft for greater penetration and durability. Also, large variations in bow efficiency, type of wheels or cams, bow length, string material and release type may require special bow tuning or a shaft size change to accommodate these variations.

The "Shaft Weight" column—indicates shaft weight only. To determine total arrow weight, add the weight of the shaft, point or broadhead, RPS insert, nock and fletching. Where two models are shown for one size, the weight shown is for XX75. Letter codes A-C listed to the right of shaft weight indicate the relative stiffness of each aluminum shaft within that "Shaft Size" box ("A" being the stiffest, "B" less stiff, etc.).

"Shaft Model" column—designates arrow model:
XX75 = Gamegetter, Gamegetter II, Camo Hunter, Autumn Hunter and PermaGraphic shafts
E = Eagle Hunter shafts
A/C/C = Aluminum/Carbon/Comp shafts

> Although Easton has attempted to consider most variations of equipment, there are other style and equipment variables that could require shaft sizes other than the ones suggested. In these cases, you'll need to experiment and use stiffer or weaker spine shafts to fit your situation.

EASTON HUNTING SHAFT SELECTION CHART

CORRECT HUNTING ARROW LENGTH — YOUR DRAW LENGTH PLUS 1" CLEARANCE

The chart is organized by correct arrow (draw) length across the top. For each length the three columns are **Shaft Size**, **Shaft Model**, and **Shaft Weight**. Entries are grouped in horizontal point-weight bands (heaviest point weight at bottom).

25½"– 26" –26½"

Shaft Size	Shaft Model	Shaft Weight
1913	XX75	217 A
1816	XX75,E	241 A
1818	XX75	
3L-04	A/C/C	180
1913	XX75	217 B
1816	XX75,E	241 B
1818	XX75	278 A
3-04	A/C/C	187
2013	XX75	234 A
1916	XX75,E	261 A
1818	XX75	278 B
3L-18	A/C/C	194
2013	XX75	234 B
1916	XX75,E	261 B
1918	XX75	301 A
3L-18	A/C/C	194
3-18	A/C/C	203
2113	XX75	242 A
2016	XX75	275 A
1918	XX75	301 B
3-18	A/C/C	203
2113	XX75	242 C
2114	XX75	256 B
2016	XX75	275 C
2115	XX75	280 A
2018	XX75,E	319 A
3-28	A/C/C	211
2213	XX75	256 A
2114	XX75	256 C
2115	XX75	280 B
2018	XX75,E	319 B
2020	XX75	351 A
3-28	A/C/C	211
2312	XX75	244 A
2213	XX75	256 B
2215	XX75	277 A
2117	XX75,E	313 A
2020	XX75	351 A
3-39	A/C/C	219
2312	XX75	244 B
2314	XX75	277 A
2215	XX75	277 B
2117	XX75	313 B
2216	XX75	313 A
3-49	A/C/C	225
2413	XX75	270 A
2314	XX75	277 B
2315	XX75	303 A
2216	XX75	313 B
2219	XX75,E	358 A
3-49	A/C/C	225
2512	XX75	265 A
2413	XX75	270 B
2315	XX75	303 B
2219	XX75,E	358 B
3-60	A/C/C	240

26½"– 27" –27½"

Shaft Size	Shaft Model	Shaft Weight
1913	XX75	225 B
1816	XX75,E	251 B
1818	XX75	289 A
3-04	A/C/C	194
2013	XX75	243 A
1916	XX75,E	271 A
1818	XX75	289 B
3L-18	A/C/C	201
3-18	A/C/C	219
2013	XX75	243 B
1916	XX75,E	271 B
1918	XX75	313 A
3L-18	A/C/C	201
3-18	A/C/C	211
2113	XX75	251 A
2016	XX75	285 A
1918	XX75	313 B
3-18	A/C/C	211
2113	XX75	251 C
2114	XX75	266 B
2016	XX75	285 C
2115	XX75	291 A
2018	XX75,E	332 A
3-28	A/C/C	219
2213	XX75	265 A
2114	XX75	266 C
2115	XX75	291 B
2018	XX75,E	332 B
2020	XX75	364 A
3-28	A/C/C	219
2312	XX75	254 A
2213	XX75	265 B
2215	XX75	288 A
2117	XX75,E	325 A
2216	XX75	337 A
3-49	A/C/C	227
2312	XX75	254 A
2314	XX75	287 A
2215	XX75	288 B
2117	XX75	325 A
2216	XX75	337 B
3-49	A/C/C	234
2413	XX75	281 B
2314	XX75	287 B
2315	XX75	315 B
2219	XX75,E	372 B
3-60	A/C/C	250
2512	XX75	275 A
2413	XX75	281 B
2315	XX75	315 B
2219	XX75,E	372 B
3-60	A/C/C	250
2512	XX75	275 A
2315	XX75	315 B
2317	XX75	358 A
2219	XX75,E	372 B
3-60	A/C/C	250

27½"– 28" –28½"

Shaft Size	Shaft Model	Shaft Weight
1916	XX75,E	281 A
1818	XX75	300 B
3L-18	A/C/C	209
2013	XX75	252 B
1916	XX75,E	281 B
1918	XX75	324 A
3-18	A/C/C	211
2113	XX75	260 A
2016	XX75	296 A
1918	XX75	324 B
3-18	A/C/C	219
2113	XX75	260 C
2114	XX75	276 B
2016	XX75	296 C
2115	XX75	302 A
2018	XX75,E	344 A
3-28	A/C/C	227
2213	XX75	275 A
2114	XX75	276 C
2115	XX75	302 B
2018	XX75,E	344 B
2020	XX75	378 A
3-28	A/C/C	227
2312	XX75	263 B
2213	XX75	275 B
2215	XX75	299 A
2117	XX75,E	337 A
2020	XX75	378 B
3-49	A/C/C	235
2413	XX75	291 A
2314	XX75	298 B
2315	XX75	327 A
2216	XX75	337 B
2219	XX75,E	386 A
3-49	A/C/C	242
2512	XX75	285 A
2413	XX75	291 B
2315	XX75	327 B
2219	XX75,E	386 B
3-60	A/C/C	259
2512	XX75	285 A
2514	XX75	317 A
2317	XX75	371 A
2219	XX75,E	386 B
3-60	A/C/C	259
2512	XX75	285 B
2514	XX75	317 A
2317	XX75	371 B
3-71	A/C/C	273

28½"– 29" –29½"

Shaft Size	Shaft Model	Shaft Weight
2013	XX75	261 B
1916	XX75,E	292 B
1918	XX75	336 A
3L-18	A/C/C	216
3-18	A/C/C	226
2113	XX75	270 A
2016	XX75	306 A
1918	XX75	336 B
3-18	A/C/C	226
2113	XX75	270 C
2114	XX75	286 B
2016	XX75	306 C
2115	XX75	312 A
2018	XX75,E	356 A
3-28	A/C/C	235
2213	XX75	285 A
2114	XX75	286 C
2115	XX75	312 B
2018	XX75,E	356 B
2020	XX75	391 A
3-28	A/C/C	235
2312	XX75	272 B
2213	XX75	285 B
2215	XX75	309 A
2117	XX75,E	349 B
2020	XX75	391 B
3-39	A/C/C	244
2413	XX75	302 A
2314	XX75	309 A
2315	XX75	338 A
2216	XX75	349 B
2219	XX75,E	399 B
3-49	A/C/C	251
2413	XX75	302 A
2314	XX75	309 B
2315	XX75	338 A
2216	XX75	349 A
2219	XX75,E	399 A
3-49	A/C/C	251
2512	XX75	295 A
2413	XX75	302 B
2315	XX75	338 B
2219	XX75,E	399 B
3-60	A/C/C	268
2512	XX75	295 A
2317	XX75	385 B
2219	XX75,E	399 B
3-60	A/C/C	268
2512	XX75	295 B
2514	XX75	329 A
2317	XX75	385 B
3-71	A/C/C	283
2514	XX75	329 B
2317	XX75	385 C
2419	XX75	422 A
3-71	A/C/C	283

29½"– 30" –30½"

Shaft Size	Shaft Model	Shaft Weight
2113	XX75	279 A
2016	XX75	317 A
1918	XX75	347 B
3-18	A/C/C	234
2113	XX75	279 C
2114	XX75	296 B
2016	XX75	317 C
2115	XX75	323 B
2018	XX75,E	368 A
3-28	A/C/C	243
2213	XX75	295 A
2114	XX75	296 C
2115	XX75	323 B
2018	XX75,E	373 A
2020	XX75	405 A
3-28	A/C/C	243
2312	XX75	282 A
2213	XX75	295 B
2215	XX75	320 A
2117	XX75,E	361 A
2020	XX75	405 B
3-39	A/C/C	252
2312	XX75	282 B
2314	XX75	319 A
2215	XX75	320 B
2117	XX75,E	361 B
2216	XX75	361 A
3-49	A/C/C	260
2413	XX75	312 A
2314	XX75	319 B
2315	XX75	350 A
2216	XX75	361 B
2219	XX75,E	413 A
3-49	A/C/C	260
2512	XX75	305 A
2413	XX75	312 B
2315	XX75	350 B
2219	XX75,E	413 B
3-60	A/C/C	277
2512	XX75	305 A
2315	XX75	350 B
2317	XX75	398 A
2219	XX75,E	413 B
3-60	A/C/C	268
2512	XX75	305 A
2317	XX75	398 B
2219	XX75,E	413 B
3-71	A/C/C	277
2514	XX75	340 B
2317	XX75	398 C
2419	XX75	437 A
3-71	A/C/C	283
2514	XX75	340 B
2419	XX75	437 A
3-71	A/C/C	293

30½"– 31" –31½"

Shaft Size	Shaft Model	Shaft Weight
2113	XX75	288 C
2114	XX75	306 B
2016	XX75	327 C
2115	XX75	334 A
2018	XX75,E	381 A
3-28	A/C/C	251
2213	XX75	305 A
2114	XX75	306 C
2115	XX75	334 B
2018	XX75,E	381 B
2020	XX75	418 A
3-28	A/C/C	251
2312	XX75	291 A
2213	XX75	305 B
2215	XX75	331 A
2117	XX75,E	373 A
2020	XX75	418 B
3-39	A/C/C	261
2312	XX75	291 B
2314	XX75	319 A
2215	XX75	320 B
2117	XX75,E	373 B
2216	XX75	373 A
3-49	A/C/C	268
2413	XX75	322 A
2314	XX75	330 B
2315	XX75	362 A
2117	XX75	361 B
2219	XX75,E	427 B
3-49	A/C/C	268
2512	XX75	316 A
2413	XX75	322 B
2315	XX75	362 B
2219	XX75,E	427 B
3-60	A/C/C	287
2512	XX75	316 A
2413	XX75	322 B
2315	XX75	362 B
2219	XX75,E	427 B
3-60	A/C/C	287
2512	XX75	316 A
2514	XX75	351 A
2317	XX75	411 A
2219	XX75,E	427 B
3-60	A/C/C	287
2514	XX75	351 B
2317	XX75	411 B
2419	XX75,E	413 B
3-71	A/C/C	302
2514	XX75	351 B
2317	XX75	411 C
2419	XX75	451 A
3-71	A/C/C	302
2514	XX75	340 B
2419	XX75	451 A
3-71	A/C/C	293

31½"– 32" –32½"

Shaft Size	Shaft Model	Shaft Weight
2213	XX75	315 A
2114	XX75	316 C
2115	XX75	345 B
2018	XX75,E	393 B
2020	XX75	432 A
3-28	A/C/C	259
2312	XX75	301 A
2213	XX75	315 B
2215	XX75	341 B
2117	XX75,E	385 B
2020	XX75	432 B
3-39	A/C/C	269
2312	XX75	301 B
2314	XX75	341 B
2215	XX75	341 B
2216	XX75	385 B
2219	XX75,E	441 A
3-49	A/C/C	277
2413	XX75	333 B
2314	XX75	341 B
2315	XX75	373 B
2216	XX75	385 B
2219	XX75,E	441 A
3-49	A/C/C	277
2512	XX75	326 A
2413	XX75	333 B
2315	XX75	373 B
2219	XX75,E	441 B
3-60	A/C/C	296
2512	XX75	326 A
2315	XX75	373 B
2317	XX75	424 A
2219	XX75,E	441 B
3-60	A/C/C	296
2512	XX75	326 B
2514	XX75	363 B
2317	XX75	424 B
2419	XX75	480 A
3-71	A/C/C	312
2514	XX75	363 B
2317	XX75	424 C
2419	XX75	466 A
3-71	A/C/C	312
2514	XX75	363 B
2317	XX75	411 C
2419	XX75	466 A
3-71	A/C/C	302
2419	XX75	466 A
2419	XX75	451 A

32½"– 33" –33½"

Shaft Size	Shaft Model	Shaft Weight
2312	XX75	310 A
2213	XX75	324 B
2215	XX75	352 A
2117	XX75,E	397 A
3-39	A/C/C	277
2312	XX75	310 B
2314	XX75	351 B
2215	XX75	352 B
2117	XX75	397 B
2216	XX75	397 A
3-49	A/C/C	286
2413	XX75	343 A
2314	XX75	351 B
2315	XX75	385 B
2216	XX75	397 B
2219	XX75,E	454 A
3-49	A/C/C	286
2413	XX75	343 B
2314	XX75	343 B
2315	XX75	385 B
2219	XX75,E	454 B
3-60	A/C/C	305
2512	XX75	336 A
2413	XX75	333 B
2315	XX75	385 B
2219	XX75,E	454 B
3-60	A/C/C	305
2512	XX75	336 A
2514	XX75	374 A
2317	XX75	438 A
3-60	A/C/C	296
2512	XX75	336 A
2514	XX75	374 A
2317	XX75	438 B
3-71	A/C/C	322
2514	XX75	374 B
2317	XX75	438 C
2419	XX75	480 B
3-71	A/C/C	322
2514	XX75	374 B
2419	XX75	480 A
3-71	A/C/C	322
2419	XX75	480 A

> If you use one of the following sizes: 2312, 2314, 2315, 2317, 2413, 2419, 2512, 2514 with an aluminum RPS insert, add the weight of that insert to your point weight, then subtract 25 grains and re-enter the point weight column within which this adjusted point weight falls.

Determining Draw Length
Length from bottom of the nock groove to the front side of the bow while at comfortable full draw.

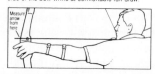

Determining Correct Arrow Length
Arrow length is measured from the bottom of the nock groove to the end of the shaft.

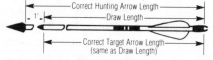

Correct Hunting Arrow Length — 1" — Draw Length — Correct Target Arrow Length (same as Draw Length)

For advanced target and field archers and clicker shooters, your **Correct Arrow Length** may be ½" to 1" shorter than your Draw Length.

Determining Actual Bow Weight or Actual Peak Bow Weight
Actual Bow Weight of a recurve bow and **Actual Peak Bow Weight** of a compound bow can be determined at your archery pro shop.

See your **EASTON BOWHUNTING** brochure for more detailed information.

EASTON ARROW SHAFT

CORRECT ARROW LENGTH

BOW WEIGHT — RECURVE BOW (ACTUAL or CALCULATED BOW WEIGHT)	COMPOUND BOW (ACTUAL or CALCULATED PEAK BOW WEIGHT)	21.5–22.5" (22") Shaft Size	Shaft Model	Shaft Weight	22.5–23.5" (23") Shaft Size	Shaft Model	Shaft Weight	23.5–24.5" (24") Shaft Size	Shaft Model	Shaft Weight	24.5–25.5" (25") Shaft Size	Shaft Model	Shaft Weight	25.5–26.5" (26") Shaft Size	Shaft Model	Shaft Weight
20-25 LBS. (9.1-11.3 KG)	23-29 LBS. (10.4-13.2 KG)	1413	75	130	1400 R 1250 C 1511 1416	A/C/E A/C/E 75 75	108 114 129 A 164	1250 R (1400) 1100 C 1512 1416 1516	A/C/E A/C/E 75 75 X7,75,E	119 121 139 B 172 C 176 A	1250 R 1611 1516	A/C/E 75 X7,75,E	125 149 A 184 A	1100 R (1000) 920 C 1711 1614 1518	A/C/E A/C/E 75 X7 75	132 142 161 C 168 B 201 A 220 C
25-30 LBS. (11.3-13.6 KG)	29-35 LBS. (13.2-15.9 KG)	1400 R 1250 C 1511 1416	A/C/E A/C/E 75 75	103 108 124 A 157 A	1250 R (1400) 1100 C 1512 1516	A/C/E A/C/E 75 X7,75,E	114 115 133 B 169 A	1250 R 1000 C 1611 1516	A/C/E A/C/E 75 X7,75,E	119 136 143 A 176 A	1100 R (1000) 920 C 1612 1711 1614 1518	A/C/E A/C/E 75 75 X7 75	126 146 155 C 161 B 193 A 211 C	1000 R (920) 850 C 1712 (1711) 1713 1614 1616	A/C/E A/C/E 75 75 X7 X7,75,E	148 148 173 B 193 A 201 C 217 A
30-35 LBS. (13.6-15.9 KG)	35-40 LBS. (15.9-18.1 KG)	1250 R (1400) 1100 C 1512 1416 1516	A/C/E A/C/E 75 75 X7,75,E	108 109 127 B 157 C 162 A	1250 R 1000 C 1611 1516	A/C/E A/C/E 75 X7,75,E	114 130 137 A 169 A	1100 R (1000) 920 C 1612 1711 1614 1518	A/C/E A/C/E 75 75 X7 75	121 140 149 C 155 B 186 A 203 C	1000 R (920) 850 C 1711 1712 1614 1616	A/C/E A/C/E 75 75 X7 X7,75,E	142 142 161 C 167 B 186 A 209 A	920 R (850) 780 C 1712 1811 1713 1714 1616	A/C/E A/C/E 75 75 75 X7 X7.75.E	152 156 173 C 181 A 193 B 210 A 217 C
35-40 LBS. (15.9-18.1 KG)	40-46 LBS. (18.1-20.9 KG)	1250 R 1000 C 1611 1516	A/C/E A/C/E 75 X7,75,E	108 125 131 A 162 A	1100 R (1000) 920 C 1612 1711 1614 1518	A/C/E A/C/E 75 75 X7 75	115 134 143 C 148 B 178 A 194 C	1000 R (920) 850 C 1711 1712 1713 1614 1616	A/C/E A/C/E 75 75 75 X7 X7,75,E	136 136 155 C 160 B 178 A 186 C 200 A	920 R (850) 780 C 1712 1811 1713 1714 1616	A/C/E A/C/E 75 75 75 X7 X7.75.E	146 150 167 C 174 A 186 B 202 A 209 C	850 R (780) 720 C 1812 1813 1814 1716	A/C/E A/C/E 75 75 X7 X7,75,E	148 166 188B 204 B 223 A 235 B
40-45 LBS. (18.1-20.4 KG)	46-52 LBS. (20.9-23.6 KG)	1100 R (1000) 920 C 1612 1711 1614 1518	A/C/E A/C/E 75 75 X7 75	109 128 137 C 142 B 170 A 186 C	1000 R (920) 850 C 1711 1712 1713 1614 1616	A/C/E A/C/E 75 75 75 X7 X7,75,E	130 130 148 C 153 B 171 A 178 C 192 A	1712 1811 1713 1714 1616	75 75 75 X7 X7,75,E	160 C 167 A 178 B 193 A 200 C	920 R (850) 780 C 1812 1813 1814 1716	A/C/E A/C/E 75 75 X7 X7,75,E	142 159 181 B 197 B 214 A 226 B	720 R (670) 620 C 3L-04 1912 1913 1814 1816	A/C/E A/C/E A/C/C 75 75 X7 X7,75,E	166 159 180 196 B 217 A 223 C 241 A
45-50 LBS. (20.4-22.7 KG)	52-57 LBS. (23.6-25.9 KG)	1000 R (920) 850 C 1711 1712 1713 1614 1616	A/C/E A/C/E 75 75 75 X7 X7,75,E	125 124 142 C 147 B 163 A 170 C 184 A	920 R (850) 780 C 1712 1811 1713 1714 1616	A/C/E A/C/E 75 75 75 X7 X7,75,E	134 138 153 C 160 A 171 B 185 A 192 C	850 R (780) 720 C 1812 1813 1814 1716	A/C/E A/C/E 75 75 X7 X7,75,E	136 153 174 B 189 B 206 A 217 B	720 R (670) 620 C 3-04 1912 1913 1814 1816	A/C/E A/C/E A/C/C 75 75 X7 X7,75,E	159 153 173 189 B 209 A 214 C 232 A	670 R (620) 570 C 3-04 1913 1914 1816	A/C/E A/C/E A/C/C 75 X7 X7.75.E	154 164 187 217 B 241 A 241 B
50-55 LBS. (22.7-24.9 KG)	57-63 LBS. (25.9-28.6 KG)	920 R (850) 780 C 1712 1811 1713 1714 1616	A/C/E A/C/E 75 75 75 X7 X7,75,E	128 131 147 C 153 A 163 B 177 A 184 C	850 R (780) 720 C 1812 1813 1814 1716	A/C/E A/C/E 75 75 X7 X7,75,E	130 147 167 B 181 B 197 A 208 B	720 R (670) 620 C 3L-04 1912 1913 1814 1816	A/C/E A/C/E A/C/C 75 75 X7 X7,75,E	153 147 167 181 B 200 A 206 C 223 A	670 R (620) 570 C 3-04 1913 1914 1816	A/C/E A/C/E A/C/C 75 X7 X7,75,E	148 158 173 209 B 232 A 232 B	620 R (570) 520 C 3L-18 2013 2014 2014 1916	A/C/E A/C/E A/C/C 75 X7 X7,75,E	159 174 194 234 B 241 C 249 A 261 B
55-60 LBS. (24.9-27.2 KG)	63-69 LBS. (28.6-31.3 KG)	850 R (780) 720 C 1812 1813 1814 1716	A/C/E A/C/E 75 75 X7 X7,75,E	124 141 159 B 173 B 189 A 199 B	720 R (670) 620 C 3L-04 1912 1913 1814 1816	A/C/E A/C/E A/C/C 75 75 X7 X7,75,E	147 140 160 173 B 192 A 197 C 213 A	670 R (620) 570 C 3-04 1913 1914 1816	A/C/E A/C/E A/C/C 75 X7 X7,75,E	142 152 173 200 B 223 A 223 B	620 R (570) 520 C 3L-18 2013 2014 2014 1916	A/C/E A/C/E A/C/C 75 X7 X7,75,E	153 168 186 225 B 232 C 239 A 251 B	520 R (570) 470 C 3-18 (3-28) 2113 2014 2114 2016	A/C/E A/C/E A/C/C 75 75 X7,75 75	174 178 203 242 B 249 C 256 A 275 B
60-65 LBS. (27.2-29.5 KG)	69-74 LBS. (31.3-33.6 KG)	720 R (670) 620 C 3L-04 1912 1913 1814 1816	A/C/E A/C/E A/C/C 75 75 X7 X7,75,E	141 134 153 166 B 184 A 189 C 204 A	670 R (620) 570 C 3-04 1913 1914 1816	A/C/E A/C/E A/C/C 75 X7 X7,75,E	135 146 166 192 B 213 A 213 B	620 R (570) 520 C 3L-18 2013 2014 2014 1916	A/C/E A/C/E A/C/C 75 X7 X7,75,E	147 162 179 216 B 223 C 229 A 241 B	520 R (570) 470 C 3-18 (3-28) 2113 2014 2114 2016	A/C/E A/C/E A/C/C 75 X7 X7,75 75	168 171 195 233 B 239 C 247 A 264 B	470 R (520) 430 C 3-28 (3-39) 2113 2213 2114 2115	A/C/E A/C/E A/C/C 75 75 X7,75 X7,75	178 187 210 242 C 256 A 256 B 280 A
65-70 LBS. (29.5-31.8 KG)	74-80 LBS. (33.6-36.3 KG)	670 R (620) 570 C 3-04 1913 1914 1816	A/C/E A/C/E A/C/C 75 X7 X7,75,E	129 139 158 184 B 204 A 204 B	620 R (570) 520 C 3L-18 2013 2014 2014 1916	A/C/E A/C/E A/C/C 75 X7 X7,75,E	140 156 172 207 B 213 C 220 A 231 B	520 R (570) 470 C 3-18 (3-28) 2113 2014 2114 2016	A/C/E A/C/E A/C/C 75 X7 X7,75 75	162 165 187 223 B 229 C 236 A 253 B	470 R (520) 430 C 3-28 (3-39) 2113 2213 2114 2115	A/C/E A/C/E A/C/C 75 75 X7,75 X7,75	171 180 202 233 C 246 A 247 B 269 A	470 R (430) 400 C 3-39 2312 2213 2215 2115 2117	A/C/E A/C/E A/C/C 75 75 75 X7,75 75,E	178 197 219 244 A 256 B 277 A 280 B 313 A

aid, the draw weight figures are changed. On a recurve bow, subtract four pounds for each factor.

The compound bow also subtracts four pounds for use of a Dacron string and/or a release aid. But ten pounds should be added to the draw weight figure, if high energy cams are on the bow, instead of round eccentric wheels. If the bow under consideration is old and less efficient, four pounds are subtracted from the draw weight figure. For compound bows that have draw lengths of more than twenty-eight inches and/or have axle-to-axle lengths of less than forty-four inches, four pounds are subtracted from the final calculated figure.

Arrow shaft selection also depends upon the weight of the arrow head, target point or broadhead. The figures are expressed in grains, and common weights range from seventy-five through 175 grains. Field points and broadheads are made to matching weights so tuning for hunting is easier. One should hunt with the same head weight as used for target practice.

On the Easton hunting shaft chart, the left columns are designated with the head weights in grains, with spaces for recurves and compounds. Draw weights for each head weight are shown beneath each, in four or five pound-increments. Arrow lengths are established from twenty-

SIZE SELECTION CHART

CORRECT ARROW LENGTH

Note (chart set-up, printed in the 30"–32" area of the first block):

> This chart was set up using modern, efficient recurve and 50-65% let-off, round-wheel compound bows with:
> - Fast Flite* string
> - Finger release
> - The following point weights:
>   - Aluminum arrows – 7% F.O.C. points
>   - A/C/C and UltraLite – 8% F.O.C. points
>   - A/C/E – Recommended insert + point weight
>
> If your equipment varies from the above, see the "Variables" section (page 4 – recurve, page 5 – compound) to determine your **Calculated Bow Weight** or **Calculated Peak Bow Weight** before using this chart.

Column length headings (with sub-columns Shaft Size / Shaft Model / Shaft Weight):

Length	Range
27"	26.5 (67.3 cm) – 27.5 (69.9 cm)
28"	27.5 (69.9 cm) – 28.5 (72.4 cm)
29"	28.5 (72.4 cm) – 29.5 (75.0 cm)
30"	29.5 (75.0 cm) – 30.5 (77.5 cm)
31"	30.5 (77.5 cm) – 31.5 (80.0 cm)
32"	31.5 (80.0 cm) – 32.5 (82.5 cm)

Each of the following data blocks lists, for every arrow-length column, the Shaft Size, Shaft Model and Shaft Weight.

Block 1

27" Size	Mdl	Wt	28" Size	Mdl	Wt	29" Size	Mdl	Wt	30" Size	Mdl	Wt	31" Size	Mdl	Wt	32" Size	Mdl	Wt
1000 R (920)	A/C/E	154	920 R (850)	A/C/E	163	850 R (780)	A/C/E	165									
850 C	A/C/E	153	780 C	A/C/E	168	720 C	A/C/E	184									
1712 (1711)	75	180 B	1811 (1712)	75	195 A	1812	75	210 B									
1713	75	200 A	1713	75	208 B	1813	75	228 B									
1614	X7	209 C	1714	X7	226 A	1814	X7	249 A									
1616	X7,75,E	226 A	1616	X7,75,E	234 C	1716	X7,75,E	262 B									

Block 2

27" Size	Mdl	Wt	28" Size	Mdl	Wt	29" Size	Mdl	Wt	30" Size	Mdl	Wt	31" Size	Mdl	Wt	32" Size	Mdl	Wt
920 R (850)	A/C/E	157	850 R (780)	A/C/E	159	720 R (670)	A/C/E	184	670 R (620)	A/C/E	178						
780 C	A/C/E	162	720 C	A/C/E	178	620 C	A/C/E	177	570 C	A/C/E	189						
1811 (1712)	75	188 A	1812	75	203 B	1913 (1912)	A/C/C	201		A/C/C	216						
1713	75	200 B	1813	75	220 B		75	242 A	1913	75	250 B						
1714	X7	218 A	1814	X7	240 A	1814	X7	249 C	1914	X7	278 A						
1616	X7,75,E	226 C	1716	X7,75,E	253 B	1816	X7,75,E	269 A	1816	X7,75,E	278 B						

Block 3

27" Size	Mdl	Wt	28" Size	Mdl	Wt	29" Size	Mdl	Wt	30" Size	Mdl	Wt	31" Size	Mdl	Wt	32" Size	Mdl	Wt
850 R (780)	A/C/E	153	720 R (670)	A/C/E	178	670 R (620)	A/C/E	172	620 R (570)	A/C/E	183	520 R (570)	A/C/E	205			
720 C	A/C/E	172	620 C	A/C/E	171	570 C	A/C/E	183	520 C	A/C/E	199	470 C	A/C/E	210			
			3L-04	A/C/C	194	3-04	A/C/C	209	3L-18	A/C/C	224	3-18 (3-28)	A/C/C	242			
1812	75	195 B	1912	75	211 B	1913	75	242 B	2013	75	270 B	2113	75	288 B			
1813	75	212 B	1913	75	234 A	1914	X7	269 A	1914	X7	287 A	2014	X7	296 C			
1814	X7	231 A	1814	X7	240 C				2014	X7		2114	X7,75	306 A			
1716	X7,75,E	244 B	1816	X7,75,E	260 A	1816	X7,75,E	269 B	1916	X7,75,E	302 B	2016	75	327 B			

Block 4

27" Size	Mdl	Wt	28" Size	Mdl	Wt	29" Size	Mdl	Wt	30" Size	Mdl	Wt	31" Size	Mdl	Wt	32" Size	Mdl	Wt
720 R (670)	A/C/E	172	670 R (620)	A/C/E	166	620 R (570)	A/C/E	177	520 R (570)	A/C/E	199	470 R (520)	A/C/E	210	470 R (430)	A/C/E	217
620 C	A/C/E	165	570 C	A/C/E	177	520 C	A/C/E	193	470 C	A/C/E	204	430 C	A/C/E	220	400 C	A/C/E	239
3L-04	A/C/C	187	3-04	A/C/C	202	3L-18	A/C/C	216	3-18 (3-28)	A/C/C	234	3-28 (3-39)	A/C/C	251	3-39	A/C/C	269
1912	75	204 B	1913	75	234 B	2013	75	261 B	2113	75	279 B	2113	75	288 C	2312	75	301 A
1913	75	225 A	1914	X7	260 A	1914	X7	269 C	2014	X7	287 C	2114	X7,75	306 B	2213	75	315 B
1814	X7	231 C	1816	X7,75,E	260 B	2014	X7	277 A	2114	X7,75	296 A	2115	X7,75	334 A	2215	75	341 A
1816	X7,75,E	251 A				1916	X7,75,E	292 B	2016	75	317 B				2115	X7,75	345 B
															2117	75,E	385 A

Block 5

27" Size	Mdl	Wt	28" Size	Mdl	Wt	29" Size	Mdl	Wt	30" Size	Mdl	Wt	31" Size	Mdl	Wt	32" Size	Mdl	Wt
670 R (620)	A/C/E	160	620 R (570)	A/C/E	171	520 R (570)	A/C/E	193	470 R (520)	A/C/E	204	470 R (430)	A/C/E	210	430 R (400)	A/C/E	227
570 C	A/C/E	170	520 C	A/C/E	187	470 C	A/C/E	197	430 C	A/C/E	213	400 C	A/C/E	232	370 C	A/C/E	251
3-04	A/C/C	194	3L-18	A/C/C	209	3-18 (3-28)	A/C/C	226	3-28 (3-39)	A/C/C	243	3-39	A/C/C	261	3-49	A/C/C	277
1913	75	225 B	2013	75	252 B	2113	75	270 B	2113	75	279 C	2312	75	291 A	2312	75	301 C
1914	X7	251 A	1914	X7	260 C	2014	X7	277 C	2114	75	295 A	2213	75	305 B	2413	75	333 A
1816	X7,75,E	251 B	2014	X7	268 A	2114	X7,75	286 A	2115	X7,75	323 A	2215	X7,75	331 A	2314	75	341 B
			1916	X7,75,E	281 B	2016	75	306 B	2117	75,E	361 A	2216	75,E	373 A	2215	75	341 C
															2216	75	385 B

Block 6

27" Size	Mdl	Wt	28" Size	Mdl	Wt	29" Size	Mdl	Wt	30" Size	Mdl	Wt	31" Size	Mdl	Wt	32" Size	Mdl	Wt
620 R (570)	A/C/E	165	520 R (570)	A/C/E	180	470 R (520)	A/C/E	197	470 R (430)	A/C/E	204	430 R (400)	A/C/E	220	400 R	A/C/E	239
520 C	A/C/E	180	470 C	A/C/E	191	430 C	A/C/E	207	400 C	A/C/E	225	370 C	A/C/E	243	370 C	A/C/E	251
3L-18	A/C/C	201	3-18 (3-28)	A/C/C	219	3-39	A/C/C	235	3-49	A/C/C	252	3-49	A/C/C	268	3-49 (3-60)	A/C/C	277
2013	75	243 B	2113	75	260 B	2312	75	272 C	2312	75	282 C	2312	75	291 C	2413	75	333 A
1914	X7	251 C	2014	X7	268 C	2213	75	285 A	2413	75	302 A	2413	75	322 A	2314	75	341 B
2014	X7	258 A	2114	X7,75	276 B	2114	X7,75	286 B	2314	75	319 B	2314	75	330 B	2315	75	373 A
1916	X7,75,E	271 B	2115	X7,75	302 A	2115	X7,75	312 B	2215	75	320 C	2315	75	362 A	2216	75	385 B
						2117	75,E	349 A	2216	75	361 B	2216	75	373 B			

Block 7

27" Size	Mdl	Wt	28" Size	Mdl	Wt	29" Size	Mdl	Wt	30" Size	Mdl	Wt	31" Size	Mdl	Wt	32" Size	Mdl	Wt
520 R (570)	A/C/E	180	470 R (520)	A/C/E	191	470 R (430)	A/C/E	197	430 R (400)	A/C/E	213	400 R	A/C/E	232	370 R	A/C/E	251
470 C	A/C/E	184	430 C	A/C/E	200	400 C	A/C/E	218	370 C	A/C/E	236	370 C	A/C/E	243			
3-18 (3-28)	A/C/C	211	3-28 (3-39)	A/C/C	227	3-39	A/C/C	244	3-49	A/C/C	260	3-49 (3-60)	A/C/C	268	3-60 (3-71)	A/C/C	296
2113	75	251 B	2113	75	260 C	2312	75	272 C	2312	75	282 C	2413	75	322 A	2512	75	326 B
2014	X7	258 C	2213	75	275 A	2413	75	302 A	2413	75	312 A	2514	75	330 B	2514	75	363 A
2114	X7,75	266 A	2114	X7,75	276 B	2314	75	309 B	2314	75	319 B	2315	75	362 A			
2016	75	285 B	2115	X7,75	302 A	2215	75	309 C	2315	75	320 C	2317	75	373 B	2317	75	424 B
			2117	75,E	337 A	2216	75	349 B	2216	75	361 B						

Block 8

27" Size	Mdl	Wt	28" Size	Mdl	Wt	29" Size	Mdl	Wt	30" Size	Mdl	Wt	31" Size	Mdl	Wt	32" Size	Mdl	Wt
470 R (520)	A/C/E	184	470 R (430)	A/C/E	191	430 R (400)	A/C/E	207	400 R	A/C/E	225	370 R	A/C/E	243			
430 C	A/C/E	193	400 C	A/C/E	211	370 C	A/C/E	229	370 C	A/C/E	236						
3-28 (3-39)	A/C/C	219	3-49	A/C/C	235	3-49	A/C/C	251	3-60 (3-71)	A/C/C	260	3-71	A/C/C	287	3-71	A/C/C	312
2312	75	251 C	2312	75	263 A	2413	75	272 C	2512	75	305 B	2512	75	316 B	2512	75	326 B
2213	75	265 A	2213	75	275 B	2413	75	302 A	2514	75	340 A	2514	75	351 A	2514	75	363 A
2314	75	266 B	2314	75	299 A	2314	75	309 B	2315	75	350 A						
2115	X7,75	291 A	2215	75	302 B	2315	75	338 A	2317	75	398 B	2317	75	411 B	2317	75	424 B
			2216	75	337 B	2216	75	349 B									

Block 9

27" Size	Mdl	Wt	28" Size	Mdl	Wt	29" Size	Mdl	Wt	30" Size	Mdl	Wt	31" Size	Mdl	Wt	32" Size	Mdl	Wt
430 R (400)	A/C/E	193	400 R	A/C/E	211	370 R	A/C/E	229									
370 C	A/C/E	215	370 C	A/C/E	222												
3-49	A/C/C	234	3-49 (3-60)	A/C/C	242	3-60 (3-71)	A/C/C	268	3-71	A/C/C	293	3-71	A/C/C	302			
2312	75	254 C	2413	75	291 A	2512	75	295 B	2512	75	305 B	2514	75	351	2514	75	363
2413	75	281 A	2314	75	298 B	2514	75	329 A	2514	75	340 A						
2314	75	287 B	2315	75	327 A	2315	75	338 C									
2215	75	288 C	2216	75	337 B	2317	75	385 B	2317	75	398 B						
2216	75	325 B															

---

two through thirty-three inches. Remember, this is arrow length, not draw length.

To determine the most appropriate aluminum shaft for the bow, the archer moves first to the column on the left that lists the weight of the arrow head to be used. As an illustration, we may choose 100 grains. Next, move down the chart to find the actual draw weight of the bow used. Then move across the chart to where the intersection of draw weight and arrow length coincide.

For purposes of illustration, let us assume the combination of a 100-grain head, a sixty-pound compound bow and twenty-nine inch arrow length. At that intersection are several number and letter designations in the Easton hunting area chart. It turns out that, for each bow and arrow combination, there are several recommended shafts. On the chart, one or two of the selections are printed in bold-face type. These shafts are used most commonly for that combo.

In our example, we find shaft sizes 2215 and 2117 are boldfaced, and at least five other shafts are listed within the block. These four-digit numbers have a distinct meaning. It will help us in our selection to understand what they mean.

The first two numbers — 21 or 22 — refer to the outside diameter of the shaft in sixty-fourths of an inch. In other

SHAFT WEIGHT & SPINE COMPARISON

This chart graphically illustrates the weight and spine relationship for all sizes of Easton Aluminum and Aluminum/Carbon shafts.

Comparing Shafts

The comparison chart uses one shaft length (29") to illustrate the relationship of all sizes. The relationship is comparable for other lengths. ◉ The weight is for a 29" length shaft without insert, point, nock or fletching. The spine (stiffness) of the 29" shaft is defined as the measured deflection (in inches) resulting from hanging a 1.94 lb. (880 gram) weight from the center of the shaft. The shaft is supported at two points 28" apart (28" span [71.12 cm]). ◉ To facilitate spine measurement on finished arrows, all spine values are determined with the two shaft supports spaced at a distance of one inch less than the arrow length, e.g., a 31" arrow is measured at a 30" span.

Bow-Weight/Shaft-Spine Relationship

When comparing the spines of various weight shafts, it is important to know that a heavy arrow should be 0.010" to 0.030" stiffer than a lighter arrow of the same measured deflection to shoot properly from the same weight bow. The **EASTON ARROW SHAFT SIZE SELECTION CHART** on pages 9-11 takes this spine difference into consideration when suggesting the proper size shaft.

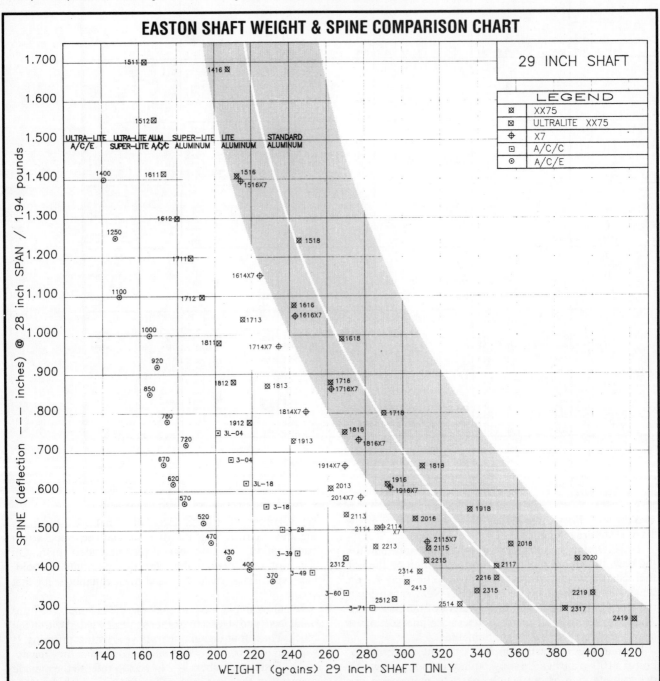

EASTON SHAFT WEIGHT & SPINE COMPARISON CHART

29 INCH SHAFT

LEGEND	
⊠	XX75
⊠	ULTRALITE XX75
⊕	X7
⊡	A/C/C
⊙	A/C/E

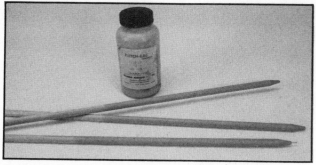

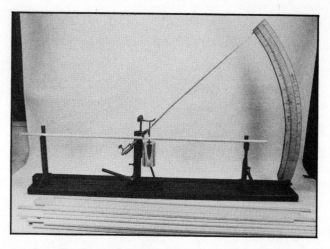

Those archers working in wood shafts often prefer to do most of the work themselves. Archers may choose to lacquer the fletch end for best fletching adhesion, above. The device at right measures spine rating of wooden arrows. The gadget may be difficult to find.

words, the recommended shafts may be 21/64- or 22/64-inch outside diameter. The second two figures list the shaft wall thickness in thousandths of an inch. Our choices are 0.015-inch or 0.017-inch wall thickness. The larger the numbers, the heavier and stiffer the arrow. Stiffness is designated as the spine of the shaft. Generally, lower draw weights will do well with lighter spines. There are exceptions to that statement, but it holds for most bows and most shooters.

As we continue to examine the Easton arrow chart, we see that there are several other shaft sizes printed in lighter type. These appear in addition to the two in boldface. These shafts will fly well from the bow under consideration, and may even be better than the 2215 and 2117, depending on the shooter and the bow.

To the right side of the box under consideration, are other figures, with the letters A, B or C beside them. These

numbers are the shaft weights in grains; in our sample they range from 272 to 391 grains for all-aluminum shafts and 241 and 268 grains for aluminum/carbon. The letters indicate the relative stiffness of the shafts within that box. A is the stiffest and B less stiff. Some boxes in the chart go to letter C, the shaft with the least spine within that group.

Additional shaft recommendations within our sample box include a 3-39 aluminum/carbon/competition (A/C/C) and 4-18 aluminum/carbon/hunting (A/C/H). Easton no longer recommends the A/C/H for hunting, but they are still available for target shooting. The aluminum/carbon arrows are lighter than all-aluminum shafts of the same length and spine. Our samples are 241 and 277 grains for our sixty-pound compound bow.

The other designation in the chart is under the heading of the Easton shaft model. These are either XX75 or E. The XX75 shafts are built of 7075-T9 alloy for most hunting shafts and many target arrows. In addition, Easton utilizes 7178-T9 for their X7 shafts and 6010-T9 for the less expensive Eagle shafts.

The lightest shafts are the Easton A/C/Extreme (A/C/E), made from extremely thin wall tubing with a wall thickness of 0.006-inch. The outside diameter at the center is 0.185-inch. The shaft actually is barrel-shaped through its length. The aluminum shaft is covered with layers of bonded, unidirectional carbon fibers and epoxy resin matrix.

For target shooters, Easton claims several advantages for the A/C/E shafts. The barreled shape, with its lighter ends, is said to produce a higher natural frequency of vibration, allowing the arrow to achieve better clearance. Further, the smaller frontal area and streamlined profile reduce aerodynamic drag. Easton reports that the more flexible rear section of the shaft absorbs a rough release, thereby causing less deviation in the flight of the arrow. Top archers feel that having the rear section of the shaft less stiff than the center or front section creates a more forgiving arrow. Jay Barrs, the 1988 Olympic men's champion, won the Gold Medal using Easton A/C/E arrow shafts.

These lightweight shafts require special nock, point and fletching components which are outlined in Easton's target and field archery selection booklet. The tapered shafts

The Easton Camo-Hunter shaft, already camouflaged and in 2117 spine rating is most popular with bowhunters.

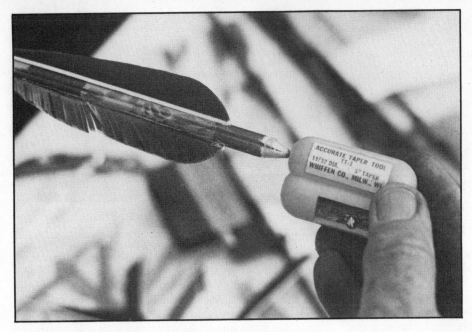

Accurate nock end taper is vital to straight arrow flight. When re-nocking an arrow, old glue must be carefully, entirely removed.

may be a bit too advanced for the beginning archer, but they have found favor with a number of experienced target archers. Such lightweight arrows must be matched carefully to the bow.

The final selection of an arrow is determined not only on how accurately and how well the arrow flies to the target, but also on what type of shooting is to be done. The 3-D target archer may wish to go with a slightly lighter shaft than the chart recommends, the flatter trajectory reducing effects of range estimation errors. The bowhunter, on the other hand, may choose a heavier shaft than the chart lists, seeking greater durability in the field and deeper penetration of the game animals. In fact, one shaft may satisfy all the requirements from a particular bow.

While Easton is the acknowledged leader in aluminum arrow shafts, it is not the only manufacturer of the product. Aluminum shafts with a fluted cross-section, made in Korea, are marketed in North America by Custom Archery under the name, X-Caliber. The shafts are said to be lighter than comparable round shafts, with the fluting adding spine to the arrow. Their cost, in most outlets, is about

the same as Easton with camouflage finish. The X-Calibers are available in camo only, in four different spine ratings. The fluted shafts were introduced in 1983 and millions of dozens have been sold since.

As mentioned, Easton no longer recommends the A/C/H shafts for hunting, although they still are available and are used on many 3-D target ranges. The A/C/C shafts cost about two times as much as comparable aluminum shafts, while the A/C/E will run about four times as much.

Somewhere between those basic prices are the newer all-carbon-graphite arrow shafts that burst upon the archery scene a few years ago and now are making big inroads. They have become popular with some target archers — they have been seen at recent Olympic and world archery competitions — 3-D shooters and bowhunters.

As of 1991, two companies are marketing the carbon-graphite shafts: AFC and Beman. AFC is a U.S. company with a Minnesota address and Beman is a French manufacturer with an Illinois headquarters. Both offer finished arrows or raw shafts in several spines.

All manner of things previously made of metal are being

The bow string is visible through transparent arrow nock on this carbon-graphite arrow. Nock groove depth, width are standard; no location adjustment is needed.

Archers switching from aluminum to carbon shafts will need to re-adjust arrow rest and plunger positions.

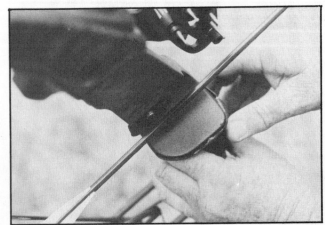

Jim Dougherty is an archery accessory supplier with a line of special aluminum arrows called Serpents. Serpents are manufactured by Easton in standard spines, but finished with snakeskin-like camouflage colors.

made of carbon fiber-epoxy resin these days, including bicycle frames, automobile parts and arrow shafts.

Beman was founded in 1985 and spent two years in research and development of the new shaft material. They began production of target shafts in June 1986. The first shafts were called Diva and are used by target archers around the world.

Much of the world of archery first heard of the carbon-graphite shafts during the next two years, as various world archers were winning medals at international tournaments, including the 1988 Olympics in Korea. According to Beman, six of eight gold medals, five of eight silver medals and two of eight bronze medals were won by shooters using Beman-shafted arrows. Most of the rest of us were introduced to the product at the 1989 Shooting, Hunting and Outdoor Trade (SHOT) Show and the National Archery Show in Las Vegas a couple of weeks later.

At those two shows, the emphasis was on bowhunting and Beman was introducing their newest product, the Beman Hunter arrow. The shafts are spined for hunting bows from thirty to one hundred pounds of draw weight. The Hunter models are produced in a range of six shafts in two diameters. Beman provides a cross-over chart to convert standard Easton aluminum shaft spines to their carbon-graphites.

According to Beman, carbon-graphite arrows have advantages in strength, stiffness, speed and flatter trajectory over those made with more traditional materials. These claims seem rather startling, considering the long popularity of aluminum shafts.

Beman's headquarters and production facilities are located in Villeurbanne, France. Villeurbanne is located in eastern France; a suburb of Lyons with a population of approximately 120,000.

The manufacturing facility is new, automated and robot-controlled, as well as temperature and humidity-controlled. The actual shaft production is by a pultrusion process that is monitored by computer. A quality control stop checks all the shafts for spine straightness and weight before they are marked and packed for shipping. The production process results in a shaft that has the same spine throughout its length, the maker claims.

The Beman selection chart is based upon a wheel compound bow with fifty percent let-off. For those using cam bows and a let-off of sixty-five percent, the next stronger spine arrow should be used. For instance, if the Beman chart called for an arrow listed as 50/70, matching 2018, 2115 and 2213 on the Easton chart for round wheel compound bows, the archer shooting a sixty-pound cam bow should move up to the Beman Hunter 60/80 shaft. Beman points out that it is better to use a carbon-graphite shaft on the stiff side, rather than on the limber.

The Beman shafts measure 15/64-inch in diameter for the 30/50, 40/60 and 50/70 designations and 16/64-inch for the 60/80, 70/90 and 80/100. These diameters must be kept in mind when ordering the various accessories for the Beman arrows and when tuning a bow.

The carbon-graphites are available as finished arrows, or cut to length as unfinished shafts. Broadhead adaptors,

Standard field or target point has larger diameter than thinner carbon shaft, requiring an adapter.

Feather fletchings may be more forgiving, but water or careless handling will reduce their effectiveness.

inserts, target points and nock caps are available as accessories.

A high-speed electric shaft-cutter should be used to cut the carbon-graphite shafts to lengths. Otherwise, there is the risk of a crooked cut or one which frays the end of the shaft.

A number of electric cut-off wheels are on the market which run at high speeds and have extremely fine saw teeth. The buyer may find them at pro shops or through several large mail order companies.

Martin Archery offers a fine-tooth manual cut-off saw which works well. This lightweight unit is complete with a shaft measurement scale, nock cradle and fine-tooth small saw, to cut any kind of shaft material. It works with the carbon-graphite shafts, as well as Easton aluminum shafts and even the fluted shafts from Korea.

When cutting aluminum shafts, the archer simply cuts through the shaft, using just enough pressure to keep each saw stroke cutting. For composite or carbon-graphite shafts, Martin advises the user rotate the shaft to score it with the saw blade first, then begin the cut. Independent tests indicate the cut-off saw works as advertised. Martin's costs considerably less than the power version and the only thing which will wear out is the saw blade itself, which can be replaced.

An adapter for a target point or broadhead must be installed, using Beman's special low temperature Hot-melt glue. The adapter is held over a flame to heat it, but it should remain cool enough to hold with the bare fingers; hotter than that is too hot. If the adapter gets too hot, the epoxy which holds the carbon fibers together may be damaged, destroying the integrity of the shaft.

Once the adapter is warmed, rub the stick of Hot-melt glue over it and push it into the arrow shaft. The adapter is quickly pulled out, then reinserted completely, rotated to assure good glue coverage and positioned for correct broadhead blade angle. If further adjustment is needed later, the adapter, not the shaft, is re-heated until the blades can be moved or replaced. Epoxy cement may be used on the nock cap and target points, but once set, they cannot be adjusted or removed.

Beman claims that one of the reasons a carbon-graphite shaft might fail is because of incorrect gluing. The adapter shaft must be coated completely with the Hot-melt glue and none of the insert metal must come in contact with the shaft wall. If any of the surfaces touch, the vibration and shock of the head striking a target — any target — is transferred directly to the shaft. With a coating of glue, the shock is absorbed, saving the arrow shaft from damage.

While the carbon-graphite shafts are flexible — relative

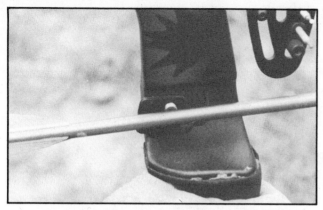

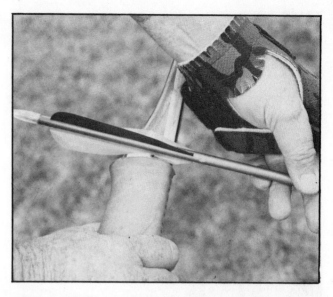

Collapsible plastic arrow rest and plunger are mounted on Jennings Unistar bow with adjustment for passage of plastic-vaned aluminum arrows, above. Plastic is not the choice for arrows which are shot off the shelf from most longbows, right.

flexibility depends upon their spine rating — they will not, Beman claims, hold a permanent bend. The shafts are not indestructible, though; they can fail. It is good safety practice to bend each arrow slightly after each shot to examine for splits. A split shaft cannot be repaired and should be discarded immediately. The head adapter and nock cap can be removed to be re-used, if they are not damaged and were not mounted with epoxy cement.

Unless an archer is using a new bow with carbon-graphite arrows, the bow which was tuned for standard aluminum arrows will have to be retuned. Because of the smaller diameter shaft, the string nock point indicator will have to be moved down a fraction of an inch. Try a sixteenth of an inch as an experimental starting point. The bow and arrow combination then is tuned as any other.

There is the question of quivers. Most arrow slots on bow or belt quivers are too large to hold the carbon-graphite shafts firmly and without rattling. The rubberized slots might be partially filled with liquid rubber or moleskin, if necessary. A number of quiver makers offer narrower shaft holders as options.

At this point, the new archer may feel somewhat overwhelmed by the arrow selection process. It sounds more complicated than it is. Once the basic draw length, draw weight and arrow head weight are known, there may be a half dozen or more shaft spines which will be satisfactory. Different shooters may find different shafts to be satisfactory from the same bow.

A particular shaft size can be picked from the Easton chart and ordered from a mail order company or may be purchased at a larger discount mass marketer. This can work well for experienced archers who know exactly what performance they seek. But beginners will be happier and save money in the long run if they locate an archery specialty shop nearby. The experienced personnel will select the best two or three shafts quickly, and the archer can try them from the bow.

With the best arrow selected, buy a dozen or two new arrows, each correctly assembled and balanced. Then head for the range for some serious shooting and plenty of fun.

The Editor has relied heavily upon Easton Aluminum's informative booklets, *Bowhunting With Easton Arrow Shafts* and *Easton Target And Field Archery* for portions of this chapter. The information is greatly appreciated. — *Roger Combs*

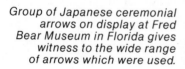

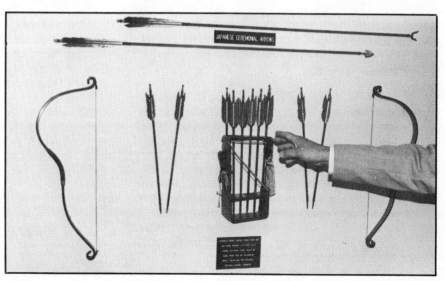

Group of Japanese ceremonial arrows on display at Fred Bear Museum in Florida gives witness to the wide range of arrows which were used.

ARROWS TO ORDER

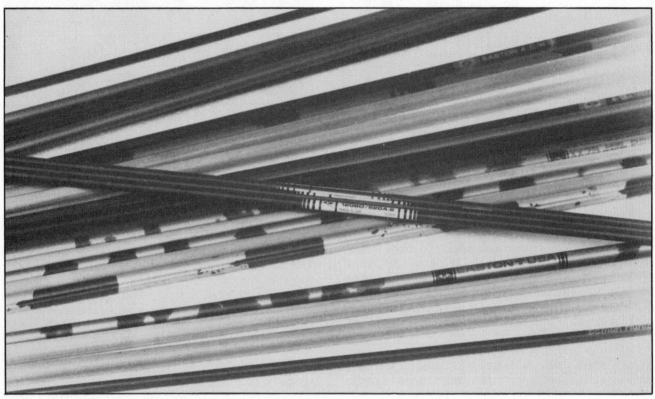

In the continuing search for better missiles, arrow shafts may be made of wood, carbon fiber, fiberglass or aluminum, or in various combinations of some or all of the materials. Production can be an archer's challenge.

THE SPORT OF ARCHERY requires two basic components: A bow and some arrows. With a bow selected, the arrows must match. Most of us may choose to simply purchase a dozen properly matched arrows and start shooting. But in the old days, archers had to make their own arrows. There is still the challenge of arrow making and many archers prefer to make their own, for aesthetic as well as economical purposes. With the basic tools, the cost of arrows can decrease dramatically and the archer will have the pleasure of knowing the arrows he is shooting are his own. C.R. Learn has made his own arrows for more than twenty-five years and still does. Read how he does it in the following report.

POSSIBLY, THE FIRST weapon used by two-legged man was a club, good at close range, but not for long distances. The next obvious choice would be the rock. There were plenty of them and they could be used as a club for bashing close targets. They could also be thrown, making them the first projectiles.

A long, heavy stick could be thrown farther and with more accuracy. The simple spear was born, later to be tipped with a rock or chiseled rock tip. Why not modify the spear, make it smaller and lighter and it would go farther? The problem was to get enough energy behind the small stick to have any advantage.

If man took a big, heavy stick, bent it into a curved con-

figuration and tied it in that position, it would make a weapon for casting the lighter spear. It may have been something like that.

The light spear was too heavy for the crude bow system, so a lighter stick was needed. Reeds, bamboo, willows or any light straight wood or cane material gave the lightness and the first arrows were brought into the arsenal of mankind. Later refinements improved the efficiency of the bow as finer tuning made for better arrows.

That was many moons ago, even before my time, but I've heard all about it sitting at hunt camps. The sport of archery has progressed far beyond this crude beginning. Not too many years ago, we had only one type of arrow material in general use, Port Orford cedar shafting. This is

Custom Archery's fluted aluminum shaft has a triple channel running the length to add spine, lighten arrow.

Wood, Fiberglass, Aluminum, Carbon Fiber — Make Your Own Arrows For Fun And Profit

Above: A few of the many shafts available from Easton. The aluminum/carbon shafts are recommended for target archery only. Carbon-fiber shafts from AFC and Beman, left, are similar in appearance, construction and flight.

a light, straight, fine-grained wood that is still in use today and preferred by many bowhunters.

Before the late Forties, a young man by the name of Doug Easton worked to perfect the first aluminum arrows to make an even stronger arrow at less weight than the cedars. The shafts would have various weights and spines that he could control.

With the advent of the plastics industry after WWII, the fiberglass arrow entered the field. It did bend, but was a bit

heavier than aluminum. Manufacturers have worked this up to a good hunting shaft and it is still on the market today.

In the early Seventies, I had the opportunity to try some full-length carbon arrows. These were made from longitudinal fibers of carbon. It was smaller than the other arrow shafts, but it would have required a bow draw weight of at least one hundred pounds to match the stiffness of the shafting. They never did get that one to fly; pun intended.

Today we have many variations and combinations of arrow shafting to pick from, depending upon what we want to pay, what we think we need and what works best for our style of shooting. Target archers use similar shafts, but become even fussier with tip weight and all the other fine tuning they do. All fields of archery enjoy a similar selection of arrow shafting materials and basically the only difference is in the spine and grain weight of the shafts.

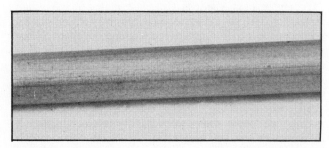

The plain, grained cedar shaft, above, is still preferred by many. The more elaborate footed cedar shafts, below, include bubinga, walnut footing by Cedarsmith. The more colorful has bubinga and maple, with a dyed maple tip.

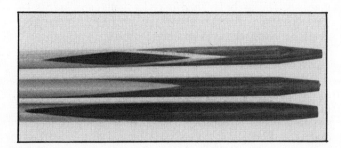

With the cedar shaft cut to length, the nock end is tapered with an appropriate device, such as a Blackhawk tapering tool, in use for more than thirty years.

The archer who will make many cedar-shaft arrows may want to invest in a grain scale to help match up mill run cedars. The long arced spine tester will be difficult to locate, but some old-time makers still have them.

CEDARS

The Port Orford cedar shafts were all we had to shoot of any quality for many of the early years. The wood is harvested from the Oregon hillsides, cured and made into little round shafts. The wood is lightweight, tough and straight-grained. There are probably other types of wooden arrows, but this is the one that has been the most enduring.

There are many things that draw bowhunters to cedar shafts. They are the least expensive. One can buy a hundred of them for the cost of one dozen of the more sophisticated shafts. They require more work to finish into arrows, but that is part of the fun of working with them.

The spine tester is set two inches wider than the shaft length and the two-pound weight is centered on the shaft as the logarithmic scale reveals the cedar shaft spine.

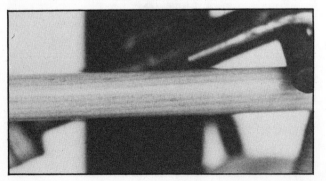

Not too many moons ago, a gentleman by the name of Bill Sweetland took the cedar shaft, compressed it in his shop and made what was called Forgewood. This made the cedar tougher and heavier for those who wanted to shoot the big, heavy bows and could never find cedar shafts strong enough. The process was around for many years. Sweetland could place the compressed area on the back of the shaft, the front and the middle for an even distribution of compression. They worked well, but the plant was sold and they have not come back on the market.

Another method used to toughen cedar shafts was to inlay; make what is termed a footed arrow. A section of hardwood was set into the front six or so inches of the shaft to make the impact area tougher. It makes a beautiful arrow when done right. These aren't cheap or simple to make and are about the most expensive of the cedars available today. They are still available.

A gentleman in Alamosa, Colorado, makes footed cedars in his shop. He uses a contrasting hardwood such as bubinga and insets this in a long tapered V along the shaft. When placed together, the foot and the shaft cut equally; you can't find the seam. To make them even more exotic looking, he adds a bubinga base, a white maple mid-section and tips it with a dyed, laminated maple tip for a triple footed shaft.

The older cedar shafts were usually three-eighths-inch in diameter. This was to get them strong enough to match bow weights. Then they found they could get them almost as tough in 11/32-inch diameter, which became the standard for most bowhunters. They also are available in lighter and smaller shafts for target and lighter weight hunting bows. The last order I had for cedar shafts came in 23/64-inch diameter, a snitch above the 11/32-inch normally available in my draw weight and length.

FIBERGLASS

After World War II, we had a new technology on the scene: fiberglass. Gordon Plastics made arrow shafts by the millions from a patented process using circular and longitudinal fibers on a mandrel that gave it the desired inside diameter. These long tubes were moved to a centerless

The spine tester will reveal the relative spine value for a set of cedar shafts so that they can be matched before shooting. The device also indicates the draw weight range best for that spine reading, as at right.

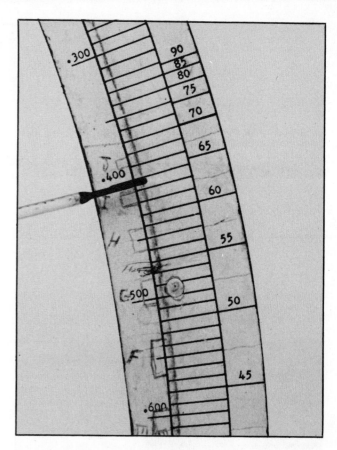

grinding machine to be trued by wet grinding, dried and sorted as to size, color, spine and straightness. They were either straight or crooked and couldn't be straightened. They were tough and made good hunting arrows. There has been some controversy about the weight and flight characteristics, but they dropped many a game animal.

The fiberglass arrow has almost disappeared from the market. If you check price sheets in magazines, you will find little selection in fiberglass shafting.

ALUMINUM

Doug Easton is considered to be the one who developed one of the toughest, longest lived and standard material in the arrow business when he perfected the aluminum shaft.

The process is simple to devise, but difficult to execute. It starts with a tube of a certain type of aluminum, purchased from the manufacturer. This tubing is drawn through special machines that reduce the diameter and the wall thickness uniformly. When it reaches a certain state, it is placed in huge bundles, heated in a furnace for a specified time and temperature, then removed and immediately quenched in a salt liquid to harden the metal.

The tubing is then cut to a specified length, one end chamfered to the proper angle to allow a nock to be cemented on. The shaft is marked with the Easton logo as well as the size and type of shaft. The first aluminum shafts were a bright color and when you handled them your hands turned black from the oxide. That was a small price to pay for an arrow that was and is used for the standard in the industry and the problem was solved long ago. When you read or see charts of different arrow producers, they compare the arrow they make to the similar standard Easton aluminum shafts.

There are various grades of aluminums. The fewer draws and quenches in the process, the softer and easier the shaft is to bend. They also straighten just as easily, but those are usually the less expensive arrow materials. The harder the aluminum stock, the tougher and more bend-resistant the arrow is. Of course, they cost more. The one arrow I have been shooting for many decades is the orange anodized XX75 shaft. It is tough and easy to find in grass, weeds or undergrowth. It can be bent, but it will straighten out nicely after a day in the field.

Not too many years ago, Carl Leckovich appeared on the scene with a new idea for aluminum arrow shafting. These were Custom Archery's fluted arrow shafts. The standard round tube is fluted — indented lengthwise — at three points in the circumference. The fluting makes the aluminum tough and more bend-resistant to give a lighter arrow a heavier spine. The fluting imparts a stiffening. They shoot fast and if you try them you might be amazed at the accurate distances you can achieve. The fluting makes it a bit more difficult to straighten a bent arrow, but by using a sleeve of round shaft, the fluted material will straighten.

Many archers shoot fluted shafts as they feel they get better flight and accuracy. They are a bit fussy in set-up, so you must tune your bow for this type arrow and forget all others. They are not as compatible as a round tube arrow will be.

CARBON

The carbon arrow is back again. A French company, Beman, came out with a little tube of carbon fibers that made into a hot-shooting arrow. It is small, perhaps the smallest of the arrow materials, but tough. They make arrows for the target types and for the bowhunter pulling any weight bow.

An American company, AFC, came out with a carbon arrow that flies extremely well, thank you. It is also a tiny "knitting needle" of an arrow shaft, similar to the Beman and it shoots hard and straight. These are now available in three price ranges that will help the bowhunter who tends to lose more arrows than a target archer might.

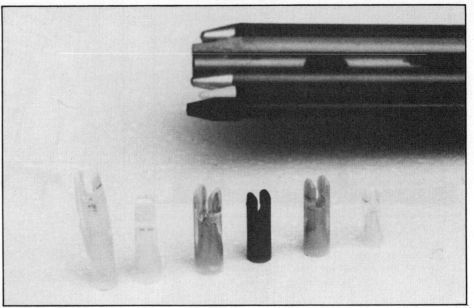

Variety of arrow nock sizes, styles, colors are available to the archer, right. Model on the left is designed to fit Gordon Plastics' fiberglass.

Different sized shafts require different sized nocks; they must match for correct arrow flight.

There are a few objections to carbon arrows, among some shooters. They are difficult to fletch in the normal manner. Since the tubing is so small, you can't really get a good helical fletch on them. The shaft should be examined after shooting for any cracks or glitches, just as we did the older cedar shafts. They may develop a longitudinal crack along the shaft. If you flex and roll them, it will show up. If the crack appears, retire that arrow; it isn't safe to shoot under any circumstances.

ALUMINUM/CARBON

Why not utilize the toughness of aluminum tubing, the light weight of the carbon materials and mate them? Easton did just this and dubbed it the A/C Hunter. They started with a tube of lightweight aluminum and placed longitudinal carbon fibers along the length. This made a light, tough hunting arrow that flies fast, straight and true.

These arrows performed as Easton had hoped, but a fly flew into the system. Would the carbon fibers break off in the meat of the game animal and cause problems for consumers? The tiny carbon fibers around the shaft became a matter of interest to the people at Easton. The shafts can still be purchased, but they aren't recommended for hunting. The A/C shafts are sold only as target arrows.

Which is the best arrow material for bowhunting or target competition? That will never be answered by anyone but the person who draws the bow to release the arrow. The only way to find out is to buy a few that you think are interesting and give them your own personal test. Do you like a light arrow, a heavy arrow, an expensive arrow or those that give more quantity? I have always felt that there are no bad arrows, only sloppy shooters. Arrow materials make a difference in arrow flight, but the only way you can find which is best is to shoot until you find what you want. If that seems too expensive, borrow some arrows from a friend to try.

The clear plastic nock, below, reveals the unusual nature of a tapered fluted shaft. Enough nock cement must be used to completely fill nock insert cavity.

Instead of tapering the all-carbon shaft, a sleeve-like plastic taper is glued over the shaft. Any attempt to taper the shaft itself will lead to fiber damage.

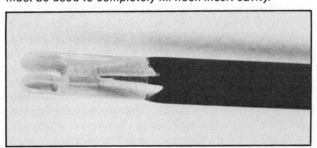

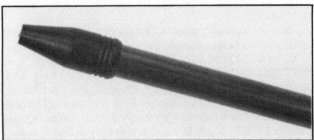

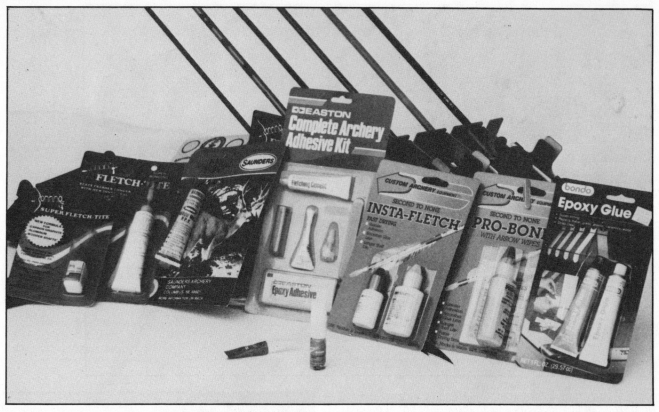

Bohning, Custom Archery, Easton, Martin, Saunders are a few of the many producers of fletching and nocking cements. So-called instant-cement and other two-part epoxy brands will work well on some arrow components.

Another way to find that perfect combination is to talk to fellow archers. Most of them have been through the same problems and can save you time and money. Pick those who shoot well on the range and consistently bring back game.

Over the years, the arrow shafts have ranged from stainless steel shafts that bent going out of the bow to others that have been proven and will remain with us for many years to come.

Now that we have an idea of the shafting available, let's look at how to make these shafts into that flying missile we call an arrow.

ARROW MAKING

Cedar is porous wood which must be sealed from the elements so it won't warp. You may buy cedars in three levels of quality: The most expensive are those that have been spine tested and grouped within five pounds more or less of the specified poundage. These shafts are also usually weighed on a grain scale and weight matched to within five or ten grains to give them the same flight characteristics.

The next range would be those that are roughly spined and weight matched, but not as precisely as the first group. The lower and least expensive are those that have been tested for basic straightness, but not spine and weight matched. These are usually classified as mill run and are a great buy if you want an arrow you don't feel obligated to chase; one you won't hesitate to shoot at rabbits in the rocks. The less work the plant does to the arrow shaft, the lower the price.

For mill run arows, you will need two tools not needed

for other types of shafts: a grain scale and a spine tester. The gain scale is a small scale graduated in grains, usually to 800 or 900 grains, in small increments. Using this scale you can match the shafts as closely as you like. For example, if you weigh out the mill shafts and they seem to run in a wide range, sort them into a smaller range and later, fine-tune them again. Most will start around 400 or 500 grains in fifty- to sixty-pound spine. Those that have more sap or water in them might go higher and you establish a "heavy" pile. Conversely, there will be some that are quite light, so make a "light" pile. Of course, those that fall into the mid-range go into another pile. You can make as many piles and weigh as closely as you like; the fun of mill run cedars. You get varying weights, but all within the range of your bow.

Cedars can have a bit of a dog-leg bend in them at times, but that can easily be straightened over the palm of your hand. Hold the shaft up to your eye and sight down the length to locate the bend. Place the arc of the bend on the palm of your hand. Apply opposite gentle pressure at the point of the bend and the arrow shaft will true out nicely.

Check these mill runs for correct spine. The spine tester is a rather simple device that measures the deflection of the shaft and will tell you the bow weight poundage for which it is best suited. If you shoot a twenty-eight-inch arrow, you set the machine's pylons at twenty-six inches with the arrow across. A two-pound weight is lowered to the midsection of the suspended arrow and the amount of deflection is read from a logarithmic scale on the unit. This scale is usually also marked with the bow poundage equivalent to make it easy.

The term "spine" may need explaining. The spine of an

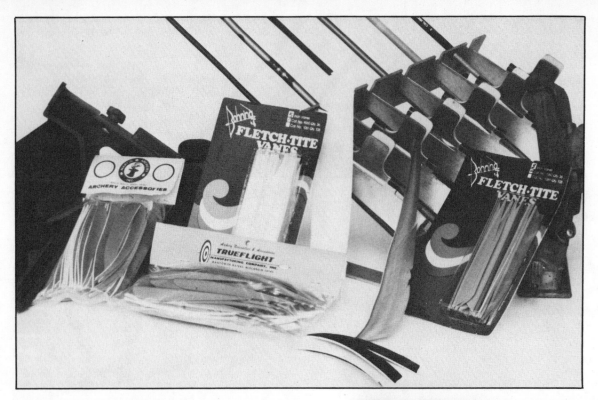

Plastic vane and natural feather fletching are available in dozens of colors, sizes and shapes, depending on shooting styles, shaft materials. Feathers, right, may be purchased full or die-cut. Shield cuts are rare today.

arrow determines how much it bends or deflects around the bow on release. This bending of the arrow around the bow is called "archer's paradox." There are many variables that determine the proper arrow spine. First, is the weight of the bow; second, the draw length of the archer. From here, it will depend on whether you shoot a longbow, recurve, compound, cam or wheels. It will also depend on the type of arrow rest you use, ranging from the shoot-off-the-bow shelf style to the sophisticated and complicated shoot-through arrow rests. All these variables enter into the discussion of spine, but let's go to the simplest and,

Trueflight supplies feather fletching to archers who are making their own arrows. Parabolic shape is popular.

some still believe, the best arrow rest: off the bow shelf.

When you shoot "off the shelf" with a longbow or recurve, you get maximum paradox and the spine is the most critical. Some feel this is the worst way to shoot, but it is the simplest. You have nothing to become lost or work loose to render the bow ineffective.

As the bow leaves the bow string, it starts to bend away from the riser. The bend is determined by the stiffness of the arrow. If it is too stiff, the spine too high, the arrow won't fly true, but will hit to one side of the mark. If the spine is too low, the arrow is too limber, and the arrow will hit off the mark at the opposite side. When you have correct spine, release system and right tip weight, the arrows

A full-length, dyed feather may be cut in any one of several shapes. The best single fletch is cut from the center of the feather. Uncut, it works well as a flu-flu.

will strike your aiming point correctly on each shot. Lower the spine and they go off target. The same is true of too heavy a spine; it will fly off to one side. You must determine what range of spine your system can handle and hit correctly.

That explanation is overly simplified, but it does the job without getting too complicated. By using the spine tester, you sort the arrows so they will fly left to right from your bow. The actual grain weight of the arrow will determine how it strikes above and below the target. Lighter arrows will strike higher and heavier arrows will hit lower. It is just as simple in practice as it is in explanation.

I have always felt fortunate that I learned bowhunting by shooting and making my own cedar arrows. It taught me exactly the values of correct spine and arrow weight. Just a slight variation in either and the arrow can miss the spot. A trued, properly weighed and spined set of cedars will shoot right along with any arrow material on the market.

A single fletch jig, right, works well when repairing or building one arrow at a time. This one is from Martin Archery. Other choices, below, may speed up production.

With the shafts separated into the various categories according to spine and weight, you can select those you plan to make up and shoot. I bundle the others and store them in a dry spot so they won't absorb moisture.

The next thing to determine is what you want to do with your arrows. You can fletch the raw wood with no sealers and use them for rock-shooting at small game. Or you can go full route and produce a good looking and durable arrow you will be proud to shoot.

The cedars should be dipped in a good lacquer paint to prevent moisture from penetrating. Once they have been dipped, they last for years and don't warp.

A golf club tube can be used for a dip tube. It is not the best, but it is cheap, simple and easily available. Place a cork in the bottom of the tube and fill it with the color lacquer you want the arrow to be. Lacquers may be hard to find now in local stores. I tried latex once and you can't believe the mess it gave me.

The Bohning Company has been making arrow materials for many years and offer the archer an unlimited variety of materials from dip tubes and lacquers in all colors to all items needed to convert any shaft to an arrow. Their lac-

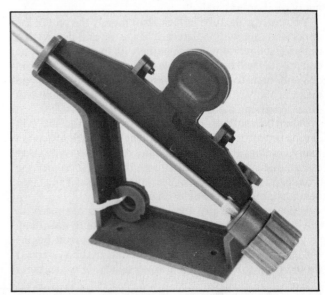

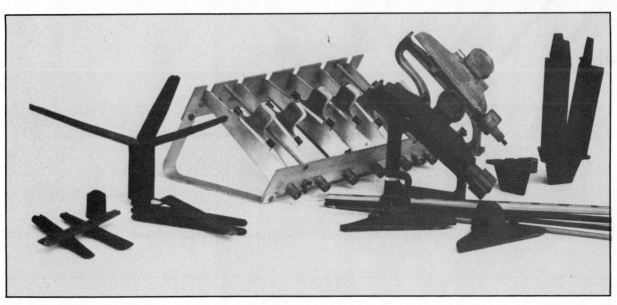

Arizona Archery's jig will hold three fletch vanes or feathers at a time, right wing, left wing or straight. Jig will accommodate any shafts, cedars to carbons.

When closed, Arizona jig may be adjusted to fit tight to any shaft. The Martin Archery triple fletch jig, below, is a new product that will fit any size shaft.

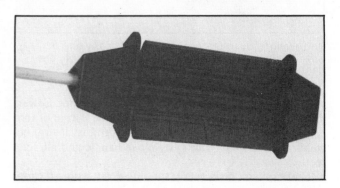

quers are available directly from the company or through many mail order catalogs.

You can dip the tube full length or merely the part of the upper end that will be fletched. Make several dips with a thinned lacquer rather than one dip with thick lacquer. The end product will be smooth, clean and attractive. Dip from one end, hang to dry, then reverse and dip again. You can make as many coats as you like. I usually do a minimum of three, reversing the dip each time.

When the shafts are dry, turn one end with a tool that will cut the proper angle for the nock. These are still offered in many catalogs or your dealer can order one for you. Buy the double type that will cut both the nock end and the broadhead taper; you will need it later. Think of it as a large pencil sharpener, set at eleven degrees.

When you have the nock taper cut, you are ready to select the proper nock for your arrow. There are many styles on the market. The entire flight of the arrow begins with the nock and it is an important part of the system. It shouldn't be ignored or passed over lightly. You can taper the nock end before or after dipping. If you do it first, you will build up some paint on the taper. On the big shafts, I prefer to cut the taper after final dipping for a better nock fit.

Place a dab of glue, Everfast or Bohning Fletch-Tite, on the nock end and twist the nock to spread the cement. Set the nock on tight. There is a grain line in cedar arrows and for the best flight, put the fine lines of that grain against the side of the bow for the stiffest spine and the most consistent flight. If you randomly set the nock on cedars, you will get wild arrows, because the stiffness will vary.

One advantage of dipping is that it helps hold the fletch on the arrow. The cement adheres better to a good lacquer than it will to any type of bare shaft.

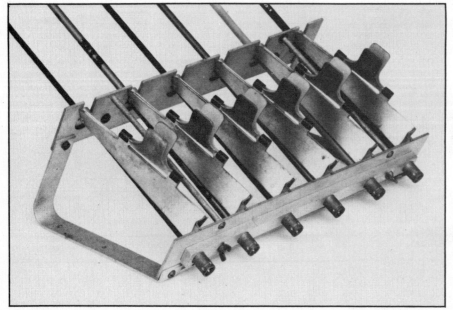

A jig such as the Gebhardt, left, will increase arrow production by six-fold. This one has been in use for more than thirty years and still performs flawlessly. It will handle three, four or six fletches.

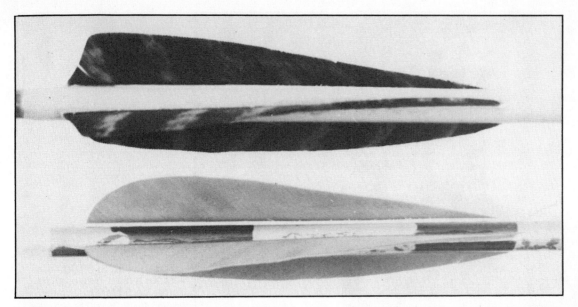

Both arrows, above, have full helical hunting fletch. Lower feathers are cut on the older shield pattern. Viewed from the nock end, right, the full helical fletch twists the feather around the shaft for better guidance.

Traditional arrow fletch is turkey feathers. These have been cleaned, ground and often dyed brilliant colors to give you a selection. They fly a bit faster than plastic fletch, but they do get wet and don't fly too well when wet.

The advantage of feathers is that they can be shot off the bow shelf when shooting that style. They fly well from any type rest or from no rest at all. If they get matted from use or from pulling through a target, they can be rejuvenated by holding the feathers over a spout of steam. They will return to original shape.

Plastic vanes aren't new on the market; they just became more popular. A gentleman by the name of Max Hamilton made a small vane called PlastiFletch many years ago, but couldn't make them big enough to handle a larger broadhead. They were relegated to target archers until the injection moulding machines became available. Now there are many brands, shapes and styles. Feathers or vanes, they both have their places.

Vanes are impervious to weather and rain doesn't hurt them at all. Moisture slides right off the vane and won't cause a flight problem. They might weigh a few grains more and you can't shoot them off the shelf or from some types of arrow rests, but these are personal things you will be able to determine yourself. Plastic vanes may be either right- or left-handed.

Feathers come from either the right or left wing of the turkey and only the four pointer or tip feathers from each bird are used. The simplest method of buying feathers is to order them pre-cut in the length you want. Most archers prefer a three-fletch, five-inch system, while others like a four-fletch, four-inch system. It is a personal choice, arrived at after testing.

Your next tool for making arrows is a fletching jig. This little item holds the fletch in a clamp which, in turn, is placed against the shaft after being coated with cement. The jig holds everything in position until the cement dries and you have a tightly sealed, permanent fletch.

There are many jigs for arrow makers, ranging from those that do one fletch at a time to those that do six shafts, one fletch at a time. Newer models place all three vanes on a single shaft in one application.

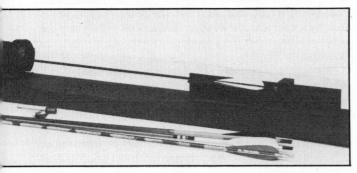

The arrow shafts, no matter what the material, must be cut cleanly to exact length. The high-speed cut-off saw from Easton revs up to handle any shafting material.

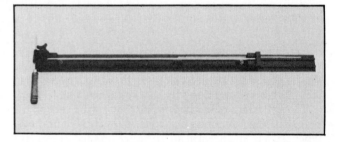

The Easton cut-off saw, left, will spin at up to 23,000 rpm without a load. Newer shaft cutter from Martin Archery, below, requires no electricity. Fine-tooth saw cuts any shaft.

The clamp you buy for any jig is determined by the type of fletch you intend to put on the arrow. You can buy right, left or straight clamps for fletching. The right is for a right-wing turkey or vane and the left clamp is for the left-wing feather or vane. It has been common practice to advocate that a right-handed archer shoot a right-wing fletch and the left-handed archer shoot a left-wing fletch. I shoot right-handed and shoot a left-wing fletch; I have for years. I tested the theory and found for my instinctive style, there was no difference. You may find otherwise with your style of shooting.

There are three methods of attaching the arrow fletch to the shaft. First is the simple straight-down-the-shaft clamp. It is highly recommended you don't use this one for bowhunting. I have seen straight-fletched shafts with broadheads almost circle back, the flight was so erratic. It works fine for target archery, but not for bowhunters with broadheads.

The second type, either right- or left-wing, is the off-set or spiral fletch. The fletch is actually angled slightly down the length of the shaft and imparts more guidance to arrow flight. There is a big difference between shooting a field point and multi-bladed broadhead. This slight vane angle will give better guidance.

The full helical fletch is considered by many bowhunters the best guidance, truest flight and best performance for any broadhead.

The helical jig imparts a twist in the fletch itself, feather or vane, right- or left-wing. I have been using the same Gebhart Multifletcher with a left-wing clamp for years. I have one jig set that imparts a radical helical on my feathers. I can shoot those arrows in any wind and they deflect but little. They seem to bore downrange and I can place arrow after arrow in a coffee can lid, one pound size, at most hunting ranges. Nearly all the game I have downed with the bow has been with those full helical fletched arrows.

For cement, there are some oldies and goodies such as the tried and true Fletch-Tite by Bohning and some new super-type cements that work well and fast.

There is another put out by Custom Archery that is a two-part cement. You run a light bead down the base of the fletch and place it in the jig, setting it properly. The second solution is then run down the side of the clamp to accelerate the speed of the glue action. By the time I have reached the sixth fletch on my jig, I can remove the first clamp, rotate the jig and start over. The normal set up time with most cements is about twenty minutes, depending on the humidity and heat. This stuff takes about sixty seconds.

Before cutting your arrow to length, you must know your actual draw length. I add one inch to mine to allow space for the broadhead. With cedars, you must allow for the taper of the broadhead, so add that to your draw length or you will end up short-shafted. It is better to cut one too long and later cut it shorter, if necessary. Do not cut all the shafts at once until you have experimented.

When you have a shaft cut and tapered, slip on a broadhead and see how the length is. You will probably find it to be right if you measured correctly. You will also find that broadhead won't seat fully on the shaft. The taper is usually longer than the head ferrule, so you merely snip the tip to get the proper fit. You should do this on all shafts as you seat the head.

If you dipped your arrow full length, it is finished. If you partially dipped, you may stain and wax the remaining part of the shaft. It should be sealed in some manner.

The best way to attach the arrowhead is Ferr-L-Tite, made by Bohning or Hot-melt by Saunders. Hot melt cements are easy to apply and the insert can be removed or adjusted at any time. Use a propane torch, set it on low heat or a candle and rotate the glue stick in the flame until it melts. Coat this on the tapered tip. Heat the broadhead until it melts the coating on the tip and twist the head onto the shaft. A dip in cold water and your arrow is done.

Fiberglass arrows are made in the same manner, but they need not be dipped. They are ground and may have some excess fibers on them, so the simplest method is to wipe them down with rubbing alcohol to clean the surface. They have no taper so you use a fiberglass insert or an aluminum nock insert for the head. You must clean the inside of the tube with some sandpaper and again with alcohol to remove the releasing agent used in manufacturing or the tips will come out.

The easiest arrow-making material is aluminum. Aluminum shafts have the nock chamfered on one end so you need no tools for that step. Most of the aluminum shafts today are hard anodized to give them color, ranging from bright gold to camo patterns, but they must be cleaned. Use a paper towel dampened with household cleanser and scrub them until no water drops form on the tube.

Fletching aluminum is fast, easy and works well, but it must be clean. Another method for cleaning is to soak the shaftment end where you fletch in a solution of phosphoric acid. Bohning makes a good aluminum cleaner based on this idea. If you don't clean the fletch area, the vanes or feathers will fall off, because the glue can't adhere properly.

Select the nock of your color and style, put a drop or two of glue on the taper and twist the nock onto the taper using slight pressure when twisting. The nock is the beginning of your propulsion system so it isn't merely a little gadget that holds the arrow on the string.

Select the fletch, feather or vane, of your choice and start making your arrows. *Never* allow your hands to touch the fletch area of the shaft or the oil of your fingers will prevent the glue from sticking and the fletch will come off in flight.

There is really no reason for dipping an aluminum arrow unless you want to make it look better. Some bowhunters say the shaftment dip gives them better adhesion of the fletch, because the glue sticks better to the lacquer than the bare shaft. You will have no problems with fletch sticking if you clean the shaft properly.

The channel of the vane is often still coated with some releasing agent used in the injection moulding process. All you need is a cotton-stick-type applicator and some alcohol to remove this residue from the vane channel.

The fluted shafts from Custom Archery clean and work the same as the round tubes. When you use a transparent nock, it appears as if the nock is broken. It isn't, but it does look different. Fluted shafts are lighter, the diameter is a bit smaller on lighter spines, but they fletch and fly well.

The full carbon shafts made by Beman and AFC are quite small in diameter. Due to the smaller diameter, they will require a change to the set-up of your jigs. The simplest system is to buy a separate jig for smaller carbon shafts.

The carbon shafts don't use a nock insert such as the fiberglass, but have a sleeve or overcollar that goes on the outside of the shaft. It has the nock taper on it. The different spine weight shafts are of different diameters so you must be certain to obtain the right sizes when ordering shafts and components.

Carbon shafts have an overcoat on them from the factory. This seals the fibers and makes them resist abrasion. It makes a good surface for the fletching cement to adhere to. If there is any problem with the little fellers, it is getting

Bohning's Ferr-L-Tite hot-melt cement has been the standard shaft insert or broadhead glue for years. Cement is heated by match, candle, torch or even campfire; permits changing broadhead blade position.

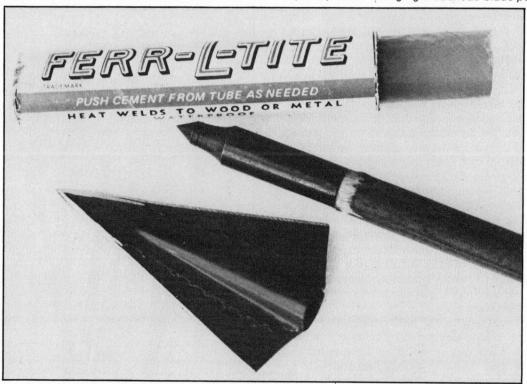

the jig set up right for diameter size. It is not possible to wrap much of a helix on them, because there just isn't enough tubing to do so. You can make a bit of an offset for a spiral fletch, but most are straight fletched. Regardless of the coating on the carbons, it won't hurt to wipe them with alcohol to remove hand oils.

When you have the nock sleeve cemented to the outer surface of the shaft and the nock has been set in place, you can proceed to fletch as before. Browning recommends using a two-part epoxy cement for the nock and fletching, rather than quick-drying glue. Beman and AFC have a low-temperature hot melt glue for the arrowhead inserts.

The Easton Aluminum A/C/Hunter is included as it is still on the market, but is not to be used for hunting. It still is an excellent shooting arrow and is fine for meets and tournaments.

The A/C/H is a combination arrow. It has an inner core of light aluminum tubing and an outer shell of filaments of carbon. The A/C/H doesn't use the tapered nock end usually found on alumium shafts, but has gone back to the Sixties and uses a combination nock and insert similar to that developed by Gordon Plastics for their fiberglass arrows of that period.

A good cleaning with some alcohol on the shaftment, including the interior of the nock end is necessary. The A/C/H is a small diameter shaft and you should check your jig setup to be certain of full coverage. You might have trouble with a full helical. Easton offers a kit with the A/C/H shafts that includes cleaner, cement and all you need to make up a set of arrows.

When we finished the cedar shafts, we cut them a bit longer, because the shaft is tapered to fit the tip. The other arrows use an insert and can be cut exactly the length needed. The insert in the shaft and the broadhead will be correct for your length of draw. Carbon and Easton A/C/H arrows use oversleeves and must be checked for length before cutting.

Cedar shafts can be cut with a hacksaw or any sharp, fine blade. Aluminum, carbon and the A/C/H must be cut with a high-speed cut-off saw. I tried using a hacksaw on a cut-off piece of carbon and it really did a messy job. The carbon filaments peeled down the short section and would have made a real mess on a shaft. High speed cut-off saws are mandatory when working with carbon shafts.

You may get by with a tubing cutter on the round aluminum shafts, but the cut won't be true and it will leave a jagged edge. You will also have to chamfer the inner section with a special tool to get that compressed edge cut smooth so that the broadhead adapter will slip into place. It can be done, but is more difficult.

Measure the draw length you need and add one-half to one inch. When you are shooting on a range or in the backyard, you can only pull as long as your arms will allow. When you draw down on old Mossy Horns in the field, you might find you can get an extra inch from your basic draw due to excitement. By cutting the shaft a bit longer, you will prevent any bad cuts from a sharp broadhead by drawing it into the hand or finger.

Cut the arrow to your length, chamfer the inside and slip the insert into the shaft. Heat the end of the aluminum tube and the insert. When they are warm, not smoking hot and black, apply a small amount of hot melt stick and place the insert in the arrow end with a twisting motion and seat it

solidly. If it gets cold too fast, merely heat it gently until it seats properly.

A hot melt glue is also recommended for carbon and fiberglass, but the shafts must not be heated too much. Use a special low-heat hot melt glue for these arrows. A two-part epoxy works the best for carbon arrow nocks. Use the fast-hardening variety.

Some archers like to crest their arrows. Cresting adds a touch of class to an arrow and will identify the archer's arrow. Each archer uses a different crest. This resting may be done either before or after fletching. Cresting patterns may be simple or elaborate.

To crest, you need a slow-turning lathe-type machine that will turn the arrow at a constant rate. Start with a wide brush and place a band of paint of your color choice at the point just forward of the fletch. When that has dried, add fine lines of different colors to individualize and identify your arrows.

If you wish, you may go further and put fine lines at the base of the nock. Some add lines in the mid-section. Most hunting arrows are not crested, but yours can be, if you wish. Target arrows should be crested, especially when shooting in a large archery tournament.

FLU-FLU ARROWS

There are times when you need a short-ranging arrow, one that will fly for a short distance, stop and allow you to find it. You can make these arrows using any type of shaft — the easiest to use are the cedar styles — and a few pieces of feather fletch.

Flu-flu fletching may be attached in several sizes, colors and patterns; imagination is the only limit. Fletching mass regulates the arrow flight distance.

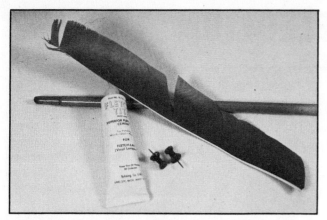

Even archers without a fletching jig can produce a reasonable flu-flu arrow. Use glue, feather and pins.

The stiff quill base is broken down by bending the feather as above. Thumb tack holds feather in place.

The basic idea of the flu-flu fletching is to give an arrow a larger mass of fletch which will move more air mass and hold back the arrow flight. You can do this in several ways; the fletch most bowhunters prefer is the feather.

Using almost any fletching jig, you can make a three-, four- or six-fletch arrow. There are always a few cedar shafts that are extra heavy, maybe just a bit on the crooked side, but too good to throw out. The flu-flu is one good way to use these arrow shafts to make what many believe to be a fun arrow.

You can dip and taper the cedar in the normal manner, nock the end and place it in your jig. Full-length feathers make the simplest and easiest flu-flu system. A full-length feather has a high section above the quill. Don't cut this as you would normally, but leave it high. Fletch three of these full width feathers on the shaft. The high fletch will reduce the flight distance of that arrow. If you want it to fly a bit further, trim the height of the fletch.

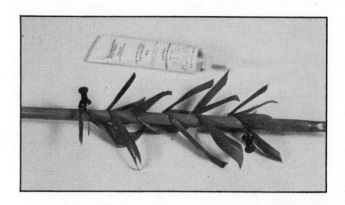

A single bead of glue is run the length of the quill. Wrap, above, is rather loose, arrow will fly farther. For aluminum shaft, below, clamp with clothespin.

If you are using the pre-cut fletching, you fletch six onto the shaft, rather than the normal three. This increases the mass of the arrow fletch and that reduces the flight of the arrow.

The main reason for the cedar shaft rather than the aluminum or carbon is that it is the least expensive. Cedar shafts work just as well for a flu-flu as any shaft material. Flu-flus work best on thrown cardboard birds and similar targets. Most ducks will out-fly the average flu-flu arrow.

Perhaps the simplest and one of the most attractive of the flu-flu arrows is the wraparound style. Twist a full length, uncut feather fletch around a cedar shaft near the arrow end where you would normally have the fletch. Pull the quill base tightly around the shaft to break down the fibers and it will curl right around the shaft. When you release the fletch, it will retain the curl.

Place the base of the quill, the thick end of the feather, on the bottom and the lighter end at the top. Run a bead of cement down the entire length of the quill. This can be a bit messy, as it will want to curl on you. When you have the quill cemented, clamp or pin the base to the cedar shaft. This is why the wooden arrow works best.

Wrap the fletch from the bottom to the top, holding it tight against the shaft. When you reach the top, you can either pin it or clamp it to hold it while drying. The tighter

you wrap the quill, the slower and shorter distance the arrow will fly. If you want to have it fly faster and farther, make the wrap a bit looser. The single feather flu-flu is simple to make, requires no jig and can be regulated by the way it is wrapped on the shaft.

If you plan to shoot the short-flying arrows, you might consider shooting them with the recurve bow. The flu-flu fletching may strike the compound cable, unless there is plenty of clearance. Pieces of feather fletching will fly all over if it strikes the cable upon release.

HUNTING ARROW SELECTION

Among the broadheads tested were, left to right: The Hoyt Black Hole, Golden Key-Futura Golden Spinner, Wasp Cam-Lok, original Bear Razorhead, Bear Super Razorhead, Satellite Archery four-blade and Satellite three-blade.

MATCHING ARROWS to broadheads for hunting can be a difficult and time-consuming task. Arrows may or may not fly the same trajectory with field points as with broadheads.

Fred and Dora Burris are well known bowhunters in Wyoming, whose stories have been published in many archery publications. They looked into several aspects of the problem and came up with considerable data to assist bowhunters in selecting the best shafts, broadheads and fletching for a number of arrows of typical length.

AFTER VISITING the Fred Bear Museum, I became sentimental about my first glass-laminated bow, a Bear Grizzly recurve. Later in the spring, I purchased a Bear Kodiak recurve to help satisfy my sentimental urge. After the bow arrived, I purchased a dozen aluminum arrows to match the bow's draw weight. All went well until I mounted my broadheads to prepare for hunting season. My tight groups went beyond Scatterville and my confidence fell to zero.

Within a few months, our son Lewis and son-in-law Dexter each purchased new compound bows. They, too, struggled to find a matching shaft and broadhead. Here's how we started to solve our shaft balance problems.

After discussing our situation, we discovered that between the three of us we had several different shaft sizes and broadhead types. We ordered a supply of four- and five-inch vanes and die-cut feathers. We proceeded to test our different shafts and broadheads. We wanted a finished shaft with broadhead attached that gave us a head weight of seven to ten percent of the total arrow.

I looked for a combination using feathers for my recurve bow while Lewis and Dexter tried plastic vanes for their compound bows. To determine the percent of head weight, we followed this procedure:

1. Measure the total shaft length from the end of the nock to the tip of the broadhead.

2. Mark the exact center of the shaft with a pencil mark. Example: If the total shaft measurement was thirty-three inches, the center of the shaft would be 16½ inches.

3. Next, balance the shaft on the edge of a pocketknife to find the shaft's actual balance point. Mark the balance point with a pencil mark.

4. Measure the distance between these two marks to the nearest one-sixteenth-inch. For our example, let's say the distance measured three inches.

5. Figure the percentage of head weight using the figures in the above examples and this formula: Divide the total shaft length — thirty-three inches — into the difference between the shaft's center and balance point — three inches — then multiply by one hundred.

$$\frac{.0909}{33\overline{)3.000}}$$

Take .0909 X 100 = 9.09 or 9.1 percent head weight.

We concentrated our attention on shaft/broadhead combinations that gave seven to ten percent head weight for these reasons: As the head weight drops noticeably below seven percent, arrow tail wobble increases and accuracy decreases. As the head weight increases substantially past

Match Arrow Shafts For Length, Balance, Accuracy And The Right Broadhead For Best Results

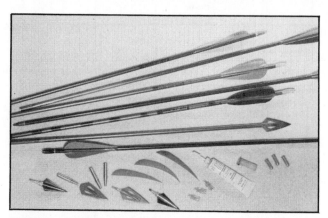

The goal of the experimenters was to establish a combination of arrow shafts, spines, feathers, vanes and broadheads to yield seven to ten percent head weight.

Each shaft, insert, nock, fletch and broadhead combo was weighed to arrive at a match. Each combination was checked for head weight, using described formula.

ten percent, the head of the arrow tends to fall or drop too quickly.

During our experimentation, we had a number of surprises. Broadheads of the same weight and length produced different percentages. This difference comes from each broadhead's own balance point due to individual broadhead design, construction and materials.

The Easton 2115 X7 shaft with four, four-inch fletching

Head weights of all combinations of shafts, fletching and broadheads were calculated and recorded, as above.

provided a little more latitude than the 2115 XX75 shaft with the same fletching.

Vanes provide many more shaft/broadhead options on the shafts we tried than those fletched with feathers.

A Martin number 9 fiberglass arrow with three, five-inch feathers, the last I had of its kind, gave 8.6 percent head weight when fitted with a Bear Razorhead. This single shaft had downed three deer for me in the past, but Martin no longer produces them.

Along with our search for an accurate hunting shaft and broadhead, I tried several different arrow rests on my recurve in an attempt to use vanes. I finally returned to a simple do-it-yourself feather rest on the bow's shelf. This decision required me to use feather fletching on my shafts. As a result, my field of options narrowed considerably.

The 2117 arrow with three, five-inch feathers provides a little latitude for my recurve. At the same time, both the X7 and XX75 shafts performed well with the lighter broadheads during our target tests.

Lewis and Dexter have several excellent options of shafts using vanes. The twenty-nine-inch 2115 XX75 shaft with three, four-inch vanes, four, four-inch vanes and three, five-inch vanes yielded percentages between seven and ten. The 2012 X-Caliber shaft with three, four-inch vanes showed promise, too. With some additional fine-tuning, both Lewis' and Dexter's compound bows will shoot many of these combinations well.

Choosing the right shaft and broadhead can mean the difference between a well placed shot and a marginal one. Finding that perfect hunting arrow combination may take some effort and create some additional expenses. But the real reward for your effort comes when you stand at full draw. Your quarry hesitates in a good position for that special moment and your arrow speeds toward its mark.

We compiled the following charts during the initial search for a balanced shaft and broadhead. This information can help you narrow down the combinations needed to find a good shaft/broadhead balance. — *Fred and Dora Burris*

Shaft	Broad-head	Weight (Grains)	Shaft Length (Inches)	Difference Between Shaft Center and Shaft Balance Point (Inches)	Percent of Shaft Head Weight	Fletch
29-inch 2016 GG Shaft						3 RH 5-inch Feather
	T-Head	125	31 3/8	3 1/4	10.4	Same
	UN-KN	160	31 3/4	3 7/8	12.2	Same
29-inch 2114 GG Shaft						4 R H 4-inch Feather
	S-Lite	120	31 9/16	2 15/16	9.3	Same
	T-Head	125	31 3/8	3 3/16	10.2	Same
	S-Lite	140	31 9/16	3 1/4	11.0	Same
	Bear-RH	145	31 7/8	3 3/4	11.8	Same
	UN-KN	160	31 3/4	3 7/8	12.2	Same
29-inch 2115 XX75 Shaft						3 R H 4-inch Vanes
	S-Lite	120	31 5/8	2 5/8	8.4	Same
	Hoyt BH	120	31 5/8	2 9/16	8.1	Same
	Wasp CL	140	31 3/8	3	9.6	Same
	G-Spin	140	31 3/8	3 1/16	9.8	Same
	S-Lite	140	31 5/8	2 7/8	9.2	Same
	Bear RH	145	31 7/8	2 7/8	9.0	Same
29-inch 2115 XX75 Shaft						3 R H 4-inch Feather
	S-Lite	120	31 5/8	3 5/16	10.6	Same
	Hoyt BH	120	31 5/8	3 1/4	10.2	Same
	Wasp CL	140	31 3/8	3 11/16	11.8	Same
	G-Spin	140	31 3/8	3 11/16	11.8	Same
	S-Lite	140	31 5/8	3 1/2	11.2	Same
	Bear RH	145	31 7/8	3 13/16	12.0	Same
29-inch 2115 XX75 Shaft						4 R H 4-inch Vanes
	Hoyt BH	120	31 5/8	2 1/2	7.9	Same
	Wasp CL	140	31 3/8	2 3/4	8.8	Same
	G-Spin	140	31 3/8	2 13/16	9.0	Same
29-inch 2115 XX75 Shaft						4 R H 4-inch Feather
	S-Lite	120	31 5/8	3 1/4	10.4	Same
	Hoyt BH	120	31 5/8	3 1/8	9.9	Same
	Wasp CL	140	31 3/8	3 9/16	11.4	Same
	G-Spin	140	31 3/8	3 5/8	10.6	Same
	S-Lite	140	31 5/8	3 3/8	10.8	Same
	Bear RH	145	31 7/8	3 3/4	11.8	Same
29-inch 2115 X7 Shaft						4 R H 4-inch Feather
	S-Lite	120	31 1/2	3 1/16	9.3	Same
	T-Head	125	31 1/4	3 1/4	10.4	Same
	S-Lite	140	31 1/2	3 5/16	10.4	Same
	Bear RH	145	31 3/4	3 5/8	11.4	Same
	UN-KN	160	31 3/4	3 3/4	11.8	Same
29-inch 2115 XX75 Shaft						3 R H 5-inch Vanes
	S-Lite	120	31 5/8	2 3/16	7.0	Same
	Hoyt BH	120	31 5/8	2 5/16	7.3	Same
	Wasp CL	140	31 3/8	2 13/16	9.0	Same
	G-Spin	140	31 3/8	2 3/4	8.8	Same
	S-Lite	140	31 5/8	2 7/16	7.8	Same
	Bear RH	145	31 7/8	2 7/8	7.6	Same
29-inch 2115 XX75 Shaft						3 R H 5-inch Feather
	S-Lite	120	31 5/8	3 3/16	10.2	Same
	Hoyt BH	120	31 5/8	3 3/16	10.2	Same
	Wasp CL	140	31 3/8	3 5/8	10.0	Same
	G-Spin	140	31 3/8	3 3/4	12.0	Same
	S-Lite	140	31 5/8	3 7/16	11.0	Same
	Bear RH	145	31 7/8	3 3/4	11.8	Same
29-inch 2115 XX75 Shaft						4 R H 5-inch Vanes
	Hoyt BH	120	31 5/8	1 7/8	5.9	Same
	Wasp CL	140	31 3/8	2 7/16	7.9	Same
	G-Spin	140	31 3/8	2 9/16	8.2	Same

Final stage of the quest for accurate hunting arrows took place on the target range. Foam broadhead target was placed at fifteen yards for easier retrieval.

Shaft	Broad-head	Weight (Grains)	Shaft Length (Inches)	Difference Between Shaft Center and Shaft Balance Point (Inches)	Percent of Shaft Head Weight	Fletch
29-inch 2115 XX75 Shaft						4 R H 5-inch Feather
	Hoyt BH	120	31 5/8	3 1/8	9.9	Same
	Wasp CL	140	31 3/8	3 5/8	11.6	Same
	G-Spin	140	31 3/8	3 3/4	12.0	Same
27¼-inch 2117 GG Shaft						3 R H 5-inch Vanes
	T-Head	125	29 1/2	2 3/16	7.4	Same
	Bear RH	145	29 13/16	2 1/4	7.5	Same
	UN-KN	160	29 13/16	2 3/4	9.2	Same
27¼-inch 2117 XX75 Shaft						3 R H 5-inch Vanes
	Hoyt BH	120	29 3/4	1 15/16	6.5	Same
	Wasp CL	140	29 1/2	2 3/8	8.1	Same
	G-Spin	140	29 1/2	2 7/16	8.3	Same
29-inch 2117 GG Shaft						3 L H 5-inch Feather
	S-Lite	120	31 1/2	2 11/16	8.5	Same
	T-Head	125	31 5/16	2 7/8	9.2	Same
	S-Lite	140	31 1/2	2 7/8	9.1	Same
	Bear RH	145	31 3/4	3 1/8	9.8	Same
	UN-KN	160	31 3/4	3 7/16	10.8	Same
30-inch 2117 GG Shaft						3 R H 5-inch Vanes
	T-Head	125	32 3/8	2	6.2	Same
	Bear RH	145	32 11/16	2 1/8	6.2	Same
	UN-KN	160	32 3/4	2 1/4	5 6.9	Same
30-inch 2117 GG 2 Shaft						3 R H 5-inch Vanes
	Bear RH	145	32 3/4	2 3/16	6.7	Same
30-inch 2117 GG 2 Shaft						4 RH 4-inch Vanes
	Bear RH	145	32 3/4	2 5/16	7.1	Same
28-inch 2012 X-Caliber Shaft						3 R H 4-inch Vanes
	S-Lite	120	30 3/8	3 1/8	10.2	Same
	Hoyt BH	120	30 5/8	2 7/8	9.3	Same
	Wasp CL	140	30 3/8	3 3/8	10.1	Same
	G-Spin	140	30 3/8	3 7/16	11.3	Same
	S-Lite	140	30 3/8	3 7/16	11.1	Same
	Bear RH	145	30 7/8	3 3/4	12.1	Same
28-inch 2012 X-Caliber Shaft						3 R H 5-inch Vanes
	Hoyt BH	120	30 5/8	3 3/4	12.2	Same
	Wasp CL	140	30 3/8	4 1/4	14.0	Same
	G-Spin	140	30 3/8	4 3/8	14.2	Same

On the final experiment, each of three shooters shot three broadhead arrows and three field point arrows. Arrow flight and target impact was then compared.

Definitions:

S-Lite 120 Gr = Satellite 3 Blade Broadhead.
Hoyt BH 120 Gr = Hoyt-Easton Black Hole Broadhead.
T-Head 125 Gr = Thunderhead Broadhead.
Wasp CL 140 Gr = Wasp Cam-Lok 2 Broadhead.
G-Spin 140 Gr = Golden-Spinner Broadhead.
S-Lite 140 Gr = Satellite 4 Blade Broadhead.
Bear RH 145 Gr = Bear Razorhead Broadhead.
UN-KN 160 Gr = Unknown Manufacture.

Definitions:

Thre or four = Number of Vanes or Feathers.
R = Right.
L = Left.
H = Helical.
4-inch or 5-inch = Length of Fletch.

Measurement conversions for fractions of an inch.

Fraction		
1/16	=	0.0625 of an inch.
1/8	=	0.125 of an inch.
3/16	=	0.1875 of an inch.
1/4	=	0.25 of an inch.
5/16	=	0.3125 of an inch.
3/8	=	0.375 of an inch.
7/16	=	0.4375 of an inch.
1/2	=	0.50 of an inch.
9/16	=	0.5625 of an inch.
5/8	=	0.625 of an inch.
11/16	=	0.6875 of an inch.
3/4	=	0.75 of an inch.
13/16	=	0.8125 of an inch.
7/8	=	0.875 of an inch.
15/16	=	0.9375 of an inch.
1 inch		

ARROW REFINISHING

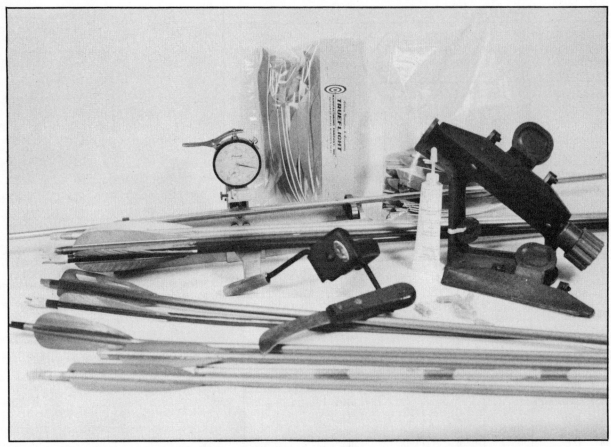

Common mishaps for aluminum arrows include slight bending and fletching damage. Repair and refinish gear should be a fletching jig, cleaning knife, new fletching, glue and a simple arrow straightener.

AFTER A FEW rounds on the range and someone with a heavy hand pulling them through the target, your arrows don't look so good. In fact, they begin to look downright ratty.

If you fletch with vanes, they probably will be turned over, possibly pulled apart. They certainly won't fly right unless they are reworked and refinished.

Arrows have a long useful life if you learn to keep them in good condition. Just because they have a slight bend in the aluminum shaft and the fletch is in bad condition, doesn't mean you have to discard them.

Cedar arrows can be reworked if they don't have any cracks down the shaft. If they are split, they must be set aside and possibly used for plant stakes. But they must not

be re-done and made into shooting arrows again; they just aren't safe. If it is merely the fletch though, they can be re-worked and re-fletched as good as new.

Carbon shafts are just as critical, maybe more so. You must check for cracks or flaws in the shaft before you do any re-work on them. Flex the shaft by bending and eyeballing to see if they have any openings or fibers trying to let loose. Once the fibers start coming undone, you should discard that shaft as unsafe. Examine fiber shafts after each shot.

Aluminum arrows are the easiest to re-work and they will give you years of shooting pleasure. The one exception is the fluted shaft that is a bit different in straightening. By using a tube sleeve over the shaft to get the unit even, you

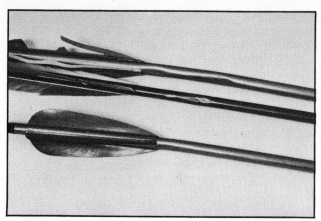

Some damage cannot easily be repaired by an archer in the home workshop. Aluminum arrows with dents or scratches, top two, should be discarded. The top arrow is a candidate for re-fletching.

Straightening an aluminum arrow shaft should be done with care. The gauge shows a plus-20 reading. Handle is pressed slowly down until indicator reaches zero.

It is a good idea to keep a new, undamaged shaft of the appropriate size on hand to re-zero gauge.

can straighten them nicely. It takes just a bit more time and effort.

When you shoot a lot, you will bang up a batch of arrows in a hurry. What I have found to be a good system is to pile these shafts — they shouldn't be called arrows unless they are ready and able to be shot from a bow — into a box or other storage until I have a batch to re-work. It doesn't take any longer to do ten than to do one, after you get set up.

The first thing to do is remove that old nock. It sometimes seems crazy, because the nock still looks good. We may have a tendency to leave the old nock on. Spend a few extra pennies and put on a new nock. Be certain to align it properly with the grain of a cedar shaft and get it snugged onto the nock taper for a good, solid and clean fit. The choice of nock is a personal one and we all have a favorite. Clean the nock off with a sharp knife or dissolve it off with some MEK. It will leave a clean taper. If you have dipped your shafts, this solvent will remove the paint just as fast, so don't use solvent on dipped shafts.

Clean the nock taper with some sandpaper or a special

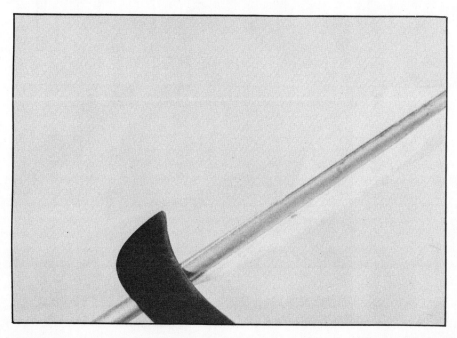

A knife blade will remove old glue and fletching from shaft. Blade will cut into aluminum if care is not exercised. Work around the shaft to clean off all the glue residue.

taper cleaner to get the end clean and all the old cement removed. If you only partially clean the nock taper, the new nock won't seat properly.

When the taper is clean, pick a new nock, place it on the taper and twist it around a few times before you add any cement. This will help seat the nock and if it is a bit rough, it will clean that. Apply a drop or two of cement, depending on the type you like, and twist the nock onto the nock taper forcing the cement into the taper and on the nock body. If you are re-fletching cedars, make a mark before removing the old nock so you will have the wood grain in proper alignment.

Once the nock cement has set and dried, you are ready to move to the next phase; cleaning off the old fletch. Most bowhunters like to do all the cleaning at one operation.

To remove the old fletch, you need a good, sharp knife. Some disagree with this technique, but it has worked for years. Running the sharp blade down the base of the fletch will cut that old fletching off at the base. You can't get all of it, because the shaft is curved and the knife blade probably isn't. Clean all remaining fletch from the shaft and scrape as much excess as you can. If you are using a painted or dipped shaft, this is even more critical.

After the scraping, I like to take a clean piece of 0000

Martin Archery's fletching jig, left and below, will speed up the operation. Fletch-Tite cement is a product of Bohning.

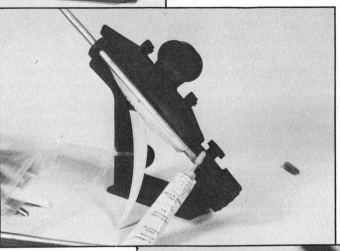

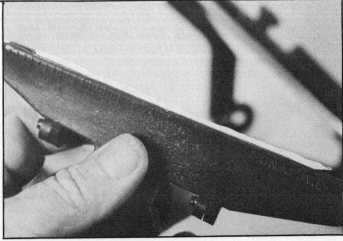

Right: The new feather fletch is placed in the clamp and a fine line of glue is run along the quill base.

steel wool and scrub the fletched area to remove any glue residue. This technique works well on the aluminum shafts. The steel wool has oil in it to prevent it from rusting, so you must use alcohol or some other solvent to remove oil from the metal or your new fletch won't stick.

Carbon shafts require greater care, since you can get too heavy handed with a blade and actually cut into the shaft. The fibers may be cut, starting a possible reaction that will run a fiber filament full-length down the shaft. Clean carefully. I leave the quill or fletch base a bit rough just so I don't have the danger of cutting the filaments.

After the cleaning solvent has dried, I like to wipe the fletch area on the shaft with some rubbing alcohol to further remove any oils or film from handling. I have always had good luck with rubbing alcohol.

The remainder of the operation is just the same as when you first fletched the arrow. Set your jig for the fletch you like, place the vane or feather in the clamp, clean the base of the vane with a cotton swab soaked in alcohol and run a bead of cement down the fletch base. Clamp the vane to the shaft and let it set until cured. When the fletch is dry,

remove the arrow and clamp and do the next fletching vane until you have the arrow finished.

Not too long ago, the thinking people at Saunders Archery came up with a new gadget for cleaning fletching from shafts. This is a slick tool that has a rounded edge on the front where you cut the fletch from the shaft. With a guide at the back, the unit looks like a short section of arrow shafting. It aligns the unit on the shaft and you move the curved cutting edge to the base of the quill or vane and neatly cut it off.

Don't throw out those slightly bent and ratty fletched shafts. Clean them up and straighten them up if they are aluminum. Throw them out if they are cracked carbon or cedar. Rework those older damaged shafts and use them for stump shooting. Get rid of the cracked cedar or carbon arrows; they can't be straightened.

My reworked arrows go into what I call my "rock quiver." These arrows are those I won't take on an extended out-of-state hunt and probably wouldn't shoot at a big-game animal. They are really great for rabbits, squirrels and other small game. — *C.R. Learn*

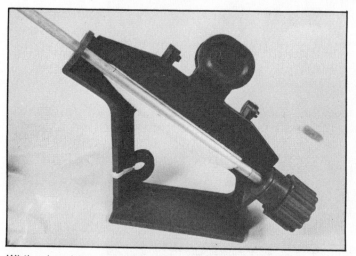

While glue dries, arrow and clamp should remain stable. Some glue requires more time to set up.

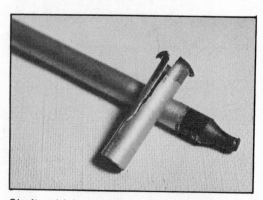

Shafts with jammed tips may be cut off, a new insert glued in and the shorter arrow may be used with an overdraw-type bow.

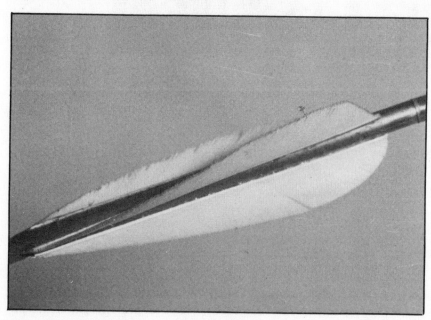

Re-fletching a damaged arrow takes only pennies and little time. The result is a new-looking arrow that will fly straight and true, left.

PRIMITIVE ARROWS

Meyer is dressed in authentically styled Plains Indian clothing he tailored himself as he draws hand-crafted arrow over his experimental bow.

LEW HANSEN lives and hunts in Utah, home to big game animals and wildlife habitat which we all might envy. Hansen came across a man called Two Deer, aka Squire Meyer, a mountain man and student of early American culture. Two Deer keeps the art of primitive arrow making alive and well. This is Hansen's report.

NO ONE REALLY knows when the first arrow was flung by a North American hunter. Evidence suggests, however, that the bow and arrow were invented near the end of prehistoric times and were introduced to ancient Americans about 1000 B.C.

At a time when throwing sticks, albeit sharpened ones, and stones was the norm, the bow and arrow revolutionized hunting, making it possible for the solitary hunter to be more effective. Compared to other means available at the time, it was a highly accurate, long-range weapon.

The evolution of the bow and arrow from its inception in the hands and minds of primitive hunters, to the sophisticated instrument it is today is an intriguing journey through time, particularly for the modern bowhunter. Every time I sit down to assemble a broadhead, I can't help but imagine myself breaking flakes of stone from a piece of flint or jasper. Threading the completed surgical steel and aluminum

Our Archery Ancestors — American Indians —
Made Their Own Arrows; Practically And Spiritually

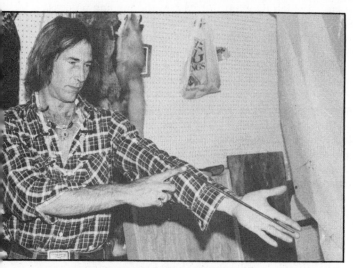

Primitive arrows, research has shown, were shorter than modern counterparts. Two Deer — Meyer — shows his method for measuring his correct arrow length.

broadhead into the insert of the aluminum shaft is a far cry from fastening a stone point to a willow shaft with sinew and hide glue, yet the image is there nonetheless.

The archaic imagery was rekindled recently while visiting a gathering of contemporary mountain men and folklore enthusiasts at Fort Buenaventura, in Ogden, Utah, a place generally given over to the celebration of the mountain man and native American cultures.

The row of tipis stood out like burnished ivory against the dark earth of the hillside, their exposed lodge poles reaching defiantly into the steely grayness of the sky. Smoke from a single cooking fire drifted on the breeze, fragrant with the scent of burning sagebrush and simmering food. Somewhere beyond the lodges a dog barked and a horse neighed anxiously as the breeze picked up, heavy with the threat of rain.

Two men sat on blankets in the brown grass before a tipi. Suspended from a stick pushed into the ground was a quiver made from an elk neck containing several arrows. One of the men, wearing an ornate choker of coyote bones and dressed in buckskins, was using a short length of deer antler to break bits of rock from a piece of black obsidian he held tight against a scrap of leather in the palm of his hand.

Taking an arrow from the quiver, I inspected it closely, rolling the shaft slowly in my fingers. The nock had been carefully carved and the shaft below had been given a slim double taper. The arrow was fletched with natural length, barred feathers, fixed to the slender shaft with thread-like sinew.

The same fine sinew was used to fasten the obsidian point to the shaft, with many precise wraps criss-crossing the carefully formed tang, securing the point with apparent perfect alignment.

The shaft was crested beneath the fletching with three bands of yellow ocher bordered in red. This was the signature of Two Deer, the arrow maker.

Two Deer is the *nom de guerre* of primitive arrow maker Squire Meyer, of Huntsville, Utah. Meyer is a regular participant of mountain man rendezvous, dressing in authentically tailored, handmade buckskins, beads and bone jewelry.

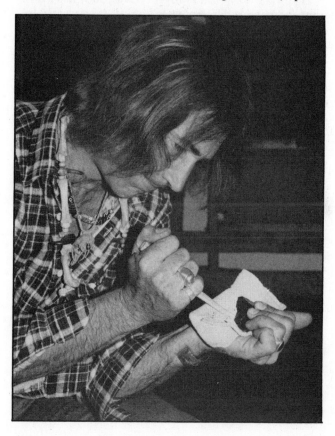

A piece of buckskin protects Meyer's hand, left, as he chips out an arrowhead. He uses a chipper made of deer antler. When finished, head is carefully matched to wood shaft, above, before the point is installed.

Meyer is able to turn out a variety of arrowhead styles and sizes. The nature of the original stone determines final outcome. Longest is 2½ inches.

His Plains Indian style arrows, made entirely by hand from materials he gathers locally or trades for at rendezvous, are accurate replicas of the arrows used by the ancient hunters and warriors of the northern plains tribes, specifically the Northern Cheyenne and the Sioux peoples.

To a modern bowhunter, one of Meyer's willow-shafted, stone-pointed arrows is a high art form, a mental journey back through time more poignant than any two-dimensional image can be.

Holding one of his arrows, drawing it over your hand as you would if you were drawing a bow, you can appreciate the integrity of the workmanship and the balance. The natural compulsion is to shoot it. Suddenly, it does not seem at all far-fetched to imagine hunting with such a seemingly frail missile. With a new respect for the old ways, you mutter, "So that's how they did it."

Meyer builds his arrows in a room converted into a shop, next-door west of the Shooting Star Saloon, whose friendly proprietress credits the Saloon's well-built hamburgers for Meyer's evident good health.

In his shop, the smell of hide glue simmering in a can placed atop the propane heater imparts a faintly sweet, musky odor to the air. Made by boiling strips of rawhide

and sinew in a small amount of water, the can is placed on a steam humidifier to maintain its liquid state once it has cooked sufficiently. Hide stretching racks lean against one wall and brain-tanned deer and elk pelts cover most of the available floor space in stacks arranged according to the stage at which they have arrived in the tanning process. Seated on a folding chair in the midst of all of this, I watched as Meyer prepared to build an arrow in the way of the ancient hunters and warriors of North America.

Meyer removed a bundle of sticks, cuttings taken from the red willow and inspected the lot. They were tightly bound in twine to assure straightness while drying. These he replaced on the shelf. Cradled in a pair of shelf brackets on the same wall was a group of ten or so uniform shafts. Each had been crested with Meyer's characteristic yellow and red bands in the area of the fletching and all had nocks prepared. Removing one of these shafts, Meyer took a seat, inspecting the shaft for straightness and bending it gently over the inside of his forearm as he repeatedly sighted down its length.

"I make them all exactly the same length," said Meyer. "I use the Cheyenne method of measuring, so for me, that's the length they are.

"Some people write that it should be (measured) from your chest to the tip of your middle finger," said Meyer.

The method Meyer uses to gauge arrow length, however, is the one described by George Bird Grinnell in *The Cheyenne Indians, Their History And Ways Of Life.* That is, from the tip of the middle finger to a point halfway between the elbow and shoulder, placing the shaft against the inside of the arm. Then, as now, arrow length depended on the stature of the individual archer and a shaft made for one man may not serve another as well.

"That's one way," said Meyer. "Everybody has a different approach, a different way."

Meyer uses materials commonly found growing in the canyons and along the streams not far from his home. Common willow, red willow and wild rose are the preferred shrubs from which he carefully selects only the straightest branches of suitable length. Other species that provide shafts are currant, plum and serviceberry.

"I have to straighten them all," said Meyer, "but I pick the straightest I can. They're all hand straightened and

Raw sinew is taken from the foreleg of a deer. Consistent work is required to separate strands.

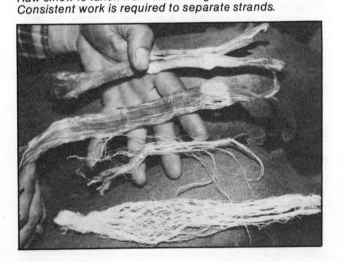

When combined with hide glue, net-like sinew provides a strong bond between wood and stone, head and shaft.

Splitting a selected feather to be used as fletching is an art few have mastered, left. Meyer uses no fletching jig, above. He sews feathers in place while glue dries.

they will all, eventually, take a curve.

"But see," said Meyer, "in the old times that didn't matter. Any wooden arrow will warp and all you do is straighten it before you shoot. Once they're straightened, it will take a while for them to re-bend.

"As long as you're going to use them that day, they're fine," said Meyer. "They'll stay straight.

"I could put a bend in this one," he said, bowing the bare shaft over his forearm to demonstrate, "and it would stay bent. Then I could go back and straighten it and it would stay straight."

Meyer does not consider himself an archer, in spite of the time and effort he devotes to building archery equipment, including Plains Indian-style bows.

"I guess I'm approaching this backwards," he said. "Rather than being an archer and thinking, 'Well, I'll make something better,' I just started making arrows for fun.

"I've been making stone arrowheads since about '76," said Meyer. He produced a bag of stone points and dumped them out on a piece of buckskin placed over the bottom of an over-turned bucket. The points varied in length from a few centimeters to one nearly as long as my index finger.

The beauty of their symmetry, combined with the fine edge and thinness of which the arrowheads had been made gave them a delicate appearance that belied their sharpness and intrinsic strength. Most of the points were of stone, such as obsidian and flint, with at least one example of a bone point.

How would a beautiful, but fragile point such as any of these perform in a hunting situation?

"It would depend on what you hit," said Meyer, when I asked him. "They will break. If you drop one on the floor, it could break, or it could make it," he said. "It's about fifty-fifty either way."

An interesting quality of stone points, however, is that when they break, the edge resulting from the fracture will likely be sharp. It is easy to imagine, then, that an arrow tipped with a stone point would retain its effectiveness even after impact with a rib or other bone of a big-game animal such as deer.

Although arrowheads can be found in dozens of different shapes and sizes, depending on their use, the maker of arrowheads finds that the stone itself, more than any other factor, dictates the shape that will result.

After a feather is split, the feather is trimmed before mounting. Although the craftsman is using a modern razor blade, Meyer has used stone knife.

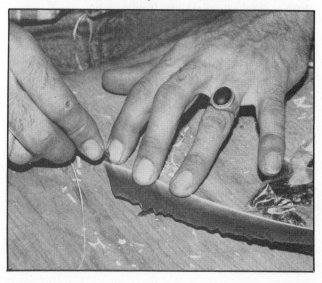

Far left: Hide glue is applied with a sharpened willow branch. Feather fletch is set into glue, followed by index feather, below. Nock is carved on shaft end and Meyer uses red, yellow cresting.

"It seems to me," said Meyer, "that I have four different shapes of arrowheads. I can't ever seem to make two identical.

"For me," said Meyer, "the way the stone works determines the way they're going to come out. These," he said, picking up two differing shapes of the same black stone, "could have come from identical blanks, but through breakage and whatnot they came out different.

"Pretty much, though," he said, "the shape of the stone determines what the point will be."

Meyer is a kind of informal scholar of Plains Indian ways and it shows in his work.

"This," he said, holding a particular point in his fingers, "is more of a Cheyenne style, whether it's of stone, bone or steel, that type is just a real simple shape."

Meyer's tool kit for making arrowheads consists of an antler-point chipper and a piece of leather to protect the palm of his hand. The stone or blank is pressed against the palm by the fingers in a sort of fist. The antler chipper is then pressed against the edge of the stone in a variety of ways to produce the desired results.

"There are different techniques," said Meyer, "depending on what you want to do." He placed a rough stone in his hand, and pressed it against the leather with his fingers.

"To start with a stone like this," said Meyer, "and get a flake, what you want to do is work across the stone, so I first push into the stone, then with an outward, flicking motion. You push down and twist out, all at the same time."

To put a cutting edge on the shaped point, Meyer uses a gentler, downward motion along each edge.

Meyer fletches his arrows with several kinds of feathers, most of which are found locally, all of them native to the West. Among the more commonly utilized feathers are those from goose wings and grouse tails. Raptor feathers would be ideal, except possessing them is illegal and pheasant tail feathers would also work well, except the pheasant is not, after all, a native species.

To fletch an arrow, the feather is first split, then cut to the

desired length. Hide glue is applied carefully to the shaft, using a pointed stick as an applicator. After the feather is in place, the glue is allowed to cool and harden, then the end of the exposed quill is secured to the shaft by several wrappings in fine, glue-impregnated sinew.

The sinew Meyer uses is taken from the foreleg of mule deer. Although just separating the sinew into strands is an arduous task in itself, the resulting fibers are worth the trouble when weighed against the inherent strength and durability of sinew and its compatibility with hide glue in bonding wood to stone.

While the hide glue continues to cool, a point is selected for the shaft. Each shaft is carefully notched to receive a specific point, thus insuring high strength and perfect alignment. Glue is again applied, this time to the inside of the

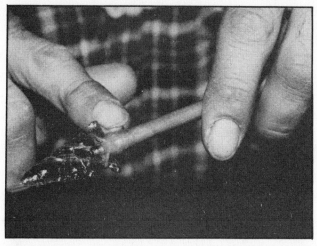

Strands of sinew and hide glue are used to affix arrowheads to shaft. Correct head shape is essential to provide a bite for sinew thread, right. Obsidian arrowhead is held with precise wraps, correctly aligned.

fresh-cut notch. The tang of the arrowhead is inserted into the notch and the glue is allowed to harden for a few moments before more sinew is wrapped tightly around the tang and the end of the shaft, forming a strong bond between the stone and the wood. To finish an arrow, Meyer applies a minute amount of hide glue to the sinew with the tip of his finger, both at the point and on the fletching. The final touch is to trim the feathers to the desired height and shape. The result is a beautiful, handmade arrow that is as pleasing to look at as it is to hold.

Meyer's lifestyle alternates between the idyllic and the practical. After living for more than two years in an Indian-style lodge nestled among the pines and aspens on thirty acres of private land, he found it necessary to leave to take a job in order to maintain his chosen way of life. So for a period of time, Meyer did seismograph work in eastern Montana, not far from the Custer Battlefield and other areas rich in Indian history.

"After living in Montana," said Meyer, "I really started to understand the philosophy, to put my mind back to the old ways. Before I left, I bought that tipi over there, " he said, pointing to a pile of charcoal-gray canvas occupying a large portion of the crowded floor. "That came off the Crow Reservation," said Meyer.

"So when I got back I made my leggings. I got into tan-

ning hides big-time," he said. "Not full-time, but big-time.

"I started getting into the Indian material culture more than anything. You can't be involved in the Indian material culture without becoming involved in the Indian spiritual culture.

"It's tied up more than you think," said Meyer. "Every material thing has its spiritual significance or counterpart. Like stone arrowheads," he said, picking up a black point from the makeshift table.

Meyer explained that by the time the white man had come onto the plains, the stone arrowhead had already become more valuable as an ornament and symbol of strength and skill, than as a working projectile point, replaced as it was by iron supplied in trade from the French trappers and other pioneering travelers. It was not uncommon, then, for an Indian hunter or warrior to be using metallic points on his arrows and lances, while wearing a stone point tied into his hair, or hanging around his neck.

Perhaps that is the greatest worth of the primitive arrows that Meyer is making. Besides their obvious aesthetic value, each one serves as a reminder that beyond the physical, there is another aspect of the chase between the hunter and the game, one that you can see only by looking back. — *Lew Hansen*

After glue has dried, sewing is removed and fletching is smoothed into shape for flight.

BOWFISHING ARROWS

WHEN YOU THINK you have all the arrows you need for the sport of archery, you may think again. There are many activities that require different types of arrows for a specific reason. One of these activities is possibly one of the most agitating, frustrating and, at the same time, one of the best ways to introduce a beginner to the sport of archery. It is the art and fun of bowfishing.

The first thing you need, in most areas of North America is a valid fishing license. You also need to know which fish are legal to shoot with a bow. Some states allow only rough fish such as carp; others allow trout and other species to be legally taken with a bow and arrow. Check your local regulations before venturing out.

The bow you use can be your regular hunting bow or, if you only have target bow draw weights, you can use one for certain phases of bowfishing. At least a forty-pound or heavier draw bow should be used.

The arrows you use are different from the arrows you normally shoot at other game or at targets. It has to be a heavy arrow to be shot into the water. If you try to use the standard hunting arrow, it will plane across the water as it tries to enter. If you are shooting from a boat or high bank straight down, you can use the lighter arrows, but most of the time you will be shooting at less than a ninety-degree angle to the water.

The simplest system is to buy special fishing arrows; most shops and mail order houses carry them. You have a choice of solid fiberglass, solid aluminum or heavy-wall aluminum shafts. You don't need any fletching as the

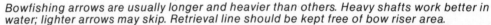

Bowfishing arrows are usually longer and heavier than others. Heavy shafts work better in water; lighter arrows may skip. Retrieval line should be kept free of bow riser area.

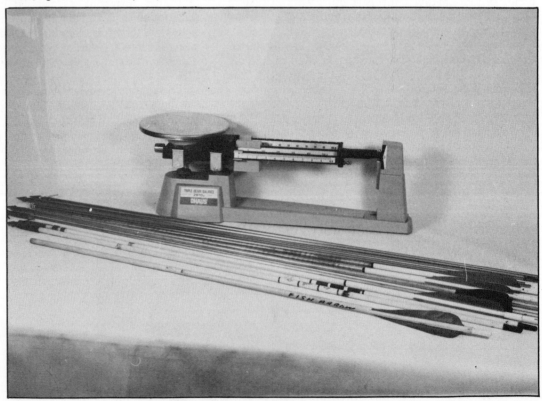

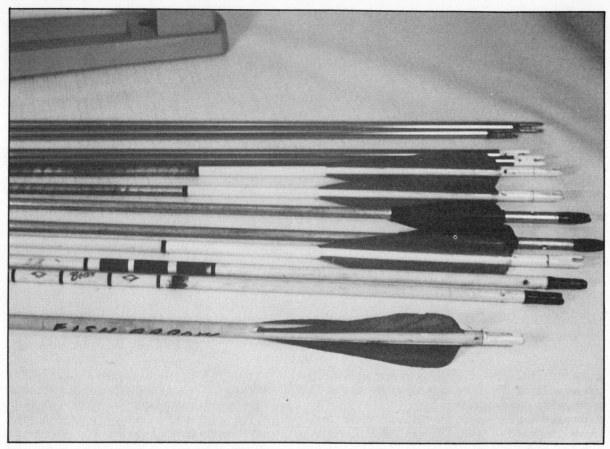

Each of the arrows above has a hole drilled through the shaft near the nock to attach heavy fish line.

arrow is fastened to the bow with a heavy fish line, attached to a reel of some type. The line is tied to the back of the shaft and tends to guide the arrows toward the target. Any of the listed arrows will work well, but after you have done some shooting, you will pick your own favorite.

In the past, we had only the solid fiberglass arrows for bowfishing. They work fine; they are tough, won't bend and seldom break. You have a taper on one end for the nock and the fish point is usually made to fit parallel on the uptapered arrow tip. The point is usually epoxied and often cross-pinned on. Your shaft will become stuck in the mud or underwater roots. The heavy fish line plus the epoxy allow you to get the arrow back rather than have it break or pull off.

There are at least two solid aluminum arrows available for fishing. One is made by Bohning Company, the other is made by Saunders Archery. These aren't just solid aluminum rods, but are of special tempered aluminum which will not bend on release. They work well and are a favorite with many bowfishermen, because of their weight.

A few years ago, Jim Dougherty came out with a heavy-walled, hollow fish arrow that has proven popular. These are made exclusively to his specifications by Easton Aluminum and are a bit different from the others. They have screw-in points just as you have in target and hunting arrows. This makes the removal of a carp from the arrow much faster; all you do is unscrew the point and slide the fish off the shaft. The nock is also different. It looks similar

to a standard heavy hunting nock, but it has a couple of holes in it to allow fish line to be run into the shaft and tied off. The upper hole is also a good securing point for the line attachment. The inside of the hollow, heavy-walled tube is threaded, as is the nock. The two go together to make a tough arrow.

Another entry is the fish arrow made by Custom Archery. It also is a hollow aluminum shaft with heavy wall thickness. It has the same type of nock system and screw-in point adapter.

Since you don't fletch them, you can buy some funny looking rubber or plastic tubes that will slip over the end of the shaft. The fish arrow is easy to work with. You buy them and go shoot at fish. The weight of the arrow is the only basic difference; that weight gets into the ounces rather than grains.

Most arrow grain scales go only to about 800 grains and that won't start to weigh a fish arrow. Use a postal scale or other ounce scale to get the weights for comparison. If you have a larger style gram scale, it will work even better. The Ohaus scale weighs into the pounds and is extremely accurate.

A solid fiberglass arrow weighed in at 85 grams; 90 grams with the point attached. The head was epoxied on so it couldn't be removed easily. The solid aluminum, without the point, weighed in at 95.7 grams and with the point went to 115 grams.

The Easton/Dougherty heavy-wall arrow weighed 51.5

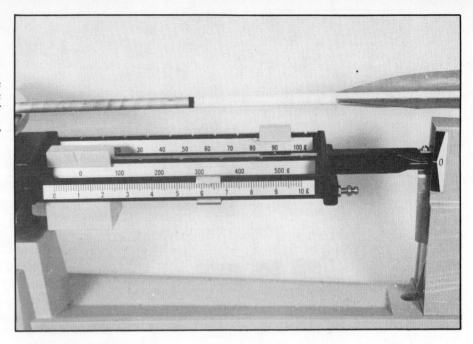

An Ohaus balance scale is used to weigh fish arrows as they are too heavy for most arrow weighing scales. Solid aluminum shaft arrow weighed in at 95.7 grains!

grams with no point attached. This was the lightest of the arrows weighed. The Custom Archery arrow was 77.5 grams, with no point attached.

To put this gram weight into the realm of our normal arrow grain weights, you need some conversion factors. There are 15.4 grains per gram and 437.5 grains per ounce. For example, the solid aluminum at 96.7 grams goes to 1490 grains — in round figures — which in turn converts to 3.4 ounces. We seldom think of arrows in ounces, but these are special arrows and they are heavy for a specific purpose.

Bowfishing is another phase of archery that is lots of fun. When you have a school of big carp swimming in a hole or along a bank, there is no way you can catch them with hook and line. But you can arrow them. When you start bowfishing, you will shoot many times, but until you get the hang of it, you will miss a lot. Once you get it all together, you can have hours of shooting and lots of fun. Furthermore, almost no one likes carp, as they damage game fish beds and deplete the young.

You might consider carrying a fish arrow in your assortment of arrows when venturing afield to different areas. A few years ago, we were camped on the high side of the Tonto River in Arizona, javelina hunting. What we had that year, was about two hours of dry mixed with three or more hours of rain. That doesn't make for good pig hunting

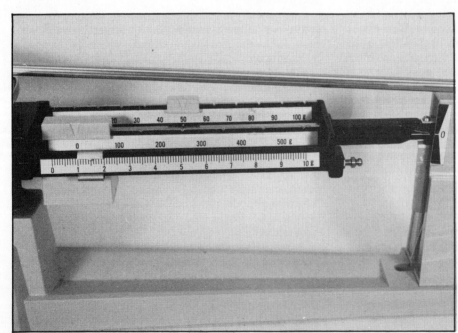

Bowfishing tournament archers use the Jim Dougherty arrow. It scales 51.5 grains, a lighter arrow.

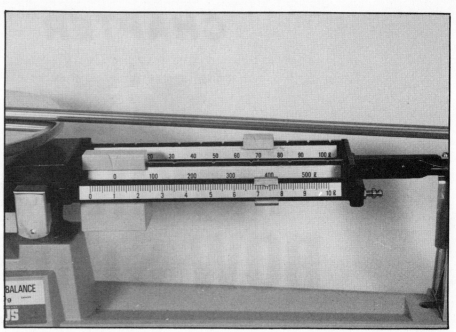

Custom Archery's fluted aluminum bowfishing shaft resists bending. New, it weighs 77.5 grains.

and we got bored sitting in camp.

While moving up and over a rock ledge to get to another draw looking for pigs, I looked down into still water to see some monster carp. There was one in there that was so big he had to back and fill several times just to turn around; he couldn't do it in one swing. He was huge.

When I got back to camp, I queried all the hunters to see if anyone had a fish arrow. I planned to go after that huge

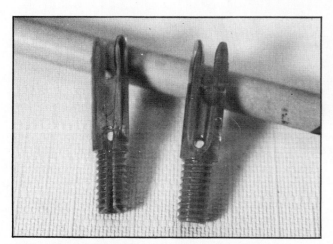

Aluminum fishing arrows benefit from the use of threaded nocks. Groove along the threads permit line to run through shaft, while the hold aids alignment.

carp and all his friends during the next rainy period.

No one had a fish arrow, so I decided to make one. I had some fiberglass arrows and managed to pull the nock off of a bright yellow shaft which would be easy to follow in the water. I tried filling it with dirt. That wasn't heavy enough so when one of the local quail hunters came by to ford the river, I bummed a couple of shotshells. I opened the end of the shells and poured the lead shot into the fiberglass tube to make myself a heavy fish arrow for monster carp.

As the luck of the hunt went, we had several more days of light to heavy rain in squalls that lasted just long enough to keep us in camp rather than in the field. During the first light squall of the day, I picked up my hunting bow, my homemade bowfishing reel and shot-loaded arrow to go shoot carp.

The carp were still there and probably are to this day, as I never got a shot! The rain had run into the river and it was so muddy I doubt if you could see a carp if it was on the surface. So much for that idea!

During one of our annual carp shooting forays I unlimbered my shot arrow and tried it out where I could see carp. It worked quite well, thank you. I shot a number of them with my shot arrow and had them on the bank.

The main difference between my emergency homemade fish arrow and the commercial types wasn't so much the weight — mine weighed in at 70 grams/1078 grains — but the length of the fish arrows. The commercial arrows will range from thirty to thirty-three inches long. Mine was my regular draw length.

Buy or make some fish arrows and have fun during the next carp-spawning period when those ugly monsters are rolling on the surface and wriggling in the shallows. It is fun; it can be productive; and you already have the gear with the simple addition of a fishing arrow or two. — *C.R. Learn*

CHAPTER 4

MAKING A BOW STRING

Part Of The Fun Of Being An Archer Is Doing Your Own Thing — Here's How To Make Your Own String Jig And First String

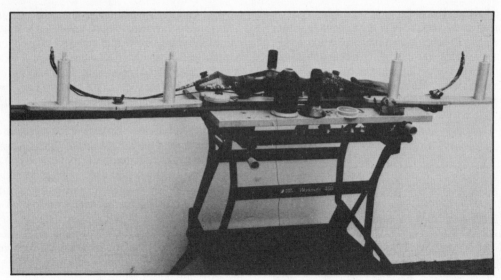

Making your own bow string can be fun and profitable. Initial equipment will be string materials, beeswax, burnishing leather, a server and, most important, your string jig.

C.R. LEARN, with his three decades of archery experience, seems to be always experimenting and researching new projects. He has constructed hundreds of bow strings and tells how to make your own the easy way.

ONE ITEM you can make as an archer is your bowstring. This is one of the easiest and the most rewarding things you can make. Bowstrings aren't that expensive to buy, but after you have purchased the basics and made a few items, you will have enough materials to construct many strings for the price of one or two from a shop.

One of the first things you need — you can build it or buy it —is a string jig. This is a tool with which to make the string — it is easy to make and you probably have the materials on hand right now. The jig allows you to make a variety of strings ranging from the short crossbow types to one that will fit a longbow.

You will need two, 2x4s, bolts and wing nuts, table or bench legs for each corner, a crosspiece of plywood or similar strong material — and you have the basics of a string jig. It helps to have a pattern to work from, so if you

The string maker has a choice of, from left above, Dacron B50, Fast Flight and Kevlar string from which to make bow string. (Right) Measuring tape with wide loop on the end is helpful over bow limb nock ends.

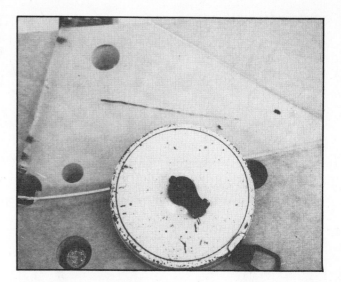

know someone who has one, borrow it, but don't be afraid to modify.

The longest string you will possibly ever make is one for a longbow. These get out to almost seventy inches, so if you think you might someday like to try traditional style shooting, make your jig long enough for these strings. The shortest would be a crossbow and you can make them on the same jig if you have that inclination. That seems a lot for one jig, but it all has to do with the length of the base and the length of the cross arms.

The base unit is made by placing the two long sections of 2x4 boards together with enough space between them to allow the cross arm to move back and forth. It will be adjustable for different string lengths. Choose the size bolt you will use, a half-inch size isn't too big since the unit gets a lot of pressure when in use, cut a hole about that wide and place it in either end of the base. Bolt through all sections to make solid end sections.

Cut the cross arms about eighteen inches long — the length is flexible — and round the ends for style if not utility. Mark the center of the cross arm and drill a hole for the bolt to pass through. You will have one moveable arm and one fixed arm, but the bolt will be in the middle of each, passing through the base and held with a wingnut for easy adjustment.

On each end of the cross arm, check the diameter of the

table leg you plan to use — you can use a long bolt, but it must be a solid section — and place it so the bottom of the attaching bolt will clear the bottom of the base on one arm. The fixed arm doesn't do anything except rotate, but it is easier to make the two legs the same.

Drill the proper hole for the leg base and bolt it to the two ends of the cross arm. This is basically your jig with the finishing touch of drilling a hole in the top of the leg over the brass leg plates to insert a short rod of about three inches. This will be the area where you will wrap the string as you lay it up for serving. When you finish, you will have an adjustable jig on which you can make any length string. If you are sold on the compound system only, you can make a much shorter jig, because these strings are relatively short compared to the recurve or longbow styles.

You may find the wooden style easy to make, but it doesn't work too well for me. I put a lot of pressure on the string when wrapping the strands around the top pegs and have literally folded the legs over when using the table leg style. I know of three other archers who made the table leg style, have used them for years and are still working. What I did was to take some old bed base angle iron, two sections of aluminum plate and some uprights made from round stock aluminum and made a jig that can't possibly be pulled apart.

You can paint, stain or otherwise make your jig look pretty, but it will work fine with no frills added. What many string makers do is attach a section of steel tape to the base section as an aid in determining string lengths.

To make a bowstring, you first need string materials; there are at least four types. The toughest and the hardest on your bow will be Kevlar. It is tough, hardly stretches at all and is most often used by target archers who will change strings after fifty or so shots. Strings do break. Kevlar is the toughest material — it doesn't break, but the strands may fray.

Serving tools are available from a number of sources. Nylon thread or one of several monofilaments is used.

The bow for which a new string is to be made is unstrung before actual nock-to-nock length is measured. Tape is placed on lower limb nock first, left, pulled along the length. Bow lengths may vary; sixty-three, left and sixty inches, center. Right: Old string is nocked on limb, pulled taut to accurately measure length of replacement string.

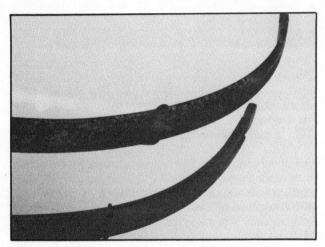

All bows are not the same. Groves recurve, top, has different limb than the Super Diablo, shown below it.

One of the newer types of string material finding favor with bow manufacturers is the Fast Flight material. It is also tough and difficult to break. It doesn't stretch much, if any, when you make it and it won't stretch on the bow. Some manufacturers do not favor Fast Flight and will warn against its use on their bows.

Many archers prefer it, because it is so light and strong. They claim at least ten or more feet per second for their arrows when using this string material over other types.

If you normally use the older styles of string materials, you will need to add some extra wraps of Fast Flight, because it is smaller in diameter. If you normally make a sixteen-strand string, you will need a twenty-strand string with Fast Flight. This isn't to make the string stronger, but thicker string permits you to use the same size arrow nocks.

Another popular type is the B66 string material. It is not as tough as Fast Flight or Kevlar, but it does give at the end of the shot when the arrow leaves the bow. This give puts less stress on bow limbs and the riser. This follow-through is considered normal for a bow and most bowyers allow for it when they make a bow using B66 string.

The old standby and still a great string material, is the B50 Dacron. B66 is also Dacron, but B50 is the old tried and true material. Most bows were made and the strings were set up for B50 and that is where the stresses are computed in a bow set-up. B50 does stretch under tension, but once it has stretched, it doesn't continue to stretch on the bow.

These string materials are made by the Brownell Company. They are constantly experimenting and trying to keep pace with the advances in bow design, giving us string materials that will make our bows shoot and perform better.

You will need another type of thread or filament material for serving the ends and the center serving of the string. Most of the time you will use a special type nylon serving thread that is heavier than sewing thread. This is also made for the archer by Brownell.

Not too many years ago, they came out with a monofilament material, which looks just like fishing line, that is pop-

To begin, the string jig base is clamped into the Workmate and arms are adjusted and locked parallel.

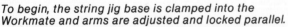

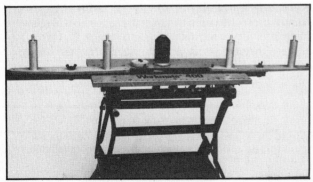

If an old working string is available, it is set in the jig, pulled as tight as possible to eliminate stretch.

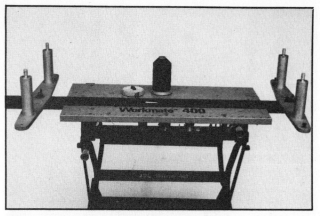

ular with archers for the center serving on strings.

The remaining tools can be found around the shop, with but one exception. That exception is the string server. This is a clamp system that holds the nylon thread of the monofilament and allows you to place it on the string ends and center serving in a tight, neat manner. They are not expensive and some archers have several with different serving materials in each.

You will need to add a ruler or measuring tape, a glue unit, some beeswax, a chunk of leather and pair of scissors or a sharp knife.

You may wish to start with a string for a recurve bow. The easy way is to first measure the string already on the bow. Harold Groves puts a Dyna Stressed limb on his

recurve bows so it has more of a hook on the end and that makes it a bit different from normal recurves. The bow we'll compare it to will be Martin's Super Diablo, also an excellent bow, but with less hook on the end.

The best way to measure the string on a bow is to take the string off and place it on the jig. The two nock loops will go over the metal tops. Turn the arms so they are parallel with the base, pull them tight and that will be your string length, less one-half inch, if you're using B50.

If you don't have a string on the bow, you could go to charts. Most compound bows are listed, but there are none for recurves. With the recurve, place a piece of tape on the nock end of the bow, pull it tightly to the other nock and measure the distance. Subtract four inches, more or less, and make a trial string to see how it fits. The Groves, for example, due to the pre-stressed limb and deep hook, needs nine inches less for the string length. The Martin Diablo needs only five less. If you don't have a string or a chart, you will probably make two or more strings until you get the length you want.

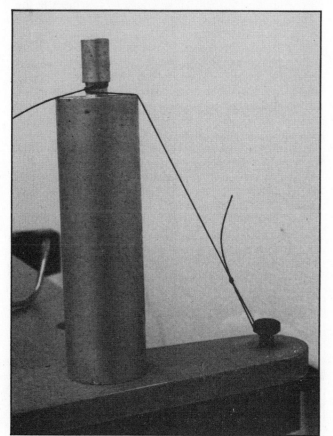

Tie a loop in the string material and attach it to the arm bolt, left. The string is wrapped around the first upright. Sixteen strands are counted, tied off, below.

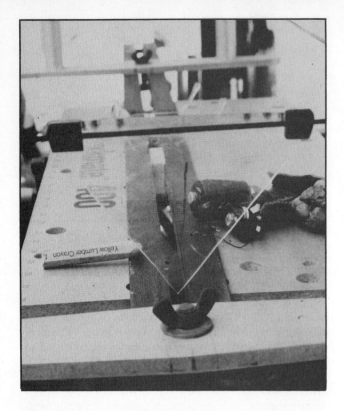

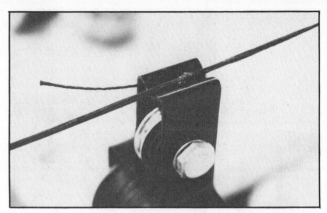

Left: Transparent plastic angle guide is placed on top loop end and string is marked against two dark ears on guide. Bohning server, above, is set on one end of string and a few turns of nylon are taken.

After you have decided on the length of your string, place the tape on one of the metal uprights on the top of the cross arm. The arms are parallel to the base. Pull the tape to get the right length, subtract one half-inch for the stretch of the B50 Dacron string material and lock the cross arms in place. You will have to pivot the arms so they are at right angles to the base for the next step. But take it easy on the movable arm so it doesn't get moved out of position. The fixed arm will present no problem; merely pivot and lock it in place.

The arms are now ready for the B50 string material. Tie one end off and make about two or three wraps around the spot so it won't slip. You should put a lot of tension on the

strings as you lay it out. This is where I used to break string jigs until I made one of heavy metal.

Put a leather glove on your right hand, take the string in that hand and pull it tight as you move around the jig. The string material becomes strands layered on the post. The left hand holds the string supply which will pull off the jig end if you hold it pointing to the jig. The B50 is pre-waxed and you don't have to worry about it falling off; you pull it off as you wrap.

I always figured that the tighter you pull the string as you make the wraps, the less stretch your string will have. Out of curiosity, I called a manufacturer of bowstrings to confirm this. They use a minimum of sixty pounds tension as they wrap their strings. This is done by machines at the plant, but the tension principle was correct; get it tight as you lay it up on the jig.

Most hunting bows are in the fifty-pound and up class and you can check the information that comes with the B50 material to determine how many strands you need for your bow. I have always made my strings sixteen strands which will handle up to sixty pounds or better, but the arrow nocks fit the same on all my strings. Consistency helps keep things simple.

Count the strands as you move the B50 around the arms. We'll make this a sixteen-strand string, so count out sixteen strands to end up on the same cross arm where you started. Move the string to the opposite post from the one on which you started and tie it off with several wraps.

Wraps of serving are continued until desired length is reached, left above. A loop of serving line is held in left hand as more nylon is wrapped in opposite direction, left. Loop is pulled entirely through, below.

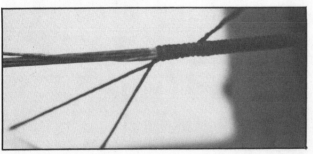

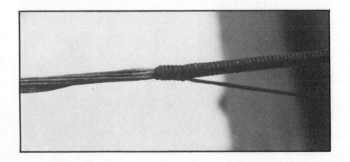

This gives you the basic string setup; all you need to do is to serve the ends. The server now comes into play; there are several different types on the market.

Easton Aluminum makes a good one, sold in archery shops. Bohning makes another style that works well. You can make one yourself, too. We'll use a Bohning, filled with serving nylon in black color. Tension is set on the spool and the forward section to allow you to pull it out with a bit of effort. Too tight and it could actually cut strands of the string. Too loose and it will result in a loose, sloppy serving.

Many archers get confused and irritated by the next steps, but they are simple if you take it slow and easy. You need to start the nylon serving thread on the area where the string will pass around the nocks on the limb tips. These can be measured and marked. A yellow wax marking pencil works great on black string material. Mark the beginning and end of the serving you are to make. For a recurve, make one loop, the upper limb one, a bit larger than the lower one.

Pull an inch or so of line from the server and lay it on the string where you have the first mark. Turn a few wraps by hand by moving the server around the string. Pull it tight by hand to get the serving started. After you have a half-dozen wraps, pull up the tension on the server to locate the curved server section against the string. Now rotate the server around the string, wrapping the nylon on the marked area in a tight, smooth lay-up. If you like, you can whip the server around the string using a wrist action, but this gets tricky,

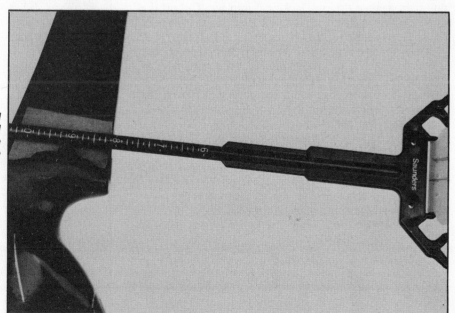

Brace height is measured with the old string braced as a guide to compare the new string. A bow square makes the job much easier.

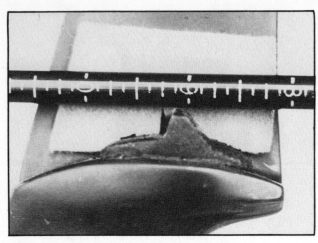

Old string measured 8⅛ inches to riser line.

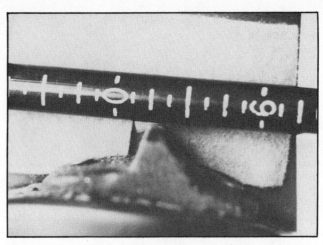

New string is braced on bow, measures 8¾ inches.

so let that go until you've made a few strings.

Rotate the server until you are about one-half inch from the end mark. Let up on the tension and pull about a foot of string from the server and cut it. You need to tie off the other end using a reverse wrap. The served nylon won't unravel, so don't worry about that now. Make a loop with the loose end the opposite way from the end of the serving. If you have the serving on the bottom, form the loop by coming over the top of the string strands. Hold the loop in your left hand and, using the right hand, wrap seven or so turns back toward the served area. Hold the loose end — you should have at least five or six inches left — and lay it alongside the served area. Wrap the nylon in a tight wrap with your right hand, continuing from the served section. As you wrap on with your hand, the loop will move off the loose wrap. When you finish, you will have wrapped the seven turns onto the end of the served area and there will be one large loop in your left hand and a long string in the right. Pull the string tightly, into the end of the serving. The loop will move down to the string at the serving end and will pull tight against the end, locking it in place. Cut off the loose end flush with the served area. Place a dab of cement on each end of the served section and it is finished.

It may sound complicated, especially the end tie-off, but it is simple once you have done it. It is the same knot or method used for tying off ferrules on fishing poles. If you have the loop and loose wraps going the wrong way, the loop won't get looser, but tighter. Merely undo the loose section and reverse the loop.

You have served one end, now go to the opposite end and do the other. When you finish, you can rotate the arms of the jig so that they are again parallel with the base. Pull the served nock ends so they are almost even at the served section. If you off-set them a bit, you get a smoother end serving. If you match them, you will get a ridge.

Pull out a few inches of line from the server, now prepare

Bohning's Tex-Tite or common beeswax is loaded on new string, as much as possible. Section of leather is run rapidly up and down to burnish, stretch string.

to serve the two strands together to make them one. You will also form a loop at both ends to fit the nocks of the bow limbs or the teardrops on a compound. On a recurve, start two inches from the end and place the nylon serving on the string. Make a wrap or two by hand to pull the strands together to form the loop and start the serve. Pull this tight as you now have the the two strands under tension trying to pull apart. Once you have the server started, you merely move down the string toward the center about six inches and tie it off as you did before.

If you make a wide loop at one end, make the second

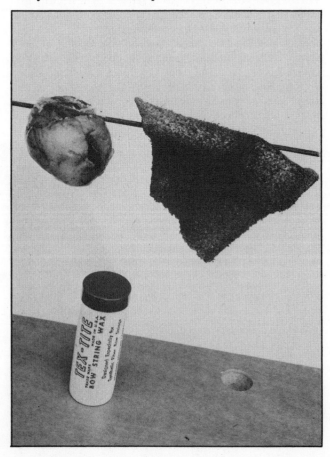

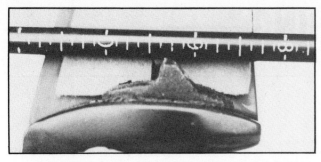

Burnishing tends to lengthen string. New string has reached a measured 8⅜ inches brace height, above. With string still on bow, right, mark extent of center nock serving. Tool makes serving task tight and neat.

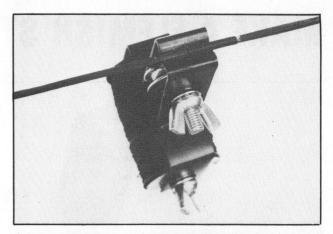

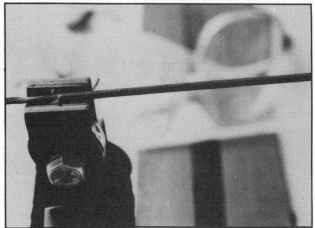

Nock serving should be long enough for any arrows and tight enough to withstand hard shooting action.

narrower to fit the bottom of the bow. If you are serving the ends for a compound, you would make them both rather small and equal to fit over the tear drops on the cable.

After you have served the ends, you can remove the string from the jig. The loops are formed and served down the string for about six inches. This distance isn't critical, but it should go beyond the string groove on the bow tips. Cut the beginning strand and the ending strand where you have them tied off.

The only way to determine if you have a proper length string is to check it with a bow square. Saunders Archery makes an excellent square that is round like an arrow. It fits on the string, lays on the rest just as an arrow would. The distance can be measured at any point, because you are checking brace height for string, not Archery Manufacturer Organization specifications. Measure the original string for reference. Remove it and put on the new one you have made.

While the string is on the bow, coat the string with beeswax by rubbing it along the full length. Wrap a piece of leather over the string and run it back and forth on the string while applying pressure. This is called burnishing the string. When you finish, you recheck with the bow square; amazingly, the string has stretched and now fits right on the button.

Mark the string in the center, just above the bow square. Place the bow under your arm as you would normally carry it and mark the bottom just below your arm. This will be the center serving area which should be long enough to prevent abrasion on the string when you carry the bow. Serve from the bottom up, using the same system as before. You get a lot of practice serving and tying off when making your own string.

By serving from the bottom up, you will have the wrap of

A short, tight string tends to get the maximum speed from recurve limb. A string slightly too long can be twisted a few turns to shorten, re-string and shoot.

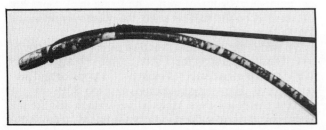

the serving being pulled tighter when you draw the bow. Re-wax the string with the beeswax and burnish it again. Take the string off the bow and leaving the bottom end on the nock, twist about nine or ten turns on the string. This will shorten the string that extra touch to bring it back to the original length. You can twist and shorten a bow string, but not too much. Excess twisting will cause the strands to rub together causing abrasion on the strands; later a broken string.

If old string is in good condition, I'll save it as a spare. The old string is nocked and ready to go. I'll shoot the new one and have the old one ready if I slice the new one with a broadhead.

Once you have the string jig made, you probably won't ever have to make another one. Practice the string serving and the tie-off. It will become easier the more you do it.

You can also try the monofilament serving materials. They make them in orange, clear and other colors. If I nick a string on the nylon serving with a broadhead, I can tie it off again in the field. If I nick one strand of the monofilament, the whole serving comes unravelled. I have had trouble keeping tension while tying off, too. Most monofilament is used for the center serving only. It does make a tight, clean serving, but I have decided against it after trying it for some time. True, you're not supposed to nick a string, but it can and does happen. That's why you carry that extra string into the field. — *C.R. Learn*

MAKE A FLEMISH STRING

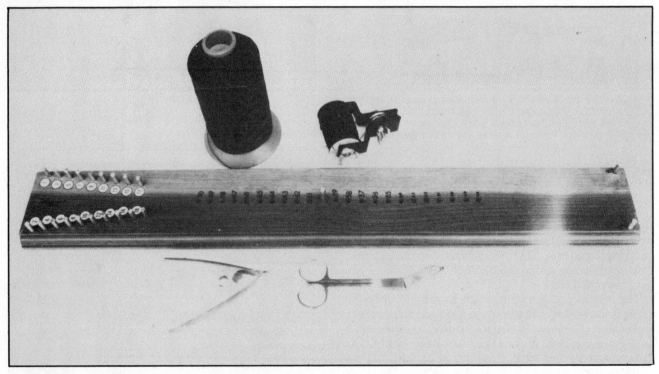

A Flemish string is a bit different and a bit more difficult to construct than the more common endless-type string.
A jig is the most difficult component to find. The one above is from Scott Chapman, Tulsa, Oklahoma. Other ingredients,
such as the Dacron B-50 string material, the center section string server, clamp and scissors are all commonly found.

MAKING YOUR OWN bow strings is challenging and rewarding for the beginner and expert archer. There is more than one type of string, as you will learn from tinkerer C.R. Learn. The less popular and more difficult type of bow string to make is called a Flemish string. Scott Chapman of Tulsa, Oklahoma, has come up with a simple string-making jig which takes most of the sting out of the task, as Learn found out.

MAKING A FLEMISH string seems complicated and confusing at first, but after you have made one or two, it becomes quite simple, perhaps easier than the so-called endless style. You need similar materials: a jig, Dacron or Fast Flight string material, beeswax, scissors or sharp knife, a ruler of some type and a string server.

Scott Chapman of Tulsa, Oklahoma, makes and sells a simple jig and the instructions to make a wide variety of hand-laid Flemish strings.

The jig is not very large compared to the endless string jig. This one measures about two feet by ½-inch and 3½ inches wide. Chapman's new jigs are made of aromatic cedar. There is a set of pegs made of hardwood that form an open V at the top or left side, some peg holes down the middle and two legs at the bottom. With this simple jig, you

can make strings up to seventy inches long or as short as forty-eight inches. There is a brass roundhead brad eight inches down the left side of the board that you will use to measure when making strings. The jig was modified to show the numbers and to mark string lengths. Your jig, when it arrives, will not have these numbers on it. You can add them if you like.

Making a Flemish string is actually making a series of string units. The number of strands depends on the style you want to make. For example, you can make a two-strand string using eight strands in the two units for a sixteen-strand string. You can also make a three-strand system using three strands of five each, which gives you a fifteen-strand string, heavy enough for bows up to sixty pounds of draw. If you want to get fancy, you can also make a string using four sets of four strands each and make double loops for the double ears on a compound string. These Flemish strings will work on longbows, recurves and compounds equally well. The string nock loops are thicker than on the endless style, the reason for making a double loop string for the compound.

We will make a fifteen-strand string for a sixty-pound bow. The string is sixty inches long in recurve style. It will fit a Martin Howatt Super Diablo bow, a popular and proven recurve. The string material is Dacron B50.

Place the board on a table or workbench and set the length peg, the one in the middle of the board, at the sixty-

The Flemish Bow String Has Advantages And Disadvantages Of Its Own

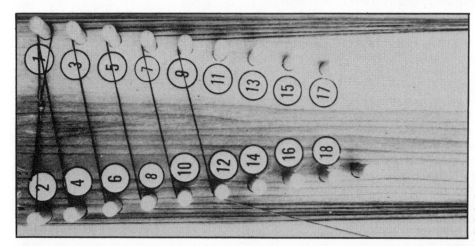

Upper end of the string strands, left, will stagger across the numbers to give a better looking tapered string. Lower end, below, set up to cut five strands.

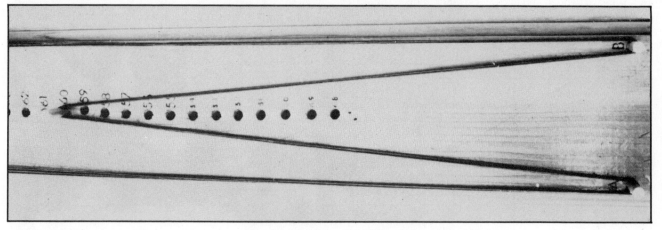

inch mark. Tie a loop on the end of the Dacron strand. This loop goes over the number one peg and across to number two. Next, it moves down to the lower right-hand peg marked A, up to the 60 marker peg in the middle, down to the upper right-hand peg marked B, up to the number one peg again, diagonally across to the number 4 peg, down to A, up to 60, down to B, up to 3, across to 6 and so on until you have crossed the 9 to 12 pegs, giving you five diagonal strands on the upper end. Hold the strands relatively tight as you lay them up, but not too tight.

You have just completed wrapping the first of three similar strands that will make up the finished string. You can move across from the eight-inch brass round-head brad and hold the string with your hand or attach it with a small spring clamp. I found that the clamp does not allow the strands to become loose.

With scissors or sharp knife, cut the strands in the middle between the large V on the left end of the jig. Release the starting strand; the loop will remain on the number one peg. Discard it. You now have five strands of Dacron B50 with a varying length on both ends when you remove it from the jig. The clamp will hold the strands until you grab them with your left hand.

Use the eight-inch board marker and measure the ad-

ditional eight inches for sixteen inches total. Hold the strands in your left hand; form a loop on the first two fingers by wrapping the strands around them, bringing the longer strands back through the palm of the hand, leaving the sixteen-inch section in front.

Heavily beeswax those five strands by holding the thumb of your right hand on the strands and pressing them to the beeswax block. Pull downward to get as much wax in the strands as possible. Beeswax holds them together for the wrapping process after. After heavy waxing, I found it simple to retain the grip on the strands and wax the long section hanging down from my left hand. By waxing them in this manner, you help hold those strands in a tighter group.

With the strands held tight, move to the unwaxed end and measure off about sixteen inches as you did with the first waxing. Use the same two-finger hold and make certain you have pulled all strands before releasing the first group. Now wax those sixteen inches just as you did the first group. When you feel you have them saturated, place the strands to one side. These will look like one single strand with the application of so much wax, but that is what holds them together.

Now make two more sections of five-strand threads and wax them. The result will be three multiple strands, three each, with five strands; fifteen total.

Twist and wrap these three strands to make the end loops — or bow nock loops — on the string. Use the eight-inch brad marker and measure each group for that distance. Hold the three groups in your left hand, using the thumb and first finger to apply adequate pressure. The second, third and fourth fingers will hold pressure also and pull down on the twisted string as you form it.

Arrange the three strands so they are separated. Grasp the upper strand and twist it away from you with the right hand until it is tight; six or seven tight twists should do it. Bring the twisted strand over the top of the other two and place it at the bottom of the three groups. Twist the upper group away from you with the right hand and pull them over the other two to the bottom. Grasp and twist the third group, twist away, pull over and place the strands at the bottom. Now continue twisting away on the upper group, pulling over to place it at the bottom. While the right hand is twisting and moving the groups over each other, the left hand is holding them firmly at the crossover junction, pulling them away from the twist to move them down the inside of the hand. Continue this until you have about an inch and-a-half of twisted and laid over strands. This is the start of the loop.

Form a loop with the twisted section. When you make a nock loop for a recurve, you normally make one loop small for the lower end, large enough to go over the bow tip to the nock. The upper loop is usually made larger to allow the loop to move up and down the upper limb when the bow is unbraced.

Bring the three strands from the upper end of the loop — there will still be about six inches left untwisted — and mate them with the three long strands of the main body. Place the short end with a long section, twist them together and they will form one thicker strand. When you have all three short ends mated with the three long sections, you are ready to form the base unit of the loop where it ties into the main string.

Place your left hand at the junction of the three thick strands. They will look just the same as when you twisted and formed the strands for the loop, but thicker. Grab the upper strand, twist away and bring it over the top toward you, pulling to make the loop joint clean and neat. Take the next upper strand, twist away and pull over the top toward you. Do the same with each section as you move down the main body of the string, forming a twisted, neat string as you go.

You must move the string back through the left hand as

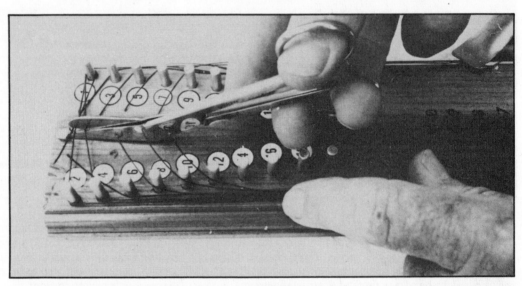

After all strands have been clamped, right, they may be cut through middle.

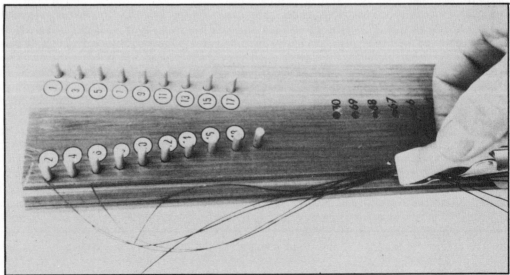

String clamp is placed at the eight-inch mark to establish the next strand length.

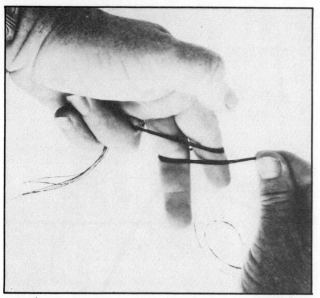

The strands should not slip or change position while being waxed. Hold the strands in right hand and make a loop around first two fingers of the left hand, above.

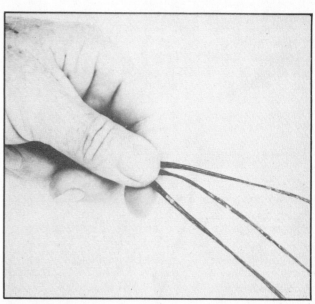

The three five-strand units have been waxed and are ready to be joined to make the loop. Hold three units in left hand eight inches from end. Maintain tension.

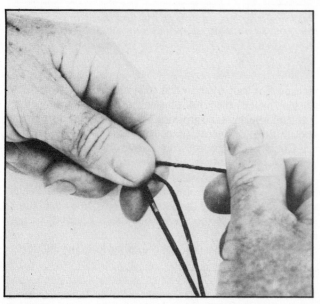

Maintain tension with the left hand while twisting each of the three strands tightly at least six times.

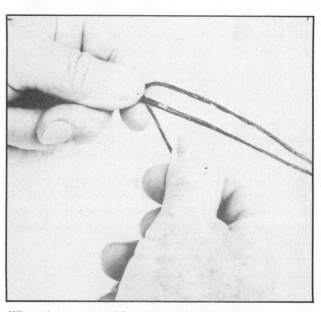

When the top strand has been twisted snugly, it is brought over the top of the other two, held firmly.

you did when mating the smaller three strands. When you have the loop moved far enough back toward the little finger, it helps to loop the end of the string over the finger and pull it down as you twist and pull over. Continue twisting, pulling over and pulling back until the end of the bulky strands is reached.

As you reach the ends of the strands, they will move off the system and maybe cause a slight single strand to stick up. Ignore that for now. When you have all three short ends twisted into the main body, continue until you have twisted and formed a section about one inch down from the last of the short sections.

Clamp the finished end with a clothespin or a large spring clamp. Place the clamp over the formed loop and grip the string where the twisted area left off. Now move to the opposite end of the string, keeping all strands even and start it all over again using the eight-inch marker for proper length. Start forming the other nock loop. Use the same twisting, pulling over system as before. You may want one loop larger, so you might make this one two inches long.

After you have the loop formed, you move to the ends of the strands as you did before and mate the three short strands with the three long strands, making three large strands for the other loop. Now twist away and pull toward

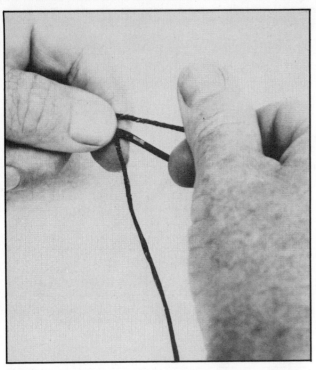

The second strand — now the top strand — is twisted in a similar manner as the first, pulled over other two.

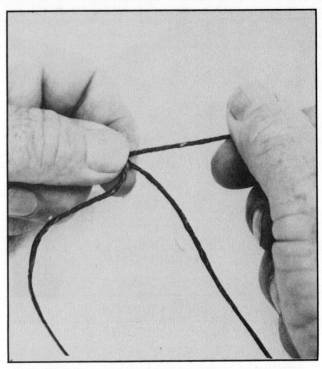

The third strand is treated as the first two. Continue the process until about an inch and a half is twisted.

you as you had been doing. You will notice the twisting and pulling will start to tangle the longer strands in the middle. Hold tight to the strands with the left hand, lift high enough so the clamp will act as a weight and move your right hand down the strands. The clamp weight will start to spin, removing the twist.

Do the same twisting away and pulling over toward you until you reach the end of the short strands. Continue about one inch more and you have the basic string formed. Now you need to twist the entire string to keep it from coming undone.

Most of us have a vise in the shop. Clamp a rod in the vise, put one loop over the rod and pull the string tight using the loop on the other end. This will pull the strands together in the middle and take any kinks out. Twist the entire string about fifteen or twenty times to get the twists in the ends set. Check and be certain you are twisting in the right direction or you will untwist the entire string.

After you have the basic twists in the string, remove it from the rod and place one loop on the bow nock. When you move the string up the belly of the bow, you might think you have made it too short, but these Flemish strings really stretch.

Brace the bow by placing the other loop on the upper

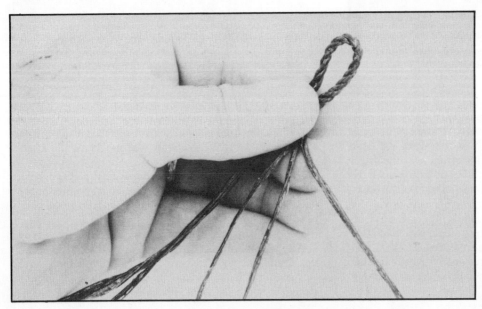

With enough twists, a loop may be formed as at left. All strands must be held tightly by the left hand for tight, efficient loop.

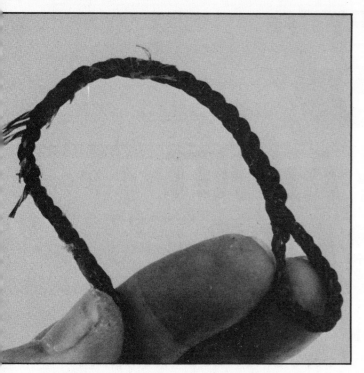

The loop on either end of the string should look like
this when finished. Attaining a neat string and loop
may take some practice. Extra string ends may be trimmed.

and, using the right twisting direction, took six or seven more twists. I rebraced the bow and after a few full draw pulls, it stabilized at the correct brace height. The Flemish string may tend to stretch a bit, so check the brace height from time to time. If it stretches, it will change the nocking point height and your arrows may become erratic in flight. If it lengthens, all you need to do is twist it up a few more turns.

The remaining step is to serve the center of the string with the aid of the string server and you have a finished Flemish or hand-laid bowstring.

If your new Flemish string is radically short or long, all you can do is make another one. Don't throw away the first string, as you may find a bow for it some day. My first Flemish was too short even for a crossbow! I don't know what I did wrong, but it hangs in the shop as a conversation piece.

One early string came out just a tad too short. Could I untwist one end and lengthen it? I did just that and had a string the right length the second time.

Which is better for a bow, the endless or Flemish bowstring? Some feel the Flemish is easier to make. If necessary, one can be made in hunt camp with a small jig and a spool of thread.

Those who prefer the endless string, say it is a cleaner string on the ends. The Flemish gets pretty bulky with all that string material at the loops. That's one of the problems with the Flemish string on compound bow cable ears.

There are several manufacturers of longbows and recurves placing Flemish strings on their commercially-made bows. There is a longbow in the shop from Rancho Safari that is of the traditional style longbow, but it has a Flemish string made of Fast Flight material. One section uses white threads and the other black threads. The result is a black and white twisted bowstring of the old Flemish style with a barber pole effect. It is an interesting, different looking bow. — *C.R. Learn*

nock of the bow limb and check your brace height. Mine came out a bit short and it concerned me at first. Run a piece of leather on the braced string, back and forth, to heat it. As you do so, the string will stretch. My original brace height was 9⅝ inches. The first string measurement came out to ten inches; too short. But when it was burnished, it stretched a bit to 9½ inches; too long. I unbraced the bow

Right: Completed Flemish
string retains plenty
of wax until first shot
snaps it off. For the
beginner, there cannot
be too much beeswax.
Modern Fast Flight
string, below, uses
black and white strands
for interesting effect.

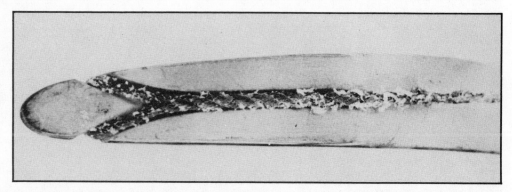

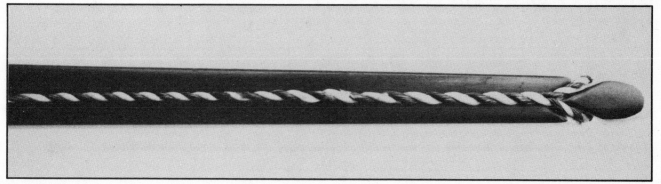

CHAPTER 5

TALKING ABOUT TARGETS

Whether Natural Materials Or Synthetic, Targets Are Indispensible. Here's What's Available And How They're Made!

Whether bowhunters or paper punchers, archers must practice and therefore require targets. They may vary from stacked hay bales, as used by this shooting club, to synthetic materials discussed.

Favored by tournament directors for nearly a half-century are backstops from Sauders Archery that are made from spiral-wound marshgrass. Any type of target face is then applied and you can shoot for years.

LIKE POLITICS, modern warfare or marital relations in the Nineties, all is compromise when it comes to selecting an archery target. The ideal would be an indestructible target that costs next to nothing and from which your shafts are extracted with the ease of a billfold by a pickpocket.

But, as you'll soon see, it doesn't happen that way. What is indestructible likely isn't portable; what is portable likely isn't inexpensive; what is inexpensive likely isn't durable; what yields arrows with two-finger effort likely

isn't suited for broadheads; and so forth.

All of which is an effort to explain why this chapter won't tell you which target is best for your particular circumstance. Unlike a geometry problem, there is no one right answer here. Only you can evaluate your needs and circumstances — and know how much you have stashed away in the "recreation fund."

One thing is certain, however: Every archer needs a target. It's mandatory...vital...requisite. Practice shooting is part of the sport; for paper punchers it's the name of the game, whereas for bowhunters it's only a means to an end — venison on the meatpole.

Bowhunting authors like Chuck Adams feel it's unconscionable to go into the woods with less than six weeks of target shooting under your belt, and eight weeks would be even better. The idea of flinging a few shafts a day or two before season opener is preposterous. Your muscles, your eye and your equipment aren't ready. It's irresponsible to bowhunt in such circumstances.

Enough evangelism — you know what's right. So let's examine the targets available. You can request literature from the manufacturers mentioned (their addresses are in the back of this book), then go to your archery dealer to have a gander.

MATERIALS

Natural and man-made materials are used for target butts today. Straw or hay bales, bales of curled wood shavings and grass matts have been used for decades, and still are today. Another natural material, cotton, has become popular in recent years. On the man-made side we have cardboard, styrofoam, nylon and self-healing plastic foam. Target faces — everything from full-color reproductions of

Paraplegics and others who use wheelchairs find archery challenging, rewarding and fun. At a special tournament, this archer aims on bullseye target affixed to Saunders' grass matt. These matts require little care, maintenance.

According to bowhunter Chuck Adams, about the only maintenance grass matt targets require is occasional wetting down, tightening of binder cords holding grass.

large game, small game and birds to anatomically correct deer and elk innards — are printed on special papers, plastics and burlap for long-term use. More about these later.

Straw or hay bales are inexpensive, widely available, relatively durable, but hardly portable. You can't readily chuck your three-bale target butt into the truck when heading for the hunting camp, but if you hunt close to your residence, this may work out.

Here's a tip from Chuck Adams, overheard at the International Bowhunters Clinic sponsored by Anderson Archery of Grand Ledge, Michigan. Adams told some of the 20,000 bowhunter attendees to buy three bales of wheat straw, which is more durable than oat straw or grass, clover or alfalfa hay, then take them to a lumberyard or hardware store with a banding tool. (A moving and storage firm also

would work.) Have the three bales banded tightly together to form a wide, flat target face.

"Wheat straw doesn't crumble like hay or oat straw, and you won't lose much to rodents," the affable Adams said, mobbed while signing autographs at the three-day fest held each June. "If you cover the bales during wet weather, you'll get several seasons' use out of them and all for less than $25."

All you need to do is change the target face attached to the front and keep on shooting. You can't fire broadheads at this butt, however, as lifespan will be shortened considerably — and you'll improve your cussing ability as you attempt to extract arrows!

Speaking of extraction, here's another tip from Joe Stiver, a bowhunting professional from Oklahoma City. "We have found that waxing our arrows periodically with a good car wax makes them easier to remove from any kind of target," says Stiver, who will later in this chapter give detailed plans for a do-it-yourself cardboard target butt. "We have also used WD40 and Teflon wet lubricants. Spray them on and leave them to dry; they work amazingly well!"

Stiver also notes that pulling arrows is made easier — and you simultaneously increase the life of your target — by correct matching of field points to arrows. "The field points should be the same size as the shaft, or slightly smaller." If the field point is larger than the shaft, pulling the arrow out is harder and you'll remove some of the target material as you do so. If the field point is much smaller than the shaft, then the "shoulders" formed where the head meets the shaft tend to "punch" some of the target face into the target butt. This makes larger impact holes and shortens the life of the target.

"The correct size to match your arrows are as follows: 5/16" point for arrow size 2013 through 2020, 21/64" for 2114 through 2117, and 11/32" for 2213 through 2419 and all Bear metric sizes," Stiver suggests.

But what about practicing with broadheads? Jim Dougherty, another top name in bowhunting and a pioneer in the sport, feels you must shoot broadheads on your hunting arrows, or you never will really know how your shaft

Left: Talk about realistic! Horne's EZ Pull pig is wild boar complete with tusks, hairy ridgeline, ears and eyes. Cotton stuffing inside polyethylene-reinforced burlap will last indefinitely. Horne's Shoot'n Gallery, above, offers variety of targets on one adult deer-sized body target.

Jim Horne looked high and low, and finally found appropriate antler material that would retain shape, not lay down. Inch-thick urethane was the lifelike answer.

"Our Curlex target butts come in three sizes — a new Portable Mini-Double, and the standard Double and Triple Bales," says Patrick Z. Coyle, branch manager for one of the employee-owned firm's twenty-eight branches nationwide. "Curlex is a good fiber that's rot- and rodent-resistant, with a long history of being one of the finer backstop materials available. Our new Mini-Double Bale was designed after numerous requests for an Excelsior backstop that would be considered portable and enable shooters to take it along to deer camps or tree blinds for practice. United Parcel Service will also handle shipment."

Perhaps the most-popular target butt ever made — at least the one that's stopped more arrows than any other — is the Saunders Archery Company's Indian Cord Fiber Matts. Available in twenty-five, thirty, thirty-six and forty-eight-inch diameters, these marshgrass matts are spiral wound and chemically treated against fungus and dry rot, then encased in burlap. Saunders' newest matt, dubbed the Triple T, is extra thick to stop even carbon arrows fired from ninety-pound compounds.

"The cost-conscious bowhunter will do nine-tenths of his practice on a Saunders Matt and use a foam plastic matt for a few hours of broadhead practice," says Chuck Saunders, president of the firm. "This combination of a Saunders Matt and foam broadhead matt will last the average bowhunter for years."

Indeed. For nearly fifty years, tournament directors have selected Saunders matts for such meets as the National Field Archery Association Indoor Shoot, National Archery Association National Tournament, Las Vegas Shoot, Atlantic City Classic, Pan American Games and the World

will fly in the hunting field. As will be presently shown, there are targets suitable for razor-sharp hunting heads — but they are not made of the natural materials being discussed here.

One more thing before moving to target materials: How to pull arrows out of targets with less effort. Both Bear/Jennings and Saunders Archery offer arrow pullers; nothing more than rectangular sheets of plastic that allow one-handed arrow extraction from the tightest matts. No more bent arrows!

Back to baled butts. A banded, three-bale target butt is hardly portable, as Chuck Adams well knows — he hauls a smaller one to be discussed later. A baled target butt the maker claims *is* portable, however, is made by American Excelsior Company.

Bear/Jennings' Easy Care Target has five-spot target on one burlap side, left, with bear logo on reverse, below. While not intended for broadheads, bowhunter can plunk lots of field points into 'em, even from the treestand.

Team Championships. About the only maintenance they require is to periodically tighten the cords binding the spirally wound grass, and keeping the matt damp so the rope grass stays swollen. Saunders also markets a variety of fixed and wheeled matt stands and supports, for either fixed locations or removal to a storage spot.

The final "natural" material finding increasing use in what are called "bag" targets is long-staple cotton. Stuffed into sturdy burlap sacks reinforced with multiple layers of polypropylene and printed with targets or painted to resemble game animals, cotton stops arrows by shock absorption, rather than by friction on the arrow shaft.

"We introduced the first bag-type target to the market in 1971," says Jim Horne, president of Horne Archery in Inverness, Mississippi. "They were called Calmont SSH Supertargets then, and were the most-popular in the country at one time. But our round shape and higher cost gave way to the more-versatile and less-expensive foam targets."

The first Supertargets — which now are called Horne EZ Pull Archery Targets — measured thirty inches in diameter and featured a shoulder view of a deer on one burlap surface, with four bulls-eye's on the reverse. "Several

The Promat target uses a nylon grid to stop arrows with friction, and they thump into a reinforced backstop. Easy arrow removal is guaranteed — try two-finger extraction.

years ago, we hired a young man to 'shoot out' one of our targets, so we could get an idea about their durability," Horne relates. "After several days, he was exhausted, his bow was worn out and our target was still stopping arrows. He quit after five thousands shots." He didn't get fatigued from yanking out arrows — the cotton filling permits two-finger extraction.

With the advent of foam targets in animal shapes, Horne Archery responded to the marketing challenge by developing an EZ Pull target that looks like an adult whitetail. Grommets on the back and legs enable shooters to suspend

Above: Stanley Hips two-dimensional targets are painted by hand are realistic reproductions. Note replaceable core with arrows. Hips created the hand-painted wolf at right, and the yellow "smiley faces" (below) are centered on replaceable cores for ethafoam targets firm makes.

the target, identical in size to an adult whitetail, from two types of optional stands or by rope from trees, rafters, et cetera.

"Since it's of the same materials as our round targets, it will last a minimum of 5000 shots before you need to replace the cover — easily done by unlacing the belly of the old target, removing the cotton, stuffing it into the new one and sewing the bottom closed," Horne said.

"While it is not for broadhead use, it will stop the most powerful bow and never damage a shaft or fletching," continues the bowhunter, whose sales tripled since introducing the target in 1988. "Because it's the same shape and roundness as a real deer, it gives a realistic shot from any

MAKE YOUR OWN COMPRESS TARGET

The following design and construction information wsa furnished by Joe Stiver, a bowhunting advisor from Oklahoma City. It's simple, functional and easy to build. It's designed for cardboard only, but conceivably could be modified for hay bales. The listed materials must be doubled to create a front *and* back press. Follow the illustration for both.

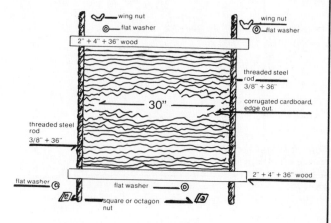

MATERIALS NEEDED

1. Four (4) 3/8-inch x 36-inch full-thread steel rods
2. Two (2) 2-inch x 4-inch x 36-inch pieces of lumber
3. Four (4) 3/8-inch wing nuts, to fit the steel rods
4. Four (4) 3/8-inch square or octagonal nuts to fit bottom of steel rods
5. Eight (8) flat washers with minimum 3/8-inch centers to fit between nuts and 2x4 lumber
6. Electric drill with 7/16-inch wood bit

CONSTRUCTION

1. Drill a 7/16-inch hole three inches in from each end of your 36-inch-long 2x4s. You can drill it on the flat surface or edgeways; edgeways is stronger.
2. Insert steel rods in the holes. On the bottom wooden piece, install first a flat washer and then the square or octagonal nut to end of each rod.
3. Fill center with flattened cardboard, edge facing shooter. When new, apply only enough pressure via the wing nuts to hold the target together. Arrow penetration can be regulated by adjusting the wing nuts. If using both a back and front press, back press should be tighter than front press,

which helps control arrow penetration and makes extraction easier.
4. Cover the target when not in use. It will last for many months and thousands of shots before needing to replace the cardboard.

WHERE TO FIND CARDBOARD

Stiver favors heavier corrugated cardboard, although he says the lighter weights also work. "Cardboard is available for the hauling at many types of stores — grocery, hardware, farm supply, et cetera," Stiver adds. "We have found that boxes holding gallon jugs of antifreeze are ideal in weight and size. They break down to twenty-eight inches long and twenty-four inches deep — a good size."

angle. Also, just like a real deer, there is no painted kill zone or replaceable core to help the shooter aim. He must pick the spot and make the same judgments as in a hunting situation."

Since then, Horne has introduced a Pig EZ Pull target, a life-sized wild pig with realistic tusks, neck hair and hand-painted body markings, and the Shoot'N Gallery target, a deer-sized body target with multiple faces on both sides.

Esafoam targets are black silhouettes of several animals, including wild boar (below). Self-healing foam is ideal for broadheads. Experts advocate practicing with them.

And perhaps the ultimate in bag-type realism is Horne's new full-sized whitetail buck target, complete with antlers. "We spent a long time searching for the right antler material, a foam that wouldn't lay down," Horne says. "I finally found a urethane in Georgia that's perfect...strong and lightweight." This will doubtless boost sales of the EZ Pull line, since Horne says his targets will "outlast your bow."

Horne was so confident of this claim that he sponsored Fred Nichols and Al Burnor of Saint Burlington, Vermont, in a quest for a *Guiness Book of World Records* team record for "Most Arrows Shot and Points Scored" in a single twenty-four hour period. They scored 60,144 points after about 6000 shots on September 29-30, 1990, breaking the old record of 51,633 points.

"We never knew how many shots our targets could take, so we agreed to participate," Horne states. "The cotton stuffing lasts forever, we know that; but how many shots could the burlap covers take before quitting? We didn't know."

During practice sessions to build endurance for the big shoot, Nichols has put more than 60,000 shots into one Horne EZ Pull target. "Yeah, the cotton was sticking out in places and we sent them a replacement cover before the successful try, but that first one took more than 60,000

One of target faces in Impact Industries' Long-Life line is crouching cottontail, above. The burlap strands will separate as field point enters, extending life. If you want to shoot broadheads, Impact offers version at right. Two-spot reverse has higher/lower placement.

arrows. Clearly, our targets *will* outlast your bows!"

Another bag-type maker is Pilgrim Archery Products of Kingwood, Texas. Cole Pilgrim makes five cotton-filled targets, one round, one shaped like a deer, another like a pig and two square models. "Our thirty-inch No Poke-R is a reversible, seven-ply that comes complete with a carrying strap and hidden stand," says Pilgrim. "One side has a three-color side view of a deer body, while the other has five, four-inch colored bull's-eyes. After several thousand shots, you can recover the target with our replacement bags or weatherized color prints." It weighs about twenty-five pounds — easy to transport.

Pilgrim's life-sized deer target is sans eyes and painted features, and can be hung from triangular-shaped rings on the back and legs. Once you stick it a few thousand times, replace the cover and you're good to go. Ditto with the Pilgrim "Hawg" target, replica of a javelina.

"Our reversible square targets measure two feet square or three feet square," Pilgrim notes. "The larger target has forty pounds of processed cotton stuffed into the polypropylene-reinforced burlap, and both sides have five, four-inch colored bull's-eyes. The smaller target is what we call our economy 'Tic Tac Target'. It has grid lines to

offer competitive shooting to all archers."

While it isn't filled with cotton, Bear/Jennings' Easy Carry Target is another bag-type and therefore fits in here. It's stuffed with polyfill and covered with burlap that is emblazoned with the Bear Archery trademark on one side, and five aiming circles on the reverse. It's especially useful for practice shots from tree stands and comes with a nylon carrying cord.

Man-made and synthetic materials are used in other targets besides the aforementioned Easy Carry Target. Cardboard, nylon mesh and several types of foam are widely used and will be discussed here individually.

A compress target for cardboard or hay bales essentially is a bale-type intended only for field points to which any style of target face is affixed. The cardboard is stacked with the edge facing the shooter, so the arrows penetrate be-

Left: Bear Lightarget II has colorful, reversible face atop foam body. Field point only, please — save your broadhead shooting for Bear/Jennings' Broadhead Target, above. You can angle it to shoot from treestands, too.

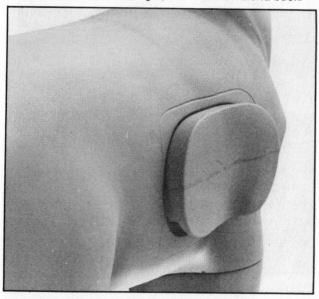

Bear/Jennings' Bowhunter Practice Target, above, has replaceable core, shown in black here. Delta's 3-D animals also have replaceable kill zones, below. These usually are of different foam density than body. Perhaps the most realistic antlers around, right, are found on Delta buck.

tween the layers, being stopped by friction. They pull out without too much effort, especially if you've waxed the shafts as Joe Stiver suggested earlier.

Cabela's, the Nebraska outdoor direct marketing giant, sells a target compressor that eliminates arrow shoot-through — common once the center of the target absorbs several hundred shots. "On hay bales, as arrows hit a concentrated area the spot becomes weak and loose, and the arrows don't stop until they come out the other side of the bale," explains Cabela's Don Frost. "But our target compressor prevents this when using either hay bales or stacked cardboard."

It's done, he says, by taking a couple of cranks on the handles located atop the target, which scrunch the materials together tighter and tighter. The compressor is designed to hold three full-sized bales up to 42½ inches long, or three stacks of cardboard. Because of the size, it's not really

portable; hence, you must ensure the bales are covered during wet weather or your target's lifespan will be shortened considerably.

Because of the simplicity of the compress target, bowhunter Joe Stiver has furnished a design for the do-it-yourselfer. You'll find it elsewhere in this chapter.

Did the idea for the popular mesh style of portable target result from some archer shooting a field point into a tennis or badminton racket? The evolution isn't clear, but that about explains how the Promat target from Impact Industries functions: Arrows penetrate the nylon screen, which slows them down, and they're stopped by the reinforced Power Pad backstop. Extraction is two-fingers easy.

Terry Thirion, of the Wausau, Wisconsin-based Impact

Industries, says his firm makes three sizes: Promat X is eighteen inches square and weighs nine pounds; Promat I is twenty-four square inches and eleven pounds; Promat II is thirty-six square inches and seventeen pounds; and the Promat Magnum is forty-eight square inches and twenty-four pounds. "We also offer two School Promats, one thirty-six square inches and fourteen pounds, and the other a forty-eight square incher that weighs twenty pounds," he notes. "These are lighter because the backstops are suited to light recurve bows such as used at camps or schools. If students are to shoot compounds, then the Promat II or Magnums are the best bets."

Impact also sells squares of Power Stop materials, suitable for backing grass, foam or bag-type targets. Measuring twenty square inches, the Power Stop backstop has "S" shaped hooks on each corner for attachment to any burlap-covered target. For foam targets, anchor the "S" hook to the material with a large nail or spike fitted with a flat washer. Hay bales may require that you tie a cord around the bale on each side, so that you can hook the "S" hooks to them. "Sometimes you need to tape all four hooks to the cord to keep the Power Stop in place when shooting," adds Thirion.

Impact also gives directions for making your own lightweight target utilizing the Power Stop. You'll find them elsewhere in this chapter.

One of the revolutionary materials used widely by target makers today is foam: urethane, polyurethane, polystyrene, styrofoam, ethafoam, esafoam, elastafoam, and probably a few other "foams." They are available in two- and three-

 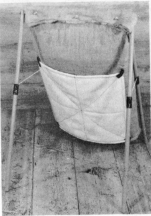 

MAKE YOUR OWN FOAM-FILLED TARGET

What follows are the do-it-yourself instructions for making an inexpensive, foam-filled archery target. It was supplied by Impact Industries, which makes the Power Stop backing materials used.

Purchase two burlap grain bags at a feed store, then fit one inside the other to provide a double-layered cover. A local upholstery shop may give you, free of charge, used foam cushions; stuff them into the burlap sacks. Hook the Power Stop securely on the back by poking the end of the hook through the burlap and squeezing it closed with pliers. Put a target face on the front and you have a bag-type target already.

If you want to make the frame, buy two ten-foot lengths of one-inch PVC pipe. Heat one piece at the appropriate points and bend to form a square U-shaped piece, to which the burlap target will be affixed at top. Cut the second length of PVC in half, forming the back legs. Drill a hole in the ends of both legs and into both sides of the U-shaped PVC at the top of the U, then bolt the legs to the U-shaped piece. This provides a frame that is both free-standing yet can be folded for easy transportation. You can tie equal lengths of rope or cord to the legs as reinforcement when open, taping these to the legs.

The burlap is folded over the top bar of the frame assembly and secured at three points using three-quarter-inch bolts with washers and locking nuts. A piece of wire will tie the bottom corners of the burlap sack to the PVC frame. Obviously, this is not for use with broadheads.

Blue Ridge by Foam Design offers black spot center white bull. Both are replaceable after repeated usage.

dimensional configurations — that means that two-dimensional are like thick cutouts in painted animal shapes, whereas three-dimensional are made to look like the critter from any angle.

Stanley Hips is the uncontested king of the two-dimensional target and he uses ethafoam exclusively. "We developed the first foam target, made of Dow Chemical's ethafoam, in 1969," reports Hips, honcho of Stanley Hips Targets of San Antonio. "Since the first one was made, everyone has copied us — even our price list!"

Hips says that ethafoam is the best material for foam targets because of its small cell construction. "This will hold up longer and close up tighter when shot with arrows," he notes. "The larger the cell structure, the bigger the hole. That's why we use only ethafoam."

This material comes in two-, four-, six- and nine-pound densities, and here's one time when "more isn't better." That is, the higher the density, the harder it is to extract arrows. "Two-pound density is the best for removing field points and broadheads, and that's why we surround a replaceable core of lighter-density ethafoam with the denser material. Our ethafoam cores will take up to five thousand shots, although broadheads will cut them up well before that quantity is reached."

In more than forty styles and sizes, all "smiley face" bullseye targets are lightweight and portable. His hand-painted animal targets feature all manner of deer and elk, bucks and does, bulls and cows, in a variety of situations: standing, eating, bedded, bugling. And how about a carp for the bowfishermen? Hips says it "looks like a fish, swims like a fish and stops arrows like a fish."

Target Systems Company is another manufacturer of foam 3-D animal targets, and you get a sense of the breadth of their line with this photo. See text for all other models they sell.

Bear/Jennings sells three foam targets. The Ethafoam Carbon Stopper will absorb the impact of all grades of arrows and is self-healing. The Ethafoam 5-spot features five replaceable aiming circles, excellent for broadhead practice although it won't handle carbon arrows. It's a variation of the Bowhunter's Practice Target, which has a rectangular, eight-inch core of self-healing polyurethane. Again, no carbon arrows.

Bear/Jennings also sells the Bear Lightarget II, a longer-lasting version of their Bear Economy Target. The former is thicker, but both are covered with replaceable faces — an FITA target on one side and four animal targets on re-verse. Neither is intended for use with broadheads or carbon shafts.

Realism is what you get with Pick-A-Spot's line of anatomically accurate targets, made of self-sealing, rigid or ethafoam materials. "You can order with or without Pick-A-Spot replacement kill zones," says Linda McCain of Pick-A-Spot Targets in Jackson, Mississippi. "Realism

On Blue Ridge animal-shaped targets, you can apply full-color photos as shown. When shot up, put on a fresh face.

TARGET SELECTION CHART

On the following chart, targets are evaluated according to their construction materials on a scale of 1-3, with 1 being best.

Type	Portability	Cost	Durability	Availability
Straw Bales	3	1	2	1
Cedar Bales	3	2	2	3
Excelsior	2	2	2	3
Grass Matts	3	1	1	2
Cotton Bag	1	2	1	2
Polyfill Bag	1	2	2	1
Compressed Bale	3	1	2	3
Mesh	1	2	1	2
2-D Foam	1	2	1	1
3-D Foam	2	3	1	2

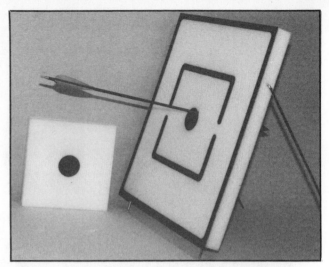

is enhanced with airbrushed detail in the proper colors."

Delta Industries of Reinbeck, Iowa, has been in the target and decoy business, plus making archery accessories, for many years. Their "RV" — for "Replaceable Vitals" — targets are true-to-life size, and the foam is colored throughout so the targets last longer. They're weather-resistant, break down for easy transporting, are intended for both field points or broadheads, and offer whitetails, mule deer, antelope, bighorn sheep, javelina and bear.

Their newest is truly amazing for realism. The Series V-RV is a full-size whitetail buck with replaceable antlers. The RV section is of self-healing foam, so you won't have to "RV" too often. This joins their smaller, ethafoam-reinforced bear, turkey, coyote, badger and raccoon, ideal for the 3-D shoot that wants the added challenge of variable-sized targets.

For the bowhunter heading to the hunting camp, Delta's Arrow Snuffer is perfect. Replaceable burlap covers encase two square feet of either self-healing foam or ethafoam.

Bear/Jennings' Economy Target is a face you can apply to any foam target for practice shooting. Even the bull can be freshened by application of new, colorful center rings.

Not for use with Broadheads!

Attach a hunting target face and you're set.

Another full-sized line of self-healing Flex/Foam targets is from Target Systems Company in Lebanon, Oregon. The buck, ram and antelope are normal broadside poses, but the firm also has a unique charging bear and bedded white-tail and bighorn. They also offer woodchuck, elk, coyote, cougar, bobcat, turkey, peccary, raccoon, standing bear, rabbit, badger, wolf, mountain goat, browsing deer, Russian boar, flying goose, carp, zebra and red fox. All are suitable for broadheads or field points, with realistic color-ation.

It's hard to top the realism of Blueridge Archery Targets' deer, bear or turkey polyethylene foam offerings. That's because they feature replaceable color photograph target faces on the six- or four-pound-density targets. Durable, lightweight and thus portable, these Blueridge targets come with adjustable metal stands for level or treestand shooting and replacement cores are available.

The animal targets join the Lexington, Kentucky, firm's line of square bullseye targets perhaps more familiar to the target archer. The Extra-Thick series uses the easiest-to-

PP&S Archery Products offers five-year replacement guarantee on life of their cores. Lots of models are available in a variety of unusual poses. Check out a typical rack!

extract two-pound-density foam in 6½- or 8½-inch thicknesses. The High-Density line uses four- or six-pound-density foam, while their Economy line is three inches of four-pound-density foam with five black dot bulls that stand out clearly against the snow-white target. All except the Economy line have replaceable cores for extended target life — presuming, that is, you hit the center more than the surrounding area!

Claiming to provide "a target for every archer," B-K Archery Products of Mason, West Virginia, sells both square or animal-shaped targets of self-healing polyethylene foam. While their 5-Dot doesn't feature a replaceable core, the Crossbow, Arrowstop, and Tru-Life Foam Animal targets all have eight-inch replaceable centers.

The Tru-Life deer, bear and turkey have colored photo enlargements laminated to foam. When you shoot 'em up, add a new face. They have a bunch of photo targets — more like posters, actually — for their Plank Foam targets. More about them in the later section dealing with target faces.

The aforementioned Impact Industries has tried to become the bowhunter's "One-stop shopping place" for any type

Thompson Targets gives bowhunters shot at decapitated deer, but with the vital areas clearly indicated as shown.

You get both right- and left-hand view, to provide some variety when shooting. These faces will last a long time.

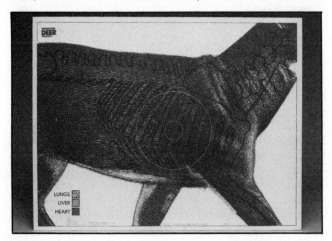

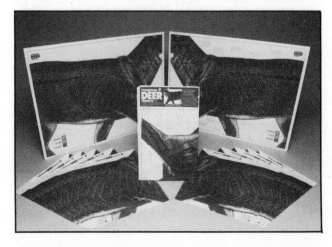

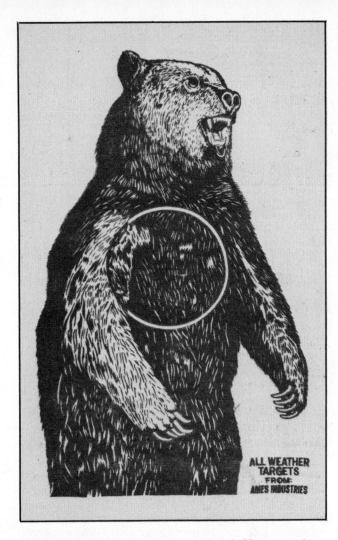

Three of the twelve targets in Ames All-Weather target face line are shown here. The firm uses colored burlap and colored inks to create lifelike images with kill zones circled. The faces will last at least one season, he says.

of target. They recently introduced their Hunter archery target, a reversible, self-sealing foam impact area that weighs a whole four pounds. It's designed for broadheads and the staggered placement of aiming dots on the reverse of the buck target extends the target's life.

Foam targets from ESA in Chicago are self-sealing, made with replaceable cores and in spot- or animal-shaped configurations. They have silhouettes of bucks or does, bear, pig, turkey, raccoon, coyote, fox, rabbit, groundhog and "harelope" (hare with horns), all three inches thick and furnished with ground stands. For club or institutional use, you can order sheets eight feet long by four feet wide. That will hold a lot of targets!

Natra-Look targets certainly are handsome full-bodied targets. Made of elastafoam, each realistic target is sculpted to the adult dimensions of whitetail bucks, does, black bear and wild boar. Each replaceable center section is made of six-pound-density ethafoam and can stand thousands of hits; although not so many from broadheads. Each target is made in three sections for easy disassembly and transportation to the range. Natra-Look targets are colored throughout, so there's no white spot when an arrow is extracted.

Another ethafoam target maker is PP&S Archery Products of Raceland, Louisiana. Their full-size targets include typical and atypical whitetail antlers, plus javelina, turkey and groundhog. Each has a five-year core guarantee.

Clearly, there are *beaucoup* targets from which to choose,

depending on your needs and pocketbook. The last element that needs discussion is the target face you procure for the front of your bale, bag or foam target. These range from simple black and white drawings to colored photographs you'll be tempted to frame and hang over your bed, wife's feelings be hanged!

Impact Industries offers a Long-Life line of faces, which they claim will last far longer than printed paper faces. It has to do with the ink and material used, they say. The special ink soaks into the burlap strands and fibers, thus it won't wear off with repeated penetrations. Also, because the woven jute strands separate to welcome a field point, the Long-Life face receives little damage from repeated use. The weatherproof faces come in three sizes with five images, including a four-dot and bullseye spot, turkey, rabbit and whitetail buck. All have kill zones circled.

Since 1983, John H. Ames of Bothell, Washington, has been selling the Ames All-Weather target faces. More detailed than the Long Life targets, there are twelve targets

Multi-Use Target Faces from Sauders vary in size, but all are paintings. Top photographers have captured trophies, as above right, which Saunders has turned into target faces on hundred-pound, heavy tag stock. The firm has many styles of "toughenized" bulls, too.

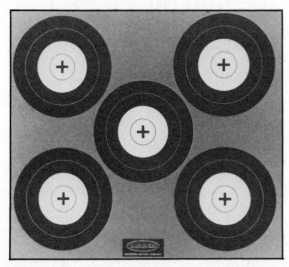

in the line. "Each artisitic animal target is waterproof ink on special burlap with the capacity to withstand thousands of shots before needing replacement," says John Ames. "For example, the forty-three-inch by forty-one-inch whitetail is created by integrating three colored inks with natural burlap tan, resulting in a beautiful target sized perfectly for a three-bale butt."

Are these targets — featuring elk, pronghorn, turkey, obscured deer, mule deer, bighorn sheep, grizzly and four varmints in addition to the whitetail — really stormproof? To prove it, Ames duplicated a full season's worth of storms by washing his targets for thirty minutes in a machine. They emerged virtually unchanged.

If you don't mind shooting at the skelton of a decapitated deer, then Thompson Targets' Buck Skins are for you. The life-sized anatomically correct targets are printed on a non-glare, synthetic material they call Leather-Tuff, which is water repellant and weather resistant. The Canton, Ohio, firm packages targets in both left and right approaches, not just one view.

Bear/Jennings offers full-color or black-and-white animal targets, plus FITA bullseyes in red, yellow, blue and black.

The Fred Bear life-sized buck whitetail targets come in four shootable poses: quartering away, head down, head up and alert, and leaping. A standing buck target has his vitals outlined in white, and the Diana Haker series has small, medium and large game displayed. This internationally known artist "designed these targets for the bowhunter, because when it comes to success in the field, nothing beats accuracy," she says. Targets include raccoon, red fox, cottontail, woodchuck, whitetail buck, pronghorn, wild boar, wild turkey, bull elk, black bear and mule deer.

The aforementioned B-K Archery's seventeen full-color animal targets are enlarged photographs taken by the incomparable duo of Leonard Lee Rue III and his son, Len Rue, Jr. There are four whitetail bucks, black bear, raccoon, turkey, red fox, woodchuck, cottontail, mule deer, bugling royal bull elk, bighorn ram, mountain lion, bobcat, pronghorn, javelina, pheasant and bushytail squirrel. They are packaged for Western or Eastern bowhunters.

Saunders Archery, of grass matt fame, also sells a variety of target faces for their long-lasting target butts. "We introduced the first full-color animal faces in 1957," notes Chuck Saunders. These are printed on one hundred-pound heavy tag stock, in sizes from fourteen by eleven inches to twenty-nine by forty-one inches. The photos are by Bill McRae, Dave Zahn, Bruce Pitcher and Mike Blair."

In animals, Saunders offers coyote, prairie dog, turkey, several whitetails, bighorn sheep, pronghorn, black bear, moose and a heart-stopper of a bull elk. They also offer painted squirrel, red fox, snarling bobcat, ring-neck pheasant and flushing turkey. Of course, they have FITA and NAA-style faces, black hunter faces, blue and white indoor faces, and metric field faces. If they're "toughenized," it means hundreds of nylon threads crisscross the paper; this makes it stronger, to last longer.

To sum up: All archers need targets. The factors of portability, cost, durability and availability you find in the accompanying chart are considered in the decision. No one can tell you what's best, only that you need one. — *Mark Thiffault*

CHAPTER 6

ARCHERY CLUBS AND ORGANIZATIONS

There Are Dozens — Large And Small — All Want To Help The Archer/Bowhunter

THERE ARE DOZENS of local and state archery and bowhunting organizations throughout North America — and the world — each with the goal of promoting and improving the sport. Many of the local groups are affiliated with national or international organizations. Some have been formed within the past year or two. Others, the National Archery Association (NAA) of the United States, for instance, are more than a hundred years old.

The NAA deals only with target archery, setting the rules and sanctioning local, state, national and international tournaments. Many bowhunters and most tournament shooters are members.

The **National Archery Association** of the United States was founded in 1879, making it one of the oldest sport organizations in the country. It is the only organization recognized by the Federation of International Target Archery (FITA) and the United States Olympic Committee for the purpose of selecting and training men and women's archery teams to represent the United States of America in the Olympic Games, Pan American Games, World Championships and other international meets. It also sponsors an annual National Championship for males and females of all ages.

The variety of archery activities involves a wide span of age groups, physical abilities and types of shooting. There is a place for everyone in the program, whether they are interested in archery as a sport, a hobby, or a craft.

Numerous state archery groups have organized and affiliated with the NAA for the purpose of bringing archery competition closer to the local level. They also provide year-long competition geared to the differing age and skill levels of their members. In some of the larger cities, local clubs are formed and many of these combine archery with a social event following practice.

The **Junior Olympic Archery Development (JOAD)** indoor and outdoor program originated in order to provide a basic organizational guide for junior archery activities under adult supervision and to meet the needs of boys and girls through the age of 17 years. It is being used by many camps, schools, churches and youth groups.

JOAD Clubs are chartered by the NAA and generally shoot once a week for developing the skills necessary to earn certificates. There are eight levels of accomplishment and each archer starts at the lowest level (Yeoman), where he/she must shoot a designated score before being allowed to advance to the next level. Archers progress at their own pace through the remaining levels until they complete the Olympian rank.

Every year, a United States JOAD championship tournament is held, generally in the Midwest, and there are numerous state and local competitions as well.

The **NAA,** with its Olympic membership affiliation, is the guiding force for these potential Olympic and international contestants.

The **College Division** of the NAA is designed to encourage the development of skilled men and women archers in the colleges and universities. This program offers a nation-wide program of competition. Each school year, numerous intercollegiate dual and three-way meets are held, as well as state and regional championships.

If a college qualifies itself through participating in the required tournaments, it becomes eligible to enter the annual United States Intercollegiate Championship. This meet is held annually and rotates to various regions of the country. Within the tournament, there are two separate meets going on simultaneously. One is for the two-year colleges and the other for the four-year colleges. Individual and team competition is provided for both men and women.

Each year the **College Division** selects a women's and a men's All-America Archery Team, as well as alternate teams. Selection to the team is made by a committee of coaches and is based on scores shot by each candidate in the required tournaments.

The **Archery Manufacturers Organization (AMO)** was formed as an archery industry trade group to standardize equipment and specifications. In other words, the intent was and is to ensure that the bow quiver of one manufacturer will fit the bow of another. Virtually all the archery equipment produced anywhere in the world meets the agreed upon standards, which has gone a long way toward stabilizing the industry and satisfying consumers' requirements.

Lately, **AMO** has moved into two other areas, both aimed at increasing the number of archers and protecting bowhunters from the increasing attacks by various anti-hunting groups.

A tournament called Bowhunters' Challenge was developed and sponsored by **AMO**, aimed at producing an exciting event to make bowshooting a year-round activity and to stimulate the growth of the sport. The Bowhunters' Challenge has had to be reduced in priority by **AMO**, because of the aggressive moves of the anti-hunters.

Mike Hillis is president of **AMO** and placed the preservation of hunting rights at the top of priorities for the organization.

According to Hillis, "**AMO** priorities are being redirected. In the face of these threats and the seriousness of their nature, we must counter these actions. Our Archery Commissioner, Doctor Jim Shubert, will head the efforts to work with the Wildlife Legislative Fund of America (WLFA). This highly professional, national body works on a daily basis countering anti-hunting attacks. Jim's experience in this area is also widely recognized. His annual meetings inform and educate individuals and groups on these issues. His involvement is absolutely essential."

Mike Hillis goes on to say, "Without a doubt, the 1990s will provide the archery community with not only some of its biggest challenges, but also some of its greatest opportunities.

"More than ever before, the sport of bowhunting is being

AMO NEWS

The Archery Manufacturers Organization (AMO) has moved from its original purpose of developing and enforcing archery specification standards, on to major efforts to save or restore hunting rights.

threatened. Ten states have proposed legislation that would restrict, limit, or eliminate bowhunting. The anti-hunting groups seem to be singling out the bowhunter because of the smaller numbers and the diversity of our sport. Not only do these external forces threaten our sport and industry, but internal conflicts within the archery community pose a problem almost as significant.

"It is my belief that **AMO** needs to take an active role in resolving both of these issues. A broad base of the hunting and archery community along with government officials are looking for someone to represent the industry. It is only logical that **AMO** step forward. Your board of directors has resolved to throw all of the people and financial resources of the organization into the arena to protect the hunting environment. Dr. Jim Shubert is working full time on this project, along with the officers and directors of the organization. However, we can't do it alone. We need the help of everyone.

"We also need the commitment of all of the interests in archery to pull together in protecting our industry. This means that many elements of our industry may have to compromise their traditional positions. This has to happen if we are going to survive.

"On a more positive note, there are many emerging opportunities for archery. The introduction of the com-

pound bow into FITA field competition opens up all kinds of new markets, both domestic and international. Continued growth and recognition of archery as an Olympic sport will help archery grow world wide.

The successful implementation of the Bowhunters' Challenge provides a tremendous opportunity, not only for exposure to archery, but also potential benefits to **AMO**. This will in turn help **AMO** increase the many programs we currently have to promote our sport."

Another organization formed to counteract the efforts of anti-hunting groups through education, is the **National Bowhunters Education Foundation (NBEF)**. The group is an independent education foundation, free of any commercial purpose or political interest. It administers the **International Bowhunter Education Program (IBEP)** to promote safer hunting by archers. Thousands of bowhunters across the world have now participated in this international self-improvement program.

Several states have made the passage of the **IBEP** classes a prerequisite to gaining an archery hunting tag. The standardized course is taught across the United States and in many countries of the world. Local information is added to the course when pertinent.

The **IBEP** was conceived in 1969 by William H. Wadsworth, while working with a group of concerned New York State bowhunters. The concept became a national program under the direction of the **Bowhunting and Conservation Division** of the **National Field Archery Association**.

The **NBEF** was established in 1979 as a totally independent and separate legal foundation, making the program available to all bowhunting organizations.

The **NBEF** controls and updates course content while volunteer certified instructor teams, in cooperation with their wildlife agencies, make the program available as part of state and provincial hunter education programs.

Another group, the **American Bowhunters Committee (ABC)** formed in 1962, later fell into inactivity and was reorganized in 1989. The **ABC** has several state chapters affiliated with it, all with the intent of promoting and protecting bowhunting. The club maintains a listing of bowhunting trophy records as well as the sponsorship of a number of state and local archery tournaments.

The **International Bowhunting Organization (IBO)** of the U.S.A. was formed to "promote, encourage and fos-

The National Bowhunters Education Foundation is responsible for bowhunter safety course content.

ter the sport of bowhunting." It has been instrumental in establishing and sponsoring several large archery tournaments in the Midwest, rapidly expanding to other parts of the country. The tournaments have become extremely popular with archers, making the **IBO** one of the fastest-growing archery organizations in North America.

The purposes of the **IBO** are as follows:

To unify bowhunter shoots and bowhunter shoot scheduling; to assist youth organizations for the promotion and encouragement of the sport of bowhunting; to schedule seminars; promote bowhunter education; National Bowhunters Education Program (NBEP) and International Bowhunters Education Programs (IBEP) projects.

Promote and participate in state and local bowhunter and hunter safety programs and provide seminars upon request pertaining to all aspects of bowhunter education.

To promote and encourage appointment of instructors in all levels of participation.

To endorse and lend assistance to "Bowhunters Who Care" and similar organizations for the purpose of fostering bowhunting.

To coordinate political issues of bowhunter concerns; aid and assist in the scheduling of shoots to prevent pos-

sible over scheduling; act as an information center for the purpose of providing a list of topics and possible speakers.

Provide coordination of activities on a voluntary basis for all bowhunter clubs — local, state, national and international — according to the purposes herein stated.

To lend assistance and the name **IBO** to shoots and activities subject to the ideals and guidelines of **IBO**.

The **National Field Archery Association (NFAA)** evolved because bowhunters of the Thirties wanted to improve their archery skills, but were not comfortable being a part of and shooting the formalized target archery administered by the **NAA**. Informal roving or field target shooting had been going on since archers took up the sport, but there was no formal group to govern and encourage any kind of standard competition.

From its temporary constitution of 1939, the **NFAA** was to be a group for those field style archers to whom

International Field Archery Assn.

*The International Field Archery Association (IFAA)
conducts field archery tournaments in nineteen countries.*

target archery has little to offer, yet to whom no sport can be complete that lacks well regulated competitive events.

Its purposes shall be: To develop rounds and regulations for competitive field style or instinctive shooting; to conduct championship tournaments using these rounds; and, in general, to do all possible to promote the field style or instinctive shooting.

Early in 1940, following the decision of the NAA Board of Governors to get out of field archery and get back to the **NFAA,** the state of Michigan started taking an active part in NFAA affairs and became almost immediately one of the strongest and most active states. It was not until then that any effort was made to formally organize the NFAA. Everything before this had been on a temporary basis. Members felt that if they were ever to become a truly national organization, they needed to start as an organization of the field archers of the country and not as a more or less local organization with large groups having no part in the job.

In 1964, Glenn St. Charles, former **NFAA** vice president, started the ball rolling toward a Bow Hunter division. Later, this was voted into the by-laws by the NFAA executive committee. Actually, this was a new name for the old Heavy Tackle division.

The Bow Hunter division was modified in 1950 to preserve a place for the style of the old instintive. The class system was deleted and replaced by the handicap — and dues were raised. Membership was at an all time high — 38,000-plus.

The old building that Roy Hoff found was turned over to the **NFAA** after he retired from the publishing business and continued to serve as the club's headquarters until March 1984, when a new, modern facility was constructed on property adjoining the old facility.

Glenn St. Charles of Seattle, Washington, is recognized as the driving force in the founding of the **Pope & Young Club,** which is the sole recording authority for North American, bow-killed big game.

Darrell Pace is a champion target archer who has competed in many Olympic and World tournaments. The meets are sponsored by the National Archery Association.

The club publishes an official records book, listing the game, its score and the hunter, his location and year taken. It has become a sophisticated, computer-assisted organization, professionally and efficiently run. Regular club membership is restricted to one hundred members, with a long waiting list. There are, however, provisions for senior members, as well as associate memberships. Regular membership requirements include the taking of at least three big-game animals with bow and arrow, one of which must be a record book entry.

The **Pope & Young Club** has grown into an active pro-hunting and record-keeping organization with no peers. It is large and influential in legislative circles.

The **Fred Bear Sports Club** is dedicated to the protection of outdoor ecology and support for wildlife management as well as all states' fish and game laws. The club encourages members to help preserve natural resources and to be bound by the restrictions contained in the rules of fair chase.

The rules of fair chase, as outlined by the **Fred Bear Sports Club,** are in the form of the following restrictions.

Any animal taken under any of the following circumstances shall not be considered to have been taken under fair chase:

Helpless in or because of deep snow; helpless in water; helpless on ice; helpless in a trap; while confined behind fences, as on game farms, et cetera; in defiance of game laws or out of season; from power vehicle or power boat; by jacklighting shining lights at night; any other method considered unsportsmanlike by the directors of the **Fred Bear Sports Club.**

Field archery, originally designed to offer off-season practice for bowhunters, has become a sport unto itself. It appeals to all levels, ages and types of archers.

The International Field Archery Association (IFAA) was founded in 1969, primarily to offer archers camaraderie of a modern international game of field archery. The entry of the United States into the group was due largely to the leadership of James Schubert, past president of the **National Field Archery Association.**

The IFAA sanctions the World Field Archery championships every other year on even numbered years. Regional field championships also are held every year. There are no individual members in **IFAA,** but membership in national organizations, such as the **NFAA,** automatically confers membership in the international group.

The IFAA has divisions of competition that allow the use of recurves, compound bows, release aids, all types of sighting devices, stabilizers, barebows, levels, peepsights and rangefinders.

The World Safari Shoot is open to all archers, regardless of their national affiliation; the rules are few and the targets are paper animals. The divisions of competition are recurve, English longbow, American longbow, compounds and cross bows. Many novelty events offer merchandise awards.

The **American Archery Council (AAC)** acts as a sounding board for the industry, as well as an information clearing house and legislative advocate for archery. Major archery oranizations are members, providing the group direction and the funds for its administrative costs.

A popular novelty event at outdoor archery tournaments is the aerial disk shooting. Arrows must be equipped with special flu-flu fletching to rapidly slow flight.

The AAC is active in the development and distribution of materials regarding archery and bowhunting. Thousands of copies of booklets on both subjects are distributed throughout the country. Members of the group provide educational programs at state and national fish and game commission meetings, conferences and at any state or province governmental gatherings where the subjects may be archery or bowhunting. In recent years, the **AAC** has placed more emphasis on safety and expanding horizons for bowhunters. The group also acts as a referral service for individuals and local groups with archery-related problems.

Bowhunters Who Care was established in 1979 as a non-profit organization to promote and preserve bowhunting through education and information. Through development of communication between bowhunters and landowners and through local school systems, the organization is attempting to reduce hunting conflicts, as well as to expand the number of acres available to bowhunters in the private sector.

Another goal of **Bowhunters Who Care** is the elimination or prevention of more states adopting the either/or hunting concept. Either/or laws and regulations require most hunters to hunt within designated boundaries (state or game reserve), with either firearms or bow and arrows, but not with both in the same season. Research has shown that where either/or rules exist, archery hunting has decreased.

ADDRESSES OF CLUBS AND ORGANIZATIONS

American Archery Council, 604 Forest Avenue, Park Rapids, MN 56470

American Bowhunters Committee, P.O. Box 1425, Henderson, KY 42420

American Crossbow Association, P.O. Box 72, Huntsville, AR 72740

Archery Manufacturers Organization, 200 Castlewood Road, North Palm Beach, FL 33408

Bowhunters of America, 1030 W. Central Avenue, Bismark, ND 58501

Bowhunters Who Care, Box 269, Columbus, NE 68601

Fred Bear Sports Club, RR 4, 4600 SW 41st Boulevard, Gainesville, FL 32601

International Bowhunting Organization, P.O. Box 8564, Middletown, OH 45042

International Field Archery Association, 604 Forest Avenue, Park Rapids, MN 56470

National Archery Association, 1750 E. Boulder Street, Colorado Springs, CO 80909

National Bowhunter Education Foundation, Rt. 6, Box 199, Murray, KY 42071

The National Crossbowmen of the USA, Longwood Gardens, Kennett Square, PA 19348

National Field Archery Association, Rt. 2, Box 514, Redlands, CA 92373

Pope & Young Club, Inc., Box 548, Chatfield, MN 55923

World Bowhunting Association, 604 Forest Avenue, Park Rapids, MN 56470

CHAPTER
7

ARCHERS
AND TEACHERS

In her heyday, perhaps fifty years ago, Myrtle Miller was an international champion.

EMERY LOISELLE is, in real life, a retired engineer with a life-long interest in and dedication to archery. He has bowhunted deer over much of the Northeast, operates an archery pro shop in his home state of Massachusetts and is Technical Editor of BOW & ARROW HUNTING Magazine. He has written hundreds of technical articles on the subject of archery, as well as a couple of books on compound bow tuning. For the past several years, he has been one of the instructors at The World Archery Center, Pomfret, Connecticut.

MORE THAN fifty years ago, Ed and Myrtle Miller had a dream. Coached by archery champion Russ Hoogerhyde, the young and beautiful Myrtle had become an international champion and was gripped by an unrelenting urge to give back something to the sport. In 1937, she and her husband — Ed passed away in December 1989 — founded TWAC, acronym in those days for Teela-Wooket Archery Camp located in Roxbury, Vermont, where yearly sessions took place for thirty-eight years.

TWAC — The World Archery Center — Has Been The Best-Known And Respected Archery Instruction School For A Half-Century!

Ed Miller, left, passed away in December 1989. At TWAC, he and Myrtle Miller have helped introduce and improve archery skills for more than fifty years.

Below: A group photo of the TWAC staff from 1987 in Pomfret, Connecticut. Author/instructor Emery Loiselle kneels in the front row, second from left.

The basic objectives were and still are to (1) develop individual shooting skills for all who wish to become proficient archers, (2) to train instructors to teach the skill of archery and (3) to present archery to the youth of the nation as a lifetime sport.

The staff and guest speakers who come to teach and lecture contribute their time and talents for free. Some of the staff members who taught in those first sessions are still on the staff today, more than fifty years later. Being avid bowhunters, my wife Eileen and I, while hunting our neighboring state of Vermont, would drive by the archery camp while hunting in the area. Open windows without glass or screens in the cabins were not inviting to my partner and it was only in later years when the school moved its operations to the Pocono Sports Camp in Pennsylvania that we caught up with these beautiful people and became staff members ourselves.

The move to Pennsylvania required a change in name for the school. In order to retain the acronym, the name was changed to The World Archery Center. A third move was made a few years ago, to a dream-like archery facility when Chris Atwood — who is assistant to Head Director of TWAC, Dr. Maryanne Schumm, and is also Athletic Director at the Pomfret School — interceded and engineered the move to Pomfret, Connecticut.

The spacious and well manicured grounds and university-style ivy-covered buildings are used during regular school months by young prep students headed for the best colleges and universities. Each year during two weeks in June, the facilities on this five-hundred-acre campus become home for The World Archery Center. Several large playing fields are set up for archery activities including a practice field, a metric course, a FITA field and other

Jim Easton, left, provided supplies for the Equipment Maintenance Workshop and narrated film on Olympic archery. TWAC Coaching Director Vic Berger, above, demonstrates excellent shooting form for students.

games such as archery golf and clout, a game wherein the shooter lofts his arrows at a ground target 180 yards away. A field archery course is set up in woods surrounding the fields. What fun, comradery and enjoyment is experienced by all!

But wait! There is not only fun. There is some serious work to be done here. Everyone works a long day which starts with a great breakfast at 8 a.m.; then all students and instructors are off to their assigned locations and duties. Daytime activities take place mostly out-of-doors in good weather on the green grass fields. Certain activities and rainy day classes may be moved into the indoor shooting range or the assembly lounge set up in the big red field

house which has indoor tennis courts.

Aside from the assembly lounge and indoor shooting area, the field house is home for the TWACkle Shop where equipment may be checked out on loan by anyone needing an item of archery tackle. A pro shop is available for students who wish to purchase new equipment or accessories. The TWAC equipment maintenance workshop is open to all who wish to make or repair equipment. Students from some of the classes learn to make arrows, bowstrings and repair equipment. An archery library is set up in the field

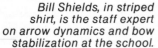

Bill Shields, in striped shirt, is the staff expert on arrow dynamics and bow stabilization at the school.

The Pomfret School is a beautiful setting, complete with ivy-covered walls, lush green lawns and archery targets.

house and next to the lounge is the snack bar and TWAC store where supplies and gifts may be purchased.

After the activities of the day and three square meals in the dining hall, prepared by the excellent in-house chef and cooks, a nightly assembly for all takes place where events of the day and the morrow are discussed. Then special movies or videos relating to archery are shown. Students have evening studying, then, until bedtime, all join in fun and sports including shooting, square dancing, games and use of the fitness center which has seventeen exercise machines and other equipment.

The World Archery Center offers courses and plans to accommodate archers of all interests. For would-be instructors, Plan 1, headed by Director Jane Morrow, B.A., physical education instructor at Northfield/Mt. Hermon School in Northfield, Massachusetts, and assisted by other dedicated staffers, is a six-day Basic Course equivalent to National Archery Association (NAA) Level 1. Designed for camp archery counselors and instructors, successful completion of the plan brings a world recognized TWAC Archery Counselor Certificate and the NAA Level 1 Certificate.

Plan 2 is designed for anyone called upon to teach or coach archery. It is a ten-day instructor course for students 18 years of age and up. Julia Bowers, master coach from Millervale University in Pennsylvania, and Linda Below, B.S., physical education instructor at Stroudsburg, Pennsylvania schools, are the directors of this course, with able assistance from other instructors on the staff. Awards for successful completion of the plan are the TWAC and NAA Level 2 Instructor Certificates.

Bowhunter and trick shooter Ann Clark, above, demonstrates good form, even without a bow in hand. She is among the guest instructors at TWAC. At left: Archery targets are official round faces, backed by matts furnished by Saunders.

Lu Wilson, left, is co-director of the advanced classes at TWAC. She is preparing a lesson plan for the 1989 session. Darwin Knight, right above, offers insights.

Plan 3, the twelve-day Coaching/Shooting plan, offers the finest training available anywhere in the world for archers of all levels of achievement interested in personal coaching to improve their performance. Enrollees in this plan may remain for any number of days, but a TWAC Diploma is awarded for twelve-day attendance. This is usually the largest group, made up of archers of all ages who desire the TWAC experience and who wish to improve their shooting and broaden their knowledge of archery. Archers in this plan do a lot of shooting and receive group instruction as well as one-on-one personal coaching from Directors C.R. "Bud" Fowkes, 1972 U.S.Olympic team coach and 1987 U.S. World team coach, and Anthony "Tony" Murawski, ACC master coach and former NAA Board of Governors member, as well as from a number of other staffers with excellent coaching skills and other specialties. Recurve and compound bow shooters/students participate in all activities and benefit from guest lecturers. Video tapes on the shooting form of each member in this group are made and critiqued; the individual may have a copy to keep.

Plans 4 and 5 — Vacation With Archery and Vacation With No Archery — may be elected for any number of days by visitors, parents and children who wish to enjoy the TWAC experience without serious work and concentration. Children's archery classes and other recreational activities are scheduled daily. All guests may attend lectures, movies, dances, audio/visual presentations, etc.

When demand for high level Advanced Coach courses warrants, additional plans are set up for Advanced Coach Certification at NAA Level 3 and NAA Level 4. This is truly top of the heap stuff administered by Lura Wilson, Advanced Coach certified (ACC) National and International judge, and Charles Pierson, ACC with forty-five years coaching experience. Archery personalities famous for their archery related specialties offer their knowledge through lectures and discussions, some only for this high level course, others for the benefit of all.

Those who attend TWAC are treated to the best instruction by the best instructors, coaches and guest lecturers with specialized expertise. Three of the few NAA Level 5 Master Coaches in the United States — Fowkes, Murawski

and Bowers — are TWAC staffers. Three of our staffers — Pat Baier, Julia Bowers and Bud Fowkes — co-authored the "NAA Instructors Manual" along with another well known archery personality, Sherwood Schoch. Some of our people are in the Archery Hall of Fame, including staffers Myrtle Miller, Lura Wilson, Ann Clark and former staffers Russ Hoogerhyde, Jean Lee Lombardo and the

A variety of archery games add variety and interest to the TWAC instruction. Aiming high are archers at the 180-yard line for the Clout Shoot, above. Linda Kellogg-Andrews, shown below, tries Archery Golf.

In 1979, Bill Wadsworth, above, presents National Bowhunters Education. At right: Sven Svenson is the Dean at Pomfret TWAC.

Many TWAC students have the chance to try out their techniques during community, youth archery classes.

Front left: Dr. Clarance Hickman, Myrtle Miller and Ed Miller discuss archery at 1978 session in Pennsylvania.

Olympic archer Jay Burris, right, demonstrates a point in discussion with Charles Pierson and Lu Wilson.

late dean Dr. Clarence Hickman. Certain former guests at TWAC including Ann and Earl Hoyt, Chuck Saunders, the late Fred Bear and Dr. Robert P. Elmer are also Hall of Famers.

The late Dr. Clarence Hickman was an inventor and physicist whose contributions to rocketry and weapons were instrumental in winning World War II, his application of science to archery explains the "archers' paradox" and opened doors to worlds of archery knowledge. He co-authored, with TWAC guests Dr. Paul E. Klopsteg and the late Forest Nagler, that greatest of archery publications, "Archery, The Technical Side." His movie, made in 1938 shot at 4000 frames per second with a high speed camera he helped design, shows in extreme slow motion how an arrow bends when leaving the bow. This film is shown at every session of TWAC.

Darrell Pace, Olympic Gold Medalist in 1976 and 1984, and NAA Outdoor and World champion Ed Eliason are coaches at the school. Current 1988 Olympic champion Jay Barrs demonstrated and lectured at the 1989 session. Former Professional Archery Association champions Vic Berger and Bill Bednar were coaches for many years at TWAC. The late renowned coach Al Henderson has guested at TWAC and another of their yearly lecturers is Len Cardinale, great archery coach and famous big-game bowhunter. Bill Wasdsworth, head of Bowhunter Education,

Well known archers from around the world participate in the school's instruction. Above: Olympian Jay Barrs shows left-handed form as fellow Olympic shooter Ed Eliason helps score, right. Ann Clark, below, explains her traveling trick shot demonstrations at the school.

comes to lecture when his schedule permits. Jim Easton guested at TWAC in 1989.

Courses include learning and hands-on practice with just about everything related to shooting and teaching archery. Subject matter for would-be instructors covers personal shooting technique, target shooting with individual coaching, shooting faults and corrections, demonstrations, mimetics, biomechanics, conditioning programs, psychology of shooting, group practice teaching, instructing the community class, video taping techniques, science of archery, history of archery, equipment selection and maintenance, tuning equipment, compound bow information, bowhunting information, field archery, archery golf, clout shooting, organizing classes and competitions and how to plan and run a FITA tournament.

Left: Lu Wilson instructs Larry Paglinawan, an advanced coach student from Hawaii. Below: Jay Barrs discusses technique.

All this activity is choreographed to flow smoothly and effectively by Head Director Dr. Maryanne Schumm under the watchful eye of Founder and Executive Director Myrtle "Mimi" Miller. Maryanne Schumm, who is well experienced in conducting such an operation by her archery and physical education activities at East Stroudsburg University in Pennsylvania, is virtually a human dynamo.

Myrtle Miller — words cannot do justice to this loving and overly generous lady. Any deserving, but underprivileged, young archer cannot be overlooked. Mimi is sure to give out many scholarships, even though she yearly picks up the tab for overexpenditures herself. Many companies such as Saunders, Easton Bear and Hoyt donate equipment for use by the students and the community class. Untold individuals, including the staff and guests, make financial donations to the scholarship fund.

One night during the session, a fun auction is held to benefit this fund. Teachers as well as students bring items, usually archery-related, to be auctioned off with the proceeds going into the scholarship fund. The bidding is high, because the purpose is commendable.

The last two days of the session are devoted to a qualifying FITA tournament sanctioned by the NAA. The mechanics of preparing and setting up the tournament are practiced by the students for hands-on experience. The actual tournament is great fun and always runs smoothly under an experienced tournament director like Allan Martin, Bud Fowkes, Tony Murawski or Darwin Kyle. This is the highlight and grand finale of the session.

Although originally slanted toward recurve bows and the world class style of archery, developments in recent years have made compound bow shooters most welcome. Indeed, the coaching/shooting plan is ideal for field archers and bowhunters wishing to broaden their archery knowledge and improve their shooting with coaching from the world's best. You will rub elbows with the archery greats and the shooter on the line next to you could well be a world class archer or Olympic champion.

Archers from all over the world come to share in the knowledge and archery expertise overflowing here. The

World Archery Center certification is recognized as a qualification standard by education institutes here and abroad. There are more than 2000 graduates of the TWAC instructor courses. It is estimated that through their work as teachers and instructors, twelve million students have learned about archery.

National Archery Association tournament director George Helwig has stated, "At TWAC you get it all. You have to see it to believe it."

And here's a quote from past president of FITA — Federation Internationale de Tir a L'Arc — Francesco Gnecchi-Ruscone: "Since 1974, when we first sent coach Mario Codespoti to TWAC, the archery status in Italy improved considerably."

CHAPTER

8

ABOUT COMPOUND BOWS

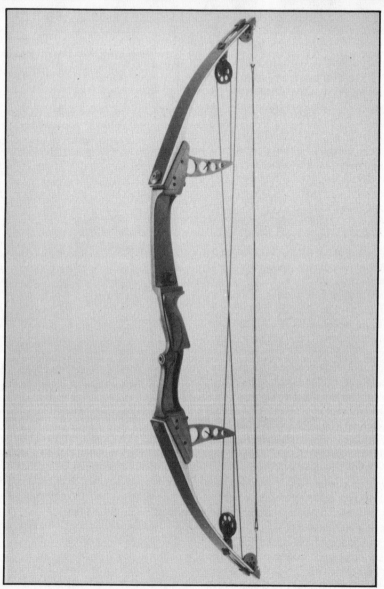

Tom Jennings' early Arrowstar design features four wheel or pulleys and two pylons. The configuration is now considered obsolete.

A Compound Bow Is Still A Bow Handler, Bow Limbs And A String — Or Is It?

THERE ARE FEW archers, engineers and experimenters with more technical experience with compound bows than Emery Loiselle. He has been an archer since before the invention of the compound bow and has tested and reported on literally hundreds of compound bows over the past nearly three decades. He has written a definitive book on the subject of tuning compounds. We all could become better shots if we understand more of the mechanics which make the compound bow work.

THE COMPOUND BOW, patented in 1966 by Holless W. Allen, was not readily accepted by the archery community at the time. Unique in concept and revolutionary in design, it was suddenly too different, too mechanical, too complicated for archers who knew and used only the simple graceful recurve or straight longbow of that era and before.

I had one of the early Jennings models and it attracted a lot of attention at the local target shoots. Archers who tried it loved the feel of the let-off at full draw and the fact that it was mighty fast shooting. But evolution is slow. Acceptance did not come fast. The odd appearance of the early models did not appeal to many archers. And what about all the mechanism! What do you do when it breaks down?

About this time I personally built a compound bow for experimental and learning purposes. This shoot-through handle with overdraw conception bow had a swivel grip and rest carriage; both could be relocated independently of each other in any direction. Based on what I learned with this bow and from experience repairing and adjusting compound bows as a Jennings dealer, I wrote and published the book, *Doctor Your Own Compound Bow.* The intent of the book was and still is to provide the archer with knowledge as to how the bow works and how to adjust, repair, set up, and tune the bow as well as improve arrow flight.

Wooden model of Allen compound design had modern features, by today's standards. The wood handle had long sight window, cut to accommodate a shorter overdraw arrow. Most advanced, fast overdraw bows of today rely on the same principles as Allen's bow.

Two drawings at right are taken from original H.W. Allen patent, dated Dec. 30, 1969. Rather than round eccentric wheels, Allen's compound bow design featured what might be considered cams.

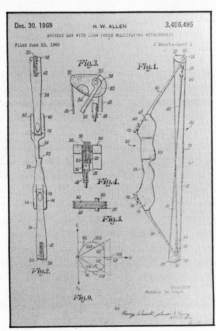

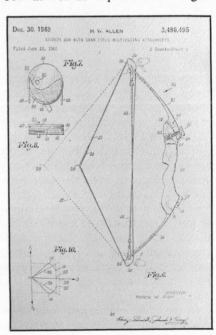

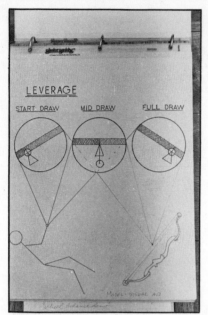

Leverage is the mechanical principle behind the bow's eccentric wheels, above. An ever-changing leverage system controls the energy storage.

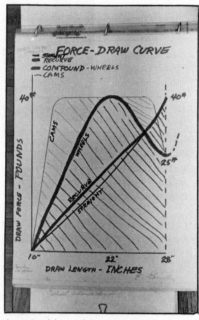

A typical force/draw curve for four kinds of bows indicates energy storage and release. It is clear that the cam wheel design stores the most energy.

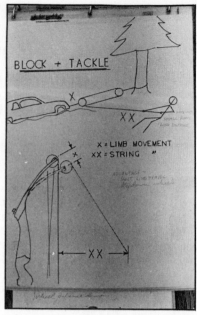

A compound bow's limbs are bent only slightly on the draw. It is similar to using a block and tackle to move a heavy object.

Many other related subjects, including arrow selection, speed, tools, jigs, tables, charts and even instruction on converting a recurve to a compound, are covered. The experimental bow, dubbed "The Monster Bow," is depicted on the cover and a chapter on gleanings from shooting and working with the bow is included in the book.

For many years, Tom Jennings was the only bow manufacturer licensed under the Allen patent. His faith in the new bow was strong enough that he devoted all his time and facilities to manufacturing only compound bows. Archers as well as organizations and state wildlife agencies were slow to accept the ugly duckling and Jennings devoted much effort, travel and expense promoting not only the product but the concept itself to archery governing organizations and the Fish and Game agencies of various states.

In the early years, compound bows were four-wheel models, highy adjustable, indeed. The cable from one eccentric went to an idler pulley installed almost at right angles near the center of the opposite limb, then to a guitar key or drum carried between the sideplates near the end of the riser. Limb bolts and fulcrums allowed adjustment of draw weight, exactly as with today's compounds. The guitar keys provided a means of adjusting draw length, within a particular range depending upon wheel size. The same keys allowed adjustment of wheel balance as well. The highly adjustable four-wheel model, however, was also susceptible to slipping out of adjustment and this, along with the appearance and complexity, kept many archers from making the switch from recurve to compound.

Jennings brought out many improvements to the original models. One of these was the use of speed pylons in lieu of the guitar keys. These were lever-type projections bringing the cable anchors closer to the string. This provided a greater cable-to-limb angle for this final cable section to

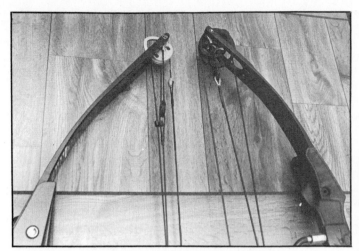

Longer bow, left, utilizes smaller eccentrics while short, fast bow needs large cams for same draw length.

Two compound bow variations are shown below: At left: Recurve limbs, tri-draw adjustable-length round eccentric wheels, yoke-fitted cable system. Bow at right has straight limbs, radical cams and long cable anchored to second axle in limb slot.

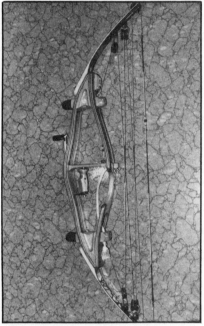

Emery Loiselle built the Monster Bow with six wheels, swivel grip overdraw and shoot-through handle.

effect an additional force vector. The pylon had an adjustment screw to pull in or let out cable as with the guitar keys.

Along about the mid-Seventies, the strange contraption called a compound bow was really taking hold and many bow manufacturers became licensed under the Allen patent and brought out their first models. A section of my book depicts and describes all these new original manufacturer's models and this section was left in the book on subsequent updates and reprints for its historical value.

Then came the two-wheelers, a simpler, more economical design with fewer adjustment possibilities, but greater stability and reliability in holding the settings and tune. These were streamlined, handsome and more highly accepted than the more cumbersome and scary four-wheelers. Had the original commercial compounds been two-wheelers, acceptance by archers and organizations might have come sooner. The irony is that Allen's original patent depicted

the very bow we are using today: a two-wheeler with cams.

At one meeting with Tom Jennings, I asked him why the first compounds were not two-wheelers as shown in the patent. His answer was that the cable guard was not known at the time and a bow built as shown in the patent left the cables in the way of arrow passage. The mid-limb pulleys set near right angles to the limb on the four-wheeler provided the necessary cable offset for arrow passage.

Jennings continued to be a forerunner in compound bow innovations over the years. His firsts include the impregnated wood riser, the bow press, tri-draw wheels, cable yoke, cable guard, the aluminum handle riser, ISO-Grid metal handles, Turcite bearings, narrow track eccentrics, needle bearing eccentrics and diecast cable string attachments. His early top-of-the-line model was the highly adjustable, four-wheel Arrowstar and the lower costing two-wheel Model T brought many newcomers into archery. The current T-Star is popular and his latest triumph has been the Unistar which has a UniCam — both cams in one — mounted on the riser below the grip.

Jennings' bow manufacturing company no longer exists. Ironically, in a lengthy civil suit with Allen, the man who risked all to bring the compound to the public, the company was put out of the production business. Bear Archery builds the Jennings lines of bows today under Tom's direction. His innovativeness and technological expertise are still in evidence and the bows are still the same high quality.

So what is a compound bow? You might say it is like a straight or recurve bow with a couple more machine principles added. Conventional and compound bows are similar in that they both have a riser, a pair of limbs and a bowstring. Both types accept the same or similar accessories and the technique of shooting is the same for traditional and compound bows. The cable and wheel system on the compound provides a block and tackle effect and the eccentric with off-center axle hole acts as an ever-changing leverage system between the bow limbs and the shooter. The compound bow with its fulcrum-mounted limbs is highly adjustable.

One man can move an automobile with a block and tackle. Pulling the rope a long distance moves the car a short distance through the mechanical advantage afforded by the device. Likewise, drawing the string on your compound provides mechanical advantage to move the short, stiff limbs a short distance.

The ever-changing leverage provided by the eccentric is in favor of the bow at the beginning of the draw and in favor of the archer as he nears full draw. In the strung position, the cable which is anchored at the opposite axle, is farther from the eccentric axle than is the bowstring. The bow limbs have the mechanical advantage and the draw becomes heavy during the first few inches of string travel. As the wheels peak over near mid-draw, the leverage forces even off, then start to change. Approaching full draw, the bowstring or pigtail is farther from the axle and the archer gains the mechanical advantage. This is what causes the nice-feeling let-off at full draw.

The advantages of the system are manifold. The bow may be left strung at all times, eliminating the inconvenience of stringing and unstringing the bow for each shooting session. There is interaction and feedback be-

Three additional compound variations include, from left: TSS Quadraflex design with mid-limb fulcrum as flexing occurs on both sides of pivot. Oneida Eagle, center, has recurved outboard limb hinged to short power limb, interconnected with cable. Cams are inside pylon plates at riser. Shorter Jennings Stealth has large cams, utilizes Fast Flight string.

Right: The bow riser design on the left accepts a standard length arrow while the overdraw-ready riser, right, is radiused to accept shorter arrows.

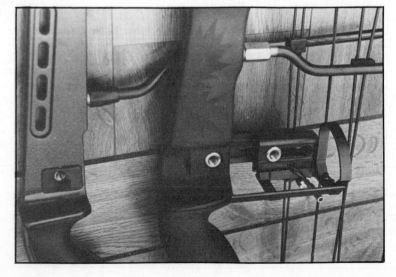

tween limbs and parts at both ends of the bow, so the bow is more stable during the draw and release. The easy hold during aim minimizes muscle tremors and makes aiming more pleasant.

The compounding system stores considerably more potential energy during the draw than does a recurve bow, and cams can be programmed to store almost the maximum a bow will ever be able to store. See the force/draw curve for such a cam. Everything under the curve represents stored energy. Such a radical cam, however, makes the draw bumpy, hard and unpleasant with such harsh transition points. To get the best of both worlds, most manufacturers offer an "energy" wheel, usually round on the string side, but cam-shaped on the cable side, representing a cross between wheels and cams.

Eccentric wheels or cams provide a better sequence of energy storage and release. We have discussed the action during the draw. At release, the energy is applied to the arrow gently, a smaller amount at first with the force increasing to full power at the peak weight position. I prefer to liken this to the thrust of a rocket. The easy, increasing thrust is gentle to the arrow and a lighter shaft with a more limber spine may be used.

The smaller arrow and the greater amount of stored energy increase arrow speed considerably. One might think the heavy limb tips carrying the wheels would be slow to recover during the shot, but actually the limb tips move only about 2½ inches as compared to seven or eight inches on a recurve. Also, due to this situation, the bow more readily converts energy to arrow speed with light arrows. A recurve likes a heavy arrow which accepts much more of the bow's stored energy than does a light arrow. This is not so crucial with the compound bow and the fast, light arrow, more forgiving of range estimating error, is more desirable for bowhunters and 3-D target shooters than the small amount of kinetic energy traded off.

Besides providing greater speed and flatter trajectory, the light arrow is less affected by wind, since it is in the air a shorter time over a given distance. This is important to the bowhunter. He can handle a compound bow five to ten pounds heavier than a recurve he might use. The relaxation at full draw makes aiming more conducive to better shot placement. These factors, plus the shorter time an animal has to react to the shot — jumping the string — makes the

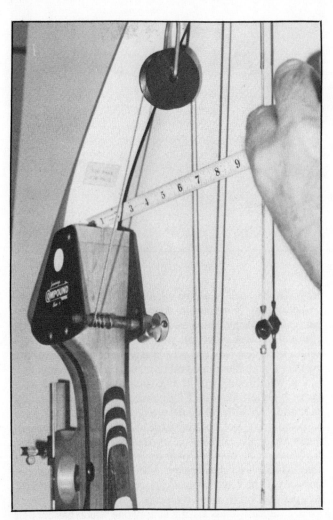

An early Jennings adjustable compound bow model featured mid-limb pulley, guitar key adjustments.

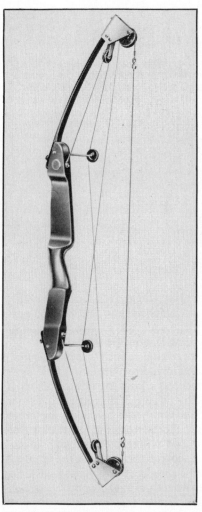

The early Allen Speedster had two pulleys, two wheels, non-adjustable.

Tom Jennings continues to design and modify his archery products. He is using a powerful bow press to relax the string on his Unistar bow. Length of pull and draw weight may be adjusted on this design.

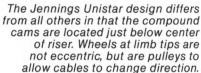

The Jennings Unistar design differs from all others in that the compound cams are located just below center of riser. Wheels at limb tips are not eccentric, but are pulleys to allow cables to change direction.

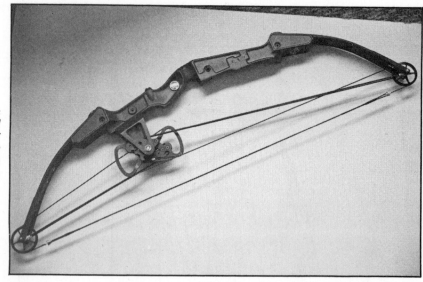

compound a humane weapon with a better percentage of vital hits.

Adjustablility, repairability and tunability are important factors. Compound bows are adjustable usually within a range of fifteen pounds draw. Most provide some means of adjusting draw length. Tri-slotted wheels provide two or three inches of adjustability and many cams come with a set of replaceable draw length modules, making the bow quite versatile in fitting individual archers. Tiller is also adjustable by turning limb bolts unequal amounts.

Bows fitted with yokes centralize the forces so that during the draw, the changing force vectors will not tilt or twist the limbs. The arrangement consists of an idler wheel installed in a loop at the end of the long cable. A short cable with drilled fittings at each end is passed through the center of the yoke wheel and anchored on the axle on each side of the eccentric. Some yokes have star slots of varying lengths and these are offered as means of making minor draw length changes. An unadvertised feature which, in my opinion, has even greater importance, is that these slots

may also be used to adjust wheel balance.

Additional innovations introduced by various companies include reusable swedges, cable guard slide blocks, optional percent of let-off, stepdown wheels, cams, draw length modules, forward grip, Fast Flight bowstrings, the overdraw and some unusual compounding mechanisms.

The trend today with the bowhunting fraternity is fast cams, high let-off, Fast Flight string, an overdraw-ready riser and an overdraw. Cams are rougher and noisier, a bit unpleasant to shoot, but they store more energy and increase speed decidedly. High let-off lets the archer use the heaviest draw weight he can pull over peak, yet with an easy and comfortable hold during aim. The Fast Flight string, because it is lighter and has non-stretch qualities, adds several feet-per-second to arrow velocity.

An overdraw-ready riser is simply one which has enough cut past center, usually a jog or half tunnel in the window at the arrow rest area, to allow pulling a broadhead into and by the riser. Even without an overdraw installed, such a riser lets you draw the broadhead into the bow almost up to the rest so you can use an arrow one to two inches shorter than you normally might use.

The advantages of an overdraw are usually related to speed. Installation of an overdraw allows use of an arrow shorter than one used with the overdraw riser per se, three to six inches or so in all. I don't recommend too much overdraw. Two or three inches helps overcome the effects of torquing and heeling. More than that increases error in the other direction. Also, shooting extremely short and light arrows approaches dry fire, rough on the bow, shortening its life.

A shoot-through rest is fine for a mechanical release aid shooter and overdraw length is unlimited, even with five-inch vanes. If you use a shoot-around rest, you should use four-inch vanes in a four-fletch pattern so the lower vane will not ride up on the rest in the strung position.

With an overdraw, you save the weight of that portion of the arrow cut off. But now your arrows will be overspined, since the shorter the shaft, the stiffer it is to the bow. Now you must go to a more limber spine, usually a lighter shaft.

So you save not only the cutoff weight, but also the difference in weight between the stiffer and the more limber shafts. This reduced weight, especially with a compound bow, translates into considerably more speed; just what is needed by bowhunters for more humane hits at unknown ranges.

When will it all end? Are we approaching rifle speeds which will hurt our generous bowhunting seasons? I feel we are almost at peak arrow velocity. Look at the force/draw curve for cams. Carrying the peak line straight across the chart represents the most energy storage possible with a bow. Such a bow would be difficult and uncomfortable to shoot, with probably no market. The radical cam of today loses only a slight amount of stored energy before and after the broad peak of the curve.

We will never approach rifle speed. For a comfortable bow, the force/draw curve cannot change tremendously. Mostly we can only hope to increase efficiency and divert a part of the lost energy to arrow velocity. — *Emery Loiselle*

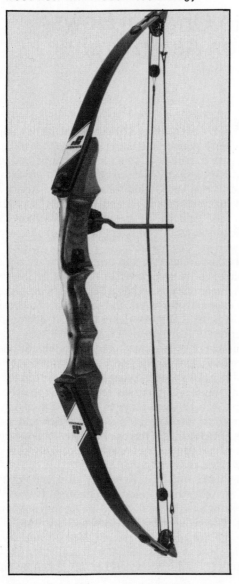

Jennings' Woody combines laminated wood riser with modern technology.

Jennings was instrumental in development of compound bows. His Jennings designs are now produced by Bear.

CHAPTER
9

LONGBOWS AND RECURVES

These Descendents Of The Original Bows Deserve Your Consideration As An Archer

Longbows, old and new; one strung on right. Older bow on left is from personal collection of Jim Easton. Next, Rancho Safari's Fast Flight bow; Martin Archery, right.

THE CHOICE of a first bow can be bewildering to the beginner and experienced archer alike. There are hundreds of compound, recurve and longbow models from dozens of makers from which to choose the one or two best suited for each of us. Many archers begin with compound bows and never shoot anything else. Others will "graduate" from recurves or longbow "school" bows into the more complicated compounds, especially those who are bowhunters.

Still other archers remain target shooters only and are committed to recurve bows as required by international and Olympic rules. Another group, a growing group, have shot compounds for years and, because of curiosity or a desire to get back to the basics of the sport, decide to try the simpler bow.

A number of large archery companies include one or two recurve bows in their line; only a few offer what might be termed factory-produced longbows. Most longbows and no small number of recurves are made by small-capacity bowyers who produce bows to order on a custom basis. The longbow, especially, is truly a "stick and a string." Except for advances in materials and technology, the longbow is what our ancient ancestors probably shot as they hunted game or went to war.

Both these simple devices are slim and lightweight, easily carried into the field when hunting. Unless the bow or the string should break, there are no moving parts to go wrong. The pioneers of modern archery, the trick shot artists and the early hunters, all used the simpler equipment, because that was all that was available. The control and accuracy of longbows and recurves can be amazing.

Material and construction style vary; all longbows are not alike. Older, used bows are often still in use and can be good buys for the collector or the beginner.

C.R. Learn has been shooting and hunting with longbows and recurves for more than a quarter-century. He has the following advice on what to look for and how best to shoot these wonderful bows.

THE LONGBOW in pure form is a stave or long section of selected hardwood, usually yew cut and cured for several years in an attic or other dry, airy space. After the curing, the stave was checked for sap wood, which was trimmed off to leave the heart wood, the strongest of the stave material, then it became a longbow. The draw weight was determined by the thickness and rigidity of the stave.

The longbow is still alive and well in the fields of archery, mostly in the hunting field. There are still longbow tournaments for what is usually termed the traditional style of archery. You may not ever see any yew or other self bows — bows made from one piece of wood — in those tournaments, but don't count on it.

The modern longbow is basically a long section of laminated hardwood mated with a belly and back of fiberglass. Some are made in the more traditional style, using bamboo for the centers. Most of these longbows are literally long, measuring out to seventy inches.

The longbow unbraced is not an elegant looking unit. It resembles a long stick, but it is much more than that. Most now have a small arrow shelf to make the shooting system consistent and there is one with a modern pistol grip as found on the recurve bow.

Perhaps the most difficult part of shooting the longbow is bracing it. Bowstringers are not commonly made for them and the best and simplest way to brace them is the "step-through" method. Place the right leg through — between the string and bow — and place the bottom limb end on the ankle of your right foot. Place the bow behind you and bring it up so it comes across your butt at about pocket level. Grab the upper tip of the bow and pull it out, bending the bow around your lower body until you can get the upper loop over the bow string nock. Not difficult, but it is the simplest and safest method. The limbs are too long for the "push-pull" method, sometimes used to brace recurve bows.

When you have the bow braced, it has all the normal items found on most basic shooting systems: A nocking point on the string and most modern longbows have the small arrow shelf for consistent shooting. If you don't have the shelf, you shoot over the left hand for a right-handed archer. If you change the grip when you shoot the bow, you will change the nocking point, if you're not careful.

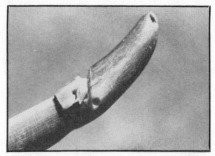

Easton's old collector bow has a horn limb tip with string groove near base.

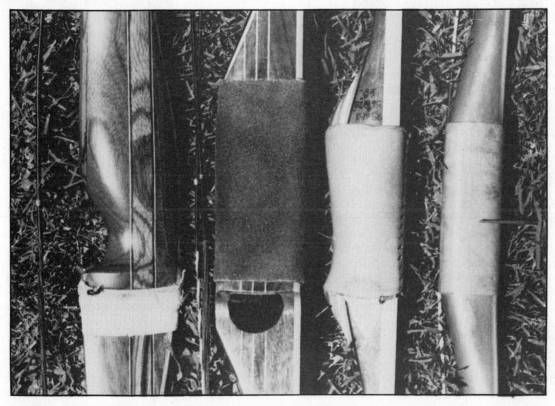

Handle styles vary. Martin, on left, features recurve-style handle with arrow shelf and rest, but it is a longbow. Next two have slightly cut shelves, leather covering. Right bow has no shelf. Bow hand is used as arrow rest.

Bracing a longbow without a stringer can be dangerous, must be practiced. First step is to place lower limb tip against front ankle, left. Upper limb is against left thigh as limb tip is pressed forward and right. If the limb slips, it will spring away from upper body, face. Pressure continues as string slides upward and seats into limb tip string nock. Both loops checked for seat, right.

Most longbow or traditional archers are "instinctive" shooters; no pins, levels, sights, stabilizers or accessories attached to the bow. They pick up the bow, line up with the target, pull back and usually release on contact with their draw check, the corner of the mouth or cheek or whatever they have developed. This is a fun way to shoot and it is fast, because the shooter does not judge the range and set the pins. Most longbow shooters lean into the bow. They appear to lean over, especially when compared to the compound techniques. That is the way it has been done for centuries and it still works.

The longbow isn't the prettiest bow in the field of archery, but it is probably one of the most rugged. There are no limbs to be twisted, as in a recurve, no cables to snap or any screws, nuts, bolts or fittings to deal with. It is a simple stick and string that takes the knowledge and ability of the archer to get the arrow into the target. The longbow may not be for everyone, but you owe it to yourself to shoot one a few times, just for the experience.

Another bow that some modern archers think of is the recurve. It isn't new, because the Saracens and Middle East archers made them. It is believed that these composite bows, made of horn and sinew, could and did outshoot the venerable longbow, but unless you happen to be a few centuries old, you'll have to go to the history books for that one.

The recurve bow is a mating of a hardwood riser that has a formed grip area for the hand, a cut-out for the arrow rest section that can be either flat or rounded and an upper and lower limb that has a definite hook or curve in it. When the recurve is unbraced, these hooks are pointing forward, away from the archer. When you brace the bow, these hooks move back and form a bent section from the stiffer

riser to the tip of the bow limbs. This is the recurve part of the bow.

If you ever pick up and shoot a longbow, you will be literally shocked at the recoil that will come back at you on releasing the arrow. This recoil is one of the things compound shooters seldom feel and it really wakes them up when shooting a longbow for the first time.

The recurve does away with this shock by making the limbs with a curve and the riser section with a deflex. The combination of the recurve — reflex — of the limbs and the deflex of the riser, allows the bowyer to eliminate that recoil felt in a longbow. Modern recurve bows have the right proportion of reflex and deflex to make them smooth shooters. FITA competitors, who are required to shoot the recurve, will literally split their arrows if they shoot at the same target all the time.

The wood for this longbow was cut in 1928 and cured for more than thirty years before it became a bow. Some collectors do not shoot, but they are shootable longbows.

Recurve variety, from left: Groves' 62-inch takedown, Brackenbury 66-inch takedown, Martin Howatt Mamba 58-inch bow, Drake Hunter Flight shortest 54-inch and Martin Super Diablo bow.

The basic recurve is one long bow, not a longbow, but a flatter limbed, carved riser with handle grip and sight window cut out. It will give you years of shooting pleasure and is one tough bow to beat. Recurves are available in any poundage to match your strength. The single unit bows are usually the less expensive.

Years ago, Groves Archery made a two-piece takedown recurve that used a sliced section at the handle area of the riser for the joint. It was double-pinned for consistent assembly each time. Ben Pearson Archery came out with a two-piece takedown that had a section of aluminum with upper and lower sections of the riser, held by a through pin.

Most, but not all, of today's recurves are three-piece takedown units. You have a center riser section that is mated in various ways to the upper and lower limbs. This system allows you to purchase limbs of different draw weights and use the same riser section. You may have a wide variety of bow draw weights with one familiar riser section from which to shoot.

The recurve bow is a pleasure to shoot. Once the bow is braced, all you need is a nocking point and an arrow rest and you are in business. From this basic bow, you can add all the gadgets and goodies you think you need.

There is one phenomenon with longbows and recurve bow systems that you might encounter. It is called stacking. Stacking occurs when the draw of the bow suddenly stops. It literally stops at some point, usually at the end of the draw or just before. You just can't seem to hump it any further back. This is due to a goof on the bowyer's part. The wrong design, wrong combination of hardwood and fiberglass or other problem and the bow may stack up. There isn't much you can do with a stacking bow but sell it to a friend. If the stack appears beyond your draw length, forget it; it will never bother you. You can make some good buys on bows from long-draw archers who say the bow stacks at thirty inches. If your draw is twenty eight, who cares? You can't get it back far enough to reach that stacking point, so buy it and enjoy it.

The main feature of these older-style bows is that they build poundage as you draw the bow back; the bow draw weight increases the farther you draw the bow. A sixty-pound recurve will build up to sixty pounds at about the twenty-eight-inch draw and continue to build the farther

you pull the string back. This, the modern compound shooter isn't used to. Not too long ago, a friend was looking for a carp shooting recurve. He checked a fifty-four pounder — usually he shoots a seventy-pound draw compound with sixty-five-percent let-off — and claimed he couldn't draw the bow to shoot it! He settled on a forty-pound recurve; a bow he could handle.

Target archers have restrictions on their equipment, so check those rules before you buy a bow that might not be allowed in some tournaments.

There are still new ideas and designs being presented. Martin Archery in Walla Walla, Washington, has increased their recurve bow production beyond what it was during the height of the recurve shooting era, more than two decades ago. They make many styles of longbows and recurves and have added a new production section merely to handle the demand for these bows.

There are many excellent bowyers around the country who specialize in certain types of recurves and longbows. Check them out and you might find the bow that fits your style of shooting. You may not find the longbow or the recurve to your liking, but you should at least make the attempt. Most archers will allow you to shoot their bows a couple of times if you ask politely. Modern, advanced technology and materials have not been forgotten by modern bowyers. Non-elastic Fast Flight strings, used on the most advanced compounds, have found their way onto longbows. The result is a faster, quieter bow with less felt recoil. Recurves and longbows are gaining in popularity as more archers give them a try.

GETTING STARTED WITH LONGBOWS

The Longbow Is A Stick And A String — But It Is Far More Than That — Here's How To Begin

Basics of longbow shooting are same as any bow; archer must maintain bow arm in position until the arrow clears the bow. Anchor point must remain consistent from shot to shot and the release must be clean. Longbow is canted slightly by the shooter.

SAM FADALA is a long-time archer/hunter who moved to Wyoming several years ago so he would have more hunting opportunities and the time to write about his hunts. He is an enthusiastic longbow hunter, preferring the "stick-bow" over all other designs. He offers the following advice to those who may wish to get started with the most basic of bows and arrows.

I'VE ALWAYS owned a stick bow. At age 6, I attacked my grandfather's oleander bush, sliced the thickest limb off and fashioned a primitive shaft-shucker. It wasn't a longbow or a flatbow. But the simple bent twig cast a homemade milkweed arrow far enough to down a backyard sparrow or two. I graduated to a commercial self-bow by age 9. That bow was, as I recall, a twenty-pounder made for high-school archery classes. The attic-sentenced lemonwood bow showed up a few decades after its last employment to serve another generation.

I'm surprised when I talk with avid compound archers who don't own an example of the classic longbow. A dedicated bowman who shoots only the compound bow is, to me, like a serious shooter with but one firearm — perhaps a .22 rimfire — but no shotgun, sidearm or big-bore rifle. I understand the appreciation of a favorite type of bow — or gun — to the exclusion of others. But if you love archery and don't have an acquaintanceship with a longbow, just for the experience of it, you're missing out on an interesting piece of tackle.

Archer friends tell me they'd like to try a longbow, if only for enjoyment and knowledge, but they believe getting good with it may undermine their ability with the compound. It won't, any more than becoming a successful handgunner will ruin the expertise of a good rifle-shot. The longbow is another shooting instrument and that's it. The longbow takes more practice, I think, for mastery, but getting good with it won't encroach on any other shooting instrument. So have no fear, try a longbow.

As with any arrow-casting device — perhaps moreso with the longbow — there's a right and wrong way to get started. Getting started with the longbow means, most important of all, buying the real thing. Today's longbow is generally a composite of glass laminated with some type of wood or woods. A true longbow is narrow of limb and thick of core, casting a fast arrow. The flatbow is another classic, by the way. Nothing said here is aimed against it. However, our immediate interest is the longbow with narrow limb and thick core.

Percentage-wise, relatively few archers use the old-style bow. However, there are still thousands of longbowmen in America. That's why there are so many bowyers in this country who build a correct example of the classic beauty. One of my friends in the archery business says there may be two hundred American craftsmen who can make a good longbow; there's no problem in locating a correct model.

There are several important criteria to consider before buying. One is length. The notion that a longbow has to look like a pole vault stick in order to qualify for the title is false. A longbow of sixty-six to sixty-nine-inches in length is fine for hunting and, when strung, is not unwieldy. It is true that a long-limbed bow has less finger pinch than a shorter bow. So if I were buying a longbow strictly for

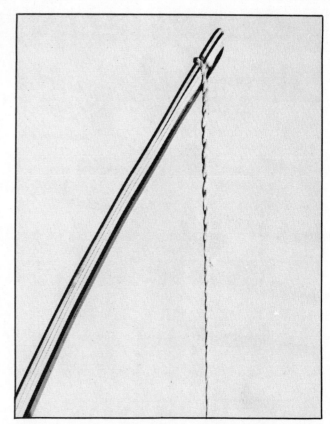

The limb tip of this John Schulz longbow appears thin and graceful, but is plenty strong and stable.

target or open-country work, I'd go with a seventy-inch model. My most-used hunting longbows are sixty-six and sixty-nine inches long, sixty and seventy pounds pull, respectively. Both shoot icicle smooth.

Longbows don't weigh much. Lightness is one of their primary attributes. Long longbows are light in the hand; that is why archers find them easy to carry. I have no more problem guiding a longbow through the woods than any of the shorter compounds. The longbow is longer, but the compound is bulkier. My sixty-nine-inch John Schulz longbow weighs only 1.5 pounds. My Jerry Hill sixty-six-inch longbow weighs a little less.

A proper longbow handles and performs remarkably well; it behaves itself. The longbow is "forgiving" of your mistakes. A slightly rough release won't send the arrow entirely off course. The longbow fits individual shooting style. You can master the straight-up stance if you must, although the relaxed posture with head tilted turns the shelf into a V-shape and puts the arrow on a straighter path out of the bow.

Arrow speed? Some longbows are fast; make no mistake about it. Don't guess. Chronograph. You may be surprised at the zip arrows achieve when loosed from these high performers. One of my longbows throws a heavy cedar hunting arrow at over 200 feet per second (fps); a light graphite shaft at 220 fps. They are historically interesting, have plenty of character, are light in physical weight, easy handling and capable of good performance. The longbow offers an archer a lot if he buys the right one.

Light in weight, but heavy in draw? A deep pitfall in getting started with the longbow is choosing the wrong draw

In Wyoming, Fadala prefers to use a traditional back quiver when shooting a longbow, although a bowquiver may be mounted. Quiver is by Jerry Hill.

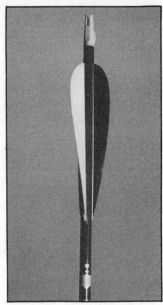

Sam Fadala custom-made this cedar shaft arrow, preferring the wood for longbow shooting.

weight. Popular opinion holds that if the longbow doesn't take plenty of muscle to pull, it's not much of a bow and you're not much of an archer.

"One of the most important things for a beginner to remember is to use a bow that is light enough to be pulled easily and comfortably," Howard Hill said. "It is better to have a bow too light than too heavy."

Remember, there's no relaxation factor in a longbow. A seventy-pound compound may "break" at thirty-five pounds, but a seventy-pound longbow holds at full draw weight. Yes, a heavy draw weight promotes smooth arrow release, because the arrow escapes the string fast when the archer's fingers uncurl. But there is no way to enjoy a practice session, or to learn shooting a longbow, if your muscles cry out each time the bow is drawn. A too-heavy bow leads to short practice sessions. It creates bad habits: failing to hold an anchor point, short-drawing — the arrow is loosed before establishing an anchor point — and premature dropping of the bow arm in order to "get the shot over with."

Getting started with a light-draw longbow, even an inexpensive self-bow, is a good idea. A light bow is also good for muscle tune-up. Some archers believe that practicing with a light-draw bow will spoil their ability to judge arrow drop with a more powerful bow. This is not true. The light-draw bow uses commensurately light arrows with a trajectory similar to a heavy bow. A light longbow promotes long shooting sessions. Before heading for the hunting field, final dedicated practice can be accomplished with the heavy hunting bow. I got rid of my light-draw bow a few years back and that was wrong. I'm looking for another forty-pound pull bow for fun-shooting in the backyard. A light-draw bow affords hours of easy practice and it does not impair the archer's ability to stay sharp with his high-power hunting bow.

Building up to a heavy bow is best accomplished with a light bow. You may be a weight-lifter, but that doesn't mean you can draw a heavy longbow repeatedly and shoot it accurately. A number of years ago, I had an eighty-six-pound bow, which I have since abandoned. At the time, I was shooting daily and the heavy bow was no problem for me. A friend and I went rabbit hunting. At the close of the hunt, he suggested we do a little stump-shooting. He said,

"Let me give your bow a try." This lad was six-and-a-half feet tall and built like a Sherman tank. Surely, he could handle a bow drawn by a 175-pound guy only five-feet, eleven inches tall. At first he was embarrassed. Then he got mad as he tugged on the bow string. But draw the bow, he could not.

An athlete in good physical condition will dominate a heavy bow faster than a fellow who is in poor shape, but if you want to master a heavy longbow, my considered advice is to start with a light model and work up. The best preparation for a physical feat is the feat itself. Don't let ego decide for you. Currently, my heaviest longbow pulls seventy pounds. I also have a sixty-pound bow. The latter will put a broadhead-tipped arrow all the way through the breadth of a deer at forty yards, but I don't think it will do that for elk. I have my eye on a third longbow; sixty-eight inches long, seventy-five pounds draw at twenty-eight-inch draw length.

Shoot the heaviest big-game longbow you can manage with accuracy, because a heavy bow throws a heavy arrow and a heavy arrow penetrates well. We hear that the heavy bow also shoots a lot flatter trajectoy than a bow of lighter draw weight, but this is not entirely correct. The spine of

the shaft must match the draw weight of the longbow. Compounds apply force to the arrow in a manner different from the longbow, so an arrow spined for a seventy-pound compound is not necessarily right for a seventy-pound longbow. A stiff cedar shaft is necessary to withstand the force of the heavy-draw longbow. Generally speaking — there are some variables to consider — a stiff cedar arrow is a heavy arrow. So the strong bow shoots a heavy arrow and the lighter bow shoots a light one. Result: similar arrow speed and trajectory. Remember, too, that a heavy arrow retains velocity better than a light one.

Riser style is also an important consideration when getting started with the longbow. The standard longbow grip may feel foreign to a compound bow shooter. When I was doing more compound bow shooting, I went for a longbow with reverse handle, because it helped me with a straight-up style; up to a point. But the last longbow I ordered has a standard riser. My reverse handle longbow is a beauty, but now that I'm shooting the longbow more than the compound, I prefer the standard grip. I suggest that a newcomer to the longbow, especially if he's a long-time compound bowman, consider a grip style that enhances the

Jerry Hill created the arm guard based on a Howard Hill model. Fadala's shooting style requires it.

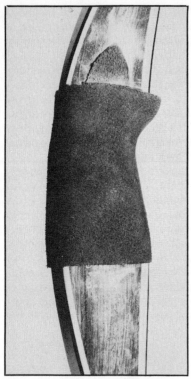

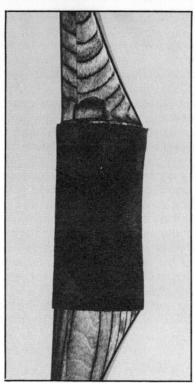

When strung, the reverse-handle longbow, above, looks as if it may have been strung backwards.

On a standard longbow, handle points inward toward shooter.

Safest and quickest way to string a longbow is to use a bowstringer.

compound bow stance with straight posture. Switching from compound to longbow is more natural when grips are similar. Jerry Hill is currently working on a longbow riser engineered to promote facile transfer from compound shooting to longbow shooting and *vice versa*. Be certain that the grip of your prospective longbow feels right to you. It's an important feature when getting started.

Draw length is another cockroach in the oatmeal. I'm comfortable with a thirty-one-inch arrow in the compound bow. When I began shooting both compound and longbow on an interchangeable basis, I stayed with the thirty-one-inch arrow, because I did not feel I could entirely switch shooting styles from compound to longbow at will. I was dead wrong. It's no trick at all to switch back and forth, any more than it is difficult for a practiced shooter to do well with a rifle on one day and a shotgun on the next day. I don't care how long your reach is — I'm a particularly long-armed fellow for my height — you can learn to shoot a longbow with a shorter arrow. Now I use the standard twenty-eight-inch arrow with my longbows.

The second I pick up a longbow, I bend to the occasion, literally. My left elbow is slightly crooked rather than locked and my head tilts a little to the right. It's that easy to shorten your draw length when going from compound to longbow. Don't try to match longbow draw length to compound bow draw length.

Newcomers to the longbow find that they have to loosen up, bend the body and just plain relax in order to do well. The longbow style of shooting, with body relaxed, knees loose, bow arm in control of the bow, but not stiff and straight, promotes the assumption of many different shooting stances. Expert longbow shooters can loose arrows

from all sorts of positions. I use only two stances: standing and kneeling. The archer who masters these will get by in the hunting field.

Anchor point may vary, too. I use the same anchor point in compound or longbow shooting, so going from one bow to the other is no problem in that regard. However, anchor point is an important consideration for the compound bow archer getting started with the longbow. The under-the-chin longbow anchor is a style used by many longbow target champions of yesteryear and hunters of the past. But I prefer to assume a high anchor point with the longbow. This style of shooting is quick and natural. Bottom line: getting started with longbow means altering shooting style, including anchor point if necessary. That's no problem if the archer keeps an open mind.

Longbows can wear sights, but most don't. Mine are clean of all aiming devices. Most longbow archers shoot off the shelf, using no additional rests or other accessories.

That brings us to arrows and fletching. It may seem painfully basic, but an archer friend tried over and over to group a batch of plastic-vane arrows from a longbow, because he'd used the same arrows in a compound bow. I loaned him several feathered shafts and he put 'em right on target. So by all means, match the arrow to the bow. Feathers are right for off-the-shelf shooting.

Aluminum, fiberglass and wood arrows all fly from a longbow, but tradition calls for wood. True, I have a set of modern graphite arrows that purr from the string of the longbow straight to the target — fast! However, cedar shafts are ideal, warping around the riser with fast recovery. I make my own cedars. I also buy beautiful commercial cedar arrow sets. Aluminum, graphite or fiberglass arrows are fine in the longbow, but the cedar arrow with feather fletching is standard. I especially like the tapered Cedarsmith shaft available from JK Chastain, 490 S. Queen Street, Lakewood, CO 80226.

Another consideration when getting into longbow shooting is the accessories. Don't initially buy every gadget you see, but do supply yourself with accessories that promote success. After years of using a glove, I've recently switched to the finger tab for longbow shooting. The compound bow shooter may feel uncomfortable with a tab or glove if he's been using a release. However, because there is no relaxation factor with the longbow, the fingers may feel the pressure. A glove or tab offers good protection against excessive pressure. A good arm guard is also essential, I feel.

A bowquiver is available for the longbow, but I like a back quiver better. The back quiver may seem cumbersome at first, but in no time it becomes a fluid part of the system. Give it a chance. Stringing a longbow is not too difficult with either the step-through or pull-the-riser-to-you methods. I prefer a bow stringer — costs under ten dollars — to avoid twisting, setting or breaking a limb, or having the bow leap away. The step-through method can be dangerous; a bow stringer is much safer.

Since the longbow handles differently than a compound, the archer may forget that the basics of shooting remain the same. The longbow is controlled by the bow arm. Drop the bow arm before the arrow is properly launched and the target is missed, as it is with the compound. Follow-through is essential. The bow should remain in position until the arrow escapes the string and flies clear of the shelf, just like the compound. Release must be a controlled maneuver — smooth, with the arrow riding swiftly over the shelf and on its way — just like the compound. A floating anchor point is just as critical when putting a longbow arrow on target as it is to putting a compound bow arrow on target.

Practice remains the key to success with either bow. Different? You bet. There are many differences between the compound and the longbow, but a good compound bow archer has every chance of shooting a longbow with skill, because the basics are the same. A romance with the longbow is not adulterous to compound bowshooting. The longbow simply adds a new and interesting dimension to the great sport of archery. — *Sam Fadala*

A modern longbow, built with today's materials, technology, can fling a fast arrow. Fadala shoots Jerry Hill bow rated at sixty pounds draw.

String silencers, such as Cat Whiskers, are good longbow accessories.

CHAPTER 10

BOWS OF THE FUTURE

Just When You Thought You Were Safe From New Designs, Along Come The Next Developments!

COMPOUND BOWS — actually the arrows they propel — seem to be be getting faster every year. Not long ago, the two hundred feet per second (fps) arrow was considered a kind of goal or landmark achievement. Today, every modern compound is able to shoot an arrow, even an AMO standard arrow, in excess of two hundred fps or greater. Many will fling a typical lightweight hunting arrow at 250 fps or greater. Reports of lightweight, short-length overdraw arrows, especially those made of carbon-fiber, flying at three hundred fps or more are not uncommon.

What's next, one might ask. Is there a physical speed limit for arrows and, if so, what might it be? Is there some new development in the works as radical as the first compound bow?

There are two directions that research and development will take. One is development and adaptation of new materials and production processes, applying them to the current design and technology of bows and arrows. Examples of this procedure are common. These kinds of changes and improvements have been going on since the Allen patent was granted.

Fast Flight string material differs from the more common Dacron string in that the Fast Flight has no stretch. When the string has been let go, it comes to a stop and the arrow is released; more of the stored energy of the bow has been imparted to the arrow. Fast Flight string will launch the same arrow a few feet per second faster than a string of another material. The non-elastic stop, however, places more stress on the other bow components and they must be able to withstand the heavier impact. Limbs, limb attachments, wheels and cables must be stronger.

The shape and size of the compound bow eccentric wheels has been evolving since Allen, Jennings and others made the first compounds. The cam wheel evolved from the round eccentrics, which evolved from cam shapes. Producing the eccentrics of lighter alloys and of carbon-fiber has reduced the mass weight of a bow. Experiments with cable attachments, lengths and locations are continuing.

The recent acceptance and spread of overdraw bow designs and the subsequent reduction of arrow length and spine weight is another development. Arrows have increased speeds and flattened trajectories. Faster, flatter-flying arrows mean more accuracy because range estimation errors are mitigated. Carbon-fiber shafts are gaining acceptance among compound shooters who embrace the overdraw concept.

A departure from the standard two-wheel compound design is Tom Jennings' Unistar. This bow puts the eccentric action together near the center of the bow, rather than at the limb tips. Shooting is smooth and even. The wheels at the limb tips are simply round pulley wheels which only change direction of the cable and string, rather than create the compounding effect during draw and release. The latest version has a sixty-five percent let-off at full draw, instead of the standard fifty percent.

Jennings says, in fact, that he has experimented with the Unistar design and achieved let-off of nearly ninety percent. In theory, one might have a hundred-pound-draw bow which could be held at full draw while holding only ten pounds. However, says Jennings, bows with let-off of much more than seventy percent are difficult to release cleanly. At eighty to ninety percent let-off, one almost must push the arrow forward to get it launched. There is barely enough tension on the string to pull it from many mechanical releases.

Another strange looking compound bow is the Oneida

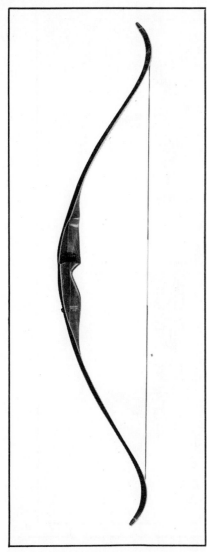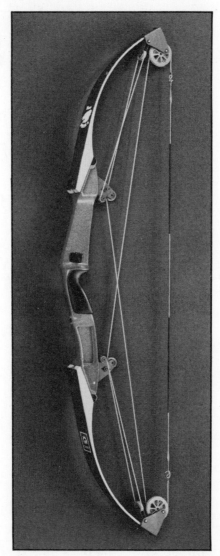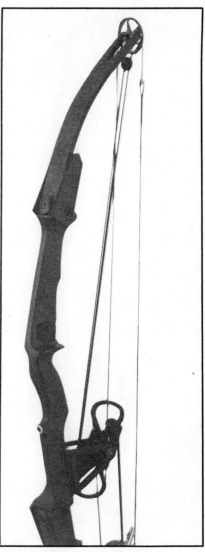

Bear Grizzly, left, is a classic recurve bow of the type preferred by many before and after the invention of the compound. A compound, center, features two eccentric wheels and six additional pulleys and wheels. The design shot well, but soon was simplified. Newer model Jennings Unistar, right, puts eccentric action in center.

Labs' Eagle bow, the design of one John Islas. It has some advantages in that the compounding action is clustered near the riser ends and a simple string nocked at the ends of two recurved limbs is exactly like the traditional recurve bow. No cables are visible between the string and riser; no cable guard is needed and there is no possibility of cable/fletching interference.

Bow & Arrow Hunting magazine's technical editor, Emery Loiselle, has given the bow a workout and declares it fit for duty. He reports the following:

"The concept of the Oneida bow utilizes short power limbs mounted at the riser ends with a fulcrum and limb bolt arrangement as in other compound bows, but from there on things are different. A second or outboard limb is hinged to the end of the power limb. A power cable from the end of the power limb goes to a cam mounted on pylons near the riser end; a yoke cable from the base of the recurve limb goes to the other side of the cam.

"A bowstring is seated in the nocks at the end of each outboard limb as it is on the traditional recurve bow. As the string is drawn, the pivoting of the outer limb causes the yoke cable at its base to rotate the cam, winding in the power cable to bend the short power limbs. A timing wheel attached to the cam carries a feed-back cable running through a groove in the riser to a similar unit at the opposite end of the riser to assure equal and stable payout of the bowstring at both ends of the bow."

An observer, watching an archer draw the bow, might think the bow appears to be breaking apart into components as the string comes back. It has a strange appearance, but shoots a fast arrow. The Oneida bows have found acceptance with many bowhunters and field archers. The bow is overdraw-ready and will propel a short, lighter weight overdraw arrow downrange at more than 250 feet per second. There are, no doubt, further refinements to this design on the drawing boards.

An inventor named John Bozek, from Michigan, is not an archer, but is obviously fascinated by the art. Bozek has several patents regarding missile launching by muscle power and more patents are pending. All his designs are

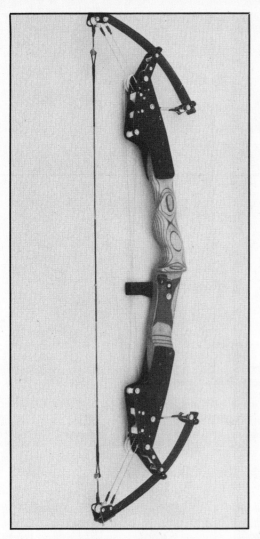

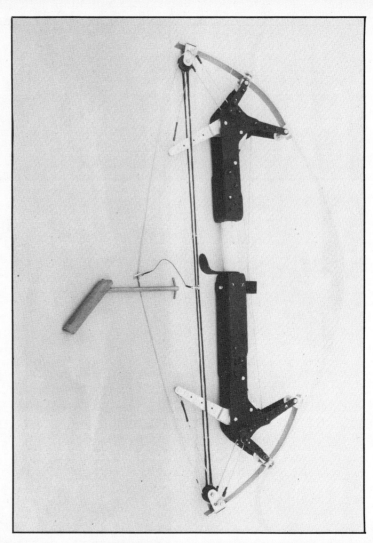

Inventor John Bozek evolves. The more conventional bow design, above, has strange looking limbs, but pulls the arrow to flight in an unusual manner. Above and right: A more unusual bow pushes the arrow in conventional way.

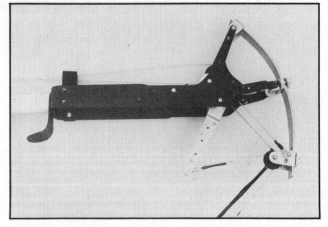

interesting, different and a few are just plain weird. He has even come up with a mechanical slingshot with variable leverage which gives a let-off in draw weight at the end of the pull backward. Another invention of his is a dual-action cocking system for heavy crossbows.

Bozek calls the device a four-bar archery bow. It functions with what he calls a rotary latching mechanism. He has built a couple of working models and has functional drawings for this and other designs. He says, "I just like to invent things."

Here is Bozek's description of the four-bar bow:

FUNCTION

The activation of the rotary latching mechanisms prevents the return movement of the intermediate swing arms when the bowstring is drawn to the resistance drop point and then released before the full draw point is reached.

CONSTRUCTION

The rotary latching mechanisms are comprised of en-

gagement disks and holding pawls.

The engagement disks are mounted on the axles on which the intermediate swing arms pivot. The disks are connected to the arms so that the paired disks and arms rotate in unison. The periphery of each disk is provided with an engagement roller, a holding notch and a disengagement ramp.

The holding pawls are mounted on axles which are supported by the riser extensions. The pawls are provided with head end rollers. The pawls are spring-loaded in an over-

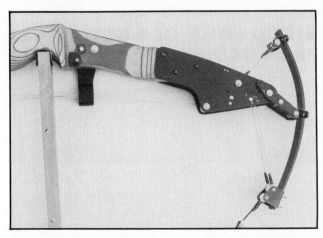

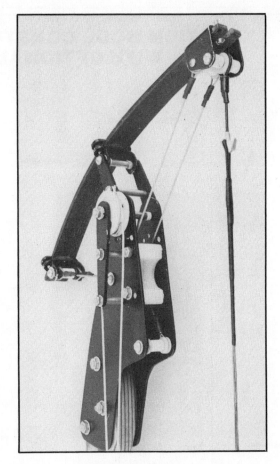

The constrained four-bar pivotal-limb bow, above and right, pivots the limbs in the middle. Both halves bend around their midpoint. More unusual constrained four-bar traction-mode bow, lower right, seems more complicated in action.

center arrangement which results in the pawls being urged by the springs to move from one extreme position to the opposite one when the transition zone is traversed.

OPERATION

When the bow is in the undrawn state, the head end rollers of the pawls are held in contact with the peripheries of the engagement disks. When the bowstring is pulled beyond the maximum resistance point, the pawl rollers are forced into the holding notches in the disks. The engagement between the rollers and the notches prevents any reverse rotation of the disks. When the bowstring is pulled toward the full draw point, the rollers are forced out of the holding notches and into contact with the disengagement ramps on the disks. The ramps force the head end rollers away from the disks until the pawl springs pivot the pawls into their disengaged positions. When the fully drawn bowstring is released, the disks are rotated back to their starting positions. During this reverse rotation of the disks, the engagement rollers on the disks contact the tail ends of the pawls. The rollers force the tail ends of the pawls away from the disks until the pawl springs take over and pivot the pawls back into their engaged positions.

UTILIZATION

The user has the option of not utilizing the latching capabilities of the bow. If the bowstring is drawn to the full draw point and then released in a normal fashion, the operation of the latching mechanisms will not be heard, felt, or sensed by the user in any other way.

If, on the other hand, the user elects to take advantage of the bow's latching capabilities, only one change in bow usage is necessary. The bowstring is released when the drop in resistance is felt. The limbs are held in place by the load cables.

The two main reasons for using the bow's latching capabilites are: 1) To minimize hand movement and physical exertion when the user can be seen by a quarry that is easily frightened away. 2) To allow a user with reduced physical arm strength to use a hunting bow that has an effective draw weight.

TRACTION MODE CONSTRAINED FOUR-BAR BOW
WITH OPTIONAL PRE-LOADING

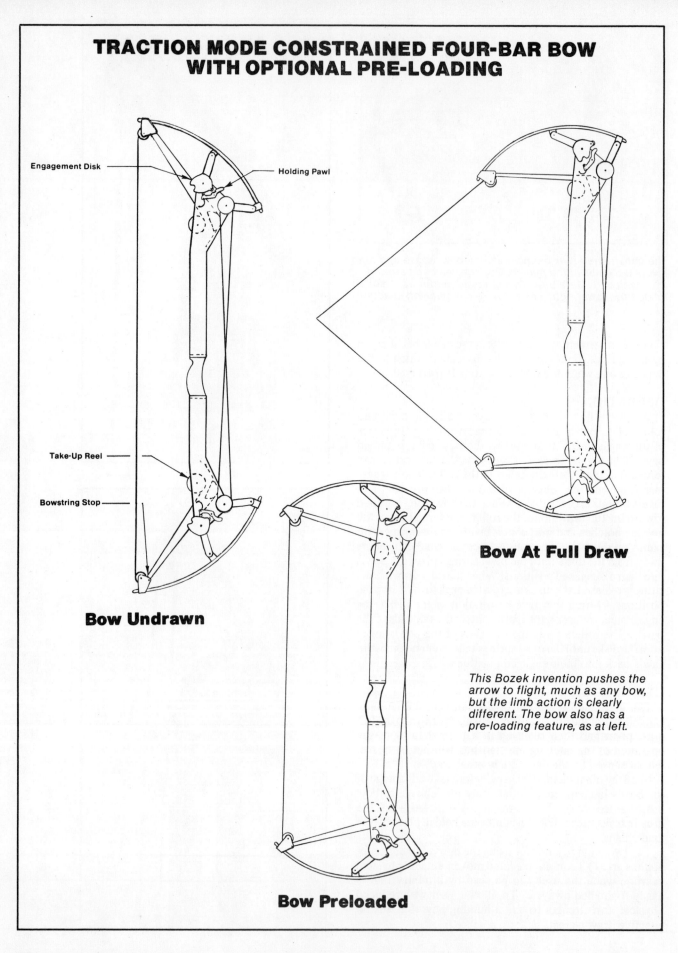

Engagement Disk

Holding Pawl

Take-Up Reel

Bowstring Stop

Bow Undrawn

Bow At Full Draw

Bow Preloaded

This Bozek invention pushes the arrow to flight, much as any bow, but the limb action is clearly different. The bow also has a pre-loading feature, as at left.

FOUR-BAR TRACTION MODE ARCHERY BOW

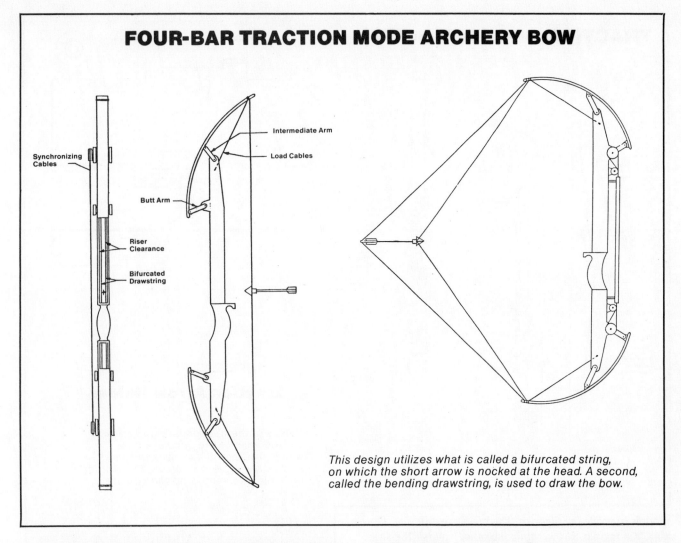

Synchronizing Cables

Intermediate Arm

Load Cables

Butt Arm

Riser Clearance

Bifurcated Drawstring

This design utilizes what is called a bifurcated string, on which the short arrow is nocked at the head. A second, called the bending drawstring, is used to draw the bow.

In the first instance, the arrow could be nocked and the bow drawn to the latching draw distance when the user is not being observed by the quarry. The final draw of the bow and the release of the arrow could then be quickly completed when the user is forced into the quarry's line of sight.

In the second instance, the user could employ different techniques for getting the bow into the latched condition beyond the maximum draw weight point. For example, the user may be able to have a stronger hunting companion perform the preliminary draw. Alternatively, the user could use both hands and one or both feet to draw the bow into the latched condition.

ADVANTAGES OF CONSTRAINED FOUR-BAR ARCHERY BOW CONFIGURATIONS

ADVANTAGES RELATIVE TO ALLEN CONFIGURATIONS

1. A drop in draw resistance at full draw is provided without the use of rotary variable leverage devices.

2. Limb stress reductions result from the bending of both ends of the limbs around longitudinal midpoints.

3. Load cable stress reductions result from the large-radius bending which occurs during the draw.

4. Unrestricted arrow movement and unhindered handling characteristics result from the absence of obtrusive load cables.

5. Reaction time improvements result from the direct drawstring/limb attachments which do not involve any rewinding of the ends of the drawstring on rotary elements.

6. Recoil shock reductions result from the appreciable outward limb motion that occurs when the limbs return to their initial positions.

7. Riser bending stress reductions result from the independent longitudinal stressing of the limbs by the isolated load cables.

ADVANTAGES RELATIVE TO ISLAS CONFIGURATIONS

1. A drop in draw resistance at full draw is provided without the use of rotary variable leverage devices.

2. Limb stress reductions result from the bending of both ends of the limbs around longitudinal midpoints.

3. Load cable stress reductions result from the large-radius bending which occurs during the draw.

John Bozek assembled working models of two bows, using principles described and sent them to Emery Loiselle for evaluation and comments. The working prototypes were not constructed for hunting purposes, but only as

TRACTION ARCHERY BOW

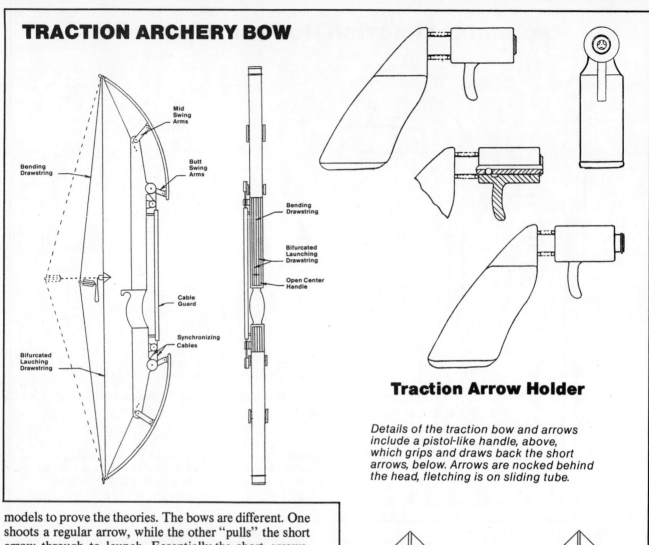

Labels on bow diagram:
Mid Swing Arms
Butt Swing Arms
Bending Drawstring
Cable Guard
Synchronizing Cables
Bifurcated Lauching Drawstring
Bending Drawstring
Bifurcated Launching Drawstring
Open Center Handle

Traction Arrow Holder

Details of the traction bow and arrows include a pistol-like handle, above, which grips and draws back the short arrows, below. Arrows are nocked behind the head, fletching is on sliding tube.

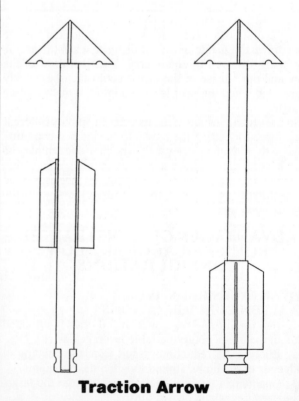

Traction Arrow

models to prove the theories. The bows are different. One shoots a regular arrow, while the other "pulls" the short arrow through to launch. Essentially, the short arrows, only a few inches long, are pulled from the shooter's hand and propelled downrange, rather than being pushed, as with a conventional bow. The Bozek arrows are nocked at the head end, not the fletching end.

Prior to use of the Bozek bow, the tail of the arrow is pushed into the holder/release device so that the spring-loaded balls can engage the groove in the end of the arrow shaft.

The holder/release device would be carried in a belt holster. When the arrow is launched, the device would be withdrawn from its holster and used to first engage the head end of the arrow with the bifurcated launching drawstring. It would then be used to pull the drawstring by the arrow. Pulling the trigger launches the arrow.

With prototypes in hand, Loiselle conducted some examinations.

John Bozek has invented a few bow designs, two of which are discussed here. Prototypes of both were sent for evaluation. Both bows have the same basic propulsion design, but the method of propelling the arrow is different. Call these prototypes Bow No. 1 and Bow No. 2.

The inventor states these are not "compound" bows as we know the round wheel model. These bows do not utilize rotary variable leverage devices which produce the so-called compound effect. Instead, they incorporate what he

FOUR-BAR LATCH

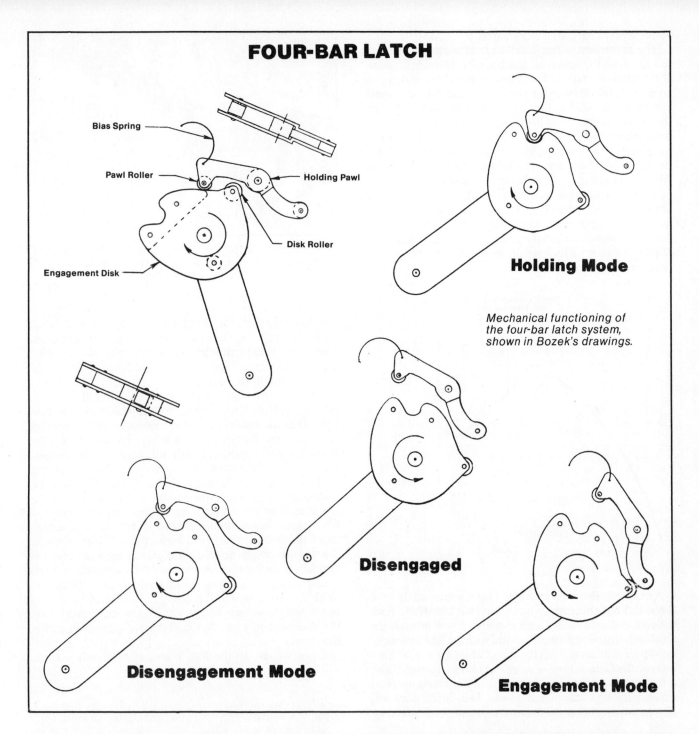

Bias Spring

Pawl Roller

Holding Pawl

Disk Roller

Engagement Disk

Holding Mode

Mechanical functioning of the four-bar latch system, shown in Bozek's drawings.

Disengaged

Disengagement Mode

Engagement Mode

calls a "constrained four-bar configuration." This designation is descriptive for two reasons: Load cables constrain the movement of the tips of the limbs and the contraint imposed by the cables determines the shape of the four-bar linkages. These linkages are comprised of portions of the limbs, portions of the ends of the riser and the four pairs of swing arms that connect the limbs to the riser.

The inventor refers to the mechanism as an "extensible limb mounting system" in which the bending of the two halves of the limb around a midcenter point distributes the bending strain equally throughout the length of the limb.

Bow No. 1, a constrained four-bar pivotal-limb archery bow, is the more normal of the two — if this term may be applied to such a different design — in that it has a wood riser is the usual configuration and fistmele or brace height is quite normal to allow shooting of a normal arrow in the usual manner.

The limb itself is a short thirteen inches long, pivoting near the center, with the limb bending on each side throughout its length, somewhat in the manner that the limbs on a TSS Quadraflex bow bend, according to Loiselle.

The butt of the limb may be connected to the riser by means of a pivotal rigid linkage. On the Bow No. 1 model, since butt linkage is subjected only to tensile stress, it is tethered by a pair of short cables.

The approximate midpoint of the limb is connected to the riser by means of the intermediate linkage. This linkage must be rigid — of aluminum bar stock on the model —

since stresses here are compressive.

The movement of the limb butt is restricted by the butt linkage when the limb is pivoted backward toward the user. If the movement of the limb tip were not also restricted in some way, the distance between the tip and the riser would continually increase as the limb pivots backward. However, the limb tip is connected to the riser or stock by one or more load cables. Consequently, as the limb pivots backward, its curvature is continually increased as a result of the bending of the two halves of the limb around the midpoint which is attached to the intermediate linkage.

As a result of the steady increase in the curvature of the limb, the force required to pull the limb backward increases as the draw progresses. However, prior to the full draw point, the intermediate linkage and the limb tip load cables align in a manner which results in any desired drop in the required draw force.

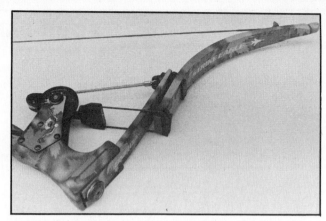

Newer version of the Strike Eagle modifies the sweep of the curved limbs to reduce the impact sound of the Fast Flight string. Pylon is moved away from limb base.

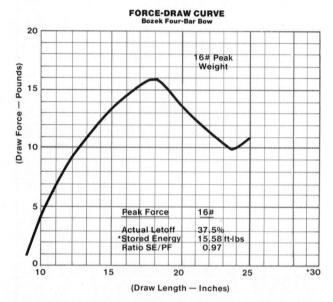

FORCE-DRAW CURVE
Bozek Four-Bar Bow

16# Peak Weight

Peak Force	16#
Actual Letoff	37.5%
*Stored Energy	15.58 ft-lbs
Ratio SE/PF	0.97

(Draw Force — Pounds)

(Draw Length — Inches)

The limbs on this bow have little mass, but are stiff due to their shortness and the acute angles of the bending cables. Even though the entire limb structure must move during the shot, the small light limb may not cause an objectionable amount of limb drag.

One of the first things Loiselle noticed while drawing the bow was that the lower limb seemed to peak over more suddenly than the upper limb. The upper and lower limb structures are interconnected with timing cables which pass through a bracket mounted on the offside of the riser opposite the rest. One of the cables was quite loose. After loosening the lockscrew and pulling the cable tighter, this phenomenon disappeared and both limbs peaked over simultaneously.

Fistmele or brace height on the No. 1 model measured 6⅞ inches. Loiselle took measurements to determine how much the limbs actually bent during draw. With the bow in the strung position, he held a straightedge against the metal brackets at each end of the limb and the measurement from the straightedge to a midpoint on the limbs was 2⅛ inches. With the string held at full draw, Loiselle made a similar check and the measurement was 2½ inches, showing that the limb bent only an additional three-eighths-inch during the draw.

Draw weight on the No. 1 prototype is only sixteen

As Loiselle drew the string, he said it appeared that the limbs did not perceptibly bend, but that the whole limb with attachments rocked back as a unit. Upon release, the total limb structure pivoted forward with the limb tips moving outward or away from the center of the bow — as happens on the Oneida bow — as well as moving forward. The outward movement eliminates much of the jarring or recoil associated with compound bows. The latter, forward, movement augments the forward movement of the string.

The Islas-design bow, manufactured by Oneida Labs in New York, is called Strike Eagle, shoots fast arrows.

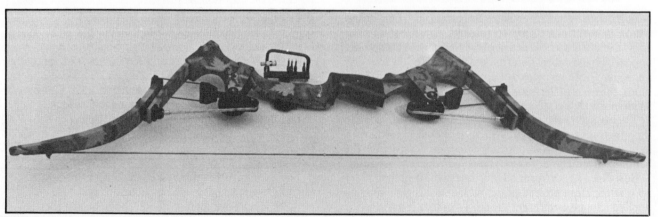

pounds with a short draw length of twenty-four inches. The model was constructed personally by John Bozek and he had no way of knowing what the resulting draw specs would be. Holding weight was ten pounds when tension on the string was maintained, but dropped to seven pounds when draw tension was slackened. This demonstrated hysteresis of three pounds at the twenty-four-inch draw sta-

tion, the relatively large amount probably being due to the light draw weight.

Loiselle plotted a force/draw curve for this particular model to get an idea how the design stores energy compared to round wheel bows. The shape of the curve is somewhat like that of an eccentric wheel, showing a fairly narrow sixteen-pound peak at the eighteen-inch station before dropping off to a ten-pound holding weight at the twenty-four-inch station. Stored energy was 15.6 foot-pounds and the ratio of stored energy to peak draw force was 0.97. This comparison factor is closer to that of a wheel than of a cam. Actual let-off considering the ten-pound holding weight in lieu of the seven-pound collapsed weight was thirty-eight percent.

Bow No. 2, a constrained four-bar traction-mode bow, is quite similar to Bow No. 1, except that it is designed to "pull" the arrow by its head, rather than pushing from the rear as with an ordinary bow. This model uses a bifurcated — divided in two — string which is located close to the riser where it can engage the head end of a short arrow. The tail end of the arrow is pulled by means of a second draw string, or by means of a holder/release device.

The inventor claims the following advantages for the traction mode: short arrows are easier to store, carry and use. The application of a tensile force to the head end of the short arrow avoids the bending and tumbling problems encountered when a thrust force is applied to the tail end of a long arrow.

This No. 2 model has a shoot-through riser. The bifurcated string straddles the arrow point to engage grooves in the rear of the head. The model tested has an additional string, a draw string, to be used for drawing the bow. A flexible cord to simulate the arrow shaft connects the head at the bifurcated bowstring and the nock attached to the draw string.

Emery Loiselle noticed the power string became limp and loose before reaching full draw with the draw string. These strings bend with varying rates and it would be difficult to maintain an exact "arrow length" between them

(Above and right) Design and interaction of the cables, wheels, cams seems complicated. All components must remain finely tuned.

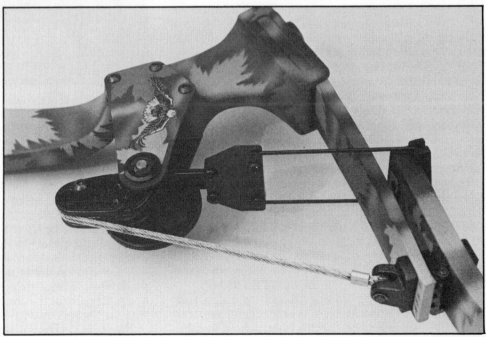

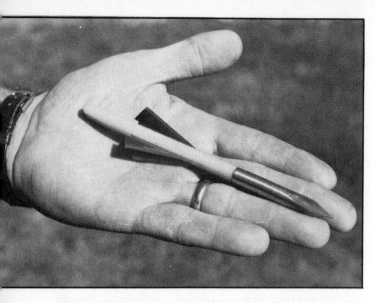

This is the Short Arrow System missile, only six inches long. The broadhead-like cutting blades act as fletching.

throughout the draw. Furthermore, the bifurcated power string does not consistently straddle the pylons as it should.

The inventor recognizes these problems and envisions the better method of drawing to be the use of an arrow puller or holder/release device which would eliminate the draw string and the need to maintain synchronization between the power string and a draw string during the draw. Omission of the draw string would also eliminate the need for the pylons and the problem of straddling.

At some future time, Bozek intends to perfect a ratcheting system for bending the traction four-bar bow which will make possible the storage of a great amount of energy and high arrow velocities.

The second bow, like the first, was also a low weight, short draw model. It is impossible with either bow to obtain meaningful velocity readings for making a comparison with conventional compounds. The inventor recognizes this limited demonstration value and attributes it to his limited resources and expertise in constructing the prototypes and reworking commercial limbs which turned out to be too limber for an adequate draw resistance. He also states that another shortcoming of the prototypes is that the draw characteristics have not been optimized. When a four-bar configuration is used, the shape of the force/draw curve is determined by several variables which he has not been able to fully explore. These variables involve the limbs, the swing arms and the load cables. In regard to each of these components, the following variables can affect the draw characteristics: (1) Limbs; overall lengths and exact locations of the "midpoint" axles. (2) Swing arms; lengths and locations of the riser axles on which the arms pivot. (3) Load cables; lengths, locations of the riser anchor points and the precise shape of the contact surfaces which determine the tension of the cable and positions from which the cables apply a tensile force to the tips of the limbs.

While John Bozek was working on his strange and unusual inventions, Jeffrey Anderson of Wauconda, Illinois, was working on something he calls the Short Arrow System.

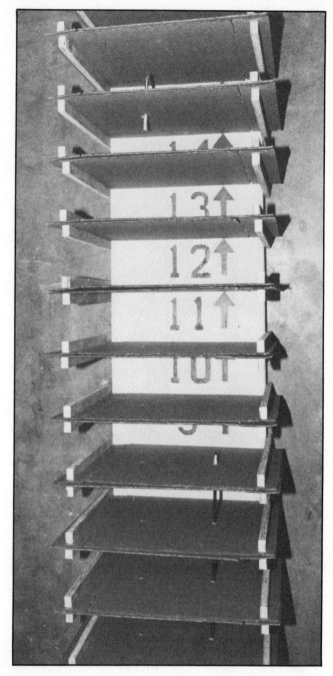

The original 22-inch arrow passed through and halted in the eighth laminated baffle. The short arrow, similar to a crossbow bolt, passed through into the fourteenth.

Anderson claims each arrow in his system is exactly the same as all the others. For bowhunters, they are said to be more stable, accurate and, most important, more humane. They are less than seven inches long!

"The arrows require no long shaft or fletching to determine the flight characteristics," declares Anderson. "And best of all, there is no fine-tuning required as with all other arrows. The six-inch arrow incorporates cutting broadhead blades that act as fletching for stabilizing the arrow during flight. These blades are preceded by a sharp point which opens the path for the arrow. The arrow can only be used with the Short Arrow guidance system.

"We have designed the arrow and its system so that we

can shoot it from a recurve, compound or crossbow. To introduce the concept, we have developed a five-minute clamp-on kit to fit the PSE crossbow family. Short Arrow Systems chose the Precision Shooting Equipment (PSE) crossbow, because of the overall quality.

"There are several advantages of the short arrow system: greater accuracy, flatter trajectory, maintained velocity and greater penetration. Tests were conducted in a controlled environment using a PSE Starfire II crossbow. The arrows used in the comparison testing were the PSE twenty-two-inch Fire-Flite 8 arrow with a Razorbak 4 broadhead and our six-inch long four-bladed hunting arrow. Both test arrows weighed 540 grains, the AMO standard for conventional hunting arrows.

"The first test was to determine the levels of accuracy of the two styles of arrows. We used a shooting bench similar to the ones used on rifle ranges. To help eliminate much of the human factor, we used a yoke arrangement with a heavy rubber cord to steady the crossbow. This device was bolted securely to the bench. The arrows were shot ten times at each range from the same crossbow, which meant removing the guidance system for the standard arrow. At thirty yards, we achieved a group of 1.8 inches with the

original arrow. With our six-inch arrow, we achieved a group which measured 0.8 inch.

"The holdover required to achieve a bullseye at thirty yards is forty-two percent less with the short arrow as compared to the standard crossbow projectile. This results in a flatter trajectory. To test the holdover required to achieve a bullseye at the various ranges, we first had to insure that the bullseye was at the same elevation as the arrow in the crossbow. Ten shots with each arrow were made to obtain a grouping at various distances. We are expressing the trajectory in the amount of holdover, in inches, necessary for each grouping to be centered in the bulls-eye. At thirty yards, the standard arrow had a holdover of 27.1 inches, while the six-inch arrow required a holdover of only 15.8 inches. This is a difference of 11.3 inches.

"The velocity loss differential can be attributed to the fact that the short arrow does not have a shaft or fletching to hinder its performance. Because the short arrow maintains its speed longer, it maintains its energy longer.

"The comparison analyzed the difference in the speed of the opposing arrows. Each arrow was shot through a Custom Chronograph Speedtach chronograph and maintained the same 'muzzle' velocity of 246 feet per second (fps). At

The production short arrow is to be 6 1/8 inches long, weight 525 grains, with a 1 1/8-inch cutting diameter.

The Short Arrow System PA16 guidance kit was tested on a standard PSE Starfire II crossbow.

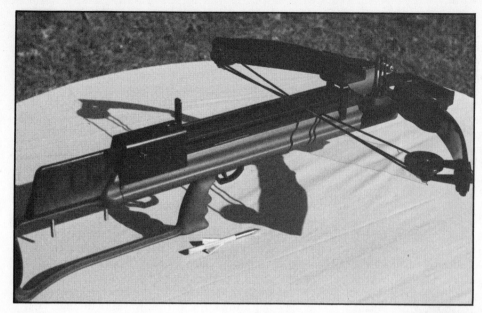

PSE Starfire II crossbow, left, has the PA16 arrow guidance system kit and optional scope mounted. An earlier development was the Bear Delta V system, below. It was fast, but did not enjoy great sales; was dropped.

thirty yards, the standard arrow lost 13.7 fps, a loss of 7.9 foot-pounds of energy (fpe). The short arrow lost 2.7 fps resulting in a loss of 1.6 fpe.

"The short arrow system maintains 6.28 fpe more at thirty yards than the standard arrow. Along with energy conservation, we must take into account that the speed of the arrow diminishes 2.7 fps in thirty yards, as compared to the standard arrow's loss of 13.7 fps at the same distance. The short arrow has less drag in flight and more penetration, because the short arrow only has twenty-five percent of the surface area of the standard arrow.

"The system has been tested, in a controlled environment, to determine penetration performance. The penetration device consists of twenty laminates of double layered two hundred-pound test corrugated cardboard set six inches apart. Both arrows were shot from the same 150-pound Starfire II crossbow. The blades of the original twenty-two-inch arrow were embedded in the eighth laminate while the short arrow's blades were embedded in the fourteenth laminate. To assure that the distance between the laminates was not a determining factor, the laminates were extended to twenty-four inches apart. This afforded the long arrow the opportunity to clear each laminate before entering the next, as the six-inch arrow had. The same results were achieved. For those who shoot longer arrows, the results of the short arrow test will be more impressive.

"There are other advantages to a short arrow. A hunter might carry many arrows and not be bothered by a bulky quiver. With the short arrow system, there is no need for nocks which can affect the flight if not installed correctly. The short arrow has greatly increased spine strength. They do not use flight characteristic-changing vanes or feathers. When the arrow is loaded in the guidance system, the arrow's sharp blades are not exposed to the archer. Due to the design of the arrow and the methods used to manufacture them, some variables found in other types of arrows are eliminated."

There are those who oppose improvements/advances in the technology of archery. The Pope & Young Club has voted to make illegal any game recording with the club which has been taken with the aid of electronic devices, includ-

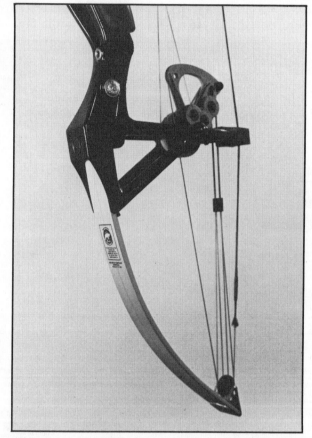

ing laser beams. They and some states have restricted the amount of compound bow let-off to no more than sixty-five percent. Some groups and individuals are lobbying state game commissions to restrict bowhunters in their states in a similar manner.

Many archers scoff at technological improvements in the sport, maintaining that the "stick and string" should be just that; a longbow or recurve bow, standard string and arrows. But most bowhunters and field archers readily accept and purchase devices and improvements which help them become better shots and better hunters.

SHORT ARROW SYSTEMS TEST RESULTS

SPEED

Test using 540 (+/−1) grain arrows

Test readings taken with Speedtach chronograph

"Muzzle" speed 246 (+/−.5) fps for both arrows

Range (yards)	Speed in fps 6 in. arrow	Speed in fps 22 in. arrow
10	245.1	241.4
20	244.2	236.8
30	243.3	232.3

ENERGY

Foot-pounds of energy (fpe)

"Muzzle" 72.58 foot-pounds

Range (yards)	FPE 6 in. arrow	FPE 22 in. arrow
10	72.05	69.89
20	71.52	67.25
30	71.00	64.72

HOLDOVER

Holdover expressed in inches

Range (yards)	6 in. arrow	22 in. arrow
10	.5	3.8
20	5.4	11.7
30	15.8	27.1

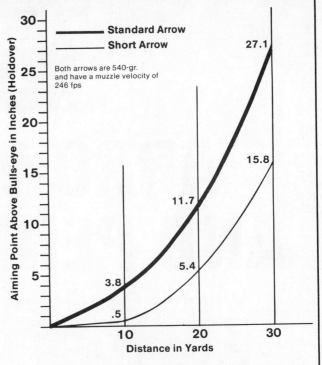

Holdover Required to Hit the Bullseye at a Given Distance

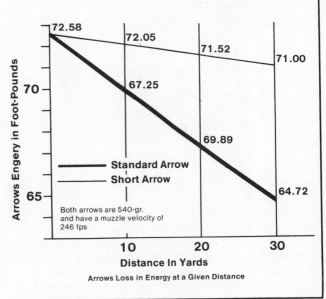

Arrows Loss in Energy at a Given Distance

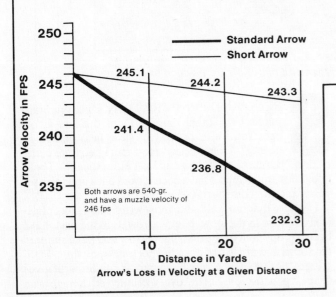

Arrow's Loss in Velocity at a Given Distance

Some inventors, such as John Bozek, design and patent these gadgets just for the challenge. Others, primarily the larger archery manufacturers, look at the changes as marketing opportunities; they want to sell more product. The consumer will decide what changes will be accepted and what will flash across the sky, only to disappear in a few months.

Some observers believe that the maximum development potential of compound bows is at hand. Little more can or will be done to improve arrow flight, given the basic design as it is.

Research and development will continue, as long as people are curious or as long as the profit motive exists.

CHAPTER 11
ARROW SPEED AND PENETRATION

Which Is Best–Heavy, Slow Or Light, Fast?

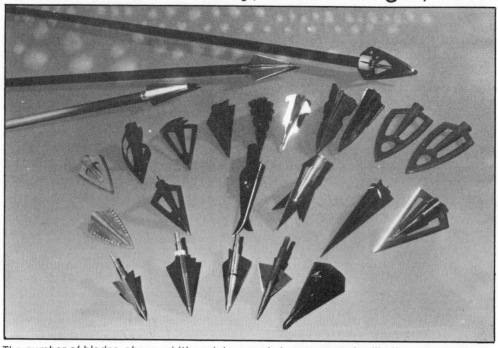

The number of blades, shape, width and degree of sharpness each will affect penetration. The bowhunter has a wide range of broadhead types and materials from which to choose.

LONG-TIME archer and bowhunter, Emery J. Loiselle, has been experimenting for years with arrow penetration theories and practice. What Loiselle has found, is sometimes surprising and often controversial. One can hear arguments on both sides of the weight and penetration question.

The questions and the answers are vital to the bowhunter and the 3-D target shooter who looks for a fast, flat trajectory error which may help mitigate errors in range estimation. A lightweight, flat-flying arrow will arc less as it flies through the air toward the target.

The controversy has raged on for years. Emery Loiselle's report should help clear up much of the mystery.

SPEED AND PENETRATION! Does one compliment the other or not? Does the fast arrow penetrate more, or does the slow, heavy arrow go deeper? Archers ask, "How can I get more penetration?" Others ask, "How can I get more speed?" These questions and disputes have been kicked back and forth for years and the controversy continues on.

I believe that most archers, most writers and most physicists believe in the slow, heavy arrow. I, in the past, have been a proponent of the fast, light arrow and have suffered the slings and arrows of disbelievers time upon time. I still go with the fast, light arrow. Under most conditions it gives deepest penetration, but the overwhelming advantage is an accurate, humane hit on game.

First, let's dispel a few myths. "How much penetration can you get with a straw?" This is an extreme. You might even substitute the word feather for straw. At the other end of the spectrum, try shooting a ten-pound lead arrow at normal game-getting distances! "The light arrow slows down faster and the heavy arrow will catch up and pass it." The first part of this is true, but "catch up and pass?" No way, not at normal hunting ranges and the light arrow will be out beyond where the heavy arrow can't go at the longest ranges.

And how about this: "Foam is not a surrogate for flesh, since the fluids in living tissue lubricate and make all shafts equal regardless of shaft diameter, length and surface friction." Water also is a lubricant. So why is it that at rainy day shoots when archers' arrows are wet, the overdraw cam bow shooters are the ones who complain that their fast little arrows are passing right through the targets or foam animals?

"All things being equal, the heavy arrow will penetrate deeper than the light arrow." The fact of the matter is that when shooting a slow, heavy arrow and a light, fast arrow, all things are usually not equal. A viable comparison must consider a lightweight and a heavyweight, including their variables, which match and fly well from the bow.

Methinks too many people believe the kinetic energy formula is actually the formula for penetration. Admittedly, kinetic energy is a basic and important factor in arrow penetration, but there are many other characteristics affecting penetration which the formula knows nothing about and does not consider.

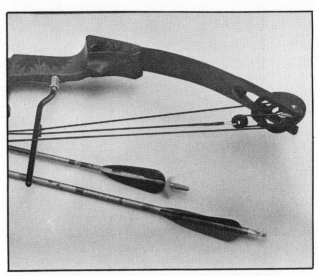

Jennings Stealth bow utilizes large cams, Fast Flight string system to generate fast, penetrating arrows.

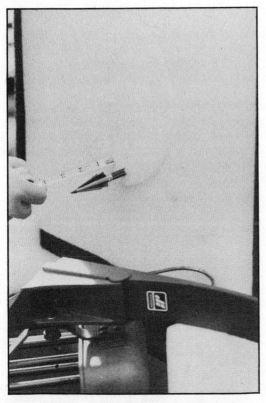

Broadhead penetration through eight inches of foam is determined by measuring the amount of shaft protruding through back.

What makes an arrow faster? Remember, we are talking about arrows which are properly spined and tuned to the bow/archer combination, be they little, light arrows or big, long heavy arrows. Add an overdraw to the bow, cut your arrows shorter to suit and you now have over-spined arrows. Besides the weight saved in shortening the arrows, you save even more weight by having to go to a more limber spine. This generally means a smaller diameter shaft, shorter and lighter in weight, needing a lighter point than a long, heavy arrow to maintain proper balance point; another saving in arrow weight. The smaller shaft presents less surface for friction. The amount of fletch helical or angle which gives spin to the arrow has a bearing on speed, as does the size and number of fletches used. Feathers are lighter than vanes and will give greater "muzzle" velocity, but feathers create more drag and the slightly heavier vanes will provide greater velocity farther down range.

What makes an arrow penetrate deeper? The basic factor is kinetic energy and the heavy arrow has more of this. Most of the qualities stated previously which make an arrow faster are also penetration-inducing factors for the small, light arrow. The small diameter shaft has less friction, as does a smooth-surfaced shaft. A ferrule up front, larger than shaft diameter, enhances penetration. Type of broadhead has a considerable effect. A fast, well-tuned arrow moves in easier and deeper during the initial spread of the target material. A lubricated shaft treated with a spray material such as Clean Kill by Royal Arms International will reduce friction in any target.

When discussing penetration, some people will throw the kinetic energy formula in your face and talk of nothing else, charging that you are defying the laws of physics. Certainly the formula for kinetic energy is the basic consideration. I use the formula in the bow reports I do for each issue of *Bow & Arrow Hunting* magazine. And yes, the the heavier arrow does indeed accept more of the bow's stored energy.

The Bow Efficiency Table figures I compile for each bow considers arrows weighing from 350 grains to 650 grains in twenty-five-grain increments. The difference in efficiency — kinetic energy divided by stored energy — be-

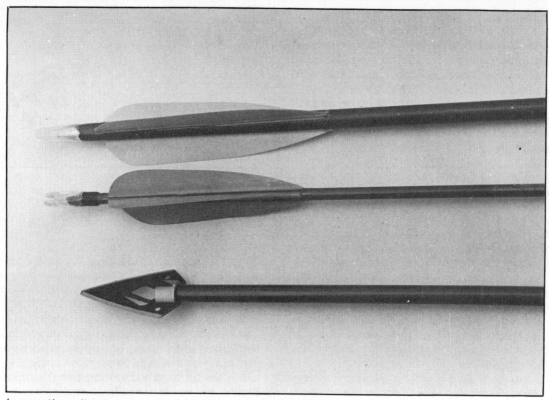

Longer three-fletch arrow, top, is shot through normal arrow rest on bow. Smaller, lighter four-vane fletching in middle is utilized with same bow and overdraw system installed. The Shear Advantage arrow, bottom, has large plastic collar which improves penetration.

tween the extreme light and extreme heavy arrows shot from a compound bow in a recent test, ranged approximately six percent. However, the range of arrow weights shown in the table is for information and heavy arrows which would tune properly to fly from the same bow at a given draw weight would fall nearer the central portion of the table. The difference in kinetic energy and efficiency would be considerably less than six percent.

It must be noted here that most of the bow reports I do concern compound bows. I recently did a bow report on a recurve bow which showed an appreciatively greater spread in the velocities of light and heavy arrows and a spread of 13.6 percent efficiency between the lightest and heaviest arrows in the table. Note that this is more than twice the loss in velocity, kinetic energy and efficiency with the light arrow and recurve bow compared to the loss with the compound.

Way back when bowyer Tom Jennings was the only bow manufacturer producing and getting the compound bow underway, he said it correctly when he stated that the compound converts more of the bow's stored energy to arrow speed than does a recurve. Velocity increase is limited on a recurve since the long limbs move seven or more inches compared to 2½ inches of limb tip travel with the short, stiff limbs on a compound.

The lesson here is that recurve bow shooters should perhaps elect to hunt with the heavy arrow. Indeed, recurve archers are usually the ones who talk heavy arrows for better penetration and rightly so. Conversely, it behooves the compound bow shooter to take advantage of his bow's capability and shoot light arrows. The information and opinions here apply to the big majority of bowhunters, those using compound bows.

Maybe we shouldn't get too scientific when talking about what arrow is best for hunting. As we have noted, there are many factors involved which are not considered by the formula for kinetic energy. I have done penetration experiments numerous times in the past. The practical lightweight arrow almost always penetrates deeper than the practical heavy arrow. By practical arrows, I mean those suited to the bow's cast which tune easily and fly properly. This usually requires that all things *not* be equal since light arrow characteristics are different than those of a heavy arrow.

Darton 45MX bow overdraw device permits arrows which are two, three or more inches shorter than normal, depending on setting.

Let me say here that there are two kinds of penetration: (1) Punch power, as through hard material such as bone and (2) penetration in soft materials. I believe the kinetic energy formula is more directly concerned with punch power and penetration in soft materials such as flesh is further enchanced or restricted by the conditions we have discussed.

As an arrow enters the target, the material is momentarily "bounced" apart and a small portion of the shaft up front slides in with less friction than is experienced further back on the shaft after the target material returns to rest. With the fast, light arrow, more of the shaft up front gets in before the big squeeze takes place.

A chronograph for measuring arrow speed always attracts plenty of archers wherever one is set up.

In making penetration tests in the past, I was amazed to find that arrows with a large ferrule and diameter ahead of the shaft penetrated deeper than other arrows. One example was the Shear Advantage arrow made by Autumn Archery in Vermont. To keep the front end of the shaft fully open for blood flow and a good trail, the special broadhead was built on a plastic collar almost one-half-inch in diameter which slipped over the forward portion of the arrow shaft. Deep penetration was apparently due to the exaggerated spread condition. Other examples are the Beman and AFC graphite shafts where the slip-over point is larger than the thin shaft diameter.

The type of broadhead has a telling effect on penetration. A large cutting diameter and a greater number of blades will decrease penetration. Low angle slicing blades are more effective than shorter blades with an obtuse angle which give a chopping action. A fixed blade broadhead sharpened to the point enhances penetration, but the flat blade may bend over when striking bone, whereas the hardened point on replaceable blade types might punch through.

Do you want great penetration? Some bowhunters don't want full penetration, but prefer that the arrow stay in the game so it will continue cutting as the shaft catches against brush during the animal's final run. Most prefer that the arrow pass completely through to afford a better blood trail from two punctures. This is especially important when hunting from a tree stand where a single hole high on the quarry may leave no blood trail from internal bleeding until sometime later.

So what's the big deal on speed and penetration? The target archer shooting known distances is little affected by all this. The bowhunter, on the other hand, needs *both* velocity and penetration. The hunter going for big-boned game at close range may opt for the big, slow arrow carrying the greatest kinetic energy and punch power. A recurve shooter should choose the heavier arrow which accepts significantly more energy from his bow. The compound bowhunter should take advantage of the fact that his bow will more directly convert stored energy to arrow velocity.

The diffference in kinetic energy between a light and a heavy arrow, both usable on your bow, is only slight. Under *most* conditions the fast arrow will afford better penetration. The biggest advantage of the small, fast arrow is more meaningful by far to 3-D target shooters and bowhunters who shoot at unknown ranges. Few of us can estimate distance exactly and flat trajectory is more forgiving of range estimating error. An error of two or three yards can mean a miss or, worse, a wound with the slow, heavy arrow, but still might be a good hit with the fast arrow.

The most important thing for a bowhunter is a vital and humane hit on game. The forgiving flat trajectory will get you this and the quarry will have less reaction time to "jump the string." Although penetration can be controlled by broadhead style selection and other means apart from arrow weight, the light arrow for compound shooters might well afford the best penetration, too. If you doubt this, add a couple of pounds to your draw weight to offset the small amount of kinetic energy traded off, spray your light arrows with a lube such as Clean Kill or Saunders Friction Fighter and go for the best of two worlds: speed *and* penetration. — *Emery Loiselle.*

Bow/Arrow Efficiency Comparison RECURVE AND COMPOUND BOW		
Arrow Weight (grains)	Recurve-Grizzly WOLVERINE 60 lb. Draw Wgt. (% Eff.)	Compound-Oregon VALIANT CRUSADER 60 lb. Peak Wgt. (% Eff.)
350	61.9	77.2
375	63.9	78.1
400	65.8	78.9
425	67.6	79.5
450	68.7	80.1
475	69.6	80.5
500	70.2	80.9
525	70.6	81.1
550	71.1	81.3
575	71.5	81.6
600	72.9	82.2
625	74.3	83.0
650	75.5	83.8
VELOCITY with *STANDARD SPECS	181 fps 71.0% Eff	215 fps 81.3% Eff.

*540 grain Arrow, 60 lb. bow, 30″ Draw.

Grizzly RECURVE bow is 13.6% more efficient with heaviest arrow.

Oregon COMPOUND bow is 6.6% more efficient with heaviest arrow.

Heavy arrow is good choice with recurve. Small drop in efficiency with compound bow makes use of small, fast arrow practical, desirable.

CHAPTER

12

BOW SIGHTS

There are many mechanical aids and gadgets which may assist the archer to hit his target with maximum accuracy.

BOWS AND ARROWS are the basic needs for the sport of archery. The next important accessory is some sort of bow sight. There are literally hundreds of sights from which one may choose. They are manufactured to fit any bow and conform to any style of shooting from a simple, basic longbow to the newest, most sophisticated overdraw-equipped fast compound.

Even those shooting primitive longbows — shooting off the shelf and aiming instinctively — actually are sighting the bow, even though it is done subconsciously. The longbow shooter must practice plenty to become proficient; more than those of us using sights.

Between no sight at all to the latest telescopic bow sight or laser beam is a large selection of sights to fit most archers' needs. Each is designed to meet certain require-

There Are Many Choices Of Sights
To Mount On Any Bow — Each Has Its Use

ments of either the bullseye target shooter or the tree stand bowhunter. For some smaller companies, a single bow sight is the extent of the product line; for the larger manufacturers, a couple dozen sight models constitute the norm.

There are sights for the target shooter with only one pin or marker; optical sights with or without magnification; crosshair sights; aperture sights; sights which automatically compensate for the aiming angle when shooting from high in a tree; lighted sights; range estimating sights; multiple pins; colored pins; light-gathering pins; dots; and circles. There are sights which extend several inches in front of the bow to provide a longer sight radius and sights that are camouflaged and protected against brush and bumps which might push the sights out of line. Colors and styles seem unlimited.

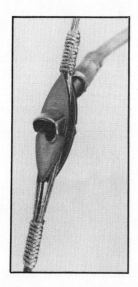

Traditional longbow shooters who do not use sights compensate for that lack by hours of practice each day. They are able to perform all sorts of amazing feats and stunts with bow and arrow, such as shooting coins out of the air; aiming with mirrors; shooting while standing, sitting, lying on the ground or from any other position. Plenty of practice with the longbow more than makes up for the lack of sights.

Most of us don't practice as much as we'd like and certainly not enough to perform some of those tricks of Howard Hill and Bob Markworth. We need a bow sight on the bow and probably a peep sight on the string.

Beginning archery students may have encountered the simple strip of paper or white tape on the bow just above the handle. By trial and error, the tape or paper was marked with pen or pencil and used as aiming lines at various ranges from the target. Each shooter would have his or her own marker; each shooter will have a different sight picture. At first, distances should be marked with a pencil so they may be changed as the archer gains experience. This is not a perfect sight system, but it does work well for beginners using school bows. Slightly upgrading the tape on the bow is a more formal sighting strip attached to the bow and marked on the white facing with pencil.

The string peep aperture, above and below, is served inside the bow string strands. Once established it must not move. Dark surgical tubing keeps the aperture in the same relationship to the eye and front sight pins on each draw. Laser sight, right, mounts on PSE bow.

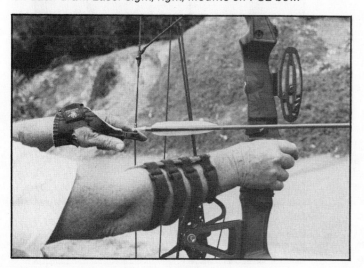

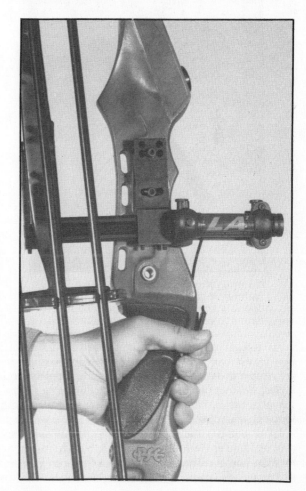

The tape may be left in place and a sight pin, a nail or other slender object slipped under the tape at appropriate locations. The pin is matched with the marks on the paper as the archer gains experience. The pins are subject to jarring and movement, with windage settings the most vulnerable. It is a technique used mostly in teaching to demonstrate how bow sights can work. Some archers use the adhesive-back paper sight tape, which has lines and spaces for yardages. Distances and windage notes are marked on the tape. As skills build, the tape markings can be changed as needed.

A more sophisticated system has a standard sight pin mounted on the bow by means of a bar or rack that is bolted to the bow riser. On the bar, the pin may be adjusted for range and windage, as needed. More advanced versions of the single pin sight are used by target archers.

Various methods of adjusting the pin or a low-magnification scope are used. Many are equipped with precise elevation markings on the bar which the archer records and duplicates each range session. More advanced models have tiny precise adjustments with locking devices to hold the pin or scope where it will not drift off the mark, as the bow is shot many times in a match.

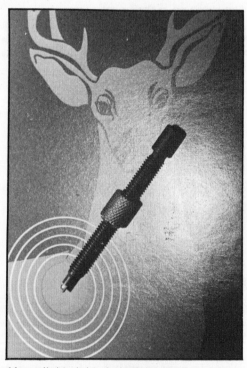

Meprolight sight pin is threaded for standard bow sight mounting, but is tipped with tritium to show brightly during low-light hunting periods.

An extension bar will place the pin well out in front of the bow for a longer sight radius. The extension bars are often adjustable in length to accommodate different shooting styles, weather conditions and bows. For some shooters, longer is better, but any unsteadiness is magnified with a long extension bar.

Extension bar sights are popular with bullseye target shooters and some 3-D competitors, but are impractical for most hunters. The long bar out front will catch on brush and branches where there is heavy undergrowth. Most

hunting requires split-second range estimation and the bow gear should be as compact and rapid to move as possible. The practical limit for an extension sight bar would be about twelve inches.

Most bowhunters will use a sight with four or five moveable pins on a protected frame. The pins are pre-set at the

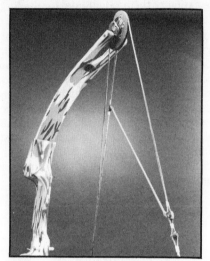

Arrowzona Archery string peep, above, uses rubber tubing attaching to compound cable. Scope-It mount, below, enables archer to use standard scope.

Below: Golden Key-Futura string peep, left, uses one bolt to hold it in place on string. Saunders' model, right, utilizes two Nok-Set rings.

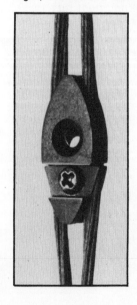

range for typical or expected hunting distances. The pins are locked in place; the locking hardware must be able to withstand vibration and shocks encountered in airplanes, buses, pickup trucks, cars, on horseback and by not-so-careful hunters. If the pins move, the hunter will miss the shot.

Hunting sight pins are set at the target range, through a process of trial and error, using known distances. Once set, the pins are locked in place for the hunt. The hunter must estimate the distance to his target accurately for the pins to do their job. The typical bow sight pin has a fully threaded shaft, colored pin head and locking nuts to hold it in place. Most hunters will set their pins for twenty, thirty, forty and fifty yards; some may opt for a ten-yard pin, depending on how flat the arrow trajectory is. Some highly experienced Western bowhunters might add a sixty-yard pin to their bows. Longer bow kills have been made successfully, but

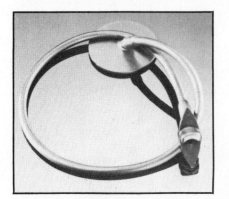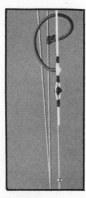

Different manufacturers take different approaches to the same problem with peeps. Above: Fine-Line's peep, tubing and limb sticker; PSE's sight and aligner. More apertures, below. Clear View, center, is always open.

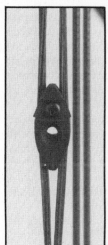

beyond that distance, luck plays a larger part.

Until development of the newer overdraw bows with fast arrows and flatter trajectories, a single set of pins — widely spaced on the sight frame — took care of most hunting or target shooting. Lately, though, this has changed. Faster, more accurate, flatter flying arrows require pin settings to be closer together; sometimes almost touching.

At times, the physical thickness of the pin assemblies is too great to allow the pin heads to crowd close enough to each other to match the ranges. Three-D target shooters do not like to rely upon "Kentucky windage," trying to guess at targets which may lie between pin settings. Sight brackets are built along two sides of the frame, so two rows of opposing pins come together in the center, the pin heads almost touching. Fine crosshair sights using thin adjustment screws also help reduce the problem.

Another development is the slanted or angled pin bar. The pins are set so the staggered tips seem almost to touch. Some light must be visible between pins or the sights will totally block out vision of the target. Some shooters shooting bows which will fling a lightweight arrow down range at more than 300 feet per second are able to eliminate a couple of pins, especially at shorter distances. Only two or three pins are required for the total range of the bow.

Most hunting and target sight setups will use pins with different colored heads to denote the various distances. Typical colors are white, red, yellow, blue and green. The archer must memorize which color is keyed to its specific range, especially when aiming at a live animal. Picking the wrong color usually will mean a miss.

Many bowhunters are in the field during early morning or early evening, hunting with less than optimum light. Regular sight pins are difficult to see against a dark, shaded background. To improve the situation, some manufacturers have used various light-enhancing techniques. Saunders Archery uses a T-shaped pin head with the long axis away from the shooter. The longer translucent head material gathers that much more existing light. Others use bright head colors, fluorescent paint or even tritium, a slightly radioactive substance, on the pin head.

Another approach is the use of fiber optics for the pins. The fiber optic tubing begins at the top of the sight frame where the most light comes from. The fiber tubing conducts the light down and curves until it faces the shooter. Maximum light reaches the archer and no artificial light is needed.

Another approach is to light the sight pins by means of tiny hearing aid batteries. The rig resembles a miniature flashlight shining on the pin heads. A red filter usually is used here to be less obtrusive to wild game — and less blinding to the shooter. If too bright, the hunter's vision will be affected; the target will not be seen. Other sights, utilizing fiber optic material, use a tiny red light on top of the fiber that results in a single red dot for a sight point.

A cautionary note is in order, though. Some states and game record clubs prohibit electronic accessories for bowhunters. This may include battery-lighted sight pins, amplified hearing devices and laser sights. Contact your state game officials before venturing afield.

Shooting downhill or uphill presents new problems for bowhunters, especially those in tree stands. Arrow trajectory to the target changes when shooting from a height of ten feet or more; the higher, the more severe the problem. These differences can be overcome with enough practice, but the hunter never knows exactly where the target will appear. Stand heights or trees may have to be changed to meet local conditions. Using sight pins set on level ground will alter the trajectory of the arrow when shot from a tree stand.

Bow sights with a pendulum pin mount will compensate for all but the highest tree stand angle. When the bow is

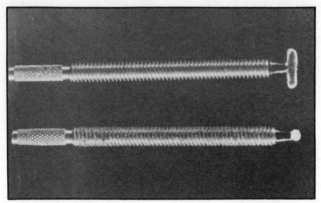

Saunders' T-Dot sight pins gather more light, transmit it through T-shaped tips, above. Full Adjust Archery offers several range-finding aperture sight pins, below.

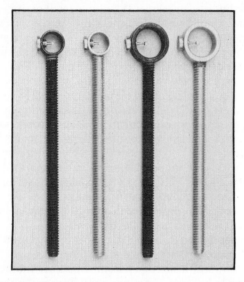

Browning Rack and Pinion sight, above, tilts pins inward to accommodate flat trajectory overdraw arrows. ProLine RF-540 dots and rings have range estimating capabilities.

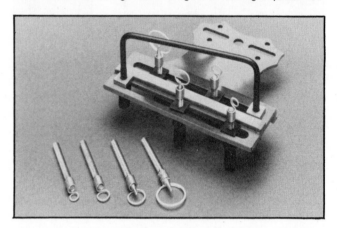

tilted downward, as from a ladder or tree stand, the plane of the pins remains constant in relation to the shooter. At ten, twenty feet or higher, the swinging pendulum sight can mean the difference in a hit or a miss. Saunders has a design which will work for any height or on the flats, equally well.

Several manufacturers, including Browning, Fine-Line and PSE, offer crosshair-type bow sights for those who prefer them. They present a sight picture familiar to rifle hunters using scope sights, but without the magnification. Crosshair sights, as with pin sights, may be adjusted for elevation and windage. On most, the windage setting remains the same for all ranges, which are adjusted independently. The horizontal hair lines may be of different colors, similar to pin sights.

Many pin variations are available to the archer. A single bead tip is but one. There are sight rings, a pin within a ring, a pin on top of a ring, a pin on top or below the shaft, hooded pins above or below the shaft. Chek-It Products has several of these variations, each intended to assist the archer in determining correct target range to getting a good sight picture.

Sight pins with tiny spirit levels are available for target shooters and hunters. The level can be used as the ten- or twenty-yard pin and helps prevent a canted bow. Canting the bow will throw the sight settings off far enough to cause a miss beyond twenty yards.

Most hunters will add a pin guard to their bows, if hunt-

ing in brush. The guard is a lightweight curved bar that protects the sight pins from being jarred or pulled out of their settings; a disaster, should it happen. In open country, the pin guard may not be as necessary, but the pins are fragile and can be bumped against a rock, a tree or even a truck door. Pin guards can be adjustable in depth and often are removable, being held by two lock nuts.

Magnifying telescopic sights are used mostly by target shooters and have not found a great deal of favor with bowhunters. At known distances, the scope sights can help hold on a small target, but because of the arcing trajectory of arrows, the scope might be more of a problem than a help. A scope sight must be set for a specific range. If the target distance is different, the arrow will miss.

If every arrow in a set is matched carefully with the same trajectory, a low-power scope can help. There are mounts available which can be adjusted quickly for changing ranges. Some scopes used by archers are non-magnifying. The optics simply help concentrate the aiming point for the shooter. Other telescopic sights for archers are available with two to five-power magnification.

As a compromise, Chek-It Products' L.E.D. sight rings might interest some archers. The sights are single rings, each with a suspended red dot aiming point in the center. Rings are available in three sizes, designed to appear approximately the size of a deer's chest at twenty, thirty and forty yards respectively. Power for the dot is furnished

Sight Master mount and crosshair sight, left, adjust quickly to different target distances. Hunting crosshair sight from PSE, near left, positively locks in settings and is designed for fast, flat-trajectory overdraw arrows.

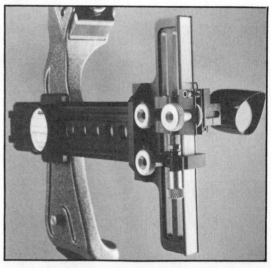

Left: Aimpoint uses firearms sight technology, special bow mount for floating dot, non-magnifying scope. PSE offers adjustable extension Terry Ragsdale target sight.

by a tiny battery carried inside the unit. The ring assembly is mounted on a standard sight pin threaded shaft to fit most any sight mount. A bowhunter might have three standard pins and one of the sight rings of the size appropriate for his anticipated hunting range.

Battery powered aiming dots, similar to those found in pistol sights, have also been tried on bows, but with the same restrictions as scope sights.

Another firearms development tried on bows is the laser sight. It may be adapted to archery by using scope rings and mounts offered by several manufacturers. Laser sights are considered electronic instruments and as such may not be legal for hunting in some states. Lasers work well with flat-trajectory firearms bullets, but will have limited application with archers because of arrow flight characteristics.

A bow sight or laser works well if the archer draws the bow exactly the same for each shot, uses the same anchor point and gets the same sight picture. However, that may not ever be possible for many of us. One needs a rear sight; a peep sight.

One archery instructor explained to a reluctant student, "If you were shooting a rifle, it would be foolish to aim it without a rear sight. The rear sight for an archer is a peep sight installed on the bowstring."

The string peep is a small plastic or metal housing interwoven into the strands of the string. Once in place, it may be served or even bolted in place so it cannot move. Several aperture sizes and styles are available, for the hunter and for the target archer. Generally speaking, the bowhunter will want a larger aperture for a larger field of view at moving game.

Close observation of the bowstring during the draw will reveal that the string tends to rotate to some extent. As this happens, the peep sight also turns. Something must be done to ensure the aperture arrives at the shooter's eye exactly the same for each shot.

With luck and a bit of experimentation, the string peep can be installed and turn just right each time. But to make sure, most peeps are installed with a string aligner attached. The aligner is a length of black surgical tubing or tubing and string that extends from the peep to the bow limb or riser. The tubing keeps the peep aperture in the optimum location as it is drawn back.

Each person is physically different, so the string peep must be mounted at the right height with no strain to see through it. It has to be eye level. Before the peep is locked in place, it should be moved up and down a bit and tested by the archer who will be shooting. Some shooters measure the height, recording it to simplify future installations.

Most archers find the addition of string peep has a dramatic effect on their accuracy and group sizes. Sight alignment and sight picture improve to the point that groups shrink considerably from any distance.

Nothing takes the place of adequate and dedicated practice, but good sights can improve most performances.

ARCHERY ACCESSORIES

There Are Jillions Of Goodies Available To Shooters Today, And Here Are A Few!

Author's Browning compound is fitted with in-line quiver for ease of transportation/arrow resupply. Note that the broadhead hood doesn't enclose razor-sharp heads all the way; thus, you must be constantly vigilant — or ouch!

PERHAPS YOU CAN remember when it was possible to go afield without all sorts of accessories hanging off of your bow and body. Photos of men like Fred Bear with tons of game collected without stabilizers, bowsights, bow quivers, et cetera, show it can be done.

But were these "the good old days?" Is archery more enjoyable to successful archers today than it was twenty or thirty years ago? The answer to this is doubtless, "yes."

What follows here is a compilation by bowhunter/editor Mark Thiffault of just a few of the accessories available to bowhunters and target shooters today. It will whet your appetite and send you straight on to a retailer where you can feast on what you find!

BOW CASES

The variety of cases and quivers available to the archer today is truly staggering — not nearly so many are the accessories available, but a veritable horn of plenty nonetheless. And they're necessary, too! Without a case, you risk damage to a sophisticated bow, not to mention the potential loss of myriad essential bits and pieces like broadheads, extra nock points, fletching or vanes, and suchlike.

For ease of classification, let's divide bow cases into hard and soft types. A hard case will be made usually of hard plastic or even metal, and is most forgiving of rugged handling. The soft cases are easier to transport, lighter in weight, capable of expanding to accommodate extra goodies and cheaper.

So what do you need? Fortunate bowhunters have both.

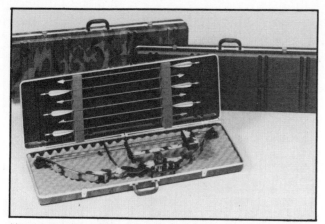

Hard case like Hoppe's Protecto Speedbow will handle the rigors of airline travel better than soft case, and has foam notches for arrow storage in lid (above). Browning's Archers-Armour polyethylene case stands upright like your suitcase when closed. It carries arrows inside, also.

If you're flying to your bowhunting spot, or carrying your tackle in the car, a hard case ensures it will arrive as it departed, with no unintentional adjustments of sights, plungers, or other integral components. Once in camp, the lighter, easier-to-carry soft case will suffice to house your bow and equipment when not out in the field.

First, let's look at hard cases long enough to handle your bow. The Bow Guard case is made by the same folks who produce the popular line of Gun Guard pistol and rifle cases. Of injection-moulded plastic with a game scene produced in the exterior, the Bow Guard brown case features sliding closures and thick foam padding. Hook and loop fastener straps are adjustable to position any bow and hold it solidly. The top of the case is made to accommodate up to two dozen arrows. It also is furnished with a small, square case for accessories like broadheads; this small case, too, is foam-filled and slotted to hold three- or four-bladed heads. The handle of the small case is slotted to act as a broadhead wrench — saves wear and tear on the fingers!

The Protecto Speedbow hard case, marketed by Hoppe's, has latch closures with eggshell foam bedding for your expensive bow. By alternating the fletched end with the business end, the lid of the Hoppe's case will hold two dozen arrows. One-third smaller than most bow cases, the Protecto is made with a Thermo pressure process that's finished either in Woodland camouflage or black that won't chip, peel or crack. There are eight other hard cases in Hoppe's line, too.

Browning's "Archer's-Armour I" bowcase has an impact-resistant polyethylene case and legs that hold it upright like luggage. The eggshell foam padding keeps the bow under control and away from the sixteen arrows you can pack on the other side. It has four latches that keep the lid closed and there are padlock holes through the handle.

For the accessory items you must take to camp, don't overlook a broadhead box like the one from MTM Moulded Products. A pair of ethafoam inserts rigidly hold up to twenty heads, plus there's a compartment for tools, extra goodies and spare parts. The box snaps shut with an integral locking system and the top is fitted with a handle. It's dust and moisture-proof when closed, too.

Cloth-type soft cases are numerous and available in a variety of finishes; mostly camouflage to match the hunter's favorite pattern. For example, Fieldline's Cordura bow case has lots of accessory pockets, a Trebark camo pattern, a self-healing nylon zipper and a nylon-lined inner compartment for the compound of your choice. It is padded with half-inch, open-cell foam.

Hoyt USA, well known for the bows it makes and markets, offers a forty-nine-inch compound bow case available either in Woodland camouflage or black. Padded with foam, the nylon, twin-handled case has three accessory pockets built-in, plus arrow storage. A heavy-duty zipper keeps it closed.

Kolpin Manufacturing has been making rifle scabbards

Soft cases like this from Fieldline have strap handles, zipper closures and exterior pouches for accessories like arrows, shooting gloves, etc.

MTM's accessory box has ethafoam broadhead sections, plus small plastic box to hold field points, nocks, etc. (above). An accessory box is integral to the Bow Guard hard case used by editor Roger Combs (right). Arrows are stored in lid, bow on foam and accessory box in cutout.

out of Berlin, Wisconsin, for many years and also offers a Deluxe Michigan Hunter soft case in Woodland camouflage measuring either forty-six or fifty-two inches in length. The durable, green corduroy interior is padded with Tuflex, and your bow is kept safe with a full-length polyester coil zipper. There are two large side pockets for accessories and, hey — if it's good enough for Michigan bowhunters, it'll satisfy anyone.

The NK-112 Sierra measures fifty-three inches long by eighteen inches wide with single-zipper closure. The bow compartment is padded with half-inch-thick foam and is Sherpa-lined, and there are brass cable guard grommets to prevent abrasions. The case, available in assorted colors and camouflage finishes, has two external accessory compartments, one for arrows and the other for small items. Luggage-style handles make carrying this Cordura case a breeze. It's from Klasic Kase by NEET Products.

Ranging, Inc., has a new accessory bag that swallows up an enormous amount of gear. It's a soft bag that features a detachable fanny pack. Crafted of nylon for durabiity and water repellency, the bag is furnished with an ethaforam container for storing broadheads, thus extending the life of the bag. Lots room for blades, nocks, and the like.

Bear Super 7 bow quiver has wraparound storage for seven hunting shafts and comes in a variety of camo finishes.

Other mainline manufacturers also offer bow cases. Bear Archery has five different soft models, three with Realtree camo finish, another with Woodland camo and one that's solid black. They carry one or two bows, with padded compartments, double handles and pouches for arrows and accessories.

QUIVERS

In the old days, quivers were used exclusively to carry arrows. They still are — but quivers today serve other functions, too.

An inexpensive, tube-type hip quiver is something every archer should own, although you probably won't take it afield when bowhunting. When you're target practicing at the range or in the backyard, a hip quiver eliminates the need for stuffing the arrows into your back pocket, poking them in the ground, or laying them flat. This writer's is the voice of a sorry, but wiser shooter — don't use any of these three methods. I managed to destroy fletching on a half dozen arrows and camouflage shafts are hard to see on the ground. Stepping on them does wonders for accuracy!

The adoption of a hip quiver serves another purpose, although most shooters may not recognize it outright. Procuring a hip quiver during early practice sessions is a sign that you're serious about archery, that you're getting started the right way. Archery and eventually bowhunting require much more than simply shooting a few arrows and heading afield. A little thing like using a hip quiver instead of chewing up arrows is an important indication of your serious-

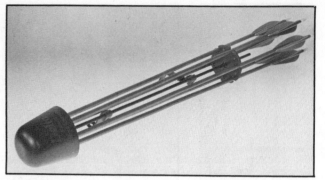

Left: On Bear's Olympus quiver, eight shafts are held in line beneath a foam-padded hood. (Above) Delta uses aircraft-grade aluminum for all but round dome for broadheads rubber gripper that holds even carbon arrows; used on longbows with hook, loop fastener.

ness. It will extend into your other required purchases, too.

But first, let's look at the quivers you can buy for mounting on your bow, carrying on your hip or packing on your back.

The tube-type hip quiver, as stated, is generally unacceptable for hunting uses; except for traditional longbow hunters. Not only would it be noisy as the shafts clank around, but broadheads would soon make their way through the bottom of the leather or vinyl material — ouch! And there's the problem of snagging on brush...all in all, tube-type hip quivers are usually unsatisfactory off the range.

NEET Products in Sedalia, Missouri, has a new 107 Field Quiver available in a variety of camo finishes that features a swivel belt loop for right- or left-side wear. Both the 107SR — 12½ inches long — and LR — fifteen inches — hold seven arrows. Moulded bottom has a foam insert, too.

The Grand Slam hip quiver from Trautman's Outdoor Creations is like a hip-mounted bow quiver, in that the shafts are held rigidly separate, broadheads secured in a foam chunk that's inside a plastic housing. The Grand Slam attaches to your belt strap with a hook and loop fastener for quick detachment, and there's a string that holds the base of the quiver around your leg. You still must be careful stalking, but the up-side is your bow isn't as heavy as with a bow-mounted quiver. Chuck Adams' Hip Quiver is of similar construction, made of tough, thick genuine leather.

In some camps weight is one of the drawbacks with bow quivers, especially with today's already heavy compound bows. Dwight Schuh, a noted bowhunter and writer, feels just the opposite — that the weight of a bow quiver substitutes for a stabilizer, the added weight increasing stability and preventing torque. "The quiver also absorbs some of the energy that vibrates through a bow, and helps to quiet the bow," he writes in his best-selling *Bowhunter's*

Traditional archers forego modern innovations, and prefer back or shoulder quiver. These are noisier, however (left). Bowhunting author Stan Warren strapped bow quiver to his compound hunting cornfield 'tails.

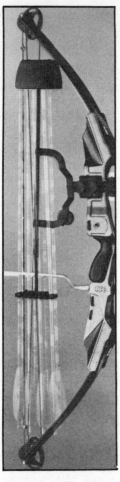

Saunders' Trophy Taker quiver (far left) is built with the arrow gripper independent from dome, holds broadheads. This reduces noise. Bow quivers are choice of most tree-stand hunters, as little motion required to nock second shaft...important only if you might miss with first shot, of course!

Encyclopedia. "In essence, a solid tight bow quiver performs some of the functions of a stabilizer."

Most archers are willing to make the tradeoff. Vision is unaffected and you can quickly nock another arrow. You also need to concentrate only on how you carry one item — your bow — through brush; not your bow *and* your quiver.

The best bow quivers are made of rigid plastic, steel or aluminum and are able to be mounted solidly with screws to your riser. You don't want it loose, making noise as you're sending an arrow toward a trophy. The rubber- or foam-filled cap that is "home" for the business end of your broadhead-mounted arrows should be generous in size; capacity of six to eight arrows minimum, plus the shroud must completely encapsulate your broadheads. If not, you'll endanger yourself or others and dull the broadheads to boot.

Bear's Olympus In-Line Quiver holds eight arrows and broadheads of any size within the foam-filled protective dome. Rubber arrow grippers hold aluminum arrows, and an adapter is available for carbon arrows. In black or Jennings camouflage pattern, the quiver's main bar is anodized for a lifetime's use. In fact, it features a lifetime guarantee!

The Pro Series bow quivers from Xi Compound Bows feature a unique dual locking system to assure a rigid, quiet connection. The hooded broadhead protector accepts larger-blade broadheads and stays pliable in sub-zero weather.

Saunders offers a nice array of bow quivers, including the Trophy Taker. Ever conscious of noise, Chuck Saun-

ders had his people develop a quiver that has the broadhead-holding protective dome independent from the arrow shaft grippers. The foam absorbs bow vibration to prevent vane noise and each broadhead is held independently in the thirteen-ounce quiver.

Quick-detachability is a feature of the Ben Pearson six-arrow bow quiver. A bracket is firmly screwed to the riser and the moulded quiver slides onto it. Your quick-detach bow quivers tend to be a little noisier than screw-mounted quivers when shooting with the quiver attached, but if

Darton's Aeromag, available in black or leaf camo, lets archers cant bow quiver forward, backward or in the conventional vertical position. It holds five arrows.

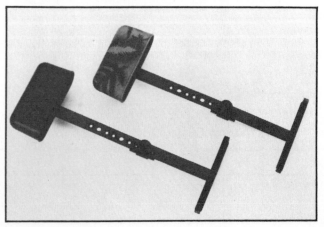

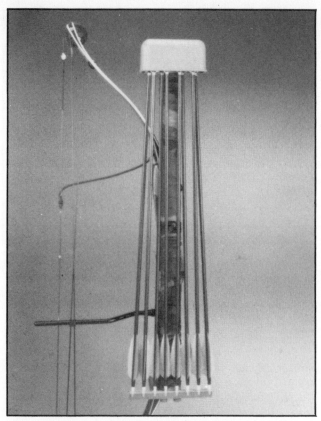

Fine-Line bow quiver is adjustable for different shaft lengths. Eight shafts are held in spacious-domed top.

you're going to hunt from a tree stand where you can remove the quiver, this isn't a problem.

Down Tucson way, the folks at PSE — that stands for Precision Shooting Equipment — have developed an all-aluminum Elite QD bow quiver. Unique in that it has an adjustable height, the in-line quiver holds eight broadhead-tipped shafts in its oversize, foam-laden dome. When the foam needs replacement, it's done easily.

Martin Archery's Super Quiver features innovations such as three compartments with snap-on lids on top of the dome for scent pads, face paint or small parts. There's a built-in broadhead wrench in the hood, plus two external arrow clips for blunts or flu-flu arrows. The Super Quiver holds eight shafts in line with rubber arrow grippers and is available in black or camouflage finish.

Bob Eastman developed the Gametracker bow quiver that detaches for easy transport. The dovetail mount and front locking rod accommodate any size broadhead with good fletching clearance. You get a built-in broadhead wrench and capacity for six arrows.

If you have more than one bowhunter in your home, and their draw lengths call for different shaft lengths, you might consider the Fine-Line adjustable bow quiver that holds arrows from twenty-four to thirty-six inches long. Eight arrow capacity, domed broadhead receptacle and vibration-free performance.

Some bowhunters prefer a different angle to their quivers. After experimenting, they find it easier to draw and shoot with the quiver tilted slightly forward or back, not parallel to the bow. If you're one of these shooters, then the new

Darton Aeromag quiver is for you. This camo or black, five-arrow quiver uses a dovetail mounting system that allows you to choose three quiver angles: canted forward, backward or parallel. It's adjustable for various arrow lengths, too.

Aircraft-grade aluminum is used for the entire Delta Industries' bow quiver except for two parts: the round broadhead dome and the plastic arrow shaft gripper. The different-looking quiver will hold a half dozen arrows and the shaft gripper is adjustable for carbon or aluminum shaft diameters. It fits most AMO standard bows and uses hook and loop fasteners for longbows.

The first time I heard noted bowhunter Jim Dougherty list what he totes to a tree stand in his Catquiver, I was sure I had misheard: light sleeping bag? Lots of dry socks? Extra outerwear? Granola and candy bars? How in hell was he gonna pack all of that in a quiver?

Clearly, the Catquiver is an arrow-holding device, plus much more. It also is a backpack that's now in its fifth evolution, using an S-curved aluminum frame system that will support up to one hundred pounds. It is adjustable to ride below shoulder level and the arrow holder carries a dozen broadhead-tipped shafts. Jim contends he can draw and nock an arrow as quickly from his Catquiver as from a bow quiver. It must've taken a lot of practice, since many of us have trouble scratching our own backs with sticks!

It would be a shame to void all the good effects of the camo outfit with a noisy hip or back quiver. See text.

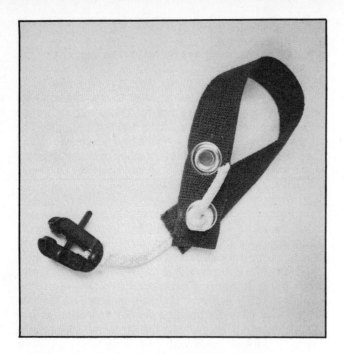

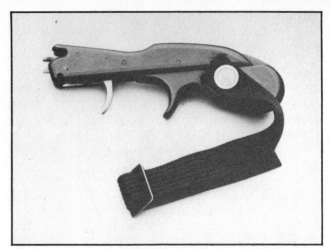

With the Catquiver, the broadheads and nocks are held firmly in foam-filled cups at both ends; the Catquiver and St. Charles back quivers both are adjustable in length. Thus, your fletching stays dry and you're toting enough shafts for an extended hunt. There is no free lunch, however. The average bowhunter will find shafts longer than thirty-three inches extend down to his *gluteus maximus,* or sticking up over his head. Also, you're limited by the construction of the arrow holder to shafts of a single length; thus, you can't carry blunts or practice arrows of a shorter length than your hunting arrows.

The Catquiver is a high-tech relative of Robin Hood's old shoulder quiver and this reach-over-and-draw quiver still is used by bowhunters. Traditional bowhunters, guys who shun compounds and recurves in favor of the straight sticks called longbows, will use heavy leather back or shoulder quivers like those made by Dan Quillian. This Athens, Georgia, accessory maker uses heavy cowhide lacing to keep the latigo parts together.

With a little practice, you can pull out and nock an arrow quick as lightning; or any other way. The drawbacks to shoulder quivers are they're noisy because the arrows smack together as you move around, they get hung up when you're bending low to clear brush and there's lots of eye-catching movement involved with drawing a new shaft after a shot. But remember: A quartet named Pope, Young, Bear and Hill used this quiver most if not all of their shooting lives and did fair to middlin' on game.

RELEASE AIDS

There really are two types of releases: mechanical, using some type of aid, and "manual," although the latter term is an invented category into which we place gloves and finger tabs. A calloused shooter who uses only bare

fingers would be put into the latter category, in which he can shoot with either a "live" or "dead" hand.

The difference between the two is in where the shooter's string hand ends up after the shot. If the hand stays anchored against the face when the string is released, the hand is "dead"; this is the author's style. If your hand moves farther back when the string is released, then your release technique uses a "live" hand. There's little difference in arrow performance, based on chronograph tests.

The release of the arrow is critical to its accuracy. Recognition of this is why release aids have been developed. Many archers pinch the nock when drawing the bow and a

Shooting with fingers can be as accurate as with release aids. This author uses finger tab over his camo glove.

mushy release inhibits accuracy. A mechanical release is crisp and clean — usually — but also is noisy, slower and can even be dangerous.

My first experience with the disadvantages of drawing back while using a mechanical release spooked my neighbor — and me. An earthen bank between our two properties provides an excellent backstop for the Horne EZ Pull whitetail buck target we shoot at. The property is about thirty yards wide, a nice, flat shooting lane.

John, my retired neighbor, often tends to his outdoor birdcages atop the bank while we're shooting. That is, he *used to* tend them during our shooting sessions. While fiddling with the cages, he observed the action in my yard...until, that is, he saw my mechanical release misfire. I had begun to draw an aluminum FS Arrow with an exposed-trigger type of release on the string. I accidentally triggered the device after about one-fourth pull and sent the arrow lofting gracefully into the air toward John. While it arced into the lawn well short of the target, John had seen enough. He hasn't again come out during our bow sessions.

Accidents are one reason for development of many different styles of mechanical release, and why many shooters prefer finger shooting. It's like learning to drive a stick shift instead of an automatic: If you learn the harder one first, then you can always drive the easier one. But if you learn the easier one first, you have a devil of a time with the clutch pedal and shift lever.

Most finger shooters use either a finger tab or shooting glove. The shooting glove has three leather cups into which you insert your first, second and ring fingers of the shooting hand. The glove is anchored around your wrist with some type of adjustable holder, often featuring hook and loop fastening material.

The leather protects your fingers as you draw and release. In time, the leather wears or becomes grooved where the string settles during drawing and this could ruin your smooth release. If the glove gets wet, it can drag on the string, too. Thus, many finger shooters apply talcum powder to their shooting gloves, keeping the leather friction-free.

There's also the complaint that sweaty fingers slide out of the glove ends. While you're fiddling, the trophy walks calmy away, right?

Finger grooves on Tru-Fire Magnum Custom release are suitable for most archers, and grip swivels for comfort.

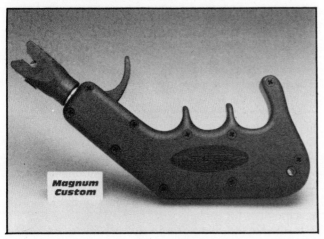

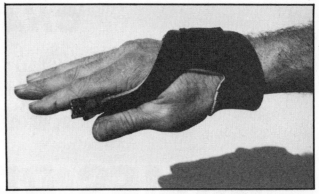

Winn Archery uses relax trigger mechanism for their all-steel release aid. This promotes smooth arrow release.

A finger tab eliminates many of these problems. It's simply several layers of leather or plastic and/or felt that protects the shooting hand while drawing and releasing the bow. It's kept on the shooting hand by inserting the middle finger through a hole in the back of the tab. It permits a smooth release shot after shot, although not as smooth as with a mechanical release.

Mechanical releases accelerate string wear, although this won't be a significant factor with most shooters. There are several "handle" types, from a wrist strap that enables the shooter to draw back with the whole arm, to a T-shaped hand grip that can be held horizontally, vertically or either. There also is a rifle-type release with a trigger guard to prevent accidental discharge.

A trigger-style release from Browning looks like a firearm without a trigger guard. The contour shape fits either hand and a wide nylon strap prevents accidental loss. Trigger travel is adjustable with a furnished Allen wrench, thus eliminating one problem with mechanical releases.

Jim Dougherty must've seen my errant shot involving neighbor John, which is the design heart of his Fail-Safe Hunter release. The trigger guard prevents the arrow being loosed by hitting a twig or branch and the trigger can't be pulled until an automatic safety device is deactivated. The trigger also is adjustable so you can duplicate rifle-like accuracy.

L.W. Lyons realizes that equal string pressure is required to prevent arrow torque, which is why they designed a center-drop jaw you activate with a side-lever. The Bulldog features a nylon strap held together with grommets and a hank of nylon rope. It weighs just five-eighths-ounce and large-fisted bowhunters may have trouble fitting the strap around their wrists without replacing the nylon rope.

Tru-Fire's Magnum Custom release is shaped with finger grooves for maximum pulling power and comfort. It swivels for use with either hand in vertical or horizontal fashion and exposed trigger adjusts easily.

Recognition of the problems with pulling or pinching arrows is why Winn Archery developed a steel release aid that has a relax trigger mechanism; that is, when the hand is relaxed, the arrow is loosed. It has a Trebark finish and is guaranteed to fit any hand or pull style.

These are just a couple of the release aids available. A trip to your local archery shop will give you lots to see and try from the major manufacturers like Bear, Saunders and others. — *Mark Thiffault*

CHAPTER 14

GAMES PEOPLE PLAY

Archery is a sport in which all competitors, men and women, even those in wheel chairs, may compete on an equal basis. Practice and technique are more important than strength. Some disabled even bowhunt.

TARGET SHOOTING may be an end in itself or a means to an end: bowhunting. Many archers shoot targets for both reasons. No matter what our reason, we all need to practice. Most archers feel they do not practice enough to shoot at their maximum capabilities. There are all types of targets and competitions available, so why not choose one which is enjoyable?

We may choose simple, informal, backyard target shooting to keep limber, to maintain archery muscles or to get ready for the game seasons. Or it might involve simply the enjoyment of shooting arrows a few minutes a day. There is nothing wrong with this activity, but many tend to become

bored in a short time and seek something more challenging. There are dozens of ways to go for the archer who wants to do something more with his new equipment.

Many young archers begin in school tournaments, shooting the bullseye-type targets, and stay with that branch of the sport for the rest of their lives. This is a sport in which a shooter can be involved into his or her seventies and even eighties; many are. This is the traditional round targets, shot with recurve, not compound bows; it's target archery. These matches may take place indoors or outside, with specific rules for each.

In the United States, target archery comes under the

When Sending Arrows Downrange Begins To Pale, There Are All Kinds Of Other Diversions Available

In areas with cold or wet winters, indoor archery meets are on tap.

who showed up on the line with new and improved gadgets on their bows or in their hands seemed to have an unfair advantage. Thus, there are categories for those with and without bow sights, those shooting finger tabs and those using mechanical releases, those with long or short stabilizers. Shooters with recurves, longbows or compounds compete only among their peers. The sport has become more than simply practice for the hunting season. It is competiton for its own sake.

Targets are paper depictions of large and small-game animals, some of fantastic size and appearance. These add spice and fun to the tournaments. Scoring rings, invisible from the shooting line, are marked on the paper targets, marked and recorded after each group has expended all arrows. Youngsters competing are permitted to shoot from shorter ranges than adults. All targets are set out in realistic hunting terrain.

From field archery, with the targets made of paper and imprinted with a number of game animal images, we move to 3-D target shooting. Here, the targets are more than

sponsorship and supervision of the National Archery Association, detailed in another chapter. Olympic archery competition in the U.S. is governed by the NAA. Strict rules are imposed to ensure the competition is between archers who use basically the same equipment under the same conditions, whether shooting in their home state or in another country against international competitors. Except for NAA-sponsored field archery events, compound bows are not permitted in these tournaments, although this is under review and may change in the near future.

Speaking of field archery, the more formal tournaments are conducted under the rules of the National Field Archery Association (NFAA) in the United States. Similar competition in other countries are under the purview of the International Field Archery Association (IFAA). Informal meets are common and tend to use rules agreed upon by the shooters.

It may seem odd to refer to formal and informal field archery, but certain rules are necessary for safety and to offer fair competition. In earlier days of the sport, shooters

The scenes above and below are of the Pete Shepley Desert Shoot-Out tournament in Tucson, Arizona. The popular meet features competition on several levels.

For added variety, the targets depicted may be of abnormal size or of animals which exist only in somebody's imagination. Monsters, prehistoric animals and life-size elephant targets have been made of foam rubber and paint. The extra-large targets are placed at distances far beyond normal arrow range. They add to the fun and challenge of the shoot.

On a typical club 3-D animal target shoot, there may be twenty-six targets in place along a forest trail. The exact number of targets is a matter of preference for the club or group putting on the tournament and depends upon how much the club can spend on targets. The course is laid out carefully so that, as archers are shooting at any specific target, they will not endanger anyone else at other targets and along the trails.

The group's management will position the targets so some are as close as ten yards; others will stretch to forty, fifty or more yards. Shots may be uphill, downhill, across canyons, between trees, over easy or difficult terrain; any type of actual hunting situation. Placement of the targets is

Three-dimensional, realistic targets may be set up in actual hunting area when animals are not in season. This tournament is held near Mammoth Lakes, California.

Practice targets are established near field archery and 3-D courses, above. Shooters, below, are free to use either/or bow, belt or back quivers for arrows.

paper prints; they are plastic and foam replicas of game animals, built to appear as realistic as possible in natural settings. Their coloring, size and poses are meant to duplicate actual hunting situations and targets.

These 3-D shoots have limited rules, except for the scoring, and have become tremendously popular with archers everywhere. Many tournaments will attract thousands of competitors for the challenge and the potential prizes. In the early Nineties, purses of up to $50,000 were not unusual.

The realistic animal targets are limited only by the imagination of the show managers and archers involved. Deer targets, for instance, may be constructed with the head up or down as if feeding, lying down as if in bed or even seeming to jump over a fence. A grouping may include does and fawns which, if hit with an arrow, will cost the competitor negative points. The animal targets may be in open, plain sight or partially hidden by brush, thus requiring the shooter to crouch down to shoot under a tree branch or other obstacle.

restricted to one or two individuals, because the distances are unmarked and unknown to competitors. Range estimation is left to the shooters.

The targets have a "kill zone" and a wound area marked on them, indistinct to the archers as they aim. Points are awarded for kill shots and wound shots. Clear misses count as no points, in most cases. Some tournaments will penalize what might be non-lethal wounding hits, by subtracting points from the score.

Fine summer weather brings out shooters who are young and old, male and female for field shoots.

Additional challenges are plenty when shooting at thrown disks, using flu-flu arrows, above. Recurve shooters without sights do better at this stop. Animal targets are marked with scoring rings, left, not visible to the shooter from hunting distances.

Small groups of shooters will travel through the course, scoring for each other, but most tournament rules do not permit discussions of the possible ranges or other aspects of the course among members of the group.

Ranges are unmarked, but wooden stakes will mark the places from which arrows are to be shot. Usually, each archer shoots two arrows at each target; one at each of two distances. The two stakes usually are placed two to four yards apart, depending upon the terrain. Some 3-D tournaments attract thousands of shooters and popularity is growing.

One group with headquarters in the Midwest, the International Bowhunting Organization (IBO), sponsors a popular series of 3-D tournaments called Bowhunters Challenge. Competition takes place in Illinois, Indiana, Ohio and Michigan each summer. The so-called world championship is at the fourth meet, with large cash prizes at stake. To qualify for the world championship, a shooter must place in the top twenty of his or her class at one of the preliminary tournaments. Prizes also are awarded at the preliminary tournaments.

Clubs across the nation are recognizing the popularity

Tournament directors with imagination are able to set up moving targets, left, appealing to archers of all ages and abilities. Most archers engaging in Olympic-type paper target shooting use recurve bows, below.

Field archery and 3-D shoots may be set up in any type of terrain, including the flat, dry Arizona desert, below.

and value of the IBO shoots and tournaments in several other states have been organized. Eventually, the championship competition actually may reflect a true national champion in the sport.

Despite the thousands of archers throughout the world who compete in archery tournaments, shooting bullseye targets from established distances under formal circumstances, millions of others seek greater variety and excitement. Some variety shoots are old; some are new; and many draw interest from thousands.

In 1987, Pete Shepley of PSE Archery in Tucson,

Arizona, decided to hold an archery tournament/event in the desert during May when the tourist season has past, but the weather has not become too hot. He called it the Desert Shootout and its popularity took off like a rocket.

Some of the popularity is the result of the time and place of the event, but part is because of the variety of the tournament. The Desert Shootout is conducted in two parts: Classes of individual archers compete in a round of target shooting, varying from twenty up to sixty-five yards.

In addition, the Team Shoot-Out round lends additional excitement. In this event, the targets are seven-inch bal-

The ultimate long-distance challenge for archers is flight shooting, below. The competitor works to get his arrow to the maximum possible range. Somewhat shorter shots are taken by 3-D novelty shooters, left.

loons set at forty-five yards. Two-person archery teams try to break two balloons each while being timed. In case of ties, speed counts.

If both shooters break both balloons, they go on to compete in the next round. If a total of three balloons break, a time penalty is imposed and the team goes on to the next round. Break two or less balloons and the team is out.

Each archer may compete on five teams with five different partners, so an "out" with one partner does not end the competition. It gets exciting as the competition is keen and cash prizes reach thousands of dollars for the top teams. The event is spreading to other parts of the country and other clubs.

Another tournament with thousands of dollars in prizes is sponsored by the Archery Manufacturers Organization (AMO) and is known as the Bowhunters' Challenge. This game combines skill, speed and accuracy needed by bowhunters. The course is laid out so the action is in view of engrossed spectators.

Commissioner of Archery, Dr. James Shubert, says, "The ultimate goal of the Bowhunters' Challenge is to pave the way for future sanctioned competitions at the local club level throughout the country. As participation increases, so do the benefits to the local clubs, national consumer organizations, local retailers and manufacturers."

Another novelty event, sponsored by the National Archery Association, is flight shooting. This event is simply shooting an arrow as far as possible without regard to accuracy. Special flight bows, regular compound bows, longbows and primitive bows compete within their classes. These events are held in the desert Southwest, usually in Nevada or Utah, and are attended only by a dedicated few.

Other types of competition will be invented from time to time, limited only to the imagination of the archers. Within the bounds of safety, there is almost no limit to the games archers can play.

SKI ARCHERY

Ski Out Of The Winter Doldrums Into This New Sport

IF YOU'RE looking for a way to keep your bowhunting skills sharp in the dead of winter, but indoor leagues aren't your thing, try archery's newest twist — ski-arc — a combination of cross-country skiing and archery marksmanship.

Ski archery is popular in western Europe where there is an established archery biathlon tour, but only recently has it made its appearance in the United States. Mike Hillis, president of Easton Aluminum's Salt Lake City division, heard about the sport while attending the winter Olympics in Calgary. He thought it sounded like a good counter-seasonal activity for bowhunters and other outdoor archery enthusiasts. So with the help of other Utah archers, they staged the first official U.S. Ski Archery competition at the Utah Winter Games on January 1, 1989.

Ski-arc is similar to biathlon; the Olympic sport of cross-country skiing and rifle marksmanship. At the Utah competition racers started at one minute intervals, skied a one kilometer loop to the range, shot four arrows, skied a 3.5 kilometer loop, returning to the range for four more arrows, then skied a half-kilometer to the finish. Shooting was done from the standing position at a thirty-centimeter target face at a range of thirty meters. Competitors carried their bows, but arrows were left at the range. Scoring was either a hit or a miss. And woe to those who completely missed the back-

Mike Hillis, president of Easton, Salt Lake City, used a compound bow, was third in Master Men group, above. Christopher Schork, right, was first in Open Men. He maneuvers bow back into backpack carrier.

SKI ARCHERY is not a new sport, except in the United States. The better-known biathlon, a combination of cross-country skiing and rifle shooting had its origin with winter military operations. Ski archery may not have real military origins, but the discipline required to do well might be similar.

Obviously, the sport can be conducted only in locations which have enough consistent snow and the proper terrain for cross-country skiing and people who can ski and shoot arrows. Given the right backing, this is a sport that could become popular during long winters.

Judith Strom attended one of the first events in Utah and came back with this report.

Winter clothing, skis and archery equipment varies according to the background, experience of archers.

There were Olympians present. Above, Ed Eliason, an Olympics archer, skates away from range on narrow skis. He finished second in Masters. First in the Women's Open category, was Marsha Groth, at the range, below.

ing target and had to search for arrows in the snow. Bright fletching is a must!

There were no equipment restrictions, permitting competitors to use a wide variety of commercially available archery and ski equipment. The skiers ran the gamut from traditional diagonal striders to cross-country racers using the newest skating styles. Archery equipment ranged from traditional recurves to hunting compounds. The biggest topic of discussion was about the best way to carry the bow. Sponsors provided specially designed backpacks used by many of the competitors, while other tried modifications of backpacker's frame packs and variations of the sling system used by biathletes for their rifles.

Since the participants came from the ranks of both skiers and archers, the scoring system was based half on skiing time and half on marksmanship. In each of the six classes — Master, Open, and Junior for both men and women — the fastest skiing time earned 100 points, with everyone else's time divided into the fastest time to get their points. If the fastest time was eighteen minutes, then thirty-six minutes would get fifty points. In the marksmanship section, eight hits earned 100 points, seven hits was 87.5 points, six hits was seventy-five points, et cetera. To do well, competitors had to have some proficiency at both skiing and shooting.

Ski archery was well received in its U.S. debut and interest has blossomed across the United States, Ski-archery returned to the 1990 Utah Winter Games and six other states also held state championshiips. The first national championship was in Utah.

Ski archery has plenty of potential for any area with snow. Fancy facilities aren't needed. A golf course can provide plenty of space for a ski loop and range area. It would seem to be an ideal way to keep in good condition in winter and may introduce archery to a new group of outdoor types — *Judith Strom*

CHAPTER

15

THE MAKERS

The Business Of Archery Depends Upon Tradition As Much As On Modern, High-Tech Production

ARCHERY is a hobby or sport to most of us, but it is also a major industry to those who are involved in the manufacturing, importing, shipping and selling of all the products we call bows and arrows. It requires thousands of production and marketing employees throughout the world to make sure everything we may need is available at our local archery pro shop or listed in that big mail order catalog.

For the most part, the industry is a child of the Twentieth Century. While the history of bows and arrows goes back before the recording of such events, most, if not all, the bow and accessory companies in business today trace their roots back no farther than the Twenties and Thirties; most are considerably younger.

In the days when Art Young and Saxton Pope were learning modern bowhunting from the American Indian, Ishi, most archery equipment was homemade. There were some professional bowyers, but not many.

Until the invention of the compound bow, all bow production was, of course, longbows or recurves. There were companies producing standard bows for sale and many of them are still in business. Doug Easton was producing his aluminum arrow shafts in the Thirties and they were being used in national and international archery tournaments everywhere.

There was a beginning rise in bowhunting activity in some states before World War II, but it was not universally accepted. It was not until after the war that archers and state game commissions became convinced that the bow and arrow was a viable hunting arm. Bowhunting spread across most states and manufacturers rushed to meet the demand for equipment.

It was the invention and acceptance of the compound bow that helped bring about the dramatic growth in archery, particularly bowhunting. As of the early Nineties, there are an estimated 2½ to three million bowhunters in the United States. That is a rough estimate, based upon the number of archery hunting licenses sold in some states. Some states do not distinguish bowhunters from others and the figures may be considerably larger than three million.

The industry recognizes the potential for customers here. True, not every bowhunter or target archer buys a new bow every year, but many do. It is an easy assumption that most archers will buy at least a dozen new arrows a year, some arrowheads, spare strings, camo paint, one or more tree stands and dozens of other accessories. It is big business in the United States and Canada.

Foreign competition is a factor in any industry and archery is no exception. Bows and equipment have been made for years in some countries, particularly England with its tradition of archery and longbowmen. More recently, product competition has come from such nations as France, Germany, Korea and others with relatively low labor costs or high labor efficiency.

The following is not intended to be a comprehensive compilation of all the firms in the archery industry; far from it. It is a brief look at a few representative, progressive companies; where they came from and how they got there.

BEAR ARCHERY

With The Name Of The Best-Known Modern Bowhunter, The Company Remains At The Forefront

The Bear Archery production plant in Gainesville, Florida is a far cry from the garage in Detroit where founder Fred Bear, right, began the business.

THE BEAR ARCHERY company cannot be discussed without reference to the founder, Fred Bear. Although the man did not have control of the company for the last several years of his life, he was responsible for its start and its overall direction. Though dead, Fred Bear still influences the philosophy of the firm.

It is difficult, if not impossible, to find one man who has had more influence on the sport and industry of archery than Fred Bear. He died in Gainesville, Florida, of natural causes after a long illness in April 1988. He suffered from emphysema and congestive heart failure.

Bear worked in his office nearly every day until the end of his life. He continued to travel the country promoting the sport of bowhunting that he loved so well and over which he had so much influence.

Born in a snowstorm in Waynesboro, Pennsylvania, on March 5, 1902, Bear moved to Detroit in the early 1920s, where he found work as a pattern maker for the Packard Motor Car Company. In 1927, he saw an Alaska adventure film made by Arthur Young and soon afterward had the occasion to meet Young. The two became friends and shot together at the Detroit Archery Club.

Young helped Fred Bear in his early attempts at making equipment and Bear soon went into business with a friend and founded the Bear Archery Company in 1933.

His worldwide bowhunting adventures carried him across North America, to Africa, India and South America. In the early days, he carried his own cameras and notebooks to record his adventures and the outdoors he loved so much. In later years, professional movie and television crews accompanied him. He was a frequent star of the *The American Outdoors* television program, as well as such programs as *The Tonight Show, The Mike Douglas Show, To Tell The Truth* and many others. More than two dozen

The day this aerial view was taken of the Bear Archery plant, the parking lot was full with employees' vehicles.

Interior view of Bear factory shows part of more than three hundred workers assembling bows, accessories.

films recount his worldwide bowhunting trips.

At the end, Fred Bear was presiding as chairman of the board of Bear Archery Company.

In 1946, the firm was incorporated and, with Bear as president, was re-named Bear Archery Company. Bear turned out custom bows, adding twelve other employees, most of whom worked with leather, to make shooting gloves, armguards and quivers.

Bowhunting was solidly established and the need was apparent for education in the proper methods of hunting with the bow and in selling its merits to the various state game and fish departments. Groundwork in this field was to make inroads on Bear's time over many years. He found

The Fred Bear Museum is located nearby Bear factory, catering to Florida visitors, archers from everywhere.

it necessary not only to create new products, but to create a market for them. He quickly learned that newspapers and magazines were interested in stories and photographs of game obtained with the bow and arrow. The fact that bowhunting has achieved the status and recognition it now enjoys among legislators, conservationists, game biologists and sportsmen is due largely to Bear's early personal efforts.

By the end of World War II, Fred Bear had decided his growing archery business was too big for the Detroit location. He also desired a closer source of raw material, such as northern maple along with a more readily accessible outdoor community. He chose Grayling, Michigan, two hundred miles to the north. The one-time lumbering and sawmill town was located on the famed AuSable River and seemed an ideal place to manufacture archery equipment and to enjoy the out-of-doors as well. The move was made in 1947. At that time, the company employed about thirty people.

Fred Bear was directly responsible for the development of design and manufacturing processes utilized by all present-day makers of high-quality archery bows. His creativity made it possible to mass-produce bows and arrows. He was awarded many patents relating to the manufacture of archery items, including the use of parallel fiberglass for both facing and backing on bows, electronic bow presses for assembly, contour sanding machines, the first archery glove, armguard and bow quiver, the first true take-down bow, a Converta-point arrow system and the Bear Razorhead, perhaps the most popular hunting head of all time. His patents covering materials and methods have in one way or another benefitted nearly all of today's bowmakers.

From the 1950s into the 1970s, Bear embarked on a series of expeditions over four continents to prove the worth of his product design and of the bow as a legitimate hunting arm.

In 1968, following a series of plant expansions in response to an ever-growing demand for Bear products, Fred Bear sold his company to Victor Comptometer Corporation. Bear remained as company president.

In 1977, Victor Comptometer was taken over by Walter

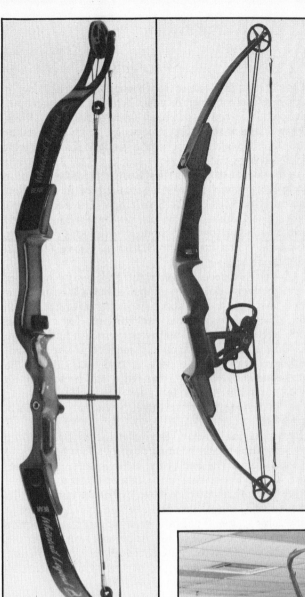

Kidde & Company, Incorporated. That same year, further expansion was coupled with a move from Michigan to Gainesville, Florida. The move was accomplished in the fall of 1978.

The Gainesville facility, designed and built to produce quality archery tackle, houses environmental control systems to regulate temperature and humidity, a specialized dust collection system and an electrostatic varnish system. The research and development department is complete with high speed filming equipment, oscilloscope, mechanical shooting machines, chronographs and other devices for material evaluation and performance. Yet, hand craftsmanship remains the key phase in the construction of fine archery tackle.

The company now employs some 350 men and women who turn out some two million bows and a like number of arrows annually for their worldwide market.

In 1983, Bear Archery acquired Jennings Compound Bows and the rights to produce all Jennings designs and products. The chief designer was and is Tom Jennings, another pioneer in modern archery development. He has become an important cog in the new Bear/Jennings combine. Jennings is one of the early experimenters and developers of the compound bow.

Jennings' innovative designs have always found favor with a number of archers around the world. His Unistar compound bow is unique. The Unistar puts the compound eccentric cam in the center of the bow, rather than at the end of the limbs. The wheels at the limb tips are merely pulleys to change the direction of the cables. The compounding action takes place at an odd-shaped, almost a figure eight-shaped cam at the center. Despite its strange appearance, the bow is extremely smooth and fast to shoot, popular with many bowhunters.

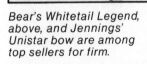

Bear's Whitetail Legend, above, and Jennings' Unistar bow are among top sellers for firm.

Some of Fred Bear's hunting trophies and early archery equipment are on display at the Fred Bear Museum.

BROWNING ARCHERY

BROWNING. The name may conjure up excellent shotguns, handguns, and rifles to some, comfortable boots to others, fly-fishing gear or archery products to the rest. Browning has it all. The man who started the company was John M. Browning, an inventor and, some say, a firearms genius. Many of his designs have not been surpassed and are still in use after more than a century.

This is not to say the company has not progressed in a hundred years. Browning produces innovative archery products based on the best of tradition and the newest in technology. Based in Utah, Browning Archery is committed to developing and building modern, fast-shooting bows and related equipment for target archers and bowhunters. The gear includes bows, arrows, accessories, clothing, knives; everything the archer needs.

How innovative is the company? As of 1990, Browning had obtained more than sixteen U.S. patents in archery equipment design and more are pending. Much of this development, for at least the past three decades, may be traced to Browning's chief archery equipment designer, Marlow Larson. Larson is also a top tournament shooter who may be seen at many of the largest competitions around North America. He has been known to adjust his Browning work schedule around the tournament schedules and hunting seasons so he can test some of his developments in the field.

Corporate and manufacturing headquarters are located in the rural town of Morgan, Utah, about an hour's drive from Salt Lake City. Morgan is not a place where one might expect to find an international corporation located. The countryside is noted for its hunting and fishing opportunities and the corporate headquarters are built around a hunting lodge of some years ago. The walls are still covered by many hunting trophies from around the world, taken by Browning workers over the years. Archery equipment production takes place about a block from the corporate offices. Every phase of receiving, processing, producing, testing and shipping takes place in the archery manufacturing facility at Morgan.

In the decade of the Nineties, Browning is moving ahead with several major innovations in the bow line. Marlow Larson is responsible for Browning's patented Kenetic Cams, now installed on several new bows. The Kenetic Cam is found on long and short draw versions of the Pro-Competition and Pro Comp SD bows. The result is fast and flat arrows.

Another new development is the Torque Synchronizer, found on several Browning compound bows. It is an adjustment device positioned about six inches down from each cam, designed to time the cam roll-over for maximum arrow accuracy. It also equalizes stress on the limb tips, all the while ensuring true cam alignment. The Torque Synchronizer loops a single cable around both sides of the cam, equalizing forces on the limbs and preventing tip twist, eliminating the tendency for cams to tilt. Browning says the device will impart target bow accuracy to hunting bows.

Browning has moved to the inelastic Fast Flight string system with a patent-pending design called the Ballistic String System. The end of the cable locks into the cam itself. Then a Fast Flight string loop connects to the cable at the cam with an attachment groove on the cable end. In the event of a string failure, there is little chance of damage to the cable system. The bow is ready to shoot again simply by restringing it. There is no loss of peak weight over the four-inch draw length adjustment with the system in use.

These days, most compound bow risers are designed to

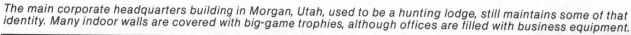

The main corporate headquarters building in Morgan, Utah, used to be a hunting lodge, still maintains some of that identity. Many indoor walls are covered with big-game trophies, although offices are filled with business equipment.

Innovations, High-Tech Combine With The Traditional For A Full Line Of Modern Archery Equipment — And More!

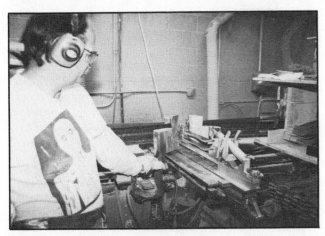

Matched pairs of Browning recurve limbs are held in jig as they are sandpapered. Operation is fast and accurate.

Laminated wood riser is drilled to specifications.

accommodate some sort of overdraw unit to shoot shorter, lighter, faster arrows. One problem has been that some overdraw devices are too long, causing the cable or string to strike the shelf — or the arrow fletching, if too long. Browning has a standard overdraw and a shorter model called the Compact Ultimate overdraw.

The Compact is designed to fit bows with shorter fist-mele, such as Browning's own Mirage series. The regular device permits an arrow of five inches shorter than normal,

while the Compact will accommodate four-inch overdraw. The Compact also may be mounted on bows with higher fistmele, if the archer does not wish to shoot an arrow shorter than four inches less than normal.

In addition, there are Browning overdraw attachments, quivers, several sights, targets, release aids, bow cases (hard or soft), bow tools, bowfishing accessories and the well known line of Browning hunting clothing and boots.

Recurve limbs are painted in spray booth, below, using carefully controlled colors. Camouflage finish is sprayed in another area. Skilled worker operates machine, right.

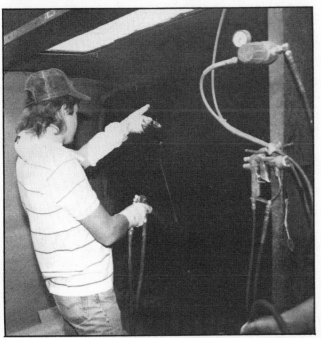

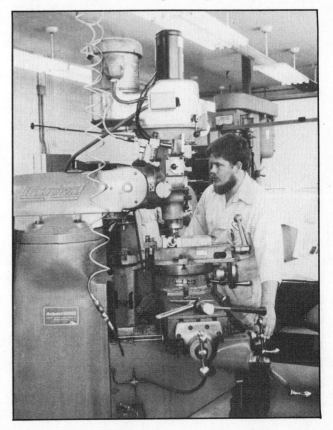

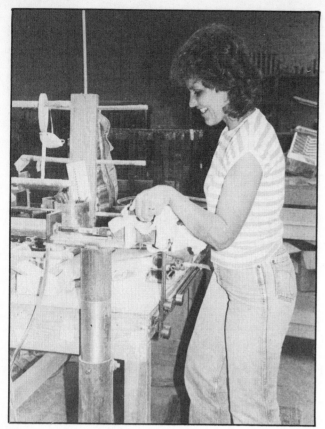

Smaller components are sanded in a padded vise, above.

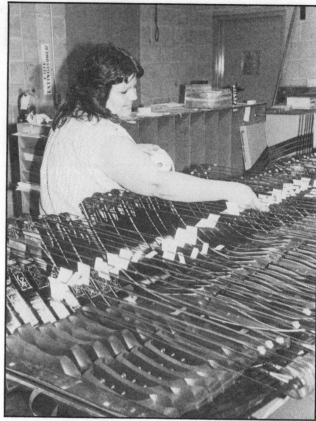

Completed bows are carefully cleaned, inspected, labeled before packaging and shipping. These bows match specs.

Browning boots are known for their lightweight comfort.

The bows are designed and manufactured at the Morgan plant. Every production phase, from start to finish, is accomplished there. Limbs are formed, cut, finished and painted. Wood or magnesium risers are produced in the plant. Cable and string assemblies are built and married to the appropriate bow models before being packaged and shipped to customers.

The factory is clean and modern, utilizing the latest in machines and safety equipment. The head of factory pro-

duction is long-time employee Horacio Macias. Don Hachtel is the archery products manager and big Mike Howell is the assistant plant manager. Each of these long-term employees is familiar with all phases of the factory's production.

Safe procedures are stressed throughout the plant. Management aims for zero accidents and zero product defects. After assembly, bows are checked for draw length, draw weight and component specifications.

Another recent Browning innovation is a move into carbon-fiber arrows. These smaller-than-normal shafts

Browning tests assembled bows for draw weight, amount of let-off and holding weight before they are shipped.

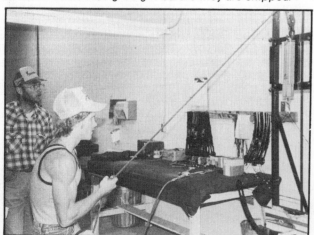

Limb edges are sanded on large belt sander. Finished parts are loaded on wheeled racks, moved to next stop.

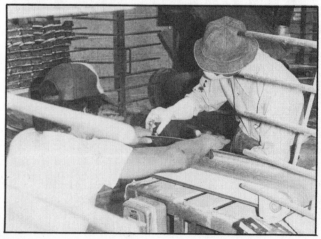

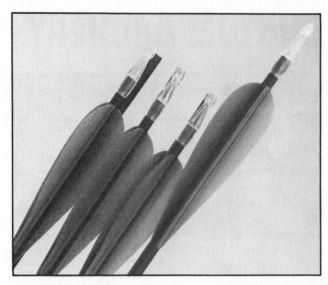

MIRAGE ARROW SELECTION CHART

To choose the best Mirage for yourself, find your bow weight in the left column, then match it with your arrow length. — Use Point Adapter #31350 — Use Point Adapter #31351

COMPOUND BOW WEIGHT	OVER DRAW				CORRECT HUNTING ARROW LENGTH							
	22"	23"	24"	25"	26"	27"	28"	29"	30"	31"	32"	33"
30-35 lb.	4029	4029	4029	4029	4029	4029	4029	5030	5030	6031	6031	7032
35-40 lb.	4029	4029	4029	4029	4029	4029	4029	5030	5030	6031	6031	7032
40-45 lb.	4029	4029	4029	4029	4029	4029	5030	5030	6031	6031	7032	7032
45-50 lb.	4029	4029	4029	4029	4029	4029	5030	5030	6031	6031	7032	7032
50-55 lb.	4029	4029	4029	4029	4029	5030	5030	6031	6031	7032	7032	8033
55-60 lb.	4029	4029	4029	4029	5030	5030	6031	6031	7032	7032	8033	
60-65 lb.	4029	4029	4029	5030	5030	6031	6031	7032	7032	8033	8033	
65-70 lb.	4029	4029	4029	5030	5030	6031	6031	7032	7032	8033	8033	
70-75 lb.	4029	4029	4029	5030	5030	6031	6031	7032	7032	8033	8033	
75-80 lb.	4029	4029	4029	5030	5030	6031	6031	7032	7032	8033	8033	

CAUTION: Shooting arrows that are too light can have the same effect as dry firing your bow. To protect your equipment, yourself and others, never shoot an arrow that weighs less than 6 grains per pound of actual draw weight.

Browning has named new carbon-graphite arrows, Mirage, provides a selection chart on the arrow carton, above. Mirage arrows are sold in packages of eight, right.

are lightweight and stiff, performing particularly well when shot from fast cam, overdraw-equipped compound bows. The shafts are products of Beman, the French manufacturer.

Browning claims their Mirage graphite arrows will provide more durability, more speed, better accuracy, flatter trajectory, better penetration and better value and longer life for bowhunters and field target shooters. The Mirage arrows are sold eight to the box, as are the point adapters. The adapters weigh thirty-six grains each and will accept any standard field point or broadhead.

The new Browning shafts are available in four spine ratings for compound bows rated from thirty- to eighty-pound draws and for arrow lengths of twenty-two to thirty-three inches. The listed spines are Beman's 4029, 5030, 6031, 7032 and 8033. Browning recommends using point

adapter #31350 for the first three spines listed — the lighter ratings — and #31351 for the two heavier. Standard fletching is three, four-inch plastic vanes.

The bright package carries assembly and repair instructions for the Mirage arrows. Browning recommends the use of any good five-minute, two-part epoxy cement to install the point adapters.

If nocks or vanes have to be replaced, Browning recom-

Horacio Macias, left, is the man in charge of archery factory production. Above: Editor Combs poses with Alan Windedahl, Bill Norton and Brad Francis, all of Browning.

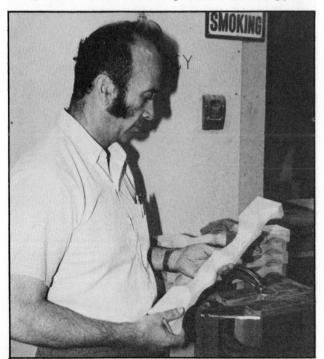

mends an instant super-glue-type, known technically as cyano acrylate. In addition to the adapters, Browning will be offering field points, nocks, glues and the bare shafts with their extensive line of archery accessories.

It is clear that Browning is committed to moving ahead with innovations and superior archery products. They are aware of the growing demands of bowhunters and 3-D target shooters and are responding with well developed and tested products.

The archery products personnel are experienced target shooters and bowhunters. They know what is needed and they are capable of providing it.

CUSTOM ARCHERY

Big sellers for Custom Archery are the fluted aluminum arrows, produced in the small California factory. The shafts are made in camouflage patterns, plastic vanes.

CARL LECKAVICH is an unlikely-looking business executive. Officially, he is the president and CEO of Custom Archery, manufacturer of X-Caliber arrow shafts — the revolutionary fluted aluminum shafts — and Magnum series round aluminum shafts. Leckavich also produces such diverse products as leather armguards, quivers and shooting gloves, a new fish arrowhead, finished aluminum arrows and cement.

In appearance, Leckavich definitely is not your average Yuppie businessman. His usual attire, whether at a trade show or supervising the building of arrows at his California factory, is a pair of Levis, sneakers and a T-shirt. He sports a short beard and his long blond hair is pulled back in a ponytail which reaches about half-way down his back. But inside that casual attire lives a technically minded, college-trained iconoclast who can develop, seek out, find and market archery products that have proved to be winners.

For several years, he has been making a line of good leather armguards, belt quivers and shooting gloves. They are made of real leather; no artificial substitutes, stresses

Leckavich. In the past, the leather products were offered in black and were popular with target and field archers, but more recently, the company has offered many of these accessories in white and camouflage for the bowhunter.

The product that really shot Leckavich and Custom Archery to prominence has been the fluted aluminum arrow shaft. While it is true that the older, better known Easton aluminum shaft still dominates the market, the

Archery Accessories Are What Make This Company Go

Left: When in position, arrows are turned out by the dozens on circular fletching tables. Carl Leckavich, below, examines address labels on arrow shipping packages.

fluted shafts have made their presence felt among target archers and bowhunters. The fluted cross-section shaft has the advantage of permitting the archer to shoot an arrow of less mass weight per arrow when compared to a standard-spine round arrow shaft. In theory, the lighter-weight shaft should produce greater velocity and less drop compared to standard arrows. The price of the fluted arrow is roughly comparable to, say, an equivalent Easton XX75 Autumn Orange arrow. Leckavich's Camo Magnum round shafts will run four to five dollars per dozen less than the X-Calibers at most outlets.

Carl Leckavich has done extensive testing to prove his point. For instance, using a sixty-five-pound compound

Carl Leckavich's company produces arrows by hand, using modern computers to assist in production control.

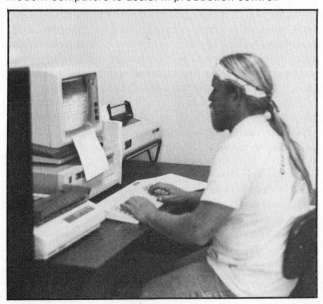

bow at fifty yards, his figures show a comparison between a conventional round shaft with a spine weight of 2117, weighing 520 grains and his 2212 fluted shaft weighing 380 grains. The X-Caliber 2212 and round 2117 spine ratings are said to be comparable. Testing showed a maximum of 250 feet-per-second (fps) velocity and a drop in trajectory of about eight feet for the round shaft, while the fluted reached 280 fps and had a drop of about 4½ feet. Leckavich has sold millions of the shafts since they were introduced in 1983.

The shafts are drawn in Korea before being shipped to Leckavich's California facility. For now, production facilities are involved in building thousands of dozens of arrows made of either the fluted or round aluminum tubing. The arrows are handmade to order by a small production crew personally overseen by Leckavich. They are sold through

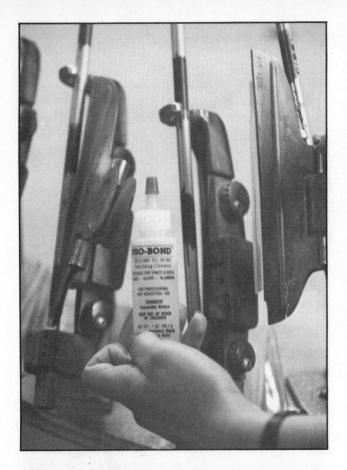

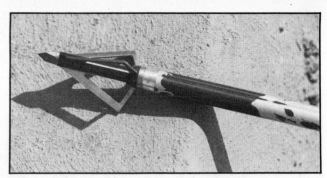

Custom Archery's newest product is an open-blade broadhead, above, well matched to fluted aluminum shaft. Arrow makers use Custom's own glue, left.

local dealers and mail order companies. Custom Archery offers shafts of black, green or brown camo, plastic vanes or feathers, all on standard-length shafts.

A custom touch of which Leckavich is proud is the extra dot of cement applied to the leading point of the vanes at the shaft. This, says Leckavich, prevents eventual peeling back of the plastic vane after heavy usage.

Fluted arrowhead inserts were developed to match the fluted shafts, although some use standard round inserts. The fluted inserts offer considerably more surface for bonding, in addition to the cosmetic improvements.

When first introduced, the fluted shafts came in for some criticism. Once bent, it seemed difficult, if not impossible, to straighten and continue to use as we are accustomed to doing with round shafts. Leckavich has come up with an answer; a simple one, at that. He has developed a simple kit which contains three sections of round aluminum tubing with the inside diameter matching the outside diameter of the fluted shaft. A shorter section is centered over the middle of the bend and the two other sections are placed to match the locations of the rollers on a standard shaft straightener. The bent fluted shaft then is rotated and straightened in the same manner as any round aluminum shaft. As with any other shaft, if the damage is too severe, the bend cannot be repaired and the arrow must be discarded.

Custom Archery has introduced a new lightweight arrowhead, the body of which is fluted. The fluting grooves, with broadhead blades, are said to improve penetration, lessen mass weight and actually add strength to the head.

The company's bowfishing head is dubbed the Whaler. Made of stainless steel, the detachable head features two collapsible barbs meant to result in less deflection and greater penetration. The design also permits the head to be applied to the shaft in a fixed mode, rather than detach. Bowfishermen using the Whaler have scored well in a number of fishing touraments around the country.

Leckavich's innovations do not stop with manufacturing all the products he has introduced for archers, but extend to packaging and shipping. He uses a styrofoam insert-separator which is placed in the center of his arrow-shipping boxes. The block has six grooves on each side for shipping a dozen arrows. Used as intended, a skilled worker can package twelve arrows in a matter of seconds, keeping costs down and insuring they arrive at their destination in relative safety.

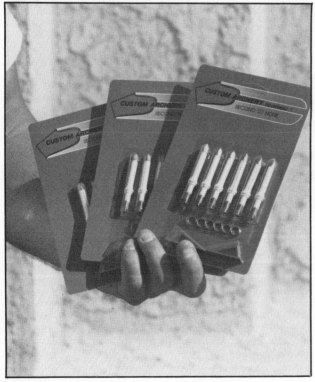

Broadheads are sold six to a package, ready to assemble. Heads were designed to be strong and lightweight, matching company's fluted shafts.

EASTON ALUMINUM

For Half A Century The World Has Shot Easton Aluminum Arrows

New Easton Distribution Center is located in Salt Lake City, Utah. Center is distribution point for Hoyt, others.

EASTON ALUMINUM may be the best known and most universally used archery product. There are traditional archers around who shoot nothing but longbows and wooden arrows of their own manufacture, but most of the rest of us fling arrows with shafts made of Easton aluminum. There are other arrow materials lately on the market, but Easton dominates the aluminum shaft supply.

Much, if not most, of the aluminum arrow shafts shot anywhere in the world are manufactured in a facility in Salt Lake City, Utah. This has been the case since 1980, when a great deal of the production was moved from Van Nuys, California.

For a bit of historical perspective, we have to look back to the early Twenties and a man named Doug Easton, an archer making custom yew wood bows and arrows in Watsonville, California. He then was making some of the top tournament arrows available in the United States. He was known as a perfectionist craftsman and soon realized he had to carefully sort and cull through a lot of cedar wood to come up with the matched shafts that the best shooters demanded.

He began experimenting with other possible shaft materials and soon was working with aluminum tubing as the answer to consistent weight and stiffness problems. In the 1941 National Championships, an early set of Easton

aluminum arrows, in the hands of a top local shooter, was instrumental in winning first place. History had been made.

Doug Easton was developing special thermal and aluminum hardening processes at the time. He designed and built a special draw bench and began arrow shaft production. There were the usual traditionalists who insisted every arrow shaft should be made of genuine Port Orford cedar or it could not be a real arrow, but the durability and consistency of Easton shafts soon were responsible for breaking target records everywhere.

In the late 1950s, Easton moved to a larger facility in Van Nuys, California. In 1965, Easton was producing the popular XX75 shafts from a new, higher strength aluminum alloy. Those shafts still are among the favorites of hunters and field archery shooters everywhere. In 1966, the Easton X7 target arrow was introduced.

In the mid-Sixties, aluminum arrow shafts, ski poles and other products were being manufactured in the Van Nuys facility on Haskell Avenue, still the headquarters of the Jas. D. Easton Corporation. After the death of Doug Easton in 1972, his son, James, became president of the company. The company was then fifty years old.

The 56,000 square-foot Van Nuys facility soon became overcrowded and there was no room to expand in the immediate community.

Studies showed that the area of Salt Lake City offered a

Easton aluminum arrow shafts are formed, sized and anodized at Salt Lake City plant. Anodizing, above, adds strength, toughness to shaft surface.

The lastest in development is the A/C/C — aluminum/carbon/competition — made of extra-light aluminum tubing with three wraps of carbon fiber. The A/C/C is ideal for field target and 3-D shooting from unknown distances.

Another new development is the aluminum/carbon/extreme (A/C/E) shaft, even more radical than other composites. The shaft is made of thin wall aluminum, wrapped with layers of carbon fiber, as are the other shafts, but the A/C/E is tapered at both ends.

The length of the shaft resembles an elongated barrel; thick in the middle and tapered down at both ends. The design has been used in international archery tournaments by world-class shooters and has done well. Tuning the new tubing is critical and requires special skills and considerations, as we have seen in previous chapters. Easton's goal seems to be to create faster, flatter flying and lighter arrow shafts.

Except for the X7 shafts, all Easton Aluminum arrows are produced from welded tubing. A shaft starts with a one-inch tube that has a wall thickness of about a sixteenth of an inch. Each piece is five feet long and will result in twelve to twenty arrow shafts, depending on finished size.

The tubes are softened — annealed — in large ovens at temperatures of up to 750 degrees Fahrenheit for eight

number of advantages. Manufacturing facilities were welcome and the labor force large, educated and healthy. The weather is mild, the cost of living reasonable and the city was fast becoming a transportation hub for all kinds of products and people.

The move to Salt Lake City was completed in 1980 and manufacturing commenced. The facility still is growing, but, at present, manufacturing occupies 110,000 square feet of factory buildings. More than 350 employees operate the plant with two or three shifts a day producing aluminum shafts, tent poles, ski poles and other products such as hockey sticks and baseball bats.

Some production still takes place at the Van Nuys plant, but all arrow shafts are finished in Salt Lake City. Van Nuys has a tube mill and some shaft sizes are produced there. Salt Lake has a tube mill and all other production facilities to produce complete arrows, as well as some other aluminum products.

Best seller for Easton is the 2117 Gamegetter II shaft, popular with bowhunters. Moving up rapidly in popularity is the XX75 Superlite, sought after as the result of increasing numbers of archers who use an overdraw-equipped bow and a desire for faster arrow speeds.

Easton continually seeks to re-design, refine and improve its products. Easton's latest is the aluminum/carbon (A/C) arrow shaft, a thin-walled aluminum tube wrapped with one or more layers of carbon fiber. This produces an arrow which is lightweight and stiff for faster flight and flatter trajectories.

The A/C shaft was developed in 1981 and soon proved its accuracy when used to win the gold medal in the 1984 Olympics. In 1987, the A/C was joined by the A/C/Hunter series, but the A/C/H was dropped by Easton in early 1990. It still is available, but not recommended for hunting purposes. It is a fine shaft for target work.

Heat treatment process imparts maximum strength to aluminum material. Timing, temperature are critical.

hours. After annealing, the tubes are drawn over a mandrel and through a die to reduce the outside diameter as well as the wall thickness.

The tubes are further drawn down several times to smaller diameters and wall thicknesses. As many as eight separate draw operations are required with several intermediate thermal processes before the tube reaches its final diameter and thickness.

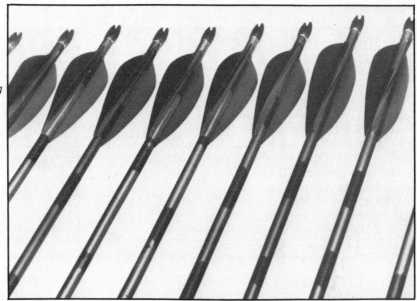

Above: After final heat treatment, anodizing has taken place, arrow shafts must be straightened. The Easton companies and Jim Easton, above right, are active in promoting the sport of archery. Easton's Gamegetter II arrow shafts, right, have become best sellers for many bowhunters.

A skilled quality control technician checks each step of the process to meet Easton's specifications. Specifics of the operation are highly guarded industrial secrets.

Heat treatment is next, with the tubing immersed in molten salt at 900 degrees Fahrenheit to get the best grain structure for the shaft. After heating, the tubes are dipped in a water quench to complete that phase of the hardening process. At this point, the first straightening step is added.

Most, but not all, Easton shafts are anodized at the Salt Lake plant. Anodizing adds color to the shaft, as well as adding strength and protection. Anodizing leaves a hard outer surface on the aluminum.

With all the modern equipment, computer operations and robotization at the Salt Lake facility, shafts still are hand-straightened. Because of their extreme hardness, the X7 shafts must be hand-straightened three different times to assure each shaft will maintain its straightness during normal use. A laser beam is used to mark the shafts with size and alloy type.

Easton shafts, as well as the products of the four other Easton-owned companies in Salt Lake City, are shipped world-wide through their new Easton Distribution Center.

The four divisions are: Easton Aluminum Salt Lake City, Hoyt USA, Easton Sports and Easton Reflex.

The distribution center, near the Easton arrow plant, covers 100,000 square feet and cost more than three million dollars to construct. The center is built of pre-cast concrete wall panels fifty feet high. The narrow-aisle, high-density pallet rack system is computer-operated. Flat floors are critical to the operation of the pallet rack system and were constructed with a tolerance of less than an eighth of an inch variance for every twenty feet. Heavy-duty forklifts are guided on the FM wire guidance system recessed into the concrete floors.

Other arrow materials continue to reach the market, mostly from overseas manufacturers. France, Germany and Korea are exporting aluminum arrow shafts to compete with Easton. Other shaft materials, all carbon fiber-fluted aluminum and combinations are under development and trial.

Still, it would be difficult to imagine another producer, foreign or domestic, who could seriously threaten the leadership of Easton Aluminum. When most of us think arrows, we think Easton.

HOYT USA

Eric Watts, above, is the new president of Hoyt USA, headquartered in Salt Lake City, Utah, not far from Easton Aluminum's production facility. The Hoyt factory, above right, is new, clean, modern concrete construction.

Hoyt shares and utilizes the Easton Distribution Center to handle production output from Salt Lake City plant.

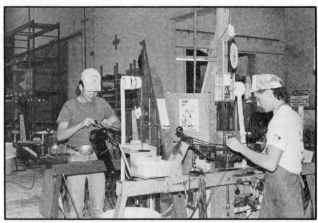

Production workers thread string and cable assemblies onto Hoyt bows. Only a few minutes are needed for task.

HOYT ARCHERY is a new, but old company, producing a full line of excellent compound bows and related equipment. The name is old, because the Hoyt Archery Company is from the firm that the famous archers, Earl and Ann Hoyt began. About a decade ago, the firm and the name were purchased by Easton and became, for a time, Hoyt-Easton.

A change in corporate structure and the name became Hoyt USA, still under the Easton corporation, but operating as its own company, producing bows and accessories.

About the same time as the Hoyt-Easton acquisition, the manufacturing facility was moved to Salt Lake City, Utah, a short distance from the new Easton Aluminum arrow shaft manufacturing plant in the same industrial complex outside the city, but near the airport.

The production facility is in a new building, with the most modern office, computer, telemarketing, inventory control and manufacturing capabilities. The factory floor has been laid out specifically for the production of Hoyt bows and accessories. Modern computers are utilized in the design and production of products, under the direction of experienced personnel.

The Hoyt Salt Lake operation has been under the direction of president Erik Watts since early 1990, when he took over from Joe Johnston. Modern machines help the production of all bow components: risers, limbs, cable and string tackle sets, cams and wheels. Painting, assembly, packaging and shipping are accomplished in Salt Lake City. Hoyt, as well as Easton itself, uses the giant new Easton distribution facility, also located in the same industrial complex as the production plants. This ultra-modern building uses the latest computers and robotics to store and retrieve packaged products, delivering them to the loading docks almost untouched by human hands. Humans are necessary to operate the forklifts, computers and to prepare shipments, but the forklifts are controlled through the aisles by magnetic strips buried in the floors. Goods awaiting shipment are stacked as much as thirty feet high inside the building and special high-lift fork machines are used to handle the cartons.

Floors and storage racks have been built on the slightest incline throughout the huge building so that new cartons need not be placed and pushed along. The facility is designed to provide "first in-first out" capability. As new

A Part Of The Easton Company, Hoyt Archery Builds In Salt Lake City

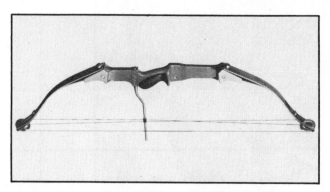

Hoyt's Pro Force Carbon Plus bow features recurve limbs and is popular with many 3-D target shooters.

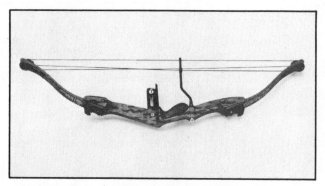

The Pro Vantage FPS + is a bow for those bowhunters who prefer to shoot the shorter overdraw arrows.

Above: Limb bolt holes are drilled in magnesium bow risers using mechanical jigs, while cable and string assemblies are built to exact specifications, below.

Fiberglass limbs are sanded and finished in large blocks at a time, ensuring uniformity throughout.

boxes are placed on the racks, the built-in incline lets the boxes slide downhill against the earlier storage. Items to be shipped are automatically found on the low end of the rack. The angle is so slight, that one would have to know about it to realize it is there.

Before acquisition by Easton, Hoyt bows were known primarily as target bows. However, the management realized that there were considerably more potential customers in the bowhunter ranks than in only target shooters, so many of the new bow models introduced in recent years have been hunting bows. The target archer has not been neglected, however. The Hoyt line includes its share of brightly painted products for the tournament shooter.

Hoyt hunting bows, especially the Pro Vantage series, have found favor with a number of well known bowhunters, including Jim Dougherty of Tulsa, Oklahoma. Dougherty has hunted over much of North America for more than thirty years and his equipment choices are the product of plenty of experience. Hoyt bows are known for their arrow speeds, reliability and functional designs.

Realizing a bow must be attractive as well as functional, Hoyt's bows feature fine finish and brilliant colors. All color finishing is done at the Salt Lake facility. Limbs are finished in special machines, dozens at a time, inspected and matched for mass weight and draw strength before painting.

Long-time Easton and Hoyt employees who have made the move to Salt Lake City express satisfaction with the change. The area features plenty of hunting and fishing opportunities, a reasonable cost of living and generally favorable weather. From a management point of view, the surrounding area contains an adequate supply of reliable and willing workers, always a factor in any manufacturing operation.

PRECISION SHOOTING EQUIPMENT

Company founder, Pete Shepley, in dark glasses, discusses some of the finer points with Tom Jennings, right, during Desert Shoot-Out archery tournament. Shepley started tournament to provide competition at a time of year when most of the North is still cold.

PRECISION Shooting Equipment (PSE) is known as the high-tech equipment innovator of the archery industry. Its reputation is based upon the drive and personality of the company's president. Pete Shepley founded the company in 1970, while still located in Illinois. He is unhesitant about adding the latest technology and material to the company's archery equipment.

All PSE products especially the bows, have a modern computer-designed look and construction which reflects Shepley's philosophy. He believes PSE's products should help the archer achieve the best possible performance, whether target shooting or bowhunting.

"Today's bowhunter has a responsibility to hunt his game as efficiently as he can," says Shepley. "Accuracy and consistent performance therefore, are essential to a successful hunt.

"We strive to produce increasingly better equipment through technical advancements in design and manufacturing."

Precision Shooting Equipment was the first to promote the popular overdraw shooting system and the handle design with offset arrow rest to allow plenty of clearance for a short, overdraw broadhead-equipped arrow. The company has become known for popularizing the innovations. PSE also features other modern trends with recurve limbs on its compound bows, radically shaped, smooth-shooting cams, letoff percentages well beyond fifty-percent and the use of Brownell non-elastic Fast Flight strings.

Pete Shepley manufactures and personally uses all the latest equipment born of the newest technology for his own target shooting or bowhunting. PSE products and the modern archery factory in Arizona all reflect this philosophy.

The present facility in Tucson was occupied in January 1989. Before moving into the 143,000 square-foot build-ing, PSE manufacturing was scattered over several locations in Tucson. The move from Illinois, where the company began, was in 1982.

The new plant is a model of the latest production techniques that are monitored and, in some cases, operated by computers and robotics. The entire operation all is under one roof, something Shepley had been working toward for several years. This simplifies many of the production opertions; raw materials come in one door and the finished products are packaged and shipped out another door for delivery to customers.

Entering the building, the visitor is greeted with an array of hunting trophies taken by Shepley on hunts around much of the world. Another wall displays old and new PSE bows, some dating back to the days when the company was headquartered in Illinois.

Metal components are manufactured at Tucson plant. Quality control is a critical consideration of the parts, examined here by PSE engineer Doug Marcoux.

Better Known As PSE, High Tech And Innovative Ideas Highlight This Company

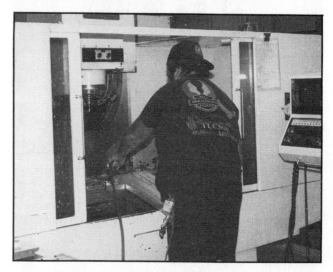

Left: PSE maintains color control by spray painting all its own risers. This brightly painted group will be used for target bows. Automated machine, above, turns out dozens of compound wheels in one operation.

A portion of the building is used for PSE dealer market orientation and product training sessions. PSE dealers are offered four days of intensive orientation about the products, as well as successful techniques for selling archery, in general. The courses are held nearly every month throughout the year and have proved popular. The effort put into the courses pays handsome dividends for PSE in the long run.

Because the facility is relatively new, the production and assembly floors are laid out for their specific functions. Materials flow through the production steps smoothly and efficiently. The latest automated machinery manufactures components designed by PSE personnel.

Shepley started PSE in 1970 while a products engineer with the Magnavox Corporation. The company operated initially from Mahomet, Illinois, in a facility of only seven hundred square feet. Within a few years. Shepley was moving some of the manufacturing responsibilities to Tucson. That move was finished by 1982.

As production and sales continued to grow, it was soon evident that the scattered, 70,000 square feet of space was neither sufficient nor efficient enough for the engineer in Shepley. The larger facility soon became available, located on twenty-seven acres of land just west of downtown Tucson. There would seem to be plenty of room for growth.

"We had simply outgrown our old buildings," Shepley says. "We now have some breathing room, plus consolidation of warehousing facilities for more efficient operation."

Inside, the manufacturing floor is light, neat and clean. By using computers to assist in the design and production of PSE bows, components and accessories, little motion is wasted during the construction processes. Bow components are manufactured and assembled within the Tucson Plant.

The Fast Cams are an example. The designer utilizes computer-aided design systems to develop the component

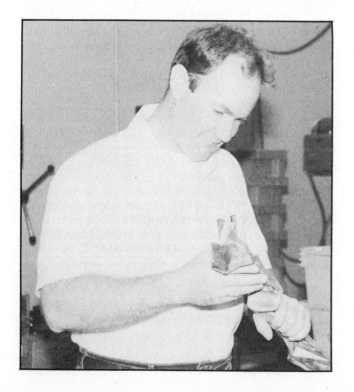

Precision cast magnesium risers are held to tight tolerances by Marcoux and manufacturing engineering staff. Riser is designed to accept PSE accessories.

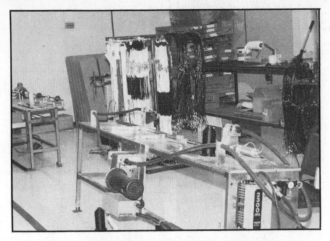

String assemblies and cable harnesses, above, are ready for installation on various bow models. Cams and wheels are manufactured in automated, computer controlled machine, right below. Cams are checked, measured and cleaned to specifications, right above.

— based upon a great deal of corporate "memory" and experience in archery. Several prototypes are built and tested until a final configuration is selected.

At PSE, most cams are machined of aluminum. To the layman, the computer-directed operation has to seem quite amazing. The process begins with slabs or sheets of thick aluminum. Two of these are attached to each side of box-like structures more than two feet high. The slabs of aluminum are bolted precisely in place, of course, before machining starts.

This box, with its aluminum slabs, is mounted on a movable base that is transported into an enclosed structure where actual machining takes place. For a typical cam-making run, there may be aluminum material for thirty cams on a side, times four sides; a total of one hundred-twenty cams at one setting.

The huge machine's cutting tools remove material around and through the cams to specifications, operating on each aluminum face in turn. Operators use compressed air to blow away stray metal scraps as the aluminum — now formed compound bow cams — is brought out of the

PSE also manufactures a line of crossbows, using special magnesium channels for the prod, or stock.

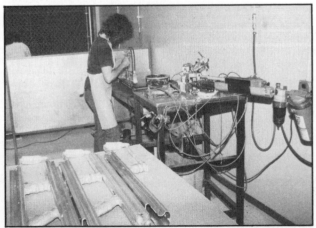

machine. Once cleaned, the nearly complete cams are subject to a final operation which finishes the side of the component while it still is part of the aluminum slab. Machining continues until the individual cams are detached, ready for installation.

All basic components of PSE's bows are manufactured at the Tucson plant, except for screws, bolts, washers, axles and so on. Components such as metal wheels, moulded wheels and cams, limbs, cable and string assemblies are all produced and assembled at the Arizona site. Pete Shepley is quite proud of this, he is quick to admit. All bear the distinctive PSE high-tech look.

A line of vinyl and leather belt quivers, back quivers, armguards, belts, tabs and gloves is offered by PSE, but bear the King name. The products also include a full line of backpacks, fanny packs and duffle bags with a choice of several camouflage patterns.

In late 1989, PSE acquired the Carroll Archery line. According to Don Vallee, PSE vice-president of sales and marketing, "There's never been a riser quite like Carroll's. The small-throated handle was popular among target archers in the early Seventies. With the advanced PSE limbs and hardware, we feel 'Carroll by PSE' bows will fill a real need."

Purchase of the company included the Carroll name, as well as machinery, handles, limbs and rights to all Carroll product lines. There is ample room in the Tucson facility for whatever part of Carroll's Archery Shepley may wish to add.

Carroll's Archery began as a corporation in 1970, pro-

The May Desert Shoot-Out attracts hundreds of archers to Tucson.

Vice president for sales and marketing, Don Vallee, below, is tough competitor.

ducing strictly recurve bows until 1972. Then it became the second company to produce compounds under the Allen patent. Carroll's was a major producer of recurve limbs during this time, supplying them for both Browning and Martin Archery.

Shepley has gained a reputation for going all-out in a professional manner for everything he does. The Annual Pete Shepley Desert Shoot-Out archery tournament is no exception. The tournament first was held in Tucson in 1987 and has grown dramatically. About 250 archers and enthusiasts took part in the tournament the first year, 400 the second and more than 650 the third year.

The Desert Shoot-Out is more than a target tournament. It is also an event where shooters, archery media and archery manufacturers get together on a casual social basis

in a delightful location in beautiful weather. It is not unusual to see executives of Easton Aluminum, Hoyt USA, Saunders Archery and PSE at lunch or enjoying a barbecue together. Tens of thousand of dollars in cash and merchandise prizes are up for grabs at the tournament, making it popular with archers from all over North America.

These events take place at the Tucson National Resort and Spa, which offers special off-season rates amid luxurious surroundings. High point of the tournament is sure to be Shepley's North American Bowhunting Adventures Big Game Awards barbecue at his ranch on Saturday evening.

Precision Shooting Equipment carries the personality of Pete Shepley, its founder and president. He is a technically oriented, pragmatic individual and PSE products reflect that fact. Additional advances would seem to be just ahead.

A popular aspect of the Desert Shoot-Out is the team balloon shoot, left. A display of past and present PSE target and hunting bows, above, shares factory wall space with an impressive bull elk trophy mount.

PRO LINE ARCHERY

Terry Ploot, Pro Line's national sales manager, examines one of company's Point Blank compound bows. Factory location is in Gun Lake, Michigan, in central state's farm country.

PRO LINE ARCHERY production facilities are located amid a rural, agricultural area of central Michigan, in the small town of Gun Lake. All design, production and shipping of Pro Line products are done at and from the factory building. It may seem an unlikely place for high-tech manufacturing to take place, but it is in the middle of some great deer hunting country with its marketing potential for hunting bows.

Bill Pierce is the president of Pro Line. As part of the corporate philosophy, he states, "Pro Line bows are sold only through independent archery dealers for good reason: They have the experience, the facilities and the motivation to aid you in your selection process. Your preference, type of shooting, draw weight and draw length...a multitude of your specific needs can only be met by your independent archery dealer. It may be a little more difficult to buy a Pro Line bow, but it is well worth the effort."

Recently, Pro Line has introduced their line of Point Blank series compound bows for hunters and target shooters. These bows feature fast speeds, a choice of Fast Flight string, wheels or cams, straight or recurve limbs. The newest models feature cut-out risers to accommodate overdraw shelves and fifty or sixty-five percent let-off.

The Pro Line products include hunting and target sights, arrow rests, overdraw devices quivers, bow cases, sta-

bilizers, tree stands and even T-shirts, caps and jackets with the Pro Line logo.

Terry Ploot, born in Norway, is the company's sales manager. He recognizes the need to bring archery to the attention of new shooters for the sport to grow and prosper. That's why, he says, Pro Line brought out the Short Stop bow kit, especially for young archers.

The Short Stop is a compound bow with sixty-five percent let-off and draw weight options from fifteen to twenty-five pounds, twenty to thirty pounds and twenty-five to thirty-five pound draws.

"The bow also is available with an optional kit that allows the bow to 'grow up' with the young archer," says

Factory floor may seem cluttered at times, but equipment and machines are laid out for maximum production efficiency. Norwegian-born Ploot was hired to set up Pro Line production facility.

Pro Line Is A Full Line Compay Offering
Bows, Accessories, Produced In Rural Michigan

All production operations including final assembly inspection, packaging and shipping is done at Gun Lake facility. Note conveyor belt in above photo.

Ploot. "By simply changing limbs and wheels, the Short Stop is transformed into an intermediate adult-size bow."

The Pro Line production facility is a new, modern building, with an interior designed by Ploot for efficient work. Most of the bow production is under one roof. Multiple-unit forming and sanding machines are able to turn out several sets of risers or other parts at once, on a production line basis. Various bow riser models are available in laminated wood or magnesium; some have optional laminated high energy limbs.

While much of the equipment is automatic, computer-controlled and programmed, all Pro Line equipment is carefully inspected along the way at each production step. This is especially critical when dealing with sanded and finished parts which are to be spray painted in camouflage patterns for hunters or in bright tournament colors for 3-D shooters. A tight quality-control program is in place at all steps, particularly at the final assembly and shipping points.

Pro Line shooters appreciate the new camouflage pattern called Field Grade, in four colors, applied at the factory. The newest Match Point Carbon 300X compound bow is available in that camo or in solid black, brown or solid gray. The compound recurve limbs are made of two layers of Gordon bias carbon bonded between Cam-Core centers consisting of thirty-two grain-oriented maple laminations. The outer layers are of Gordon fiberglass. These materials all produce a fast-shooting bow, favored by bowhunters and target shooters.

A few years ago, Pro Line acquired MKM Products, which manufactures tree stands and bow sights. All the tree stands are designed to not damage the tree. The stands are lightweight, easy to carry and climbing or non-climbing models are available.

For years, Pro Line has also produced a line of crossbows for hunting. While crossbow hunters have been criticized by some archers, crossbow competition is sanctioned by the National Archery Association and enjoys considerable international following.

Young archers may enjoy archery with Pro Line's Short Stop bow, designed to expand for growing children with optional longer limbs and wheels.

Pro Line bows are attractive and well made. The company has been around a long time and the bows are finding popular acceptance among archers in many parts of the country as well as in Canada and Europe. Forward-looking company management should keep turning out products consumers are willing to use.

SAUNDERS ARCHERY

One Of The Real Old-Timers In Archery, Chuck Saunders Has The Most Modern Accessories

CHUCK SAUNDERS is truly one of the pioneers of the modern archery movement. He has been in the business for more than half a century, manufacturing some of the best known arrow target matts and hundreds of innovative archery accessories. Saunders personally is a supporter of many youth programs and is the driving force behind the Bowhunters Who Care organization.

One of Saunders' earliest, successful products was the target butt, first produced fifty years ago. The product still is on the market, better than ever and called a Spiral Wound Indian Cord Fiber matt. They obviously have stood the test of time; Chuck Saunders explains why:

"Making a good matt has always been tough. Now it is even tougher. Today's bows are heavier and use lighter arrows which hit targets at speeds twenty-five percent faster than ever before. As matts are made tighter to stop the faster arrows, they become more difficult to withdraw the arrows. If an arrow is stopped too quickly, the heat loosens the point and may stay in the matt as the arrow is withdrawn.

"The Saunders approach to this challenge is three-pronged: First, we produced a tighter, thicker, tougher matt that stops even the fastest graphite arrows — the new Triple-T Indian Cord Matt. Next, we designed our Arrow Puller, which makes it easy for the archer to pull the arrows out of the target. Finally, we developed our Friction Fighter shaft treatment, which reduces heat so the points stay on. This also reduces the amount of the arrow-stopping material which sticks to the super-heated shaft."

Matts and targets are obviously a large part of Saunders' business, but the company offers many other handy and helpful devices to make archery easier for most shooters. Saunders points out that all the company's accessories are made in the United States, including such diverse things as bow cases, gloves and arm guards, the famous Saunders finger tabs, quivers, strings, bowfishing gadgets, sights and the popular T-dot sight pin.

The cable guard slide has rollers on both the cable and rod section, resulting in smoother, almost frictionless action. Most bows using it, says Saunders, will show a slight increase in arrow speed. The wear on plastic-coated cables after 10,000 cycles was checked and was too small to detect.

Many archers use a bow sling. Saunders' is made of an aluminum U-frame that fastens to the bow at the stabilizer hole. A flexible tubing encircles the shooter's wrist. A stabilizer may be screwed into the attachment bolt of the sling.

Another accessory which is used in conjunction with the cable guard slide is a cushioned cable stop. The stop brings cables or cable slide to a slow stop, which helps prevent secondary vibration from building up. Position of the stop can be changed to achieve proper over-travel. Another

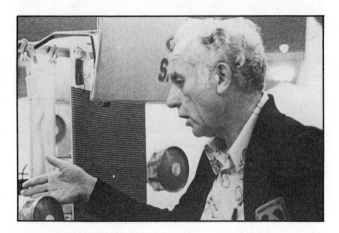

Typical of Saunders' innovative accessories is the cushion cable stop, below. Gadget reduces vibration and cable overtravel. Chuck Saunders, above, brings more than fifty years' experience to the industry.

benefit gained from using the stop, says Saunders, is that vibration sound is reduced as an aid to bowhunters, especially those shooting overdraw bows.

Chuck Saunders remembers: "In the early Forties, we would rest the arrow on the index finger of our bow hand. Back then, a bow was either left- or right-handed. If the feather fletching wasn't properly trimmed, it would cut the hand as the arrow passed by the bow. Later, a small shelf was cut out of the bow riser section which led to the Folbert cut-out window. This led to a variety of arrow rests, the first of which was made by Larry Welsch. Now there is a bewildering assortment." Saunders has several for target archers and bowhunters.

Archers who do not shoot overdraws, but who shoot the newer cutout bows, will appreciate Saunders' Lucky Launcher arrow rest plate. The plate will accept most arrow rests and attaches to a threaded rod or to a pressure button. The arrangement allows the archer to adjust the arrow rest in or out to the best position for straight arrow flight. The foam mounting becomes a built-in pressure plate to absorb arrow slap. It works well with Saunders' own pressure button, called the Arrow Pilot.

YORK ARCHERY

One Of The Oldest Archery Manufacturers Is In Front With Modern Developments

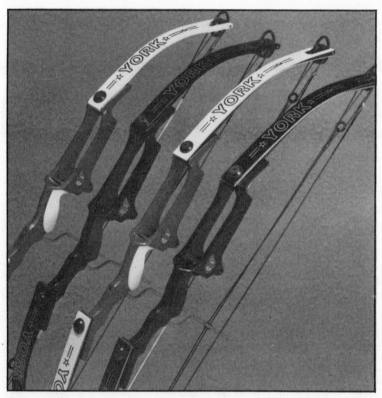

York's Shoot-Through-Overdraw (STO) bows are unique to the company and have been good sellers to target archers and bowhunters. Arrow is enclosed in riser.

WOODCRAFT Equipment Company, manufacturer of York Archery equipment, is the nation's second oldest archery manufacturing company. The privately owned, Independence, Missouri, firm traces its roots to the early 1920s, when a Boy Scout, Dudley Smith, developed a record-breaking fire-by-friction set. Smith's set was so much in demand by other Scouts that he began producing them in a barn behind his house. The next logical step led the young businessman into producing finished and unfinished archery equipment for the Boy Scouts.

By 1926, Dudley Smith had taken on two new partners in order to meet the fast-growing archery demands in scouting. In 1928, Kenneth B. Smith joined the company and soon became its sole owner and manager.

The popular bows of that era were made of osage-orange and lemonwood. In its early days, York Archery manufactured a variety of longbows, as well as arrows, leather goods and other accessories. These items first appeared in the 1930 York catalog. Also listed in the early catalogs was equipment for playing field hockey.

By 1956, York had begun phasing out the lemonwood bows and producing the then-revolutionary recurve bow. Just as the longbow evolved into the recurve, York's Boy Scout business evolved into a high volume school supply business. A contributing factor to York's team and school business is the fact that they still manufacture a full line of fiberglass and composite recurve bows, as well as cedar arrow shafts.

With the arrival of the compound bow in the 70s, York, under the leadership of second generation owner, Ken Smith, Jr., has continued to contribute to the development of archery. Recent achievements include: first solid fiberglass split limb used on a compound bow (1979), first center-flex graphite limb design with self-axle hole (1980), first cable guard built into handle riser (1981), first programmed cam two-wheel compound bow (1982), first tri-draw adjustable cam (1984) and first mass-produced shoot-through overdraw-handle riser (1985).

CHAPTER

16

CUSTOM LONGBOW AND RECURVE BOWS

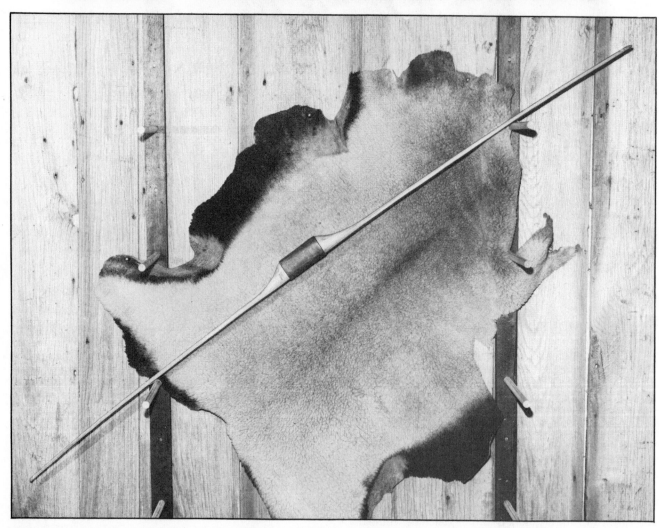

Mike Fedora is a bowyer making custom and semi-production recurve and longbows. Most are made to order for specific shooters. The typical prospective buyer will already have considerable experience.

To Get That Extra Special Something In A Bow, You'll Have To Order One Made By A Bowyer

WITH A FEW exceptions, most longbows and recurves are custom made, one at a time, by a single craftsman. Production is low and the time from order to finish may be considerable. But demand is high and increasing for the traditional bows. Even some large compound bow manufacturers are expanding their longbow and recurve production schedules.

C.R. Learn has been shooting longbows and recurves for years, some of which are custom made. His report will help the prospective customer avoid pitfalls and needless expense.

THE BOW HAS a name on it you have never heard, but it has smooth, graceful lines and looks great. It is a recurve with long sweeping hooks on the unstrung limbs. It looks as if it must be fast. You brace it and notice the grip feels comfortable, much different from many of the recurves you have held. When it is braced, it pulls smoothly and evenly, with no stacking; it just feels great in your hands.

Many bowhunters feel that any handmade bow is a custom bow. This is not true, since all bows require hand work whether they are a recurve, longbow or compound; there is no other way to get the proper tiller into the limbs and have it perform correctly. Large companies usually use a furniture carving machine to shape sixteen or more bow risers at the same time. Others utilize monster sanding machines that form a riser in one pass with several belts doing the shaping they are programmed for.

What constitutes a custom bow? As a rule, a custom bow has features that you don't normally get in a production bow. Production bows go through a basic type of what might be called a production line. One work section does risers, another forms and shapes the limbs while another takes care of assembly and tillering. The last phases would be the final finish, testing, packaging and shipping.

The custom bowyer works similarly to the production factories, but he usually makes one bow at a time following it step to step until he has a finished unit. The work is slower and therefore the cost is usually higher, because he can't possibly compete with the system used in large plants. As a rule, the custom bowyer is an individual with different ideas about how a bow should be built. He will incorporate his idea into making a bow, test it and, if he is satisfied, will advertise by word of mouth locally. Some go national by utilizing the various archery publications. The number of bows they make is not large, but usually are high quality.

There are a few custom bowyers out there who make a "different" type of compound, but the majority prefer to work with the time honored recurves. Others specialize in the traditional longbows. You buy what you want directly from the maker you prefer.

Let's look at the recurve, because it has seen a positive rise in demand from both the larger and smaller recurve makers around the country.

You may find it difficult to find a single unit recurve, that is a riser tapering out into the limbs, not a takedown. These are popular among devotees of that type and are excellent bows. If there is a disadvantage to this type of bow, it is that

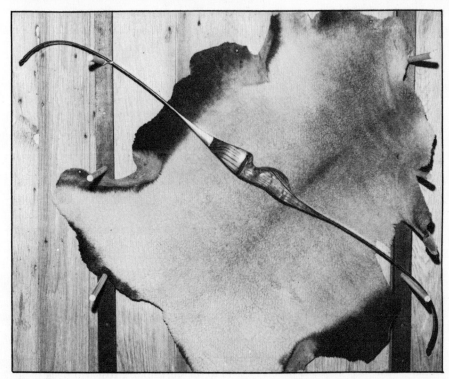

Beautiful recurves such as this Fedora require special jigs and forms to build. New interest is shown in one-piece, long, single-unit recurves by target shooters and traditional bowhunters.

you must buy the precise draw weight you will shoot; you can't change unless you buy another bow.

It might be safe to say that most of the custom bows made today are of the three-piece take-down style. This has been popular over the years and continues to be a favorite with archers. With this unit, you get a riser of a certain length; you can buy extra limbs in different draw weights to match your preference. You might start with a set of forty-five-pound limbs to get your muscles toned and to learn the basics of archery. When you feel you are ready for a heavier draw weight, you merely order the added poundage you want. You may have to send the riser back to get a positive fit of limbs to riser, but that will depend on the bowyer.

If you want a custom grip on your bow, you can have that made to your specifications. There are different methods of accomplishing this and you will have to follow directions the bowyer sends you. It can be as simple as sending a pattern of your hand to submitting another bow that has the grip you like so the bowyer can duplicate it.

If you are into target archery and plan to compete in

short bows are easier to move through brush and close terrain.

Many of the single unit recurves were quite long; a popular length was sixty-eight inches. That might be harder to find today, but they are out there if you hunt for them.

Most bowyers make the more popular bow lengths, because that is what bowhunters order most. To make a longer or shorter limb than they advertise isn't a simple matter of extending the base length of the limb. They must make an entire form to set up the laminations for each limb length. Some might do it and charge only the extra cost of making the longer or shorter limb, but the customer might also have to pay for the forms. The longer your draw length, the longer the recurve bow you should shoot. You will find them normally in sixty, sixty-two and sixty-four inches. They are the most popular.

Custom bowyers make bows because they like to. Some, if not most, make bows on a part-time basis in the evenings and on weekends. Most hold down a full-time job.

Due to the small number of bows they make, most cannot live by bows alone. Occasionally, a bowyer will hit

The graceful lines and curves of this Jim Brackenbury recurve make it a work of art, beauty.

The Brackenbury recurve features take-down limbs, held by almost invisible recessed Allen bolts.

FITA tournaments or Olympic-type events, you must use the bows specified by the rules for that type of shooting. If you are a bowhunter, you are bound by no rules as to length of limb or such, but some states do have minimum draw weight restrictions for hunting bows. When you get ready to order a custom bow, these are some of the things you must consider.

Bowhunters have favored the shorter bow lengths, say about sixty inches, for many years. This may have been influenced by one of our great bowhunters, Fred Bear, who favored and sold that length bow. There is one thing to remember regarding bow length: The longer the bow, the smoother the draw will be. The short bow enthusiast — overall length of fifty-four inches are common — will say

upon a style, shape and type of custom bow that bowhunters and target archers prefer and be able to become a full-time maker, but not often.

Another thing you will notice about custom recurves are some really wild innovations. There isn't much really new if you have researched archery over the ages, but some of these radical bows are, to put it bluntly, just plain weird. All that really matters is how they perform and the archer must be the judge of that.

The cost of a custom bow is usually higher than a production model, because the bowyer can make only so many. He has to charge what he considers a fair price for time, effort and knowledge. The bowyer makes bows that he is proud to send to the customer. Most will back their product with a good warranty.

The longbow situation is similar to that of the single unit recurve; there just aren't that many longbow manufacturers. One that comes to mind is Martin Archery, which includes several models of longbows in their catalog. Longbow shooters — they prefer to be called traditional archers — tend to be quite fussy about their equipment. Longbows still require the same traditional production work from laying out the laminations, glueing and curing forms, sanding and tillering to get the final shooting bow.

Wilderness has a full line of one-piece and take-down bows.

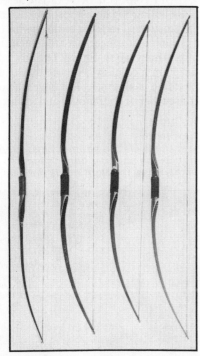
Dick Palmer produces a full line of custom longbows for most needs.

Longbows are just about the toughest bows you can buy. You may not want to throw your bow down a hill, watching it bounce across gravel, rocks and come to rest in a stream, but if you should have that happen, you could probably pick up that bow and shoot it with no problem. Longbows and recurves aren't for everybody, but they are definitely available in many shapes, styles and prices for those who want them.

Martin Archery recently added a new wing to their production plant to try, emphasis on try, to keep up with the demand for the recurves and longbows. They are one of the few manufacturers who make all types of bows from the simple longbow to the most sophisticated compound. Over the years, I have shot many types of their bows and have hunted for several years with one of their more popular recurves, the Super Diablo. They do offer some sixty-eight-inch bows and a takedown that has been recently updated.

What amazed me during a conversation with Gail Martin was the fact that they do customize bows for archers who wish them. They have done this for years, but haven't advertised it. They will give you a special grip or other features if you contact them. One word of caution: On any custom bow or any type of customizing you want done, it will become your bow forever, because it deviates from standard models.

The Sagittarius longbow from Jerry Gentellalli's Rancho Safari is a smooth shooter.

The custom bow goes beyond standard styles, lengths and features. Some are radical, but if they work, so much the better. Most are great shooting bows and it will soon become the one you carry in the field for many years.

Not too long ago, I got the crazy idea of having one longbow that would shoot either left- or right-handed as far as the arrow rest and grip are concerned. This isn't anything new; just go look at a summer camp or high school that offers archery and you will find ambidextrous bows. All I have to do to change from left to right hand shooting, is to flip the bow over for what I want. It shoots fine, but certainly isn't everyone's choice. If I take it to a tournament, it certainly gets a lot of comments, not all of them favorable.

When you decide you just have to have that custom bow, try to find a local bowhunter who has the type of bow you are interested in and see if he will allow you to shoot it. That's the best way. If you decide you want a monster hundred-pound draw weight for shooting mastodons, you might have to go the custom route. They usually charge extra for bow weights above those they offer in their catalog. Save your money, call or write to the bowyer and discuss what you want. That will help him make your custom bow and will help you become a satisfied customer.

Customs aren't for everyone, but they are usually well built, with an excellent finish. If you go the three-piece takedown recurve style, you can order several bow limbs for a single riser. You might want a light set for targets, a fifty-five pounder for game to deer size and when you go for elk or bear, maybe sixty- to sixty-five-pound draw weights will be better.

Custom is just that; a bow made to fit your hand, your need and perhaps, most of all, your ego.

INSTINCTIVE SHOOTING

Do Instinctive Archers Aim Or Don't They? Can Anybody Learn The Fast Trick Shots? Give It A Try — It Might Work!

C. R. LEARN thinks that the fewer gadgets and accessories the archer uses, the better shooter he will become. Learn claims he shoots instinctively at game and at man-made targets. Some are able to do it, but some cannot ever learn the technique used by the great modern archers of the century. Give it a try, he says. You may get good at it. But remember: This kind of shooting requires plenty of practice.

THE RABBIT comes out of the brush, dashes to the end of the hollow log and stops, looking around at what has disturbed it. He is sitting by his bolt hole and anything can trigger his movement into that hollow log; you will miss rabbit dinner. The bow comes up, the draw is started immediately with the bow canted and your eye on the rabbit at all times. The finger of your draw hand touches the corner of your mouth and the arrow is off

The instinctive shooter must learn which is his or her dominant eye, which may not be the same as dominant hand. Point, with both eyes open, at a distant object.

The finger stays still while the shooter closes the right eye; note how the pointing finger seems to jump to the right. In this case, the right eye is dominant.

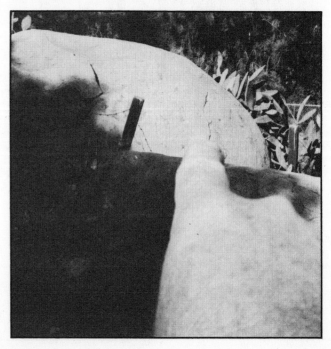

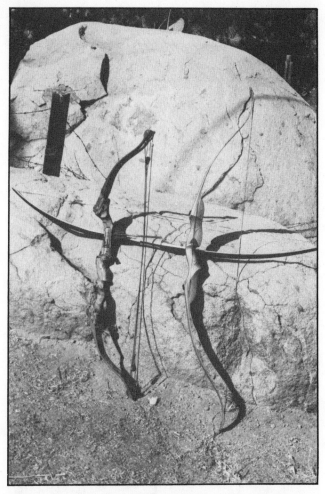

Longbows, recurves or compound bows all may be shot using the instinctive sighting method. The longbow is more closely associated with instinctive shooting.

and on its way. The rabbit soon becomes a great dinner treat; you have been eating too many canned meals on your hunting trip anyway.

How far away was the rabbit? The bowhunter didn't notice and really didn't care. How did he know when to shoot or release the arrow? That was triggered by the contact of the draw hand, in this case, the index finger touching the corner of the mouth, the anchor point. The arrow was released on contact. How does the bowman know when to shoot, how far to aim the arrow and where his sights are? Good questions, ones that aren't always easy to answer, because we are dealing here with what is termed, instinctive archery.

There are knowledgeable bowhunters who state that there is no such thing as instinctive shooting. Everybody aims, they say. The simple answer to that is look at films or video tapes of Howard Hill, Fred Bear, Ben Pearson and one of the followers of those great archers in more modern times, Bob Swinehart. Their feats speak for themselves. They were all instinctive archers.

The first thing you must know is that some people will never be instinctive bowhunters. You can practice all you want and will never have what it takes to hit the target using this system. Don't feel bad; that's why they put sights on bows. It is not a disgrace to use sights. Often, they are what keeps a bowhunter in the sport. You won't know if you can shoot instinctively until you try.

One of the first things to determine is what is termed lead eye. This is also referred to as dominant eye. It can be either the right or the left. You could be right-handed in everything you do, but still have a left eye dominant. That might be one reason you couldn't shoot instinctively. One of our modern bowhunters whose name you will recognize, Jim Dougherty, shot right-handed for some time, switched to left-hand shooting and shot even better. He is still a southpaw in his bowhunting technique.

To determine which is your dominant eye, point your finger at a target ten or more feet away. You can point it at the clock on the shelf in the living room, for example. Hold that finger rigid and close the left eye. If the clock is aimed right down your right finger, that is your dominant eye. Without moving the hand, close the right eye and open the left. You will note the clock seems to shift in relation to the point of your finger. You would totally miss that clock face if you shot at it. In fact, you would miss the entire clock if it wasn't a big one. This is a simple and positive test to see which is your lead or dominant eye.

Another item that goes with instinctive shooting is one that you have been told to avoid like a social disease — "snap shooting." This has good and bad aspects. The bad type of snap shooting usually occurs when you buy a bow that you really can't handle. The draw weight is too high for you to control, so you get into the bad habit of releasing the arrow when the weight builds to a difficult point and you let the arrow fly even though you haven't reached your anchor point.

This is the worst type of draw and shoot system. The best cure for it, perhaps the only cure, is to forget the macho, ego nonsense and get a lighter draw weight, one that you can control and hold to anchor. If you shoot a compound, you have the advantage that you can lower the draw weight to one that will allow you to use proper draw and release technique. As your muscles tone up, the poundage can be increased until you reach the level you desire. If you are shooting recurves or longbows, you have to either lift weights or get a lighter draw weight bow.

The proper method of snap shooting, that used by the "old timers" who could shoot dimes and aspirins out of the air, ducks on the wing and all sorts of fantastic shooting, used the proper snap shooting system. There could be some argument that the bow will deliver its peak power at the time of draw and immediate release. If you draw and hold for several seconds, does the bow lose power or does it remain the same? A good point to ponder. To answer, look at flight shooters who shoot only for distance. They shoot bows in the monster draw weight ranges as well as more moderate draw weights, but they actually draw the arrow into the rest. As the tip of the arrow reaches a predetermined point on the rest, they release the arrow literally on draw. That is what can be termed controlled snap shooting and that is what you need to develop.

With controlled snap shooting, you can draw on a running animal, hold and follow to get your lead and let fly when the lead is correct. If you draw and shoot when the animal is first sighted and starts its flight, your arrow will hit where he was, not where he is. You need to learn to hold long enough to get proper lead. That comes with time and practice.

The classic target archer stance is illustrated as the bow is held vertically using a loose grip, sights level.

In this position, the feet are unchanged, but the bow is slightly canted, opening up the view of the target.

Most snap shooters and instinctive bowhunters shoot longbows and recurves and cant the bow from the grip. Sight shooters basically must hold the bow vertical in order to have the sight picture in the right perspective. Cant the bow and your sights will be wrong. The instinctive bowhunter can shoot a bow in almost any position, from vertical to horizontal, if the need arises. If you have a chance at the perfect game trophy and a large tree limb is in the way, the sight shooter must move to avoid the limb to get the proper bow/sight alignment. The instinctive archer merely drops to one knee or to his butt and shoots below that limb, canting the bow to avoid any contact on release. You figure out which is for you and do it.

Can you shoot a compound instinctively? There have been articles printed stating you can't and that you can't snap shoot a compound. That's strange. I have been doing it for years, but in a different manner. Yes, you can shoot the compound instinctively, because the system works the same regardless of the bow used. I have found that the peak of the draw on a compound bow throws off my so-called sight picture and I do have to allow time for the bow to settle down. That allows me to regain the stability of the bow. Compared to sight shooters, it isn't a long time.

Can you cant a compound? Of course you can! A compound is merely another form of stick and string and it will cant just as easily as any other bow. Some of the radical let-offs we have today on compounds does get the snap shot/instinctive archer off base. They have to regain the sight picture, but they do it and don't even think about it as a rule. You can have close to identical shooting styles with almost any bow. There may be exceptions with the forward handles and overdraws, but you could probably work out a satisfactory system for any bow.

How far was that rabbit from the hunter and how did the hunter judge the distance? Here is where you can become involved in some hot conversations in a hunt camp if you have a variety of hunting styles represented. The instinctive bowhunter actually uses the rangefinder in the eye to judge distance. If you close one eye, you can't judge distance. Did you ever look at the two "eyes" of a mechanical rangefinder? There are two openings that use angled mirrors to determine the actual distance. This system was used on cameras for many years to focus on the subject.

There are several ways of judging distance to a target without sights or rangefinders. Some hunters can't get the hang of it and resort to optics to judge distance. But that

Longbow shooters might open the foot stance, cant the bow and bend slightly at the hip, "shooting into" the target, a style typical of most traditional archers.

Recurve shooters will use a similar shooting stance.

takes time and personally, I have never seen a deer, elk, bear or even a rabbit that would wait for me to take the range, pick the right pin, hold vertical, come to draw, hold to settle the sight and release. Maybe I've been doing something wrong all these years.

When you bring the bowhand up and align it with the target, you can use what is called a gap system. You learn by plenty of shooting and using the same equipment all the time, learning just how much gap you need between the tip of the arrow and the body of the game. In truth, when you are close, your gap will have the tip of the arrow below the game. When far, your tip will be held over the game. With practice, you really can drop that arrow in with accuracy.

There is a term, point of aim, that was used before the compound came on the scene. I haven't seen it in years, but it is still there. What you do is place the tip of the arrow on the target — or center of a large target — and back off until the arrow drops into the center of the target. That will be your *point-on* distance. Beyond that, you will hold over the game to have the arrow drop on target. It really is quite simple, but it takes time to develop these little techniques.

Those who believe there is no instinctive shooting could almost be right. But if you aren't using a sight and hit what

you aim at all the time, what else do you call it?

When I started bowhunting many years back, there were few, if any, sights for bows. If we wanted a sight, we stuck a piece of tape to the back of the bow, found one of those large colored pins, stuck it into the tape so it wouldn't move and used that for a sight pin. It worked, too. Eventually we had a series of pins stuck into that tape for various ranges. There was one big problem; you couldn't lay your bow down or all the pins would move and you had to start over.

That was too much of a nuisance, so most of us learned to use the gap system, the instinctive, controlled snap-release shooting technique. When I draw on an animal, I never see anything but the spot I am aiming for. The arrow is placed in the string — I fletch with feathers, so could care less about a hen or cock feather position — the arrow is placed on the shelf rest. There are no buttons, no channels or anything but a piece of Teflon tape secured to the riser and a piece of moleskin to prevent noise on the bow window.

The bow is drawn, still without removing the eye from the target. When the thumb of my right hand touches the corner of my mouth, the arrow is on its way. My eye

It is possible to shoot instinctively from a kneeling position, as demonstrated in these two photos. The canted bow gets closer to the ground and under overhanging limbs. Arrow has no head and camera uses a self-timer.

remains on the target as the flight of the arrow is followed unconsciously. Distance isn't considered, but I feel that over the years I have learned to use the left arm as a rangefinder. My left arm raises the bow to the correct angle, an instinctive gap system. It directs the distance control. The draw weight of the bow and weight of the arrow must always be consistent for this to work and it does work well, thank you.

A few years ago while javelina hunting in Arizona, I was headed back to camp late in the afternoon, almost dusk, with a light drizzle starting. I had found little sign of game, so I had started picking up and carrying selective chunks of cactus to use in making knife handles. I had several stuck into the belt of my fanny pack.

As I walked down a small ridge, I caught a glimpse of black to my left. Pig or barrel cactus? This turned out to be a javelina snoozing at the base of a green barrel cactus. It was rather late in the day for a snooze, but he was a pig. I carefully set down the cactus and the cigar I had been puffing. I had stopped hunting hard and was heading for camp. I slipped my XX75 2018 arrow out of the bow quiver, nocked the arrow, never taking my eyes from the pig as it snorted and moved below the cactus. The wind was in my face, so that much was right. I moved to within what might have been fifteen or twenty yards. The pig started getting restless so I came up with the bow, drew and, as the thumb hit the corner of my mouth, the arrow was on its way. I had wanted to hit him at the spot behind the shoulder. He was lying down and the arrow couldn't pass through.

I watched the hot pink fletch close on the target as it hit where I had aimed. The pig grunted, stood up, turned around and plopped over dead. A heart shot. While I was skinning and cleaning the javelina in camp, some other hunters stopped by and we talked about sign and pig herds. One of the hunters noted I had no sights on my bow. After discussing the shot and possible distance, he asked, "What if you had missed?"

That never entered my mind. I am not a target shooter and miss many times at targets which aren't going anywhere anyway. I find that after days in the field, I never think of missing. I am confident of only a clean, sure kill. That is what hunting is all about; food in the freezer and fun in the hunt.

Last year, pigs were hard to find, but I found two herds in one day. The first was in the early morning and there was no way to get an arrow through the thick brush. They faded away and I never picked them up again. That afternoon I checked another area and literally walked into at least ten javelina. They were right there, feet, not yards away and standing rock steady so I wouldn't see them. I pulled an arrow from the quiver, nocked, keeping my eye on a big pig, brought the bow arm up, drew, anchored and shot in one motion. With game that close, they can and will spook and run at any time. I didn't hit the javelina at three long paces, but I did hit a tough, mesquite limb about the size of your little finger, dead center. The arrow blew apart, the pigs grunted and ran off.

That twig was never seen, but after the pigs left, I could see it plainly when I retraced my location. If there is any one thing you need to develop in instinctive shooting ability, it is total concentration on your target. That concentration eliminates all other objects and you zero all thought, eye control and everything else to that target. Eliminate all extraneous noise, vision and hearing. This is what I feel is needed to get the game in the bag. Recently I have found myself looking at game animals like they were on a chart, picking out the vital areas as if I had X-ray eyes to find the best shot placement. It does help to know where the vital organs on a game animal are. Some bowhunters haven't learned this yet.

There is another problem that I have found. That problem is movement of the game on which you are drawing. I walked around some scrub oak on a ridge in Colorado and found a three-point bedded down casually, holding low so I wouldn't see him. I followed my usual routine; remove arrow from bow quiver, nock on string, bring bow to shooting position, canted to the right at the top.

The draw is almost complete and the arrow milliseconds from being released when Mr. Buck wiggles his left ear. Mule deer have large ears, the better to hear with, but I can tell you that there is one, probably a nice big four-point or better now, that has a pierced left ear. When he wiggled that ear, that is where my eye and the arrow went. It made a neat hole in the middle of that big, floppy ear. What can you do but laugh? He certainly wasn't hurt, except for his pride. If someone ever bags that pierced ear buck, they are in for a surprise.

There are several deer, a few javelina and various small game that have similar weird ears that wiggled just as I was ready to release. Ear piercing seems to be my alternate hunting technique.

What does it take to become an instinctive archer? Patience is the first criteria. Concentration is high on the list, both in shooting style and the target. You can cant or hold the bow straight, but canting seems to go with the system as it opens up the vision better. The eye isn't blocked by the limb and riser compared to a vertical hold. Learn controlled snap shooting or learn to hold and release when ready. Snap shooting can get away from you and cause many problems that take longer to correct than you can imagine. After that, practice, practice, practice.

My first varmint shot with a bow was a ground squirrel sitting at the edge of his hole. I drew, aimed, shot and concentrated on that little target. When I hit it, I realized it had been almost one fluid, totally controlled reaction from sighting to picking up the squirrel. Most of my bagged game has been the same. I have no conscious feeling of reading distance or anything but total concentration.

How good are some of the instinctive bowhunters? Two friends of mine were shooting a tightly contested broadhead target round. Both shot recurves, used canted, controlled snap release and were really deadly at just about any distance. A perfect twenty score on a deer target and the remark was made that the only way to beat that shot was to split the arrow. So that is what the other bowhunter did; he split the arrow that was perfect in the twenty ring. Luck? When an archer calls his or her shot, makes that shot just as it is called, there has to be more than luck involved.

Pick up your bow, regardless of what type it is, go to a safe area and place a small target on the butt. Walk away and without knowing the distance, turn, draw, anchor and release as soon as you have the right sight picture. You may miss, you may come close. You never know until you try. When you learn the technique, you will have more fun, spend less money on gadgets and possibly get more game than you ever imagined.

Terrain and game may force the archer even lower, into almost seated stance to shoot. Positions need practice.

If the limbs are short enough, C.R. Learn shows that bow may be held vertically, if awkwardly, when seated.

CHAPTER

18

HUNTING FOR ARCHERS

Hunting May Not Be For Everybody, But There Are Some Reasons You May Want To Try

NOW THAT YOU have become a proficient archer, what comes next? Shall you continue with your archery career, improving skills on paper targets, or perhaps move on to 3-D target shooting? There are numerous choices for every type of archer. One choice you should consider — as approximately three million Americans have — is bowhunting.

Archers bowhunt for many reasons. Many enjoy the outdoors, the woods, the prairies; being away from the everyday struggle to make a living. Others seek the solitude of hunting a game animal alone or with one or two partners, but without the pressure of hundreds of other people. It is quiet, restful recreation with plenty of fresh air and exercise.

In most states, the typical archery deer season opens in late summer, well before rifle season. This may be followed by a black powder hunt, then the firearms season and, later, perhaps another archery season late in the year.

Even California, a state not noted for the length of its deer seasons, has special archery-only seasons which allow the bowhunter to spend as many as three months in the field. Some Southern states are even more liberal, with four or five months for some areas of bowhunting.

If the bowhunter cares to compete with rifle hunters during the firearms season, many states permit it, although the chances of shooting a deer with an arrow while other hunters are shooting rifles or shotguns can be rather slim. But it can be and is done with success. Point is, most states and provinces allow plenty of time for the archer to hunt.

Not only is time a favorable factor, so is location. Most governing bodies restrict the distance from roads and buildings where firearms may be discharged. Some places prohibit gun hunting altogether, but permit bowhunting.

The County of Los Angeles, for instance, prohibits all firearms hunting within the county, but offers a long archery-only deer season within sight of some of the heaviest populations and expensive real estate in the country.

Deer, as we shall discuss in the next chapter, are the most popular bowhunting game animal, although not the only one. There are other big-game seasons in North America, as well as dozens of small-game animals legally hunted. Elk exist in huntable numbers mostly in the Rocky

Utah bowhunter, Willie Norton, is all smiles as he displays this mule deer buck trophy. Norton is one who enjoys extended archery seasons.

Mountain states and the West. Some plains states are home to hundreds of thousands of antelope. Bears, mountain sheep and goats, caribou, moose, mountain lion, musk-ox, wild boar, javelina, alligators and even some fish and birds have been taken by bow and arrow. Rabbits, ground hogs, prairie dogs, coyotes and other pests and varmints are fair game for the archer.

Other continents, too, have their special archery hunts. Bowhunters are active in South America, Australia, Africa and some countries of Europe. Eastern Europe is more receptive to archery hunting than are countries in the west.

Informal studies have shown that the average archery deer hunter will require seven years of trial before he or she is able to take that first deer. This is not to say you will not fill your tag the first time out — it has happened — but it probably will take longer. This should not discourage you. In the meantime, you will learn plenty about animal habits and habitat, about the seasons and the terrain you are hunting, about your equipment and about yourself. You will spend some wonderful days and nights in the fields and forests, communing with nature. Taking game is important, but most bowhunters feel the effort, the act of the hunt, is as important as filling the game bag. Good hunting!

BOWHUNTING EQUIPMENT

For The Hunter, There Are Several Extra Things Needed For Success — Here Are Some Of Them

YOU WILL NEED more than a bow, arrows and related archery equipment to become an archery hunter. At times, the list may seem endless. More and more equipment and gadgets are on the market each year to help us become better, more efficient bowhunters.

Every bowhunter needs a good pair of hunting boots. There are people who hunt in sneakers and running shoes, but they are rare. A good pair of hunting boots will keep your feet warm and dry; absolutely essential to your health and comfort while hunting. Boot needs vary with the climate and terrain in which you are hunting.

If most of your hunting is to be in the desert West, a pair of mountain hiking boots of top-grade leather is preferred. They should have rubber soles with deep lugs for the best

Two basic types of hunting boots with different uses. Rubber bottoms and Cordura nylon uppers, left, are best for wettest conditions. Kangaroo leather, above, provides lightweight, comfortable hiking all day.

footing on loose, steep terrain. The brand of soles most commonly sold is Vibram; a pattern made popular about twenty years ago for hiking boots and still favored by many hunters. The leather is thick enough to give protection over rough ground and above the ankles to reduce the possibility of turning your foot while climbing.

Some will argue that the lug soles are too hard and make too much noise while trying to stalk an animal. Softer, crepe-like rubber soles may be better for some. If hunting in wet climes with plenty of rain and/or snow, the pac-type boot is the way to go. These are the rubber-bottom boots with leather or heavy nylon fabric for the tops. The good ones will keep your feet warm and dry all day in the wettest weather.

Wear wool socks inside any hunting boot. Even in the hottest weather, thick wool socks will insulate and actually cool your feet, protecting them from blisters much better than any other material.

The next item is camouflage clothing. To be sure, not every bowhunter agrees that camo is an absolute requirement. A look at some of the famous bowhunters of this century will reveal Saxton Pope, Arther Young, Howard Hill and Fred Bear not clad in camouflage clothing as we know it. But they relied on subdued, blending outerwear and knew a thing or two about good hunting techniques. Before World War II, there was little or no camo clothing available to archers, unless they made it themselves.

There are dozens of camouflage patterns and colors available; more are introduced almost every month. The key to success is slow movement when the game is not looking and blending in with the plants when they look up. One camouflage pattern may not be satisfactory with every season and every location.

The desert Southwest is predominantly brown. The Northwest is mostly green during deer-hunting season, with the possibility of snow at any time. The Midwest and East will show typical fall colors of brown, red and yellow during most of the deer seasons and always have the chance of snow. The Southeast may be greener, may show the fall colors, but have only the slight chance of light snow in some years. Pick a high-contrast pattern which seems to reflect the dominant colors of your region.

Look for material that is quiet. Some camo clothing is far too loud when brush or thorns rub against you in the field.

Well-washed, all-cotton wool or fleece material will be quieter. It if rains or is cold, plan on wearing long underwear and/or rainproof gear *under* the camo clothes, so leave room when you buy your camo outerwear. Other bowhunters in your area are good sources for advice before you buy.

Don't forget about your hands and face. In some areas, camo makeup paint is preferred; in others, hunters use a mesh face net. The net has quick on-off advantages, but may distort your vision when shooting unless open around the eyes. Practice with a net on before committing to the hunt. Most bowhunters use camo paint. In cold weather, camouflage gloves are a requirement.

The argument over scents rages on. Some deer hunters swear by them and others do not. There are basically two kinds: lures and cover scents. Luring scents are based either on typical game food, such as apples, corn or cedars, while others are of does in estrus to attract a buck. Doe scents must be used only during the time of year when does are in estrus, or they are not likely to fool a buck. Cover scents are intended to mask the human odor so frightening to game animals. One of the earliest cover scents for varmint hunters was skunk smell; it takes a dedicated hunter to use it. There are dozens of scents on the market. Some work some of the time in some places. Again, seek the advice of successful bowhunters in your area to see what works.

The question of accurate range estimation is answered only one way: a mechanical range-estimating device. There are few makes on the market — some are rather bulky, others fit on the bow in the way of a decal or pictures of deer on the bow. The pictures vary in size and the hunter simply matches the deer viewed with the appropriate picture, then reads off the estimated range. Most bowhunters, unless adept at accurately estimating range, will benefit from a rangefinder of some sort. More hunting shots are missed because of faulty range estimation than any other single cause.

No hunter should leave the vehicle or the camp without emergency equipment and they're easiest carried with a small backpack or hip pack. Minimum survival supplies include space blanket, waterproof matches, knife, compass, et cetera. Most will fit in lightweight hip pack, also known as a fanny pack. Pack along a spare bowstring, broadhead wrench, rangefinder, binoculars, camo paint, finger tab, first-aid gear, maps, small bottle of scent, insect repellent, Allen wrenches, snacks and the like. A couple pounds worth of gear may save your hunt or perhaps save your life.

The choice of a tree stand depends on the game you will be hunting and in what part of the country. Tree stands are the gear of choice for whitetail hunters in the East and Midwest. They generally are not used by mule deer hunters of the West, although there are exceptions in both areas.

The simplest tree stand is just a notched board that is wedged in the crotch of a tree. Firmly in place, the board will hold any hunter for a short period of time, but most archers will soon tire of standing immobile on a small platform. These stands are easily portable and quite cheap.

Next is a stand that's placed in the tree semi-permanently. The hunter must climb the tree, perhaps with the aid of screw-in climbing spikes, then lash the stand to the tree. These stands usually are left in the same location for most of a season.

Camouflage pattern selection will depend upon terrain, growth pattern in area, above, below, right. Rangefinder, below right, is for archers.

Camo net, above, covers hunter's face. Below: Day pack has snow camo.

A simple platform tree stand, above, is attached to trunk. Tower stand, below, is found in thick brush areas with no trees.

Many bowhunters favor use of deer attractant scents. Above: Dominant buck by Robbins and estrus doe, below, by Buck.

Some bowhunters favor large folding hunting knives, such as those by Buck Knives, above, Browning, below.

A lightweight tree stand may be backpacked into the hunting area each day, moved perhaps once or twice a day and packed out each evening. The portable stand is made of aluminum tubing and weighs less than the more-permanent steel stand.

Either of these stands may be offered in a climbing version. That is, it is constructed in such a way that it may be used to help the hunter get up a tree. Usually the foot section straps to the feet. A separate hand or arm section is used to pull the body upward. The foot section is tilted and locks into the tree trunk as the arm or hand portion is moved upward again. It's sort of like a caterpiller crawling up a tree.

The ladder stand has two subtypes. The regular ladder stand is just that; instead of climbing the tree trunk, the hunter props the stand against the tree and climbs up via the lightweight tubular ladder attached. In many areas, it is illegal to spike or otherwise damage trees while climbing and a ladder stand is ideal. And some trees are too difficult to climb without a ladder. However, ladder stands can be a bit bulky and difficult to carry through heavy undergrowth without help.

Another type of ladder stand is the free-standing tower. These are used in the hill country of south Texas, where there are no trees to climb and the hunter must get above the thick, high brush. The stand rests atop a pyramid or triangular structure with a ladder attached to one side. The seat on top may swivel for shots in any direction.

Deer calls and deer antler rattling devices have been used successfully in several areas of North America, although some are illegal in some locations. Antlers, genuine or artificial, are struck and rubbed together in the manner of two bucks fighting over a doe in estrus. The object is to lure in other bucks that think there is a doe in heat nearby. Other lures are tubes or mouth diaphragms which, when properly blown, imitate contented bucks, bleating does and crying fawns; all to make a buck think a doe may be near.

A bow-carrying strap is handy on long hikes or trips into the tree stand area. The strap should leave both hands free while walking or standing.

Many bowhunters rely on some sort of wind direction indicator. It may be as simple as thin thread tied to the upper end of the bowstring, or a tiny plastic bottle of talcum. The talcum powder is squeezed into the air and the wind direction quickly determined.

It is always a good idea to carry a small flashlight with you, no matter what time you start out or expect to get back. Aside from the possible emergency uses of the flashlight, it may be essential for following a blood trail after dark.

Don't forget a small camera in your day pack. Be optimistic! You *will* down that game and there is no better way to record those memories than on film.

As time goes on and you become more experienced, you will add some favorite items and delete others on your list of hunting gear. It can be easy to carry too much, although emergency equipment should always be carried, no matter how short and easy the trip starts out to be. — *Roger Combs*

WHERE DO BOWHUNTERS COME FROM?
Young Or Old, More Bowhunters Are Needed

TO KEEP NUMBERS increasing in the sport of bowhunting, new archers or converts from firearms hunting must continue to join us. In the past, the largest percentage of new bowhunters have come from the ranks of gun hunters, although there always have been those who have hunted only with bows and arrows.

Such states as Pennsylvania, Wisconsin and Michigan routinely sell nearly 250,000 bowhunting licenses every year. In the South, bowhunters are a fast-growing segment of the outdoor populations.

New bowhunters must be recruited for the sport to flourish. Ohio hunter Bob Grewell looked into the challenge and this is what he found:

The young hunter had been successful with firearms, but working with bow and arrows teaches him the more intimate rewards of one-on-one, close-range hunting.

UNFRIENDLY, CHILLING winds gusted along the brushy fenceline where the first-year bowhunter sat in a ground blind, almost hugging himself to keep warm. It was not the first day he had hunted, but only now had this 16-year-old taken up deer hunting with a bow. He had taken whitetail bucks with a shotgun each of two previous years and loved the sights, sounds, odors and sensations of hunting this elusive game animal. But between the meanness of the weather and the lack of deer sightings, he was becoming discouraged.

He considered his decision to switch from gun to bow and realized maybe the only reason was because he had been fascinated with his father's enthusiasm about bowhunting.

Now, though, he was cold, discouraged, cramped and bored. Deep down inside he felt sure there was a positive reason why he'd chosen this more demanding method of deer hunting. His limited association with experienced bowhunters had led him to believe this form of hunting had many invisible qualities that hunters must experience to understand their meaning fully.

Suddenly, his thoughts were interrupted by a flash of movement. A large, grayish-colored shape seemed to be floating down the fenceline as if being blown toward him by the wind. The teenager immediately lost all sense of discomfort. His body warmed suddenly, and his cramps disappeared.

The fine ten-pointer never knew the young bowhunter was lying in wait. The buck nosed along the fenceline in a natural, carefree manner. The closer he moved, the more tension invaded the hunter's mind and body.

The young bowhunter was awed! This close to a secretive whitetail, he could distinguish the texture of the buck's body hair. He studied the buck's chest heaving as it breathed. He could even see the buck's eyelashes when his target stopped and scanned the landscape. That's how close he was! The tension, excitement, beauty and thrill melded with the fact that he was able to get this close to a mature buck! He knew now why his dad loved this type of deer hunting so much.

Taking a few more steps, the buck stopped broadside at twelve yards. The bow was positioned and the excited young hunter was ready to draw. His eyes were fixed on the chest cavity of his quarry, just as he had been taught. He remembered that he shouldn't look at the animal's antlers. Concentrate on the kill-zone, he'd been told. The young hunter brought his bow to full draw just as the whitetail turned its head in the opposite direction.

Clack! The arrow fell off the bow rest and tapped the side of the bow. Pandemonium broke loose, as the deer vaulted from side-to-side, escaping down the fencerow.

Stunned, dejected and angry, the young hunter sat, still with his bow at partial full-draw position, for almost a minute.

He had lost this time. But hadn't he also won? He realized then he was hooked on bowhunting because of a first-hand close hunting encounter that he never had experienced before. There was more to this sport than just hiding, waiting and shooting a buck. He couldn't wait to get home and explain the whole sequence of feelings and events. He knew his father would understand.

I don't believe there are many things on this earth as exciting to a bowhunter as *any* morning of whitetail season. Even more exhilarating is being within range of your first buck of the season. A hunter's age or experience doesn't seem to have much influence on reactions, either. Even a creaky-boned older hunter will lie awake at night, stimulated by the anticipation of being able to hunt with a bow. The internal motivators in each of us tend to rekindle our strength, energy and enthusiasm. This must tell us something about the impact of bowhunting upon humans. Most of us have experienced this feeling of "hunting lust." We feel bowhunting's uplifting sensation and gratification, no matter what our age. Not every human feels the same way we do, though.

Ideally, we want to inject our love of the sport into others; we particularly want to to share this gift with our children. But do we push and prod and try to force others to accept and participate in bowhunting? Human nature's rebellious traits can interfere and turn off desires if we push too hard. Too much, too soon, can alienate some people.

Possibly the ideal way to share all of bowhunting's benefits is to entice a person through positive association. We should not force a novice to become involved, but persuade one by actual contact with the sport. We can do this best by sharing bits and pieces, getting a potential recruit to view practice sessions, read material about bowhunting while we provide occasional explanations about our sport and share the many facets covering equipment choice. The most persuasive impact comes from first-hand experience, in my opinion.

I truly love bowhunting. My wife will suggest that I often overindulge, but it is a special part of my life, as with thousands of other hunters. I know many, including myself,

Young and/or inexperienced minds will benefit from verbal and visual involvement with other hunters, above. Formal bowhunter education classes will help improve the new hunter's dedication to bowhunting.

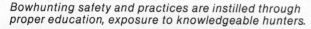

Bowhunting safety and practices are instilled through proper education, exposure to knowledgeable hunters.

who used to be die-hard gun hunters. We had never picked up a bow. I still own several guns and still love the solid, hefty feel of a gun in my hands. Although my guns don't get as much exercise during deer season as my archery equipment, they still are a vital link to my outdoor activities.

Easy as it is to believe in the lethal effects, the aesthetics, organizational strength and the importance of the bow and arrow to modern hunters and wildlife managers, as well as

Left: Time spent in the field with experienced hunters results in knowledge of the woods and of safety rules for bowhunters. Rules of the game, above, are learned.

how much personal reward and satisfaction bowhunting gives each hunter, bowhunters should not come off as arrogant or domineering when trying to persuade a non-bowhunter to take up the bow.

An introduction to bowhunting should be slow and easy, presented as an exciting alternative to gun hunting's basically short seasons. I never have felt it necessary to sell bowhunting; it can sell itself. Bowhunting's addictive forces make a much better hunter out of inexperienced as well as veteran gun hunters. They learn to be patient and careful. I have observed that anyone who will participate in bowhunting normally becomes much more excited about hunting in general, a more conscientious person and a more dedicated outdoorsman.

Hundreds of thousands of bowhunters truly find this archaic form of hunting extremely pleasing. Just to sit alone in some secluded blind or tree stand deep in a private woodland deer haunt reduces stress in mind and body; it tends to change attitudes for the better. When social pressures and other human disregards raise your blood pressure, bowhunting can be like a visit to your doctor. Hunting deer with a bow puts a hunter in a different world; an environment where your success depends on your skills, experience and method. It is so symbolic of the essence of hunting that you do another person a great favor when you introduce him to the sport.

We need to expose our sport to others in a positive manner; instillment through association. If every bowhunter introduced just one other non-bowhunter or young person, our sport would benefit in so many ways. Those who grasp and stay with an activity are those who are taught properly from the start. Youngsters of today who don't hunt — specifically don't bowhunt — often tend to be negative about the sport. This is especially true when they haven't been introduced to the sport properly; they have been sub-

jected to ignorant, negative remarks, or they have been pressured to hunt with a bow.

The philosophy that association and acceptance of an idea and activity are based on gradual introduction enables the individual to pursue the endeavor in a more dedicated manner. Most bowhunters who are taught about the sport stay with it, haven't been forced to participate. No one should have bowhunting pushed on them.

If I never spent another day afield in bowhunting for the rest of my life, I would cherish the idea of a young inexperienced person adopting the sport simply because he or she wanted to bowhunt, not because of being forced to participate.

Young people today could use association with the bow as a means to learning responsiblity, respect for themselves and the animal they hunt, self-confidence and developing a better understanding of life as a whole.

Many youngsters, such as the one below, have their first exposure to hunting game while using firearms.

Young archers who are able to experience all facets of the sport will benefit, even if they watch and listen.

I feel fortunate that my sons always have loved the outdoors, and for that, I am grateful. I'm sure each of us who has children, knows of a neighborhood youth who has listened to stories of your bowhunting activities. Their natural curiosity leads them to listen.

I always had hoped my own children would pursue bowhunting. In many ways, I exposed them visually or verbally to practice sessions, hunting preparations and conversations with hunting friends. Not too long ago, my oldest son was teetering on the verge of bowhunting. I wanted so much to have him cross the line, but I didn't want to make him feel I was forcing him.

When my son badgered me to hunt for whitetail, he never once mentioned using a bow. All he ever did regarding hunting deer with a bow was to watch and listen. I was glad he wanted to hunt, because I knew he would gain valu-

Things well known to the experienced hunter, such as how to properly hide, must be taught the new bowhunter.

The important safety rules cannot be over-stressed to the new bowhunter. In a tree stand, a safety belt is absolutely essential, as this instructor demonstrates.

able knowledge. He did take a bowhunter education course one year, but I was disappointed he hadn't shown more interest in hunting with a bow. The last thing I wanted was to make him feel I was forcing him to adopt my favorite sport. All I could do was make sure my bowhunting conversations and actions contained the proper etiquette. My concern was needless, because his prior audible and visual association with archery apparently had been ingrained. His previous gun hunting success on whitetal bucks was only the means through which he had made his final decision to choose a bow.

I have become friends with serious bowhunters who feel comfortable having children listen and look up to them. Their conversations, confident attitude and concern for others has always stirred my two sons' curiosity, just as I have noticed other youngsters sit up and take notice. Throughout their growing years, just being around bowhunters has apparently had a positive influence on their interest and knowledge of the sport.

The impact serious bowhunters have on non-bowhunters and youth is of vital importance in making a conscientious future bowhunter. Where our future bowhunters come from can depend greatly on each of us; our comments and actions. The way we present ourselves to them, what we say and what we do can change a young or non-bowhunter's life in either a positive or negative manner.

As for our first bowhunting son, he is now head-over-heels in love with the sport. Practicing, reading about archery and spending time afield has become much more exciting for him. Applying his continuously gained knowledge and hoping to rectify last year's mistakes next season, he has taken up bowhunting on his own. It gives me a good feeling to know there will be one more hunter in the woods each fall; one who truly appreciates and loves this exciting sport. — *Bob Grewell*

CHAPTER 19

BOWHUNTING DEER

The Most Popular Big Game Anywhere Are North American Deer — They Are Plentiful And Challenging

Typical mule deer habitat will include the high country terrain with its evergreens, grassy meadows. In many areas of West, water is hard to find.

DEER ARE, without doubt, the most popular big-game animal hunted in North America by hunters using modern firearms, black powder guns or bow and arrows. The animals are also the most populous big-game animal on the continent, produce some of the best-eating game meat one may find anywhere and help provide bowhunters with challenges aplenty.

Deer habitat extends from coast to coast, from Alaska through Mexico, in all states except Hawaii. There are more than thirty different species and subspecies throughout North America, but the three major hunting categories of deer are the whitetail, mule deer and blacktail; the blacktail is actually a subspecies of mule deer, with a wide-ranging habitat and definite habits of its own.

In many areas, particularly in the American West, the three deer families' habitat overlaps, often considerably. Whitetail deer, in particular, seem to be expanding their range westward, sometimes all the way to the Pacific Coast. Blacktails and mule deer often share all their habitat and may be hunted together. Separate game tags are generally not required.

In the Twentieth Century, enlightened game managers and sportsmen have been able to increase the population of deer, especially whitetail deer, dramatically. In some locations, their efforts have been too successful, with deer considered by many southern farmers little more than crop-eating pests. But the steps have led to vast huntable deer populations in the Midwest, Southeast, the East, including New York State and Pennsylvania, north into Canada and south through much of Mexico. Whitetail deer herds in

MULE DEER HABITAT

WHITETAIL HABITAT

some areas have outgrown the ability of the habitat to support them, with the number of deer killed by vehicle accidents almost matching the hunting harvest.

There are more than a dozen subspecies of whitetail deer, with major branches in Virginia, Kansas, the Dakotas and the Southwest. The whitetail deer in Arizona are the smallest subspecies, called Coues deer. They are considered by most hunters as the most difficult to take of all deer.

Whitetail are creatures of habit and normally do not travel far from their home habitat. Most will spend their lifespans within a mile or so, unless forced to leave by the actions of nature or man. Even so, they will most likely return to familiar surroundings as soon as possible. They prefer heavy foliage near food sources, including agricultural crops; soybeans and corn are favorites. They like wooded areas and occasional open flatlands.

Typical mule deer behavior is different from that of whitetail. Mule deer are travelers; some have been reported traveling as much as a hundred miles in search of more food, better weather or to escape the influence of man. They normally browse over vast territories for food and may not follow regular patterns of travel as whitetails are prone to do. Typical summer mule deer habitat will be high in the most rugged mountains, as far from humans as possible, but in fall and winter, they will move lower and are often seen in rural areas and along highways. Mule deer favor open, rugged terrain, broken by some forests. They may attack some agricultural crops, but not as aggressively as whitetails.

The blacktail is sometimes larger than other mule deer and has many of the same characteristics, but with a black tail. They have the large pointed ears of the more numerous mule deer, but favor the western coastal territories of California, Oregon, Washington and British Columbia. A separate subspecies of blacktail is found in Alaska and parts of British Columbia: the Sitka blacktail. When they can be found, blacktail deer are in heavy timber and logged-over terrain. Hunting techniques more closely resemble whitetail than those for mule deer. Because of the terrain, blacktail are more creatures of habit, but not as solidly as the whitetail.

Some deer-hunting techniques remain the same no mat-

Deer hunters must learn to use full camo, including hands and face, when hunting, no matter the habitat.

ter which type of animal hunted. Basically, one needs a bow of at least forty-five pounds draw weight; fifty or more is preferred, on up to eighty or ninety pounds for some Western hunters. Good, matched arrows with the sharpest broadheads, a quiver, camouflage clothing and the ability to hit a target out to some reasonable distance are all the same wherever you are hunting. In some areas, hunting whitetail deer and some blacktails, tree stands are mandatory. In others, a comfortable pair of hiking boots will be as necessary as the bow.

The ability to move quietly through deer habitat, to remain calm and quiet while observing or waiting and a knowledge of the game being hunted are required of all deer hunters.

Hunting skills are the same for any, but techniques for each may vary. Differences are primarily those divided between hunting whitetail or mule deer.

WHITETAIL DEER

Many areas of the South contain trophy whitetails, available to bowhunters. Mississippi, a state with enlightened game management, was home to these two.

WHITETAILS are the most populous deer in North America and seem to be expanding in numbers and habitat, mostly through the efforts of enlightened game departments and influential hunting lobbyists.

Whitetail deer roam over most of eastern, midwestern, southern and central North America. Hunter numbers — archery hunter numbers — reflect this abundance, with more than a half million archery tags annually sold in the combined states of Pennsylvania and Michigan alone. More than 300,000 archery deer hunting tags were sold in Michigan in a recent year, a figure which moves the state into the "most bowhunters" column.

The Midwest has long been famous for its whitetail deer hunting, with good reason. In more recent years, though, the South has been moving up in bowhunting numbers. Certainly, some states such as South Carolina, Alabama, Georgia and others have the most liberal bag limits for deer hunters.

Overall deer populations have increased steadily because of wise game management as well as better habitat for the animals. It is often necessary for game managers to increase hunting seasons and bag limits to maintain a balance. Actually, in terms of herd mortality, hunters come in fourth. Mother nature is the greatest danger to deer, with winter snows devastating many herds from time to time. The automobile is second to weather, especially in heavily populated whitetail states. Dogs, wild and domes-

tic are the third destroyer of deer; humans come in fourth.

Major crops in the South include soybeans, corn, cotton and various grains; all crops attractive to deer. Deer take their toll on agricultural crops and most farmers welcome hunters, especially bowhunters, as a tool to keep deer populations in bounds. Many large farm holdings have regular hunting programs with comfortable lodges, managers and hunting guides catering to the resident and non-resident hunter. A good hunting program can be an income-producer for the farmer.

Mississippi is not usually the first state that comes to mind when bowhunters get together to talk about whitetail hotspots. Not a lot has been written about the area which, in fact, abounds in the illusive game.

Whitetail deer in Mississippi in particular, are doing well. This trend is due to several factors. They are plentiful, healthy, enjoy growing populations in most areas and, on some well managed private and public ranges, are producing trophy antler racks. The state's Department of Wildlife Conservation encourages enlightened game management on privately owned farms and clubs, including the necessary food crops and either-sex game harvesting.

One of the most common and earlier symptoms of a dwindling food supply is a decline in buck antler development. In fact, say Mississippi game management experts, when a deer herd has been above carrying capacity for several years, even older bucks may grow only spike antlers. Adequate food is the key factor.

Among The Deer Of North America, Whitetail Are The Most Plentiful And The Most Hunted

Many of the private areas of Mississippi are leased or owned by hunting clubs, practicing modern deer management techniques. One such is the Pecan Grove Wildlife Club at Fort Adams. Located in the southwest corner of the state, it's just north of the Louisiana state line and on the eastern banks of the Mississippi River. The club is owned and developed by businessman George Haynes of Baton Rouge, Louisiana. Haynes obtained the old 7000-acre plantation several years ago and has implemented programs to improve deer, wild turkey, duck, fishing and small game habitat.

The state's deer season for archery opens around the first of October and runs until mid-November. Those who hunt with archery and/or black powder are permitted to take up to five bucks per season, plus three does.

The regular firearms season opens the day after archery season closes and runs until past the middle of January of the following year. If they wish, archers may hunt also during the firearms season with bow and arrows, but they must abide by the gun season rules, which include the wearing of a specified minimum of hunter-orange outer clothing. Only bowhunters and muzzleloaders may take the extra three does per season.

The Pecan Grove Wildlife Club lodge is located about an hour south of Natchez, Mississippi, and about an hour north of Baton Rouge, Louisiana. It is just northwest of the early settlement of Fort Adams on the banks of the Buffalo

Some privately owned hunting areas will have several permanent tree stands built over likely deer trails.

The lodge at the Pecan Grove Club is built on stilts, above, because the area will flood when Buffalo River rises. Byron Latour, below, arrowed small whitetail.

River. Both cities have frequent airline flights from and to any place. The club acreage includes access to Lake Mary and the banks of the Mississippi River for plenty of fishing opportunities.

During the drive to Fort Adams, George Haynes outlined the club's program for conservation and game management. All wildlife is left in its natural state. Deer food plots are planted, as is millet for ducks, crimson clover for turkey and deer. Haynes has initiated a timber management system, selectively cutting certain areas to enhance hunting potential. Timber cutting thins out some areas, allowing more deer browse to grow.

Haynes has taken steps to construct a number of water control structures on the property, with better hunting in mind. The club property is located along the banks of the Mississippi and Buffalo Rivers and, because of that, subject to partial flooding from time to time. When the property was farmed, the flooding brought silt and topsoil down, creating rich farm land. Flooding also helps to restock the many fishing ponds, lakes and streams in the area.

Lake Mary is one of the large ox-bow lakes at Pecan Grove. Ox-bow lakes, explained Haynes, are formed when the river, after years of flowing around a sharp bend, eventually floods through the curve in an effort to flow in a straight line. The original river bend is left isolated, leaving an ox-bow-shaped lake. There are hundreds along a river as extensive as the Mississippi. Lake Mary is full of bass, bream, crappie and catfish, as well as a locally popular fish called *sac-a-lait*.

Crossing the Buffalo River and turning off the dirt road to the parking area of the lodge, one is struck immediately by the fact that the building is constructed upon log pilings which raise it about twenty feet above ground level. The guest rooms, large dining room and meeting room are all on the higher level. The meat processing area and recreation/indoor archery range room are at ground level.

Haynes and his staff have spent time surveying the property during all seasons to determine the natural deer travel routes, feeding and bedding areas. In some places, they have constructed rather permanent tree or free-standing stands to take advantage of this knowledge.

Before opening day, the guides are out, making a final survey and marking the route into the tree stand locations with red tape so hunters can find their way in the pre-dawn darkness. Undergrowth is heavy because of the rich soil and the seasonal rainfall. In some areas, access routes have been cut through the brush to enable hunters to make their way without becoming soaked while passing through the wet growth.

Undergrowth along Mississippi River is thick and jungle-like. Shooting lanes must be cut near permanent stands.

The little town of Fort Adams Mississippi is said to be one of the oldest in the state. Lodge is rustic, but with modern facilities, excellent hunter accommodations.

The lodge itself can accommodate up to a hundred people during the hunting season. Rooms are comfortable, set up with double bunk beds and enough bathrooms to handle a large group. The lodge also features a meeting or seminar room, a dining room large enough for many hungry hunters and food as delicious as one can find anywhere.

The rut comes later in the year in this part of the country — usually cooler weather does not arrive until late December — and the rut may extend into late January. October is a bit early for establishing mock scrapes.

Heavy rain changed the standard routes and hot spots which had been scouted over several weeks by guides at the Pecan Grove Club property. Some of the lower pockets were flooded and the deer were using different routes to and from bedding areas.

Hunters may use the permanent stands at the club or they may bring their own climbing and portable stands. Or they may not use a stand at all, choosing to still-hunt areas of their choice. Some stands are within a few minutes' walk from the lodge, while others require a four-wheel-drive vehicle to drive a half-hour or so to reach suitable spots.

The club manager and his crew plot out likely areas on maps before opening day and assign guides and transportation to each hunter.

Those who have the longest travel time are launched earlier in order to be on their stands well before first light. The wise bowhunter will bring a small flashlight in his day pack or pocket so as to easily follow the marked trail into the stand. The unfamiliar terrain can be confusing, especially in the dark and rain. Guides will offer to escort each hunter to the stand, but another human only adds to the amount of scent left on the trail.

Hunting the deep South in October is almost sure to include rain, at least part of the time, so a bowhunter is advised to bring lightweight, rainproof camo clothing. The weather is warm, but if you get soaked and a breeze comes up, you can become chilled and remain uncomfortable during your hours on the stand.

A product welcomed by all is mosquito repellent. As

Wooden tree stands are complete with benches on which to sit, platform has room enough to move, shift around.

progressive philosophy of harvesting a large percentage of does each year, until the quality of bucks shows improvement.

To over-simplify the program, it boils down to reducing the number of females and male spikes in any given year; the expectation being that the remaining does will fill out the habitat by giving birth to more twin fawns. Theoretically, the next-year fawns will be fifty percent males. As this serious culling continues for four to six years, the buck-to-doe ratio and the quality of trophy bucks improves dramatically. The state encourages the practice by permitting three does per year during the archery and primitive weapons seasons, with some other special antlerless seasons in certain locations.

Good habitat is essential to the development of trophy whitetails. Some of Pecan Grove's cut-over areas have been allowed to produce better browse. Some nearby farms have acres of soybeans and corn, which promote healthy growth among the deer herds. The club also uses mineral-fortified salt licks, proven successful for improved antler development.

In some areas of the South, the whitetail herds are not noted for their quality; just their quantity. Left unmanaged, some of these herds produce small deer, with a preponderance of females. Without hunting pressures, they soon eat and reproduce their way past habitat capacity. With progressive management, private hunting clubs are able to

soon as the rain stopped, the temperature rose and large, yellow-looking mosquitoes found the stands. These suckers seem able to penetrate even heavy cloth. Repellent is effective on all exposed skin and on camouflage sleeves and trousers.

After daylight, I was able to hear, but not see some of my fellow hunters as they apparently released arrows. I learned later, as the truck picked each of us up for the return run to lunch in the lodge, that none had any more luck than I. There were no deer taken on opening day. We each returned to stand in the afternoon and remained until well after dark, but nobody scored.

The following day dawned bright and clear, although there were still plenty of low areas with too much water. The weather was cool and a warm jacket felt comfortable in the early morning. Later it warmed up a bit, but the day remained comfortable in full camouflage clothing. With the rain, walking and stalking quietly through the woods was easier, because everything underfoot was wet and soft. On the other hand, deer, too, move more quietly through the same woods.

This day, my hunting partner was Richard Sapp of Bear Archery in Florida. As we were on our way along a path not far from the lodge to take up adjacent tree stands, we jumped two whitetail does which had been hidden in the underbrush. If they hadn't run, we probably never would have seen them, even from ten or fifteen yards away. Neither of us had arrows out of the quiver, so we did not have a shot, but their presence gave us encouragement.

State game department officials oversee and approve or disapprove local hunting club activities, while offering advice to managers about how to improve the quality and quantity of deer and other game. Pecan Grove and other neighboring private clubs generally subscribe to the state's

Trees and vines grow tall and thick in Mississippi, for ideal whitetail habitat. Deer feed on nearby farm crops.

Bowhunter uses Woolrich's Shadowbark pattern, above, in Tennessee and Brigade Quartermasters' ASAT, below, in Mississippi. Hunting guide John Sloan, right, prefers the ASAT pattern when after Southern whitetail.

produce plenty of healthy trophy bucks.

Most of the growth in Mississippi in October was still predominately green, although there were some early signs of changing colors. I chose to wear the ASAT camouflage clothing pattern from Brigade Quartermasters, because of its durability, light weight and ability to blend in with most habitat. When wet, the ASAT material dries quickly and the design includes lots of pockets to carry exta gear up a tree.

Undergrowth was always wet, whether it was raining or not. I was happy to have on a pair of LaCrosse hunting boots, which never let in any water. They are rubber on the bottom, with Cordura nylon uppers. They are fast to lace and, with wool socks, my feet never got cold, no matter

how rainy it was or how inactive I was on the stand.

The ground floor of the lodge includes an indoor archery range, lighted for night practice. Many of us availed ourselves of the facility. That, unfortunately, was the only archery shooting I was able to do on this trip. Bill Bynum, who had hunted here before, took a doe on the second day.

Just before dark that same day, I heard one of my neighboring tree standers let an arrow fly, followed by sounds of running feet that indicated a hit deer. When the truck arrived after dark, we all used our flashlights to follow the blood trail for what seemed like hundreds of yards, until the returning rain washed the sign away. As happens sometimes, that was a deer we did not recover.

The fourth day of the season, the day I was scheduled to head back to the Baton Rouge airport, a taxidermist from neighboring Lafayette, Louisiana, Byron Latour, downed a small three-by-three buck. It wasn't a giant wall-hanger, but it filled the venison larder.

In another part of the South, the two states of Kentucky and Tennessee have several similarities, not the least of which is their enlightened game management programs. In both states, good deer management programs have led to plenty of whitetail, some in trophy size, to attract hunters from all over the country. Hunting licenses and deer tags are plentiful and inexpensive, especially when compared with some other well known whitetail hunting states.

The seasons in both states are relatively long and there is plenty of private as well as public land available to the bowhunter. National forests and various state wildlife management areas are plentiful in both states, with ideal whitetail deer habitat.

In Tennessee, guide John Sloan leases two privately owned areas totaling more than 4000 acres of prime hunting habitat. He has exclusive rights to these two locations and guide hunters there through the bow, black powder and rifle seasons. The seasons run from October to the following January, with Sloan in the field with clients much of that time.

The weather, Sloan warned me, could be fickle during deer season. The early October weather in the South is usually warm and comfortable, but the area has been known to experience almost any kind of weather, including rain, high winds and even some snow at times. So I was expected to travel prepared for almost anything the weatherman could throw at us. As it turned out, I brought too many warm clothes.

John Sloan had scouted his hunting area well before opening day and had a good idea of where to set up tree stands with the most likely chance for success. Before my arrival, he had guided for several clients and all had chances for shots. No guide can guarantee any hunter will get a deer, but Sloan has excellent results at getting hunters shots at deer. The rest is up to the hunter.

Sloan's deer camp is an old house offering all the comforts of home, plus his culinary skills. Sloan is a good cook, although he offers nothing fancy; just plain good food. The camp has sleeping facilities for up to four hunters at a time. When I was there, there was one other hunter in camp; a man from Illinois who had heard of Sloan through friends who had hunted in Tennessee in previous seasons.

The terrain we hunted offered different conditions in two leased areas. The first is mildly hilly, reached through a farmed area that is basically flat. During summer, deer are seen feeding on the farm crops, but during hunting season, there is considerable harvesting going on and deer change their movement habits.

Sloan had established two or three tree stand locations within view of a well used crossing and plenty of deer tracks. Deer were known to travel the route shortly after daylight, on their way out of the agricultural fields to their daytime bedding places. Sloan set up each location about three hundred yards apart, in order to cover most of the crossings. We were in the stands well before daylight to be able to spot the first movement.

The first morning, I spotted a number of does, a couple of spotted fawns and at least two nice bucks passing by. Unfortunately, they remained at least a hundred yards beyond my tree stand.

Later in the morning, when Sloan picked us up on the way to lunch at the camp, he said he had similar experiences during the first hunt. He spotted a rather large six-by-six buck easing along the stream, but did not have a shot. We returned to the same area for the evening hunt, but results were the same, so Sloan decided to try another place on the second day.

The new property was at a greater distance from the camp and was not being farmed at all. The land was much steeper, crossed by numerous small streams and heavier growth. We saw plenty of deer sign and the hills were grown with oak trees providing plenty of acorns, a whitetail favorite. The land is a series of rather steep ridges and what roads there were followed the ridge lines. This left plenty of hiking and climbing for the hunters between ridges.

There seemed to be several well used deer trails through the woods, so I was set up on a ridge, while the second hunter was placed on another ridge, several hundred yards away. At about 9 a.m., I heard some commotion and voices in the valley between us.

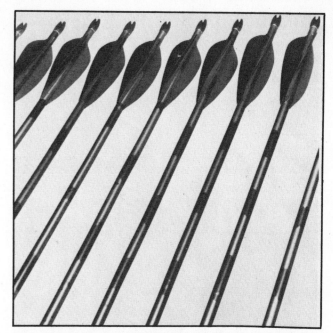

Easton Gamegetter II arrow shafts, already in camouflage pattern are popular with whitetail hunters in the South.

The hunter with Sloan had taken a shot at a deer and thought he had wounded it. The three of us spent an hour searching the ridgeline where the deer disappeared. On hands and knees, we turned over leaves and brush, seeking any blood sign. Eventually, we were able to spot some drops, forming a trail down the opposite side of the hill on which we were searching.

Sloan is a good tracker and, using the leap-frog technique, we were able to follow the track for some distance. Sloan directed one of us to remain at the spot where the last blood sign was located, while he searched ahead for new drops of blood. In places, the trail was plain to see; in others, small drops were far apart.

After a couple of hours of fruitless searching, we could locate no more sign. We kept returning to the last known spot and carefully searched, moving in ever widening circles to try to spot more blood, but to no avail. Nobody likes to lose a wounded deer, but we eventually had to abandon the search with no further places to look.

We hunted the same area during the evening and returned to our first spot the next morning, but could not manage to arrow a whitetail. Sloan's hunter returned to Illinois that afternoon; Sloan and I hunted again that evening and made plans to drive to Kentucky the next day.

The drive from Sloan's camp in northcentral Tennessee to southeastern Kentucky was about four hours long. It gave us time to work out some hunting tactics and plans.

The terrain, according to Sloan and borne out by personal observation, was similar, but with more agriculture than his area of Tennessee. The place we were to hunt is called Deer Creek Lodge — appropriately enough — in an area of intensive farmlands. The man who runs the hunting lodge, Tim Stull, hunts his own farm and leases hunting rights to several other farms and woods that provide good habitat.

The weather in late October in both states was beginning

Southern woods are full of the things whitetail deer prefer to eat: oak trees and acorns, during bowhunting season, Ulti-Mate 365 cover scent is applied to boot toe, above, for walk into tree stands in Tennessee.

to look like fall, most of the leaves turning color, although they were not yet losing much of the foliage.

Sloan and I had both worn the ASAT camouflage pattern in Tennessee. It seemed to hide us well in his state and we saw no reason to change the pattern in Kentucky. The mostly browns and darker vertical lines seemed just right for the cover we were hunting through.

Another wearer of the ASAT pattern was Mickey Pope, a hunting partner of Sloan's who also joined us. Pope was the first in our party to down a deer.

The accommodations at Deer Creek Lodge are excellent. A hunter may choose to do his own cooking and house-keeping, staying at the lodge bunkhouse. He may live locally and simply pay the reasonable trespass fee on the property or he might opt for the full treatment, staying at the main lodge building and take great meals with Stull and his people.

John Sloan has hunted often at the lodge and knows the area well enough to be one of their guides when the need arises. We did a bit of scouting the evening of our arrival and located some likely areas near some harvested corn-fields at the edge of the woods. These woods were crossed by several old logging roads and trails that showed plenty of fresh sign.

There were at least a dozen hunters in the lodge the next morning, but the properties are large enough to accommodate them all. Tim Stull coordinates the locations where his guides take their hunters. We all left before daylight, but not before we loaded up on some great breakfast.

Sloan set us in our stand locations before it was light and we settled in for what was to come. About eight in the morning, I thought I could hear some commotion in the

direction of Mickey Pope's stand. I saw a couple of distant deer, but when I met Sloan out on the road at mid-morning, Pope was late arriving. A half-hour later, we spotted him struggling down the trail, pulling something. It was the deer he had arrowed a couple of hours earlier.

The deer was field dressed and loaded into Sloan's pick-up for the drive back to the lodge where we had lunch and a nap before the afternoon hunt. We followed the same pattern and hunted the same general area the three days we were in Kentucky.

The last day, Sloan guided us much farther into the woods, where we each set up tree stands at likely deer travel routes. Just before noon and time to head back to the lodge the final time, I heard some sort of motorized vehicle coming my way down the trail.

It was Sloan luck. He had arrowed a doe — they are plentiful and legal game in that part of Kentucky — a short while earlier and wondered how he was to get the carcass back to the truck. Just then, along came a hunter from an adjoining property, who was riding a three-wheel Suzuki all-terrain vehicle. They hitched up the deer to the vehicle and Sloan didn't have to sweat at all.

Over on the other side of the lodge property, Ben Watson was arrowing a nice three-by-three buck. The rack was not tremendous, but it had a nice-size body. Kentucky regulations require each deer taken to be weighed and checked in at an authorized game-checking station. This animal field dressed at just under a hundred pounds on the official scales.

The weather was mild to warm during our time in both states. We could have wished for cooler temperatures; the rut was not due to start for some time in this weather.

John Sloan, left, took a small doe for camp meat, while local car dealer Ben Watson downed a young, healthy buck. Watson had to officially weigh in the buck, right.

Distances to good hunting areas of Kentucky and Tennessee are not that far from surrounding states. A careful hunter could hunt three or four different states in a season. The resident and non-resident fees are not expensive. The Deer Creek Lodge had hunters from California, Tennessee, Pennsylvania and Ohio, as well as Kentucky, while we were there. Whitetail do well there and hunting opportunities and hunting numbers are increasing.

Moving farther west, the place is Bent Creek Lodge, Alabama, near the small town of Jachin, a few miles east of Meridian, Mississippi.

Our hosts were lodge owners/operators Leo Allen and Johnny Lanier, who both grew up in the area.

"As we grew older, we were not hunting as much as the land would allow," they say. "After much planning, we decided to go to a custom hunting operation. We have grown from an old rustic clubhouse to a new modern lodge. As we have grown, more land has been added and now we hunt over 22,000 acres."

Bent Creek Lodge includes an 8000-acred trophy area where only bucks with eight points or better are harvested. The area includes more than four miles of riverfront on the Tombigbee River, known as Dean Swamp. The area never has been open to the public. Years ago, when wildlife was

Sloan, left, and Mickey Pope swing the first deer shot at Kentucky's Deer Creek Hunting lodge into pickup truck.

not so plentiful, game was trapped here and used to populate the state in areas that had little game.

The repopulation and modern game management measures by the Alabama Department of Conservation and Natural Resources has proven enviably successful. Deer seasons are quite generous. The early bow season begins around the middle of October and the firearms season about a month later. Both seasons run until the end of January, the limit on deer being one buck per day. Bent Creek Lodge is included in the state's game management program and doe tags are usually available to hunters. Bent Creek also offers some outstanding wild turkey hunting in the spring.

Lanier and Allen are heavily involved in the day-to-day operation of the lodge and its game management plans. Annually, they plant about a hundred cleared fields with deer-appealing feed. In early mornings and late afternoons, these fields are loaded with feeding deer. However, the distances across are mostly one or two hundred yards — much too long for an archery shot, but ideal for a rifle or black powder arm. Different methods are required for the bowhunter. Developing and teaching these methods was the task of a couple of instructors at Bent Creek, Ronnie Groom and Bob Sheppard.

Bob Sheppard is an avid bowhunter who has conducted these seminars at a couple of locations in the South, over the past fifteen years. Combined, the two men have taken more than 150 whitetails with bow and arrow, plus more than three hundred others with a rifle. They offer a common-sense, no-frills approach to bowhunting.

Bent Creek offers three days of instruction and deer hunting, including lodging, at a most reasonable price. The lodge is restricted to no more than twenty hunters at a time.

A group bowhunting assemble for photographs at the Bent Creek, Alabama hunting lodge, above. Early season hunt included special seminar for first-time bowhunters. Techniques for hunting "edges" were presented, right.

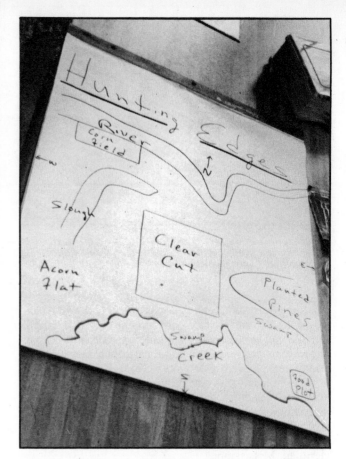

Bob Sheppard, who happens to be a cardiologist, restricts the number of hunter/students at Bent Creek to twenty for the formal classes. The lodge is open to bowhunters through the archery season at a reasonable fee per day. The fees include overnight lodging in a new, modern hunting lodge and three delicious meals per day.

Classes alternate with hunting sessions for the three days. Most of us were checked into the lodge in time for a noon meal on the first day, leaving some time for an afternoon hunt. With so many acres under management, guides are able to put each hunter into an area that is not hunted more than twice a week.

Hunters were asked to bring their own portable tree stands for their own convenience, as well as for liability reasons. In this part of Alabama, ladder-type tree stands have found favor. One of the classes before our first hunt was on tree stand placement and safety; appropriate for what we were about to do.

Some of the Bent Creek property is farmed, some is abandonded farmland, more is old-growth forest, plus previously logged-over acreage. It is only mildly hilly in some spots and, unless thinned or cleared by man, the undergrowth is thick in most places. Creeks and streams run throughout the property.

We were told to expect some rather warm days, possibly rain, but with the chance of some early-season cold. It has been known to dip below freezing in this part of Alabama, but usually later in the year.

Before we were guided out to our first afternoon hunt, we spent some time on the target range outside the lodge. The folks had set up a number of 3-D targets in a wooded area near the back door. These could be shot from the ground or from one of the several tree stands already in place for a later class. The first day, we were treated to an archery exhibition by Marlow Larson of Browning Archery. We all now know why he is a champion.

The hunters at Bent Creek ranged from novices to veterans. The school is structured as a blend of classroom with in-the-woods sessions around the morning and afternoon hunts. The main meeting room of the lodge building is adequate for the two dozen participants and instructors.

Bob Sheppard said there were thirty-two bowhunters who took advantage of Bent Creek through the season. Everyone had an opportunity for at least a shot at a deer, eight had more than one shot and three used up all their arrows. Sheppard assured them all beginners miss deer; a part of the game.

For my first afternoon hunt, the guide dropped me off a short distance from one of the open, planted fields. With plenty of daylight left, we agreed he would hunt the next hill over and we would meet at dark for the drive back to the lodge. The green field had a slight rise in the middle and I remembered to approach carefully. Sure enough, as I topped the rise, I spotted three does chowing down on the greens. Trouble was, they were at least eighty yards away, almost in the middle of the field.

I ducked down and crawled forward twenty or thirty yards, but there was no way I could get any closer. Every time I tried to take a peek, I was caught by three pairs of eyes. The wind was in my face and the deer did not seem alarmed by my presence at first, but by the time they were about fifty yards out, they decided to leave this strange moving object behind.

Bob Sheppard's seminar covers hunting the edges. He stresses that any change in terrain can create an edge. Such an edge may be a treeline, a waterway, an acorn tree patch or any other thing that might cause deer to follow a given path. I attempted to outwait the next group of feeding deer in the evening, but by that time, the wind had changed and I saw no more.

Sheppard and Groom present a wide variety of valuable bowhunting information during their three days of seminars.

Cardiologist Doctor Bob Sheppard demonstrates ladder tree stand techniques during his Alabama presentations.

Classes include scouting and patterning whitetail movement and how it changes as the season progresses. A productive spot in October might yield nothing in January, they teach.

We were taught how to recognize good browse for whitetail, including how to find mast crops; then how to locate, set up and hunt that good spot. We learned the importance of hunting into the wind, no matter how good the browse might be in a particular location.

Tree stand use and safety were stressed throughout the seminars. Tree stands are broken down into categories of climbers, hang-ons, ladder types, sling types and those that are permanent. Sheppard had examples of each type in trees at the target range so that all students could try them out.

Hunting an open field calls for different techniques than hunting from a deep-woods tree stand. In this country, the best plan seems to be to try to locate the travel routes the deer will use to enter the fields just before dark, then place a tree or ground stand within easy arrow range, upwind of the pathway. More often than not, most of us carefully select and climb a good tree, only to spot the deer on the other side of the field — 150 yards away.

Technique for tracking wounded animals was taught in the classroom, as well as in the woods. Recognizing active buck scrapes was discussed, although the rut was at least a month away when we were in Alabama.

In any deer management area, determining age of the deer killed is an important information tool. Checking out deer jaws for age, as well as age and health of the herd, were demonstrated. The various age classes of the deer herd were described and this information evaluated to give the hunter an understanding of how it relates to the established management goals.

One of the most popular discussions was led by Browning's Marlow Larson. His subject concerned matching equipment and tuning the individual bow. He stressed the importance of a coach, a trusted advisor or at least a knowledgeable professional dealer to help with that first bow and arrow purchase. He insists the rookie bowhunter may not get the correct match of equipment and accessories without competent help, no matter the brands selected.

I saw deer during each morning and afternoon hunt and missed a couple on the second day. The final day, Leo Allen took me where he said there was an almost legendary "monster buck." It's a story you hear at every hunting camp, I thought to myself.

I was doing everything right, I thought. I had a spot where I could watch a natural funnel from the deep woods into the large, open field. I had good cover and remained quite still for hours. Light was fading rapidly and I must have blinked a few times. Suddenly, he was there, in front of me, less than thirty yards out. I was shielded by a branch, but every time I tried to raise and draw my bow, he seemed to be looking at me. We played a kind of peek-a-boo for fifteen minutes before the buck browsed out into the field, beyond bow range. I built some character that evening.

Bob Sheppard believes that there is no magic to taking deer with a bow. He says, "Consistent success comes with experience, hard work and repeated exposure to the real thing."

Some of the better bowhunters in the country have difficulty explaining the nuts and bolts of their technique to others. Bob Sheppard and Ronnie Groom do not have that problem. They are good teachers; you learn without realizing you are being taught. They have missed, selected the wrong tree stand location and have come home wet and empty-handed like the rest of us.

Alabama offers a limited, seven-day, non-resident hunting license for a reasonable fee, good for any game. Leo Allen assures me the monster buck is still there. — *Roger Combs*

Non-resident hunting fees and bag limits are extremely reasonable in Alabama, with favorable whitetail habitat.

MULE DEER

Brad Francis, a Browning Archery employee, with mule buck with velvet antlers taken on Utah family ranch.

MULE DEER are found mostly in the western part of Canada, Mexico and the U.S. Much of the habitat is dry, rugged, semi-desert and some is quite mountainous. With a few exceptions, much of the habitat is on public property: national forests, Bureau of Land Management acreage, state lands; areas not in the hands of private owners.

Typical mule deer habitat is open, often covering thousands of acres. While the deer populations may be large, the vast areas to be hunted are what cause the problems for bowhunters. Adequate pre-season scouting will improve the hunter's odds, but not everyone can afford the time or expense of spending so many days or weeks scouting, often at considerable distance from home. Mule deer are not territorially conscious and may not be where they were scouted before hunting season opened.

There are a couple of solutions to the problem: Hunt the same general area year after year, becoming intimately familiar with the habitat and the game. Similar conditions each year may lead to deer being found in familiar surroundings. Or you may locate and rely on guides or friends who live in the hunt area. They will save considerable time and expense, eliminating non-productive habitat and will often be familiar with excellent private property hunting. The hunter will cover more ground in a shorter time, traveling on horseback. Nine or ten miles at altitudes above 10,000 feet might take all day on foot, but require only a couple of hours by horse. Most good mule deer hunting areas of the West will be serviced by one or several horse packers whose services may be obtained for reasonable fees.

Mule deer are so-called because of their large radar-like ears, which seem able to pick up the slightest sound. Their eyesight and smelling ability also must be reckoned with. The bowhunter will do well always to remember to hunt into the wind. With strong breezes, it is sometimes possible, even on dry ground, to approach mule deer bucks well within bow range, moving slowly and cautiously, keeping low and moving only when the quarry's head is down. Complete camouflage coverage is essential for the mule deer bowhunter.

Arrow ranges will probably be longer than for whitetail deer and the most successful method is to spot and stalk the deer. Therefore, a good pair of binoculars is always an

Mule Deer Habitat Of The West Is Wide And High, Requiring Different Hunting Methods For Success

asset to the western hunter. Save wear and tear on the body by utilizing binoculars long and carefully before physical movement.

Shots of forty or fifty yards are not uncommon for mule deer hunters and the bowhunter should practice enough at these ranges to feel confident with them.

Seasons may or may not be open to bowhunters while the rut is on. Most archery deer seasons in California, for instance, are closed long before the rut. The hunter cannot count on the deer's mating urges to improve the odds for a shot. Portions of the state open for bowhunting as early as mid-July, with extremely hot and dry conditions the rule. The hunter must be prepared for water shortages, dry ground and wildfire danger in much of the West.

Bowhunting deer is hard work anyplace, but big mule deer are likely to be found at high altitudes and the hunter needs to be in good physical condition to cope with the steep terrain and the lack of oxygen in the mountains. Mule deer also are found in valleys and foothills, but the hunter can count on plenty of walking or riding to locate them.

Nevada and Utah are two states with notable mule deer populations and the non-resident hunter is welcome. Hunting techniques for most of the the West will be similar to what is successful in those two states.

Nevada deer hunting opportunities are not actually a secret that somebody is trying to keep the rest of us from knowing, but the result seems almost as if they were. Nevada is one of the better trophy mule deer hunting states. While the Pope & Young Club record book certainly is not dominated by animals taken in Nevada, the state is well represented, especially in recent years.

The Nevada Department of Wildlife and its deer management program seem to be doing things right. The state is divided into hunt management areas, with a season and quota for each. Bow season is handled separately, with fewer units and fewer numbers than are assigned to firearms hunters.

Tag quotas are assigned for both residents and non-residents. Getting drawn for the firearms non-resident quota is rather difficult, but being included in the archery quota offers reasonable odds with a good chance of a tag.

Deadlines for archery quota tags are rather early in the year. Residents and non-residents must submit applications and fees by June 15. The drawing is a week later. A $5 filing fee is required to process your application for the quota drawing.

ASAT camouflage pattern works well in northern Nevada.

Hunting the high country for mule deer will be more comfortable in outfitter-packed tents, equipment.

Shots at Western mule deer will probably be longer than in other regions. Archers must be prepared for mostly spot and stalk, with plenty of frustration.

Nevada is a huge state with miles and miles of miles and miles. Most of us have limited exposure to Nevada; spending weekends in Reno or Las Vegas among glittering lights and frantic gamblers. That may be one of the reasons that the state's hunting possibilities are so well hidden; they are hidden by the lights of the gambling casinos!

A lot of the state is covered by desert, but other areas comprise high, beautiful mountains and valleys, ideal mule deer habitat. The state is too large for any hunter to scout, unless one is a native or knows a hunter who will share the knowledge. The alternative is to locate and rely upon a reputable guide. Much of Nevada is public land and open to any hunter who follows the rules, but time and money are saved by following a guide who already knows the area.

As an example, Kim Smith's family has owned and operated the Cottonwood Ranch in the northeastern corner of Nevada for several generations. They have been guiding and packing into the nearby Jarbridge Wilderness since 1952. The ranch is in an isolated area of Elko County, about seventy-five miles northwest of the small town of Wells, Nevada. Utah and Idaho are not far away.

The Jarbridge Mountains comprise the largest concentration of peaks over 10,000 feet in Nevada, offering scenery to match the hunting. The mountains are home to more than 22,000 deer, including many in the trophy class. Food, water and weather favor the species.

In nearly four decades of guiding, the Cottonwood outfit has had a ninety-percent success rate overall. It is, of course, somewhat lower for bowhunters. The area is accessible only by horseback, but the Smiths have a comfortable ranch lodge from which hunting parties are packed and guided to high mountain spike camps for hunts in the Jarbridge Wilderness.

The ranch provides the horses, packers, guides and plenty of home cooking. The only thing the hunter needs is a sleeping bag, personal gear and bowhunting equipment.

While competition for a non-resident firearms tag is tough, archery applicants might expect a ninety percent selection chance. In most years, the archery season in Nevada is mid-August through early September. Some hunters will select the last week of the season, because it includes the long Labor Day weekend and because the later time might mean cooler, better hunting weather.

The weather can be variable at that time of year, so the hunter should pack a lot of extra clothing and gear. If not needed, much of it may be left at the ranch rather than hauling everything on the pack animals.

Nevada mule hunting almost always requires services of a pack outfit to get into high mountains. Travel is not all smooth, above, as cowboys learn, below.

Because it was nearing the end of the bow season for the year, the deer were a bit spooked, the season I was there, but the good news was that I was the only bowhunter in camp. Toward the end of the five days, muzzleloaders were showing up, as the season was to start the day after I left. We saw a lot of good bucks.

One thing the Nevada bowhunter must be prepared for is tough traveling. The spike camp is a mountainous five-hour horseback ride from the trail head. Unless one rides a lot, the body will be complaining long before camp is reached. But that is a small price to pay for the quality hunt.

Travel by horseback can be tough on flatlanders not accustomed to the high altitudes and steep terrain, but it will beat backpacking for thirty, forty miles.

Much of the West's mule deer habitat is high and dry most of the year. Stalking across high desert terrain presents plenty of challenges for the archery hunter.

When Kim Smith said the meals would be delicious and the guides would take care of everything in the camp, she was not exaggerating. The spike camp was set up when I reached it; two previous groups had been there. A sleeping tent, a mess tent, close-by spring water point and sanitary facilities were ready for occupancy. Meals featured plenty of good cowboy cooking and there was always more than a normal human could eat.

The camp is at about 6000 feet altitude and the hunting spots are higher, so the mountains take some acclimatizing for the flatlander. A lot of the travel is by horse, but it still is necessary to pace oneself to avoid too much stress.

At certain times of the year, the country can receive a lot of rain and snow. But in September, it was dry — and had been for many months. The predominant habitat colors are shades of brown, so I chose to wear a camouflage suit of ASAT, from Brigade Quartermasters. The ASAT pattern is primarily brown and darker brown, with vertical streaks of black, resembling shadows and branches. The colors seemed made for the terrain. The military-like ASAT clothing has plenty of pockets to carry those bowhunting essentials and emergency items, too.

I was prepared for severe weather, but it remained mild with cool nights and warm days during the week in the mountains. Some rain would have been welcome so identification of fresh tracks would have been easier.

We saw plenty of deer, including good bucks, each day. Most were too far away for an arrow shot, but at least we knew the animals were there. We glassed some that seemed impossible to approach in the rugged terrain.

Our pattern consisted of an early wakeup by the guides who had coffee already boiling over the campfire well before daylight. We saddled up and were on the trail into the high mountains, to a likely destination just as the sun was peeking over the ridges. We dismounted and approached each ridge cautiously, because we soon learned that most of the canyons and valleys beyond held deer.

I managed to miss an easy ten-yard shot the second day out. Mike, the chief guide, set me up at an ambush location and returned with the horses to a ridge where we had seen several bucks. He rode around a peak, hoping to drive a buck or two toward my location.

After more than an hour, I was slipping into carelessness when a nice four-by-four suddenly appeared in front of me, not ten yards away. I don't think he knew I was there in the shadows as I drew and aimed. I must have had buck fever, because the arrow flew three feet over his back as he stood there. Before I could nock a second arrow, he was gone. So much for filling my tag on the second day.

The afternoon before we were scheduled to re-pack and return to the ranch house, we went back to the same ridgeline to see if the deer had returned. They had and I decided on a long stalk down the facing valley wall. I was looking into the setting sun and the faint trail was only partially visible. To make matters more difficult, the hillside was entirely of loose broken shale, noisy and slippery.

The good news was that the wind was in my face and the deer were bedded down in the shade of an old pine stand. The hillside was so steep I finally just had to slide down on my butt, a couple of inches at a time, hoping the loose rocks wouldn't alert the bedded deer. It took more than two hours to drop down a few hundred feet.

By the time I was within sixty yards of where I had last seen the deer, the sun was below the facing ridgeline and it was beginning to get dark. Shortly, the deer were up and starting to browse just below me. What little growth there was between me and the game was only about six inches high and didn't offer much cover. Each time I moved closer, broken rocks would clatter ahead of me and the deer would look up at the sound. They did not spot me, however.

It soon would be too dark for a shot and, as I tried to close that last twenty yards, the deer knew something foreign was on the hill. They did not bound off, but they browsed along, moving down until the range was at least a hundred yards. I had no chance of getting closer and finally signaled the guide to bring a horse down the imaginary trail for a ride back to the top.

At the top of the ridge where the guides had remained,

they had watched my every move. They agreed it was a most exciting stalk, even though no trophy resulted.

Nevada mule deer offer surprises and challenge for the bowhunter who is lucky enough to have his name drawn for the early archery season.

As mentioned, Utah is not far from the Cottonwood Ranch in northern Nevada. The state has a reputation for some wonderful mule deer habitat north and south, east and west. The terrain is similar to much of Nevada; rugged, steep, plenty of desert, but with the chance of cold, snowy fall and winter, especially in the north.

The mule deer hunter should leave camp with a small pack filled with emergency equipment, spare gear, as well as water canteen. Binoculars are also essential.

Much of the country northeast of Salt Lake City is in private hands, homesteaded years ago by pioneer families. Much of it is still in the descendants' hands; other large ranches have been turned into commercial hunting ventures. Either way, the area contains plenty of mule deer,

many in the trophy class. There is also plenty of public land, national and state forests, typical of much of the West. The state is vast and the trick is to find a knowledgeable commercial guide or a friend of a friend who will take you to a prospectively good hunting area without wasting a lot of time in unproductive country.

One of the pluses to hunting in Utah is that it is a state where most of the residents hunt and fish. They welcome non-resident hunters and little of the anti-hunting sentiment encountered in other states is evident. Hunting licenses and deer tags are reasonably priced and are easily obtained, even for the non-resident.

Northern Utah, Nevada mule deer habitat can be open, below left, or forested, above. Usually great distances must be covered in vehicles or on foot to find deer.

Brad Francis is one of those whose ancestors homesteaded a large tract of northeast Utah a couple of generations ago. He bowhunts every chance he gets and was kind enough to guide several of us through his family's ranch, not open to the public.

The habitat contains plenty of deer, large and small, with a satisfactory buck to doe ratio. The country features deep, stream-fed canyons ideal for cattle, surrounded by steep cliffs and mountains where mule deer prefer to live. The country is criss-crossed with dirt roads and ranch trails, lending itself to rather easy scouting by four-wheel-drive vehicles.

The winter range for these mule California mule deer has been invaded by luxury homes, above.

Monster buck trophy, above, hangs in Morgan, Utah bank.
Most mule deer bucks are quite a bit smaller, right.

Two methods of hunting are used. In some areas, the spot-and-stalk methods pay off, while in others, tree stands have proven productive. The tree stands are usually permanent wooden structures, placed over cattle waterers or feed bins. When conditions have been good to the area and feed and water are abundant, the tree stands may not be the best way to go.

Spotting a mule deer and getting within bow range are, of course, two different problems. On a recent hunt, we saw dozens of mule deer during the early bow season, often spotting six or eight bachelor bucks at a time. All the does we saw had one or two fawns with them, indicating a healthy herd. But more often than not, the sighted deer were high atop the cliffs or far down a canyon with the wind blowing the wrong direction. Most were difficult or impossible to approach.

The guides had scouted the area for weeks and knew where deer were likely to be found, saving the hunters plenty of time. Some found success establishing an ambush site above a saddle, awaiting deer at daylight.

I found success on the last morning of the hunt. My guide took me a final time up one of the numerous box canyons where deer had been spotted on previous mornings. As

luck would have it, a small buck, still with velvet antlers, was spotted about halfway up the hillside, not far from the road.

Earlier, I had blown several stalks, because the wind changed or I had made too much noise trying to pass through sagebrush and dry leaves. This final morning, the wind was calm just after sunup.

We later guessed that the young buck had never before seen humans and was not afraid of this strange camouflaged object on the road. For sure, he had not been shot at by firearms hunters in this area.

The buck held still while I drew and aimed, taking a step or two as I was about to release. I lead him a little as I let the arrow fly and it flew true as the buck stepped into a perfect lung and heart shot.

He ran less than a hundred yards, never out of my sight, and piled up not three feet from the canyon road. The buck was dead within minutes and all we had to do was field dress and hoist him into the back of the pickup truck for the drive back to camp. The six other hunters in camp also were able to fill their deer tags on the trip, not typical of most deer hunts. Utah can be a great place to hunt mule deer.

CHAPTER
20
AMERICAN ELK

Found Mostly in The West, This Game Animal Has Its Own Challenges

ELK MAYBE be the second or third most popular big-game animal in North America for all who hunt, whether with firearms or bow and arrows. Less than a hundred years ago, elk roamed over most of the West in huge numbers. However, the march of civilization reduced their numbers until only a few remained. Fortunately, enlightened governments and game managers took action and elk numbers are on the upswing, with additional starter herds thriving in new areas.

There are two basic subspecies of huntable elk in North America: the Roosevelt elk and Rocky Mountain — also called Yellowstone — elk.

The Roosevelt species is found mostly along the Pacific Coast of northern California, Oregon, Washington and British Columbia. Rocky Mountain elk have a much larger range, being found from Arizona up through most of the Rocky Mountain states and into Canada. Small herds of Tule elk thrive in California, but with only limited hunting opportunities.

Elk are big; often three to four times as big as typical deer. A mature Roosevelt bull may tip the scales at 1100 pounds; a full grown Rocky Mountain bull may reach seven hundred pounds on the hoof. Alive, viewed from a bowhunter's perspective, they look even bigger.

Considerable elk hunting is done with outfitters moving far into the wilderness for up to three weeks, using pack horses and mules. Such hunts are major undertakings and are usually quite expensive. However, plenty of bulls have been taken by bowhunters who were drawn from a state's limited tag quota. Hunting with a single hunting partner, such individuals have downed wonderful trophies.

The bows, arrows and equipment for elk hunting are basically the same as for deer, although most hunters prefer a bit heavier-drawing bow. Shot placement is more critical — the heart or lung shot is mandatory — but ranges usually are within thirty yards. As usual, the hunter needs absolutely razor-sharp broadheads, good boots, complete camouflage, excellent archery skills and a fit body. In many cases, elk live at altitudes of up to 12,000 feet. Seeking and stalking animals at that altitude is stressful and difficult.

ANTHONY BISCOTTI

Arizona, Colorado, Idaho, Montana and Wyoming are the primary elk hunting states, with Utah and New Mexico showing great promise for the Rocky Mountain subspecies. Oregon and Washington are tops for Roosevelt elk.

Arizona seems to outshine all other states when it comes to elk hunter success ratios. Recently, the Arizona Game and Fish Department estimated the elk population at 20,000 animals. Most of Arizona's elk herds live at elevations of 6500 to 7000 feet, making them easier to approach than in some other mountain states. Northeast Arizona and northwest New Mexico have similar habitat, favorable to elk.

Mature elk can become quite large. This life-size foam field archery target illustrates how big a bull can be and is good for practice.

Elk hunting tags are available primarily on a quota basis, with applications usually required by June, or even as early as April in some states. Given the importance and expense of an elk hunt, bowhunters should allow about a year for planning and administrative details.

By far the most popular technique used for elk in recent years is calling or bugling. Bugling is used to locate as well as draw bull elk within bow range. This particular technique will work from shortly before the onset of the rut — usually around the first part of September in most elk regions — through late October. Later in the season, effectiveness of bugling seems to diminish.

Elk make all sorts of sounds: squeals, grunts, screams and whistles. Imitations of these sounds can be learned by spending time in elk habitat or from instructional audio tapes. The bull elk becomes quite aggressive during the rut, protecting his harem of cows and seeking to drive away any competing bull. A skilled bugler often can call a large bull in close, as long as the hunter remains downwind.

Elk-calling effectiveness may be decreasing due to the number of elk hunters now using this technique. The bulls have become educated to hunters' tricks in many areas and are more difficult to fool. One also must be careful to not call in other elk hunters!

The spot-and-stalk method of hunting often is successful for elk. In dry habitat, elk sometimes may be located near waterholes and mud wallows. It is possible to approach within thirty yards of elk, if you are downwind and move silently and slowly. Bulls with cows are extremely difficult to fool, because several cows will be looking in all directions at once, ready to give warning of any approaching camouflage blob.

Elk have been killed by ambushing. The frequented waterholes sometimes may be observed and a ground blind established before daylight to await thirsty elk. The hunter must be aware of the morning wind direction and use care to not spread his human scent around the area during the approach phase.

A downed elk upwards of a 1000 pounds presents a formidable transportation challenge. The animal must be field dressed and cooled out quickly, the cape and antlers cared for and the meat moved as soon as possible. Without pack animals or a couple of hunting buddies to help, backpacking everything out will take at least three or four trips.

It can be tough going, but elk meat is some of the best wild game anywhere and elk antlers on the wall are dramatic trophies.

Jim Ludvigson of Dewey, Arizona, shows off his 1990 elk trophy. The bull was listed by the Pope & Young Club as new world record; second in Boone and Crockett records.

FERAL GOATS

GOATS, SHEEP AND PIGS, in their feral state, allowed to roam free, become huntable game in many areas. Usually, they are enclosed within fences, but on property open enough to offer genuine hunting challenges. For the bowhunter, these animals are often in open season when other big-game seasons are closed or the area is closed to all firearms hunting.

Most of these game preserves or game farms are privately owned and operated for profit. The goats, sheep and pigs are either raised on the premises or purchased from suppliers. The preserves do their best to provide a fair chase situation for hunters, even though the area is surrounded by fences.

One such typical game preserve is the Big Horn Canyon Ranch in Southern California. It is popular with bowhunters who wish to keep their mental and physical skills tuned for deer season and for those who wish to take an unusual trophy.

Chuck Wagner is one of the partners operating the Big Horn Canyon Ranch hunting preserve in Cherry Valley, California. He began the morning by showing us the entrances and the general boundaries of the ranch, which has more than five hundred acres fenced and several thousand more acres unenclosed. Over the years, several of the animals he has imported have escaped and prospered outside the wire, but inside the general hunting area, he has five kinds of sheep, four types of goats and a huntable population of wild pigs. The animals have been captured in other hunting areas of northern California and Texas. The habitat must be to their liking, as they are doing well on the grass and sage brush-covered hills and valleys of the ranch.

Before arriving at the ranch, inland from the California coast and about midway between San Diego and Los Angeles, none of we four hunters had anticipated the ruggedness of the terrain. It is similar to Catalina Island. Catalina, too, has huntable populations of Spanish goats and wild pigs.

The ranch hills are covered with green grass in the spring, with plenty of sage brush and other tall bushes to hide the animals. Game trails are easy enough to find, but there are thousands of branches and side paths from which to choose, so tracking is not a viable hunting technique.

The most acceptable method of hunting such steep terrain is to climb up the hillsides to a high vantage point, from where, hopefully, a goat, sheep or pig may be spotted. As in any other kind of hunting, a good pair of binoculars is an essential piece of gear, not only for spotting game, but for judging the trophies.

Before we started our hunt, the four of us decided to limber up a bit with a few arrows into a practice target. The practice butt was made of a double burlap outer fabric filled with something called Trocellen, a closed-cell polyethylene foam. It not only stops any arrow from any bow, but the filling lets go of an arrow shaft so easily you can pull it out with two fingers. After several thousand shots, the outer burlap will have to be replaced, but the inner filling should last a lifetime.

We soon discovered we were able to spot several distinct and separate herds of Barbado, Moreno, Corsican, four-horn and Rambouillet sheep; Spanish, Catalina, Angora and Toggenburg goats. The two groups of pigs seemed to band together until alarmed, when they would scatter faster and farther than any of the other animals. Chuck Wagner told us the pigs were the biggest challenge

Left To Their Own Devices, Feral Goats Can Provide The Bowhunter With Fun And Challenges

to any bowhunter and we soon learned that he knows what he's talking about.

Because of insurance restrictions, only bowhunting and crossbow hunting are permitted at Big Horn Canyon Ranch. Some of the cover is high and heavy enough to prohibit all but the closest range shot, while at other places, a shot of thirty to forty-five yards could be made.

Wagner had advised us that equipment with the flattest arrow trajectories possible would be advisable, with our sharpest broadheads, especially if hunting sheep or pigs. The goats did not have the toughest hides, but the sheep carry heavy wool coats, while the pigs are fast and elusive, requiring fast, accurate shot placement.

Ranges on uphill and downhill shots can be deceptive. The hunter should be experienced at estimating range or should carry and use a reliable archery rangefinder to double-check his estimates. Following a blood trail in this dry country is usually not much of a problem, but we are all interested in a quick, humane kill whenever possible.

Wagner had told us that many of his hunters are basically gun hunters who wish to experiment with bowhunting. Others are bored with the in-between time after the close of deer hunting. Some like to use the time to hone their skills in spring before the first California deer bow season opens in July.

Jeff Barclay and I, after climbing up, down and up another peak, finally spotted a small group of wild, black pigs pushing through some thick brush about forty yards below us. We could catch short glimpses of them through the openings, but could hear them plainly as they took their time moving our way. Pigs, I'm told, do not see well, but have a keen sense of smell. They were upwind of us and seemed unaware of our presence.

Finally, one of the larger pigs paused in a semi-open area of two merging trails below and to my right. I drew back the three-fletched Easton 2016 Gamegetter shaft and let fly. The arrow flew well over the back of the pig. I had grossly overestimated the distance. In a matter of seconds, well before I could nock another arrow, the pigs were gone, out of sight and sound. That turned out to be the only shot at a pig I had the rest of the day. Pete Fosselman and Mark Thiffault had a shot at another bigger pig several hours later, but it, too, avoided getting hit. We all agreed that Wagner was right when he said the pigs were the greatest hunting challenge on the ranch.

An hour or so later, Barclay was glassing a hillside near the far boundary of the ranch, when we both spotted Fosselman a ridgeline over. He was making a stalk on a Spanish goat that appeared to have a decent spread of horns. The experienced Fosselman now was clad in a new archer's bowhunter suit in the popular Trebark camo pattern. Although there were no trees around him, he appeared to blend well against the spring green grass, older sage brush and dry branches on the hillside.

Despite his caution, Fosselman soon was spotted, maybe winded, by the goat and he and his friends took off over the ridge. We were able to watch Fosselman and Thiffault top the same ridge several minutes later, this time, moving

Terrain in private game reserves can be as rugged as any other. Animals will be fenced in, although some do escape. Goats were introduced to California by early Spanish explorers to provide future food.

slower and with more caution than before. The goats had stopped to browse a bit not far down the slope.

Fosselman said later that he felt he had a good chance to make a successful stalk from the ridgeline. This time, he took almost a half-hour to get to within arrow range of the goat before straightening up for a twenty-yard shot. The arrow, tipped with Barrie Archery Rocky Mountain three-blade razorhead, struck a little high, just behind the shoulder on the right side.

We all sat down to wait twenty minutes, although we knew the direction the goat had taken after it was hit. The arrow had passed completely through and there was a clear blood trail which we followed after our wait. As luck would have it, the goat piled up not far from the access road and it was easy to locate in an open, grassy area.

Before long, we had a pickup truck nearby and the goat was loaded aboard for the ride back to the ranch entrance for field dressing and caping. Fosselman thought enough of the head to decide to take it to his taxidermist for preservation and mounting.

During California's early deer season, ranch bowhunters also are offered access to the unfenced several thousand acres behind the preserve, providing they possess the appropriate California deer tag.

There are certain hard-core bowhunters who shun preserve hunting for various reasons. However, most such areas are well managed and offer plenty of challenge to any bowhunter, plus providing a place for early or off-season hunting. The cost can be reasonable and the experience can be priceless.

HUNTING BLACK BEAR

A group of nine hunters to the southern Alaska islands managed to bag eight black bear trophies.

BEAR HUNTING with bow and arrow may be the second most popular game in North America. And the popularity seems to be growing each year in many states and provinces. There are large, huntable black bear populations in the East, Midwest, parts of Canada, the West and especially in Alaska.

There are other kinds of bear in North America: the Alaska brown bear, polar bear and grizzly. But hunting these animals is highly specialized, expensive, difficult and rare. Hunting some of the species, with bows or with firearms, is no longer legal in many of the traditional areas where they were found not long after the turn of the century. For instance, both Art Young and Saxton Pope have entries in the Pope & Young Club record book, but both the specimens were taken in 1920 and both were killed in the Yellowstone National Park, Wyoming, where such hunting is no longer permitted. Pope and Young had obtained special permission for the hunt. The three species' records fill less than one page of the bowhunting record book, while the more common black bear listing fills nearly two dozen pages with thousands of entries. We will restrict our discussion to black bear hunting.

In Canada, the provinces of Saskatchewan, Manitoba, Ontario, Quebec and Alberta have notable populations of black bear. Many American bowhunters travel north for the bear seasons, spring and fall. In the U.S., hunters in Virginia, Wisconsin, Idaho, Utah, California, Colorado, Michigan, Minnesota and Alaska, among others, will find populations of black bear, many in the record book size.

Lately, the efforts of some anti-hunting groups have resulted in the reduction or elimination of archery bear hunting seasons in some locations; California being the most notable. Whether or not the bow seasons will be restored or the restrictions will spread, remains to be seen.

There are three basic bear hunting methods generally in use: Hunting over bait, spot and stalk, and the use of trained dogs to tree the bear. In some localities, baiting is illegal and in others one may not use dogs. Where legal, there may be restrictions on when either technique may be employed and the rules may change from year to year. The potential bowhunter must be literate in the latest hunting regulations in the area he is to hunt.

Springtime may be the best season to use the baiting method, because bears are recently out of hibernation and should be hungry. In some areas, bait hunting is successful in the fall, too.

Another method of bear hunting is the chance encounter. In times gone by, many California archery deer hunters would simply purchase a bear tag, because it was not expensive and often the deer and bear seasons coincided. Therefore, if the hunter encountered a bear while after deer, he could legally take one. Many bear in California were taken that way, when it was legal to do so.

The bait method is practiced more in the East and Midwest, with larger human populations and less open country. Almost anything bears will eat is used as bait: carrion, sweet bakery goods, honey, fish, garbage and artificial scents. The bait must be contained in bear-proof containers, securely fastened to large boulders or trees or the bears will carry the food off, beyond arrow range. Typically, the hunter will be in a tree stand within arrow range, high enough to be safe and for the human scent to carry well

Black Bear Are Plentiful In Many Areas And Have Become Favorite Archery Game

During a brief period of sunshine, the boat's skipper refueled his on-deck generator, right. The boat served as a floating base camp and messhall, providing a dry, warm break at night.

Coastal islands are largely uninhabited by any humans, except for the odd fisherman or lobster trapper who may have to take temporary shelter.

above the bait. It is a matter of waiting for the game to come in to eat and hoping for a good shot from the stand.

An exciting and challenging method is spot and stalk. This technique cannot work in all locations, because one might search for years and never see a bear. But where bear are plentiful, it is extremely rewarding to the hunter.

Alaska is many things to many people; and parts of that huge state are paradise for bowhunters who hanker after black bear. On a recent trip north for spring hunting, a group of hunters spotted dozens of black bear along the south coastal islands and nine hunters in the party managed to take eight bear. They were able to spot and select from among several animals before taking a shot.

There is no "bow season" in Alaska; only hunting season. Alaska officials do not prescribe what kind of arm is used during any specific season, as long as it is legal under current regulations. Technically, a bowhunter may find himself competing with a rifle hunter, but in actual practice, this seldom happens. There are too many miles of empty space to be concerned with crowded conditions while hunting; this is especially true of the area of southeastern Alaska, much of which is made up of various sized islands.

The black bear season in this part of Alaska runs from September 1 to June 30. The spring season begins April first. From past experience, I would guess the spring bear hunts are the most productive. Registered guides are required for non-resident black bear hunters and the area is so vast that some help from knowledgeable local hunters will save time and money.

Our host on this hunt was Chuck Wagner who, with his partners, has formed Alaskan Coastal Adventures. The outfit has located an area southeast of Juneau, operating all the way down to Wrangell and Ketchikan which fairly teems with game. We saw plenty of black bear, deer, ducks, geese and other game and also sampled the salt- and freshwater fishing of the area. There are thousands of miles of shoreline to explore. It is an area well known for fabulous salmon and halibut fishing, with plenty of trout, char and steelhead in the coastal streams. Wagner recommends taking plenty of fishing gear on any hunt to Alaska.

Alaska Airlines flies in and out of most cities in Alaska and has plenty of experience with hunters and fishermen.

For our trip, Wagner had lined up a comfortable sixty-foot boat as a floating hunting camp. The boat offered comfortable living, with excellent meals prepared by the boat operator. It rains a lot in that part of Alaska, but the boat remained dry and warm.

For those who preferred, Wagner located some island cabins to serve as on-shore base camps amid the black bear habitat. This spring hunt was at a time when the black bears were coming out of hibernation and many were spotted as they browsed on the new grass of small island beaches. Some of the beaches are tiny; measuring twenty by a hundred feet in size. The rest of the shoreline is steep and heavily overgrown, cliffs dropping directly into the water, leaving only sharp rocks showing at low tide. Access to these island shorelines is limited to small boats, but Wagner and his crowd know all of the best landings. Most can be approached by shallow-draft skiffs, also part of the equipment.

Some of the group hunted with rifles, some with hand-

Wrangell, Alaska is primarily a fishing village for most of the year. Its airport services jet airliners on regular basis, catering to hunters.

Left: Dick Wormington, asphalt paving contractor and bowhunter, is co-operator of Alaska outfitting service. He was charged by black bear after hit.

guns, others with bow and arrow. Unlike the situation in many of the Lower Forty-eight, firearms may be carried by the bowhunter in this rugged, sometimes dangerous country. A powerful revolver is highly recommended. Four bowhunters and two reps from the booking agency were dropped off at their own island, several hours by boat from Wrangell, during the latter part of May. They stayed in a primitive crabber's cabin until picked up seven days later. They carried all their own food and equipment for their stay in camp.

All the bowhunters took a bear except one, who had several shots and a lot of bad luck. Rather than scouting the shoreline from a skiff, the cabin bowhunters made their way along the rugged shore on foot, searching the terrain with binoculars. When a bear was spotted, feeding on the new grass, it was up to the hunter to plan and execute a stalk, staying downwind and moving as quietly as possible toward the bear.

That part of Alaska at that time of year gets a lot of rain and wind. Temperatures do not reach below freezing, but the rain and wind can lower a person's body temperature to a danger level, unless proper clothing is worn. A pair of waterproof boots is essential with stress on ruggedness.

Chuck Wagner and his crew alert the hunter to the absolute requirement for the right gear for a successful Alaska trip. Count on it being wet. And when it is not wet, it will be raining! A month or more of steady rain is not uncommon in that part of the state. Keeping dry and warm is a matter of being outfitted from head to toe in waterproof clothing.

Some bowhunters wear hip boots or waders such as those more commonly used by fly fishermen, but they can become too heavy after many hours of walking and a tear in the fabric is worse than not wearing rubber boots at all.

Alaska boatman, Bruce Jamieson, pointed out that his experience prompts him to rely upon soft, foam rubber waders to keep dry and warm.

Two other items of equipment essential for any bowhunter, but particularly the Alaskan variety, are a good hunting knife and a high-resolution pair of binoculars. A knife will do more than simply skin-out and field-dress game; it may save a life under adverse conditions. I carried a Chris Reeves Mark IV in a leather sheath for this particular hunt. Handle and blade are formed from a single piece of steel; it is an extremely tough knife. It performed all its tasks without a hitch.

When confronting rain, wind and saltwater, an inadequate pair of binoculars can be ruined in a hurry. Light-gathering capabilities are more important than a lot of magnification for the kind of hunting we were doing. The days were long, but it was either overcast or raining most the time. A set of five-power Ranging Dawn and Dusk rubber-armored binoculars did the job better than some eight- and ten-power glasses. They are light enough in weight to be carried without fatigue all day and could reach out into darkly shaded coves and clearings to spot black bear when others could not.

Each hunter came home with memorable experiences. At least two will make campfire stories for years to come. Dick Wormington of Beaumont, California, hunts with a custom JW compound bow and has taken a number of mule deer as well as several California black bears. He is not a rookie bowhunter.

Wormington's bow draws eighty-four pounds at twenty-nine inches of draw, shooting Easton 2216 shafts tipped with Bodkin broadheads. He uses no bow sight, but does have a Flipper II arrow rest and a Martin Archery Kwik-Lok bow quiver attached.

Successful bear hunters are tired, wet and cold, but return with plenty of stories and trophies.

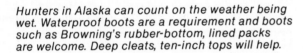

Hunters in Alaska can count on the weather being wet. Waterproof boots are a requirement and boots such as Browning's rubber-bottom, lined packs are welcome. Deep cleats, ten-inch tops will help.

During the third morning on the island, a couple of bears were spotted ambling across a low-tide sand pit from another nearby island. The wind was right and Wormington figured that if he set up an ambush just on the edge of the woods on his side of the crossing, the bears would walk right into range. He did and they did as expected.

One of Wormington's shafts lodged behind the bear's foreleg, just where it was supposed to. However, the bear became enraged instead of dead and spun around to snap and bite at the protruding arrow. In one movement, he had snapped off the shaft and began to look for the source of his irritation. Wormington unleashed a second arrow, hitting right on, but by then, the bear knew what was hurting him. He charged across the remaining distance of sand toward the bowhunter.

Wormington, who had no place to retreat, also was armed with a .357 magnum revolver. The bear was not slowing down nor turning away, as Wormington drew the big revolver and fired three rounds into the bear's chest. The bullets seemed to have no effect. It took two more .357 slugs to convince the bear to turn away and run into the underbrush, where he expired not far out of sight. The hunter had his bear tag filled.

Ed Gaines, another Californian, had a story even more bizarre to tell about his bowhunt. Gaines hunts with a PSE Laser bow set at sixty pounds and thirty inches of draw. He uses Easton 2117 shafts with Barrie Rocky Mountain Razor Heads; three blades at 130 grains. Gaines adds a Pro Line five-pin sight and a Lonnie Jones stabilizer on the bow.

After several days of hunting, he spotted and stalked a nice-size black bear from behind a fallen log. When hit, the bear ran up a big fir tree, stopping thirty feet above the ground. This not only proved that black bears can climb trees, but that they also can be mighty fast doing it.

The bear died in the tree. His forelegs were draped over two heavy limbs and it looked like he was there to stay. Gaines began to plan ways to get the heavy carcass down. He was considering throwing a line up over the limb or climbing up the tree with some sort of block and tackle when one of the guides, Rob Shelley, arrived on the scene.

Shelley was carrying a .300 Winchester magnum rifle. He simply sighted in one of the heavy limbs which was supporting the dead bear and let off a round. The brittle limb shattered and down tumbled the bear. Little damage was done to the pelt in the fall and the technique was safer than trying to winch down 250 pounds of carcass with a broadhead inside it.

An Alaska non-resident hunting license costs $60. A black bear tag will be $200 additional, with the option of purchasing a second tag if the hunter desires. License agents are found in even the smallest towns at sporting goods and hardware stores. The necessary paperwork also may be taken care of through the Alaska Department of Fish and Game in Juneau, well in advance of the trip north. However, local sporting goods dealers have the latest intelligence on who is taking what game or fish and where.

Non-resident hunting and fishing fees in Alaska are reasonable. Once in Alaska, the booking agent takes care of everything except taxidermy and return transportation. Food and lodging are excellent and more luxurious than one might expect. Personnel are qualified to care for trophies and meat and will be helpful in getting everything to the airline for transportation home. Alaska is expensive by Lower Forty-Eight standards. Everything has to be shipped north, adding considerably to consumer cost. The hunter will be wise to purchase everything needed at home before departing on a trip to Alaska.

BOWFISHING

FISHING WITH a bow can and has been done on several lakes and waterways in the United States and Canada. The type of fish allowed to be taken are rough or scavenger fish: carp, gar, buffalo fish and suckers. Most states will not permit game fish such as trout, salmon and the like to be taken with arrows, but the aforementioned scavengers are legal.

The rough species are extremely damaging to gamefish and wildlife biologists welcome any destruction of the roughs. There usually is no limit on the number of carp, so you can shoot as many as you want, thus helping other fishermen. In many places, the rough fish seasons are open all year.

The usual target for bowfishing is the carp. This fish can become huge, weighing thirty, forty or more pounds in some waters. It will give any angler a real battle, with plenty of excitement for the bow-wielder.

During spring and summer, when the species is spawning, carp-shooting tournaments are popular among archers. In some contests, big cash and equipment prizes are awarded, luring hundreds of bowfishermen to the waterways. The top shooters can take home incredible prizes and money, including boats, motors, trailers, equipment and cash. Carp shooters have been known to rid some impoundments of tens of thousands of pounds of carp on a single weekend, improving trout fishing considerably later in the year.

Carp can and are eaten by some, but the meat is quite bony and oily, requiring special preparation. This particular fish once was considered quite a delicacy in parts of Europe, but few Americans favor it. Fish from a tournament that cannot be donated to needy causes usually is plowed under the soil for fertilization purposes.

During spawning season — the waters beginning to warm up in spring — carp may be seen rolling just under or above the surface in shallows near the shore. Their actions

Carp, above, are the main target of bowfishermen, to the benefit of game fisheries. Shallow waters warm up early in spring as carp begin to spawn. Men and women compete on equal basis, below, in bowfishing competition.

A wide-beam, flat-bottom boat equipped with outboard and trolling motors works well for most bowfishing.

are destructive to trout egg nests along the water's edge.

Along flat, shallow shorelines, the archer may wade in while fishing. This works well in some areas with warm water, but wading can stir up sediment and may obscure the carp for later fishing. A stable fishing boat such as a Jon boat or bass boat is popular in most money tournaments.

In recent years, serious carp shooters have begun building stands or towers on their boat decks. This puts the archer well above the water surface, providing a better angle from which to see the shallow-swimming carp.

Due to the reflection of light through water, one must remember the fish is actually below where it appears to be. The archer must aim below the fish or risk a miss. It takes experience and there will be plenty of misses before the tricks are learned.

Any bow with a forty- or fifty-pound draw is satisfactory for fishing. Heavier draw weights are not necessary; plenty

Carp And Other Rough Fish
Are Great Warm Weather Targets

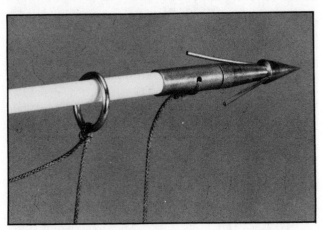

Fishing line is attached to Bear removable barbed arrowhead at shank, pays out through sliding ring.

Complete bowfishing kit by Bear Archery may be fixed to bow with tape: arrow, fletching, line, head, reel.

Archers, above, have assembled shooting towers on their boats to give a better viewing, shooting angle to water's surface. Fishing team, right, takes aim.

of shots will be taken during a day and muscles may cry out in pain with a heavier draw. Some believe a recurve bow is better because of the faster, more simple action. There are fewer lines and cables to become entangled during the fast action before and after a shot. Others favor the compound bow with sixty-five percent let-off, because they can hold on the target longer without tiring while waiting for the fish to surface or show for a shot.

Special fishing arrows and heads are required. Most bowfishing arrows are of heavy, solid aluminum or fiberglass. A lightweight arrow may skip on the water and too light an arrow will not penetrate the shallow water to the fish. Small plastic fletching or no fletching at all is used, because the shots are at short range and the arrows have no time to stabilize.

Barbed arrowheads are essential to keep from losing the fish — and the arrow — after it is shot. These heads, incidentally, usually are illegal for other game in most places. Most fishing heads are removable, so the fish can be pulled off the arrow. Or the barbs may be collapsed so the fish can be removed from the shaft. The arrow and bow must be connected with heavy fishing line in order to re-

trieve the fish. The line should be the heavy braided type, as some of the fish are heavy and strong and you do not have the advantage of a flexible pole with which to play the fish until it is tired.

The arrow, line and, hopefully, a fish all are retrieved with some sort of reel attached to the bow. There are several types of reels, from the simplest round rim which holds the line to a more sophisticated commercial fishing reel which attaches to the stabilizer bushing. On the latter,

the line is cranked in the same as with a fishing reel. Repeated shots will be faster and easier with the latter set-up.

The most important item of gear for bowhunting may be a pair of polarized sun glasses. The treatment of the lenses tends to reduce the amount of reflected light off the water, giving you a much better look below the surface. Without the glasses, you are likely to see only those fish which roll or jump to the bright surface of the water.

Don't forget plenty of spare parts, shafts and barbed heads. It may be a long trip back to the boat dock. Remember the sun screen and use plenty while on the water.

VARMINTS

Jim Dougherty is a former, many-times varmint calling champion, now residing in Oklahoma. Coyote is the most commonly hunted varmint.

HERE IS MORE to bowhunting than deer, elk, bear and other big game. Varmints have been a favorite bowhunter target for years, challenging hunting skills and calling skills.

Russ Thurman, an editor with *Gun World Magazine* talked to several expert callers while researching the subject and has filed the following report.

THERE'S A REMARKABLE epidemic that spreads through the ranks of bowhunters each December. Some are stricken as early as the second week of December; most are able to resist the galloping anxiety until the middle of the month while some even wait until after Christmas. But it's there every year. Deer season is coming to a close.

As each day ends, that last deer tag gets heavier to carry. The burden shows. Early morning coffee gatherings aren't quite as light-hearted as they were in September, October and November. Some guys play it cool, but there's still an edge in their voices. The worst cases stare off into the woods a lot and their sentences never quite get completed. All have an extra dose of crow's feet around their eyes. It's not a pretty time.

The worst is the end of the season. Last chance. Gone are the hopes for a trophy that can be hung on the wall. Now, anything to hang a tag on would do just fine. While there are some selected seasons in certain parts of the country, deer season ends, tragically for some, at the fading of light on the last day of the year.

For those who wait until the next deer season to go bowhunting, life goes into neutral. But it doesn't have to be that way. While big-game hunters may find it hard to believe, some of the best bowhunting is just beginning. It's time to go varmint hunting.

The hunting of varmints — coyote, bobcat and fox — can be every bit as adventurous and challenging as stalking a big mule deer or rattling up a whitetail. Bowhunting and varmints are a great combination; a contest at close range. This means learning how to call in animals, then drawing down on them when they often are just a few yards away. With firearms, varmints can be taken at greater distances, but it's not quite the same as when hunting with a bow. The closeness of the animal — knowing you got it there with a call and taking it with a bow, an updated version of an ancient weapon — is most rewarding.

In addition to keeping stunned bowhunters from walking around in a daze until the next deer season, hunting varmints can actually make you a better big-game hunter. It'll keep your shooting skills tuned, enchance your camouflaging techniques, increase your in-the-woods senses and add many pages to your knowledge of animals. This all will help when you're perched in your favorite tree stand or stalking through a mountain pass. Next time, you probably won't end up as one of the sad end-of-year-tag-gang, either.

You'll also gain a better feel for your bow and bow accessories. You don't have to change or add any equipment to your regular bowhunting outfit except for varmint calls. And it's important to use your big-game equipment. Just because a coyote, bobcat or fox doesn't have the stature of a whitetail, doesn't mean it's all that easy to bring down. Many varmint hunters have been amazed by coyotes that survive through-and-through arrows. This means you must use sharp broadheads, not some cast-off you've been using for target practice. The arrow head must be sharp so it'll do what you want it to do on a deer — cut two clean, gaping holes.

All your equipment must be camouflaged; no shiny parts. For the most part, you're going to be on the same level as the incoming varmint. With their keen hearing they will have pinpointed your call and they will be on sharp lookout for their prey. This is not the time for a scraped riser edge to reflect sunlight. After a season of big-game hunting, double check all your equipment for areas that may need to be touched up with camouflage paint or tape. Make sure your bow is quiet. Replace any badly worn self-adhesive fleece around the sight window and arrow rest.

There really is only one additional piece of equipment you may want to add to your setup and that's a light for night-time varmint hunting. Mark Thiffault, varmint hunting editor of *Gun World Magazine* recommends the three-battery Keller Legend I which runs off three AA cell batteries. It's a mini flashlight, eight inches long and has a green-camouflage finish. This waterproof light has a beam

Hunting These Game Animals Will Sharpen Skills And Occupy The Hunter During The Off-Season

that can be adjusted from spot to flood just by twisting the head.

Now, before you rush off to buy a high-powered torch that'll throw a spot on the moon, check the laws in the area you intend to hunt. The laws concerning using a light and night-time hunting are not the same throughout the country. It's even more important to fully understand all the laws related to hunting varmints. In all but a few areas, bobcats are protected year-round, but with some seasons available. There's a lot more of an opportunity to take foxes; coyotes are by far the most plentiful.

When hunting varmints, camouflage is just as important as when going after big game. In a great many varmint hunting areas, there's not a lot of cover, so blending into the environment is critical. You can wear camouflaged clothing or subdued clothes that match the area. You probably won't have to bundle up quite as much as you did for sitting in a tree stand. Usually, you won't be in one spot for long when hunting varmints; probably no more than thirty minutes. In most cases, you'll also be returning to your vehicle for a ride to the next spot. Regardless, use the same common sense rules for hunting in cold weather: Dress warm enough for the worst condition, but don't become overheated. Sweat can freeze on your skin, causing chills and worse.

Make sure your hands and face are camouflaged. Headnets are favored by some folks, but they can be distracting. Camouflage makeup works fine, especially for hands unless you've learned to shoot effectively with gloves; a feat that takes a tremendous amount of practice.

Scents are used by many varmint hunters, although there's a great deal of debate as to whether they really do any good. Murry Burnham, the legendary Texan who, along with his brother Winston, has a remarkable career of taking all types of game, says scents have always played an important part in his varmint hunting plans.

"Any time you're going to have animals close, such as when you're calling or bowhunting, a scent can give you that little edge that makes a difference," Burnham writes in his book *Hunting Secrets*.

"Nowadays many different animal scents are on the market. My old standby is skunk scent. Years ago, Winston and I would either pack a dead skunk or squeeze its dark-yellow musk into a can. Imagine what we smelled like! But after some experimenting, we discovered that we could place the carcass or can of musk downwind from our calling position. If a predator tried to circle up our scent, the stinky skunk would play tricks on the animal's nose and confuse it just long enough for one of us to get a shot."

Jim Dougherty, a many-time champion varmint caller and renowned bowhunter, thinks scents are not that useful when hunting varmints. "Some folks use scents either to try to attract varmints or to mask human smell. I don't think scents are effective on varmints."

Dougherty writes in an upcoming book, "Coyotes are going to circle and when they pick up the downwind odor, they're going to sort through it and pick you out. As far as

I'm concerned, using scents with varmints only means you have to put up with the smell and it doesn't help get the varmint closer." By the way, Dougherty and the Burnhams have hunted varmints together for many years.

Decoys are other tools that hunters use to bring varmints within bow range. They can be as simple as several feathers tied together and attached to a bush to blow in the wind, or as elaborate as stuffed rabbits. Regardless, a decoy is designed to distract the varmint's attention away from the hunter. As mentioned, a varmint will have pinpointed your call and will be looking, concentrating on your location. A decoy can divert that attention, if just for a split second, giving you the needed time to send an arrow on its way.

Some hunters have combined decoys and electronic callers to really attract varmints. A dying rabbit call placed near a rabbit skin can have a coyote thinking about a banquet dinner instead of any danger that may be crouching in the nearby brush. Electronic callers are especially useful when you're hunting alone. Before you use an electronic caller, though, check the laws in your area. While the caller

Another sought-after varmint is the bobcat, held by Dougherty. Big cat was taken with a Custom Bighorn take-down recurve bow in Oklahoma.

is not attached to the bow, some states still consider it to be an illegal electronic aid.

Even if you can use an electronic caller, calling in an animal yourself is an exciting aspect of bowhunting for varmints. Learning how to call is not that difficult, especially when there are so many instructional cassette tapes available from experienced hunters. Calls are not expensive, so there's not a lot of investment; however, to really get the job done, you'll need several types of calls. Once you've practiced with cassette tapes, find someone who has called in varmints. Most hunters enjoy showing a newcomer the way it's really done.

It's important to understand the animals you are hunting: where they live, what they eat, their habits and why they respond to varmint calls. Coyotes, bobcats and foxes are predators; they're hunters. They spend most of their time searching for a meal. Rabbits, rodents and birds are on the top of their menu. Foxes also will eat berries and fruit. Coyotes are always searching for larger game. They will attack even young deer and old or injured adult animals.

The best months for hunting varmints are late winter through early spring. This will vary in different parts of the country depending on weather. But even in areas where it's extremely cold, varmints can be taken without — this is the best part — having to face the bitter early morning cold. Varmints, for the most part, aren't out prowling around when you would normally be hunting deer. They begin looking for breakfast after the sun has warmed things up a bit.

Varmints respond to calls because they think it means a

Kelly Dougherty is following in his father's footsteps and puts another coyote in the bag.

meal is in the offing. They're attracted to what sounds like an injured animal. Murry Burnham, however, is convinced many animals respond to a call, because they're just curious.

"When I'm trying to call coyotes in south Texas, using bird or rabbit distress cries, it isn't unusual to lure javelinas. I've brought them close enough to touch," he writes in his *Hunting Secrets* book. "I've also had jackrabbits and cottontails respond to a call...I've also had coyotes come in that seemed more curious than hungry. But knowing how sounds are developed isn't that important. Results are what count. You must realize that the actual sound need not be perfect."

While it's important to learn how to call — to make those distress sounds — it's not as important as knowing where to call. Predators can be found just about anywhere, from coastal sand dunes to high country timber. But within each of these areas, there are hot spots. It's like reading a lake or river for likely fishing areas. You're looking for spots where fish are holding for protection and for access to food. It's the same with predators. They're always on the alert for danger so they are most often near cover, but, because they are predators, they're also looking for the next meal.

In open country, where you find a lot of coyotes, foxes and even cats, you need to pick the most likely places where varmints are on the roam. It may be a brush-filled wash that bends around a rock-strewn series of hills. Or it may be a decayed fence line over-grown with sage. Then there's the woods, with its many trails, a clearing every so often, mostly packed with thorny brush. These are all likely homes for varmints; they provide protection and food.

Once you've found an area where there are varmints, you need to decide where to locate a stand for calling. Remember, you're not stalking varmints, you're calling them to you. So while a woods may be packed with foxes, it may not be the best place to hunt them. There's a lot of cover for them to use when they approach your position in response to a call. You need to pick a spot where you have good concealment, but also good observation and enough room to shoot your bow.

It can be difficult to find all these in one spot, so you may have to use a less concealed location just so you have the room to get an arrow off at the right time. That's why camouflage is so important. In most cases, varmint hunters pick stands that have some cover, without being hemmed in by brush or woods. That often means varmints will have to cross open areas to answer a call. This adds to the challenge and the excitement.

"I don't have any idea how many coyotes I have called up in thirty-five years of hunting them," wrote Jim Dougherty in *Bow & Arrow Hunting Magazine,* "but I know the next one will give me the same thrill as that first one did, when I see him coming to me hard across a winter prairie."

Pick a stand and place yourself in the direction where you think the varmint will be approaching. You'll want to be facing into the wind. Have the least likely approach route to your back; probably the most open area. The placement of the sun can also be important. In the morning and late afternoon, it is best to have the sun at your back. This will provide deeper shadows for your stand and reduce

Smaller bobcat was called into range of tree stand while Dick Clark was hunting whitetails.

the visibility of an approaching varmint. We're talking best situations, here. It's rare you'll be able to work all these factors to perfection, but they're good to keep in mind.

How you sit in a stand can mean the difference between collecting varmints or just a frustrating day in the field. You'll want to sit so you're comfortable and still able to draw and release an arrow with the least amount of body movement. Getting too comfortable may mean too much added movement and a varmint streaking in another direction. Get in a comfortable position and test it by drawing your bow. Can you cover the most likely approach area? Is your elbow banging into a tree limb or scraping loudly against brush? Can you sit that way for thirty minutes?

If you're hunting with another person, you'll need to have a safe/concealed spot for your partner. In most cases, one person does the calling while the other is ready to shoot. A hunting group of three is about the most that should be used on a stand. Usually, one person is back doing the calling with the two shooters up front. Use common sense when placing shooters; safety is most important. A shooter must know the limits of his shooting area to

prevent endangering the other hunter.

Now it's time to do some calling. The number of ways to call — how long, how loud and how often — is almost endless. Most experts agree, however, it often doesn't matter if you haven't perfected the techniques. Once you've gotten some training from cassettes or an experienced caller, just start calling Start with a loud blow on a call, pause, then blow again. If there are varmints in the area, they'll hear you.

"Many times you can sort of regulate how fast the animal comes to your call by the way you call," says Murry Burnham. "Constant calling brings the animal in more rapidly. On and off calling makes it react more deliberately. Blow a few distress squeals, wait a minute or two, then blow briefly again. Spend more time looking than calling."

Coyotes and foxes will usually answer a call within ten minutes. They'll come in at a trot or even faster, because they run their prey to ground. They know exactly where the sound came from and they'll be headed for it, ready to pounce. That's why it's useful to have a decoy or another person calling. They can distract the coyote or fox just long enough for the shooter to release an arrow. If a coyote detects you or senses danger, he'll exit fast. So will fox, except they'll often remain in the area. More than one fox has returned to answer a second, even a third call. If you haven't had a coyote or fox answer your call within fifteen to twenty minutes, it's probably best to move to another stand.

Bobcats are stalkers; they're slow and deliberate. You have to call them longer. Experienced cat hunters recommend blowing a call loudly for fifteen minutes then changing to blowing softly. Often a bobcat will suddenly appear near your stand, staring at you with piercing eyes. It's kind of spooky. Like most felines, bobcats have an indignant air about them. Instead of dashing off in the face of danger, they'll often just sit and allow you several shots before disappearing into cover. You'll have to have a lot more patience to hunt bobcats. Remain at a stand for at least thirty minutes.

Whenever you finish a stand, don't just stand up and walk off. Take your time and look sharply. Have signals pre-arranged with your partner so you don't stand up and scare a varmint off that only he can see. Circle away from the stand a short distance, moving downwind, then move quietly back through the stand. You'll often take a late arriving or overly cautious varmint using this method.

If you're walking to your next stand, walk into the wind while searching for another area from which to call. In most cases, depending on terrain and how strong the wind is, stands should be a quarter of a mile apart. A lot of varmint hunters select stands within easy walking distance of roads. This gives them access to extra gear, a warm vehicle between stands and hot coffee.

Varmint hunting is a lot of fun. It'll keep you sharp for all other types of bowhunting and challenge your outdoor knowledge and hunting skills. There's not a lot of money involved to get started and you don't have to be an expert to be successful. Many well known bowhunters got their start hunting varmints and many of them still consider it to be some of the most exciting hunting to look forward to each year. It is also a great way to avoid being stricken by the end-of-deer-season epidemic.

JAVELINA

The javelina makes a dramatic trophy for the den wall, left. Lora and Pete Shepley, above, take advantage of Arizona javelina population.

THE COLLARED PECCARY, more commonly called the javelina, inhabits desert portions of Arizona, New Mexico and Texas, as well as much of Old Mexico, thriving on the fauna of the area. With javelina hunting seasons open in the winter when seasons for most other animals are closed, they seem to offer ideal hunting for the dedicated bowhunter.

Leroy Janulewicz is several times California and national varmint calling champion, with more than three decades of bowhunting experience. He does not often miss an opportunity to travel to Arizona or Texas in January for a chance at javelina. His experiences will help any bowhunter who wishes to take the challenge.

THE HISTORY of javelina hunting has come a long way in the past seventy to eighty years: From undesirable pest to the smallest big-game animal in the United States. In the 1920s, this small big-game animal was harvested for its hide and meat for commercial purposes, most of which was shipped to the East Coast. But thanks to some state fish and game departments, this slaughter was halted to protect the animal. Winter is javelina hunting season.

The collared peccary, *pecari tajacu sonoriensis,* javelina migrated from Central America centuries ago and continued into Mexico. This hardy animal has slowly continued into the neighboring states of Texas, Arizona and New Mexico. The javelina is a pig-like looking creature, easily identified in the hunting field. They have a thick coarse hide of grayish brown and bristled hollow hair. During the winter months that coincide with the hunting seasons, they grow a white collar in front of the shoulder area, thus giving them the name of collared peccary.

Javelina are equipped with a set of upper and lower tusks in the two-inch class, which are used for protection and obtaining food. Javelina can be a ferocious animal at times, but are not vicious. It protects itself or a small pigling with those razor sharp tusks. I wouldn't recommend putting my finger in a wounded hog's mouth to see if it bites.

Javelina stand only about two feet at the shoulder and will average from thirty to forty pounds, field dressed. Don't underestimate this relatively small, compact critter. It can outrun an Olympic track star on flat ground! These desert hogs are mostly vegetarians, but have been known to eat lizards, rodents and carrion of other dead animals. For the most part, their diet consists of prickly pear cactus and its fruit, roots, bulbs, tubers, acorns, grass, mesquite beans and filaree, to mention a few favorites out of several hundred varieties of vegetation that make up their diet. Hogs also like to snack on grubs and small insects.

Javelina have poor eyesight, but can catch quick movements up to about seventy-five yards. They have a hard time distinguishing slow movements at ranges under seventy-five yards, but can pick out humans. Their hearing is not keen, but they can hear something unnatural at a great distance, if not preoccupied while feeding, heads buried in a

Javelina hunters will search for tracks and signs of feeding on the desert floor. The animal eats all manner of cactus, roots, bulbs and tubers.

Bowhunters Are Challenged By This Little Big-Game Animal Of The Desert

cactus patch. With two strikes against them, these critters make up for it in the smelling department. Their little noses can smell you coming from over two hundred yards away, if they are downwind. This can be one of the most important factors when you come upon a bunch of hogs. If you feel the slightest breeze hitting the back of your neck, you had better start looking around to see what's going on.

The popularity of hunting javelina with a bow and arrow has grown rapidly since the late 1950s. Javelina have become one of the most popular animals to hunt and archers are attracted from all over the country to the states where they can be found. Each year, I run across archers from the East Coast who actually drive to Arizona to fling arrows at the desert hog. I really am amazed when a hunter spends all that money to hunt, but doesn't know the first thing about his quarry. I've talked to guys who don't even know what a javelina looks like!

I've been hunting javelina with a bow and arrow for more than twenty years. We all learn from mistakes. With many javelina to my record, I learn something new every season about these fascinating animals.

Javelina will usually travel into the wind when moving to a feeding or bedding ground. This will enable them to catch any sign of danger. The peccary does have some enemies, such as humans, mountain lion, jaguar, packs of coyotes and the bobcat. Hogs will usually travel in groups or sounders that can range from ten to thirty head. This is primarily for protection. I once spotted a lone coyote from a distance, stalking a group of ten feeding hogs, in hopes of scoring a nice desert pork chop. The dog was not fooling anyone. A couple of big boars sent him the other way with his tail between his legs.

You may find a lone javelina feeding or bedded down with not another hog in sight. This loner will more than likely be a large boar that has been run out of the sounder for some reason. It may have lost the fight with a younger, dominant boar that challenged it for the older boar's do-

Binoculars may be used to search across canyons for feeding animals. Gray javelina may be hard to spot in shadows, but watch for movement.

main. It may have a sickness or disease. A good friend of mine, while hunting in Arizona a few years ago, spotted, stalked and shot a huge lone boar that was feeding. When we approached the downed hog, I almost passed out from the odor emitting from the worst smelling hog ever! After gutting it and cutting the musk gland out, it still stunk. Back at camp we skinned and cleaned it with fresh water and the meat was still so rank nothing could be done with it. However, while skinning the big old boar, I found numerous old and new battle scars on his tough, thick hide. There were

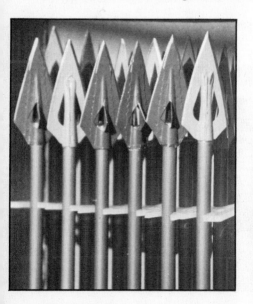

Desert hunting will be rough on arrows. A large supply, tipped with sharp broadheads, left, will be required. Javelina have tough, armored hides, difficult to penetrate. Watering holes, below, will reveal pig tracks.

Hunting equipment for javelina is basically the same as for any big game. When no other seasons are open in other areas, the Arizona season is a happy change.

numerous puncture wounds all over his body.

The big boar weighed forty-five pounds field dressed. I figured his live weight to be approximately sixty-five pounds. The largest boar I have taken weighed forty-six pounds field dressed. Hunters can easily calculate a javelina's approximate live weight by establishing the field dressed weight and dividing it by .70. This formula is pretty accurate. It is possible to find javelina that are heavier than average. Hogs that you find around cultivated crop fields and near residential areas receive supplemental foods to their regular diet.

Sounders of javelina will usually have their own territories within any given area. They will usually travel between a quarter and half mile to a feeding or bedding area. Javelina have a musk gland that will exude a musky, skunk-like smell when frightened or to mark its territory. Hogs will mark their bedding grounds, feeding areas and watering sites. It is not uncommon to smell where they are, or where they have been. The musk gland is located on the rump about six inches above the tail. This gland should be carefully cut out after gutting so it won't taint the meat.

When hunting javelina, I take along scents that are natural to the area that I'm hunting. There are numerous scents on the shelf of your favorite archery shop. I would suggest having pine, cedar, juniper, sage, deer and dirt-

type scents in the camp. I also have used neutral soaps for bathing and washing clothes, to help eliminate the strong human odor which javelina can detect so well. Scents really work after walking around the desert for a few days. I will take leaves or berries from brush as I'm walking and crush them in my hands to add a little extra natural scent.

Camouflage clothing helps as well, to break up the human outline. Even though the hog has poor eyesight, it can still detect something unnatural when you get in close to a bunch.

Your hunting equipment is important. I like a fast, flat-shooting bow that will push a good aluminum arrow, tipped with a sharp broadhead. String silencers on your bowstring are a must! I've had good twenty-yard broadside shots at feeding javelina and had them jump the string.

The terrain hogs occupy will not be like the eighteenth hole at your favorite golf course. Javelina country has lots of rocks and cactus. That is why you need a good broadhead that you can keep sharp. A good pair of binoculars is another important piece of equipment. Don't leave camp without them!

Now that the basic essentials are in the back of your mind, it's time to hunt this Gray Ghost of the desert. The nickname fits the javelina because this small animal has the ability to hide and camouflage itself well. They also have the ability to disappear after being spooked. There are only three ways that I know of to hunt these hardy critters, depending on the terrain you are hunting.

The first method is to have a group of hunters fan out and walk slowly across flat areas into the wind, in hopes of spotting a bunch feeding or bedded down. This method works well in parts of Texas and southern Arizona with a group of eight or ten hunters.

The second method is glassing with binoculars from hilltops and ridges to locate them, then throw a good stalk on the javelina. This is where your good pair of binoculars come in handy. You let the glasses do the walking for you. Javelina will usually move to where the sun hits a hillside at morning's first light. They also will try to catch the evening's late light atop a ridge or hillside. I've noticed that it's hard for javelina to get going after a good night's sleep, unless they have had their share of morning warm sun and some grub. I've even known some humans to have the same problem!

Once hogs are spotted, plan your stalk with the wind in

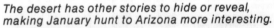

The desert has other stories to hide or reveal, making January hunt to Arizona more interesting.

your favor. When slowly stalking into a bunch of pigs, be aware of those little objects that look like pieces of cactus. I've had little piglings the size of cottontail rabbits run right back to mom or dad to tell on me and there went my perfect stalk. If the hogs spook, they will make a loud whoofing sound. If you stand still and imitate the whoofing noise, a few may return in order to regroup, which will allow you a second chance. I've seen many pigs make that fatal mistake.

The third method of hog hunting is to call them to you with a varmint call. The latter two of these techniques are my favorites and they account for many javelina for my friends and me.

I have always been fascinated with calling in a whole group of hogs. It's a sure way to get the old blood pumping and someone will always get a few shots! There are several theories as to why the Gray Ghost is attracted to a varmint call. I have a few of my own.

The first theory is that a bunch of javelina may think a member of the sounder is being attacked or in trouble. Young adult hogs and juveniles are notorious for getting into trouble. This could range from being caught in a trap to being torn apart by a mountain lion. I had the pleasure of assisting an old trapper once, when a young adult sow had one of its legs caught in a coyote trap. The sow made sounds like a garbled jackrabbit call. Talk about mean and nasty! With a pole snare around its neck, it was finally released unharmed after several exciting dusty minutes!

A territory theory also is possible. Another sounder of hogs may have trespassed into the wrong area and began fighting among themselves.

Another theory is that a javelina hears a dinner call. I have talked many hours with old timers who claim to have actually witnessed javelina kill and eat jackrabbits and cottontails that have been caught in traps.

You don't have to be a calling champion to call in hogs. Your basic jackrabbit or cottontail call will work fine. Just use it as if you were calling in a coyote. You don't have to be that particular about the type of country you're hunting. If in flat country, just make sure you're in some brush and have an arrow nocked. Javelina will be on you quickly, so be ready for some hot action. If you're in low mountain country, I would get on top of a small mound or ridge. I like to be a little higher so I can see from which direction a pig may be coming. I have been surprised more than once with a bunch of hogs popping their teeth and breathing down the back of my neck.

When a group or a single comes to a call, it can be intimidating as hell. With bristles all hackled up, popping tusks and whoofing, it can become confusing. It's easy to get excited. When javelina are running at you, or spooked, the bristled hair will stand up on their backs and make them look twice their size. Many archers make that mistake and shoot high, only to come up with hair on their broadhead. Aim a little lower and right behind the shoulder. I usually wait as long as I can and when the target hog gets to within about twenty feet, I let go. The average shot will be twenty to thirty feet, so wait until you have a nice broadside shot. Those straight-on shots are tough; it's like trying to split a playing card!

Javelina don't bleed much after being stuck with an arrow. Don't become discouraged if the blood trail is poor. The hollow bristled hair will soak up blood like a sponge.

After tracks were found at the waterhole, this hunter set up a natural blind to await returning animals. Wind should be blowing from across pond.

In most cases a hog will run only seventy-five yards after being hit. Try to keep sight of a hog as much as possible. Watch the direction where you last saw him, so you will have a point of reference. If you see him bed down within thirty yards, he's in bad shape. Just watch him and wait as you would for a deer. I've seen guys run right after a shot hog and they end up chasing it all over the cactus-filled hills.

I like to combine the glassing and calling methods. If I don't spot a group of feeding hogs and it's getting into the late morning hours, I break out the old varmint call. Sometimes you can bring javelina from out of their beds that you had missed while glassing. It's so easy to walk by a bunch of pigs that might be in a wash or canyon and only a stone's throw away. Not every javelina will come into a varmint call. I've blasted on calls and had them run the other way. At least I learned where they were bedded down. I had no intention of walking in the direction of where they had come from.

Javelina meat, when properly prepared, can be excellent table fare. Surprisingly, the meat doesn't resemble or taste like domestic pork. It is lean and light tan in color when cooked. It should be cooked well done! Some people find the gamey odor and flavor of the meat objectionable, but most of these complaints can be eliminated by properly preparing and cooking the meat. Javelina meat is excellent when barbecued or baked to your favorite recipe. The meat is popular in several Mexican dishes and when cooked with sweet and sour sauces in a crockpot, it's out of this world.

Javelina are hardy animals and I have a great respect for these little critters. If you never have hunted javelina and want an exciting hunt, give the Gray Ghost a try. — *Leroy Janulewicz*

GLOSSARY OF TERMS

AFTERHOLD — n. position of arms, hands, body and head after the string is released.

AIM — v. to superimpose a sight pin on the center of the target; when not using a sight it is the placement of the tip of the arrow on a particular point for a given distance.

ANCHOR — v. to place the index finger of the drawing hand on a definite spot on the body, usually on the face, when at full draw.

ANCHOR POINT — a definite spot on the archer's body (usually on the face) which the index finger of the string hand touches at full draw.

ARM GUARD — a piece of stiff material used to protect the bow arm from the slap of the bow string upon release; usually made of leather and worn on the inside of the forearm of the bow arm.

ARROW FLETCHING — n. see Fletching.

ARROW PLATE — n. the piece to which the arrow rest is attached.

ARROW REST — n. a projection on the bow or arrow plate upon which the arrow lies while it is nocked on the string.

ARROW NOCK — see Nock.

ARROW SHELF — the horizontal projection at the bottom of the sight window which can be used as an arrow rest; usually found on hunting bows.

BACK — n. the side of the bow away from the bow string.

BARB — n. 1. part of a point of a fishing arrow; 2. one of the hair-like branches growing from the shaft of a feather.

BAREBOW — n. a method of shooting which does not include a bow sight.

BELLY — n. the side of the bow nearest the bow string, now called the face.

BLUNT — n. an arrow point that is not pointed, usually a metal cap that fits on the end of the arrow shaft. Used to stun and kill small game at short distances.

BOW — n. a device made of a piece of flexible material with a string connecting the two ends that is used to propel an arrow.

BOW ARM OR HAND — the arm or hand which holds the bow.

BOW NOTCHES — see Notches.

BOW RACK — a device to hold bow or bows while not in use.

BOW SLING — see Sling.

BOW SIGHT — a mechanical device placed on the bow with which the archer can aim directly at the target.

BOW SQUARE — a device, usually shaped in a T, used to measure string height and nocking height.

BOW STRING — the string of a bow, usually made of Dacron.

BOW STRINGER — a device used to string the bow for shooting.

BOW TIP PROTECTOR — a small, pliable cap that is placed on the tip of the lower limb to protect it from excessive wear produced from contact with the ground or floor.

BRACE — v. see String.

BRACE HEIGHT — see String Height.

BROADHEAD — n. a sharp, bladed metal point used for hunting live game.

BULLSEYE — n. the center of the target, the area with the highest scoring value.

BUTT — n. any backstop to which a target face is attached.

CANT — v. to tip or hold the bow to the right or left of vertical while at full draw. The reference to right or left is determined by the position of the top limb; n. the direction in which the bow is tilted.

CAST — n. the ability of a bow to propel an arrow.

CENTER SERVING — the serving on the central area of the bow string which protects the bow string from wear.

CENTERLINE — n. the relationship of the bow string to its limbs; usually a line which evenly divides the limbs when the undrawn bow is viewed from the string side (face).

CENTERSHOT BOW — a bow which has the lower part of the sight window cut past its centerline.

CLASSIC FORM — a method of shooting with as little deviation as possible from normal body position.

CLICKER — n. a small strip of metal, mounted on the sight window of the bow in front of the arrow rest, that gives a precise indication of when full draw is attained by snapping off the point of the arrow with an audible click.

CLOUT — n. a form of target shooting in which the arrow is shot into the air at a 48-foot target on the ground from a distance varying between 120 and 180 yards.

COCK FEATHER — see Index Fletching.

COLLAPSE — n. loss of muscle control prior to release of the arrow; v. to lose muscle control to release of the arrow.

COMPOSITE BOW — a bow made of more than one substance, not necessarily a laminated bow.

COMPOUND BOW — a hand-drawn, hand-held bow that stores more energy than a recurve bow through the use of two cables and two eccentrics.

COURSE — n. the range on which field rounds are shot, usually composed of 14 or 28 targets.

CREEP — v. to allow the arrow to move slowly forward before the release; to not maintain the draw length before release.

CREST — n. the colored bands around the shaft of the arrow which aid in its identification.

CUSHION PRESSURE POINT — a pressure point which will absorb some of the shock of the arrow as it passes after release, usually plastic, leather, et cetera.

DEAD RELEASE — a release in which the drawing hand remains at the anchor point.

DRAW — v. to pull the bow string back; n. the distance the bow string is drawn back.

DRAW CHECK — a device attached to the bow which indicates attainment of full draw.

DRAW WEIGHT — 1. the weight, measured in pounds, used to bring the bow to full draw; 2. the weight on a bow, using 28 inches as a standard draw.

DRAWING HAND — the hand which holds the string during the draw.

END — n. a set number of arrows that are shot before going to the target to score and retrieve them.

EXTEND — v. the place the bow arm and bow in shooting position before beginning the draw.

FACE — n. the surface of the bow toward the bow string.

FIELD CAPTAIN — the male official in charge of an archery tournament or the men's line of a large tournament.

FIELD ARCHERY — an archery round in which the archer shoots from a variety of distances at targets in woods and fields; designed to simulate hunting conditions.

FIELD POINT — a point that is shaped similar to a target point, but is as heavy as the broadhead.

FINGER TAB — a flat piece of smooth material which protects the fingers of the drawing hand.

FINGER SLING — a small strap that attaches to the thumb and index finger of the bow hand; see Sling.

FLETCH — v. to glue a feather or vane to an arrow shaft.

FLETCHING — n. the feathers, plastic vanes, or other devices attached to the arrow shaft which stablize the flight of the arrow.

FLIGHT SHOOTING — shooting for distance.

FLINCH — v. to move either the bow or release arm just before or at the release, usually caused by anticipation of the clicker or fear of hitting the bow arm with the string; n. the movement of either the bow or release arm before the release of the arrow.

FLU-FLU — an arrow with untrimmed feathers which restricts the distance it will travel; used to shoot aerial targets such as game birds.

FOLLOW THROUGH — movement of the drawing hand and arm after the release of the string.

FOOT MARKERS — lines or devices to indicate where the archer wishes to place his feet at the shooting line.

FREE STYLE — a method of shooting using a bow sight to aid the archer in aiming.

FREEZE — v. to be unable to move the bow to the desired position while at full draw and aiming or releasing the bow string smoothly.

FULL DRAW — the position of the archer when the bow string has been drawn and the draw hand is at the anchor point.

GAP — n. the vertical space an archer sees between the tip of his arrow and the target, used in barebow shooting.

GAME — n. a designated set of ends in a round that allow the round to be evenly divided; outdoors each distance shot usually constitutes a game.

GLOVE — n. three leather fingers that are held on the drawing hand by a strap around the wrist, used for protection of the drawing fingers.

GRAIN — n. the smallest unit of weight in the United States; one ounce equals 437 grains.

GRIP — v. to hold the bow, used in reference to holding the bow too tightly.

GROUND QUIVER — a device, usually metal, that is stuck into the ground and holds the arrows and/or bow.

GROUP — v. to shoot arrows in a pattern; n. the pattern of the arrows in the target.

GUNBARREL — n. a method of aiming used in barebow shooting in which the nock end of the arrow on the string is placed close to the eye and the archer sights down the arrow shaft.

HANDLE RISER — the thick mid-section of the bow.

HEEL — v. to exert pressure with the heel of the hand on the lower part of the handle during the shot.

HELICAL CLAMP — a curved clamp used for fletching arrows.

HELICAL FLETCHING — a fletching applied with a helical clamp in a fletching jig.

HIGH ANCHOR — an anchor where the drawing hand touches the cheek when at full draw.

INDEX FLETCHING — the feather or vane set at right angles to the slot in the arrow nock.

INSTINCTIVE — adj. a method of shooting in which no aiming method is used, where the archer looks at the target and shoots; sometimes erroneously used to include all barebow archers.

JIG — n. name given to devices used for fletching arrows and making strings.

KISSER BUTTON — an indicator or protrusion placed on the bow string so it touches the lips or teeth while the archer is at full draw; usually made of plastic.

LADY PARAMOUNT — the lady in charge of a tournament or the women's line in a large tournament.

LAMINATED BOW — a bow made of several layers of different material glued together, usually two layers of fiberglass and a hardwood core.

LET DOWN — returning from full draw to the undrawn position with control and not releasing the bow string.

LEVEL — n. a small glass vial filled with fluid, but leaving one bubble of air; used to determine if the bow is being held vertically.

LIMB — n. the upper or lower part of the bow that bends when the bow string is drawn back; the part of the bow where the energy is stored.

LOOP — the woven or served eyes at the ends of the bow string that fit into the notches when the bow is strung.

LOW ANCHOR — an anchor position where the drawing hand is under the jaw bone.

MASS WEIGHT — the weight of any piece of equipment if placed on a scale; usually used in reference to the bow.

MAT — n. the circular disk of straw to which the target face is attached.

NATURAL STANCE — the position of the feet on the shooting line that allows the archer to come to full draw and aim without moving the bow horizontally to reach the bullseye.

NOCK — v. to place an arrow on the string; n. the attachment to the rear end of an arrow which is placed on the bow string and holds the arrow on the string.

NOCK LOCATOR — the mark or device that indicates where the arrow is to be nocked on the string.

NOCKING HEIGHT — the distance on the string from the ninety-degree angle, formed by a straight line from the arrow rest to the string, perpendicular to the string, to the bottom of the nock.

NOCKING POINT — the area of the string covered by the nock.

NOTCH — n. the groove or ridge that holds the bow string when the bow is strung.

OFFSET FLETCH — a fletching applied at an angle to the arrow shaft with a straight clamp.

OPEN STANCE — the position of the feet on the shooting line where the left foot is behind an imaginary line extending between the archer's right foot and the center of the target.

OVERDRAW — v. drawing the arrowhead back past the front of the bow; draw into the bow; n. amount of arrow length reduced from regular arrow when used with overdraw device.

OVERDRAW DEVICE — n. a shelf attached to the bow riser extending back toward the archer and permitting a shorter, stiffer arrow to be shot from the bow.

PEEK — v. to move the head or bow arm to watch the arrow either in flight or where it hits the target; considered a bad habit.

PEEP — n. see String Peep.

PETTICOAT — n. the non-scoring area of the target.

PINCH — v. to squeeze the index and middle finger against the nock of the arrow during the draw and/or hold.

PIVOT POINT — the point on the face side of the bow handle which is farthest from the string when the bow is strung.

POSTURE GRID — a device having a series of vertical and horizontal lines for the evaluation of posture deviations.

PLUCK — v. to pull the string out and away from the anchor position as the string is released.

POINT — n. metal tip of the arrow.

POINT-OF-AIM — 1. a method of aiming in which the point of the arrow is sighted on an object, usually on the ground, to allow the arrow to hit the target; 2. the object that is placed on the ground when using the point-of-aim method.

PRESSURE POINT — the spot on the arrow plate against which the arrow lies and presses when the string is released; can be cushioned or spring-loaded.

QUIVER — n. a device used to hold arrows.

RANGE — n. a place for shooting.

RANGE STICK — a stick used for finding the aiming spot at different distances when using the point-of-aim method.

REBOUND — an arrow that bounces off the scoring area of the target face.

RECURVE — n. the end of the bow limb that bends away from the archer when the bow is held in the shooting position.

RECURVE BOW — a bow that has recurves.

REFLEX BOW — a bow whose limbs, when unstrung, point in a straight line away from the face side of the bow starting at the handle.

RELEASE — v. to allow the string to leave the fingers.

RISER — see Handle Riser.

ROUND — n. the shooting of a definite number of arrows at specified target faces from set distances.

ROVING — n. an archery game of shooting at natural targets in fields and woodlands.

SEMI-RECURVE BOW — a bow that is neither straight nor fully recurve.

SERVING — n. the wrapping of thread around the loops and center of the bow string to protect it from wear.

SHAFT — n. the arrow, excluding the point, nock and fletching.

SHAFT SIZE — a number given to a particular arrow size to allow ease in selection and use.

SHELF — see Arrow Shelf.

SHOOTING LINE — the line from which the archer shoots.

SIDE QUIVER — a quiver which is fastened to the archer's belt and hangs at his side.

SIGHT — n. see Bow Sight.

SIGHT BAR — the piece of the bow sight to which the sight block is attached.

SIGHT BLOCK — the movable portion of the bow sight which holds the sight pin.

SIGHT PIN — the part of the bow sight that is superimposed on the center of the target when the archer aims.

SIGHT WINDOW — the cut-out section of the bow above the handle.

SKIRT — n. the cloth extension which holds a target face to a circular mat by covering the outside edge.

SLING — n. a strap fastened to either the bow or the archer's bow hand that keeps the bow from falling after the release; used if the archer shoots with a relaxed bow hand. See Finger Sling and Wrist Sling.

SNAKE — v. the way an arrow buries itself under the grass.

SNAP SHOOTING — shooting without pausing to aim carefully.

SPINE — n. 1. the stiffness or amount an arrow bends, determined by hanging a 2# weight from the center of the arrow and measuring the bend; 2. the part of a feather or vane that is in contact with the arrow when fletched.

SPIRAL FLETCH — see Offset Fletch.

SPRING-LOADED PRESSURE POINT — a pressure point containing an adjustable spring.

SQUARE STANCE — the position of the feet in which an imaginary straight line would touch the toes of both feet and extend to the center of the target.

STABILITY — n. the ability of the bow, in its design, to perform consistently.

STABILIZER — n. 1. a piece consisting of a weight which is extended some distance from the bow by a relatively lighter rod, mounted on the handle riser, usually extending either forward or backward; 2. any weight attached to the handle riser to minimize torque.

STACK — n. a characteristic of bow performance that shows an increasing rate of change for each increment of draw weight, generally considered undesirable for shooting comfort.

STANCE — n. the position of the feet, usually in reference to their relation to the target.

STRAIGHT BOW — a bow that is neither recurve nor reflex; when unstrung the bow is straight.

STRING ALIGNMENT — the placement of the string when at full draw in relation to either the bow sight or the bow.

STRING — n. a cord used to shoot a bow; see Bow String; v. to place the string in the proper position for shooting.

STRINGER — n. a device to aid in stringing the bow.

STRING HAND — see Drawing Hand.

STRING HEIGHT — the distance from the pivot point to the string of the bow when it is strung.

STRING NOTCH — see Notch.

STRING PEEP — a piece inserted between the strands of the bow string at eye level through which the archer looks while aiming.

STRING SERVING — see Serving.

TAB — see Finger Tab.

TACKLE — an inclusive term for archery equipment.

TAKE-DOWN BOW — term used in referring to a bow which can be taken apart for convenience of storage or travel.

TARGET CAPTAIN — the person who decides who is to call the evaluation of each arrow, record the scores and draw the arrows from the target.

TARGET FACE — n. the piece which is attached to the mat and indicates the scoring area.

TARGET MAT — see Mat.

TILLER — v. to shape the limbs of an unfinished bow.

TIP — see Point.

TOE MARKERS — see Foot Markers.

TORQUE — n. an undesirable twisting of the bow by the bow hand, or of the bow string by the string hand.

TOXOPHILITE — n. a lover of the bow; archer.

TRAINING ARM GUARD — an arm guard which covers the elbow as well as the forearm of the bow arm.

TUNE — v. to adjust the arrow rest, pressure point, string height and nocking height to achieve good arrow flight.

VANE — n. a type of fletching, other than feather, usually those made of plastic.

WEIGHT — n. see Draw Weight.

WINDAGE — n. the left-right adjustment of the bow sight or the pin on the bow sight.

WORKING RECURVE — the recurved portion of the bow limb that straightens to some degree as the bow string is drawn.

WRIST SLING — a sling that attaches to or encircles the bow and passes over the bow hand and/or wrist; see Sling.

YARN TASSEL — a large tuft of yarn that is used to clean mud, dirt, et cetera, from arrows.

MANUFACTURER'S DIRECTORY

BOW MANUFACTURERS

Alpine Archery, Inc.
P.O. Box 319
Lewiston, ID 83501

Astro Bows, Inc.
3257 George St.
La Crosse, WI 54603

Barnett International, Inc.
1967 Gunn Highway
P.O. Box 934
Odessa, FL 33556

Bear/Jennings Archery, Inc.
4600 S.W. 41st Blvd.
Gainesville, FL 32601

Black Widow Bow Co.
HCR 1, Box 357-1
Highlandville, MO 65669

Bows By Groves
116 Veranda N.W.
Albuquerque, NM 87107

Jim Brackenbury
8326 S.E. 252nd Ave.
Gresham, OR 97080

Browning
Rt. 1
Morgan, UT 84050

J.K. Chastain
490 S. Queen St.
Lakewood, CO 80226

Darton Archery
3261 Flushing Rd.
Flint, MI 48504

Fedora Archery
Box 151, Rt. 1
Richland, PA 17087

Golden Circle Sports
Box 400
Kooskia, ID 83539

Golden Eagle Archery
111 Corporate Dr.
Farmington, NY 14425

High Country Archery
P.O. Box 935
Lewiston, ID 83501

Howard Hill Archery
248 Canyon Creek Rd.
Hamilton, MT 59840

Jerry Hill Longbow Co.
231 McGowan Rd.
Wilsonville, AL 35186

Hoyt USA
475 N. Neil Armstrong Dr.
Salt Lake City, UT 84116

Indian Industries, Inc.
817 Maxwell Ave.
Evansville, IN 47711

Martin Archery, Inc.
Rt. 5, Box 127
Walla Walla, WA 99362

McPherson Archery, Inc.
RR 4, Box 12
Austin, MN 55912

Oneida Labs, Inc.
235 Cortland Ave.
Syracuse, NY 13202

Oregon Bow Company
250 E. 10th Ave.
Junction City, OR 97448

Dick Palmer Archery
824 N. College Ave.
P.O. Box 1632
Fayetteville, AR 72701

Ben Pearson, Inc.
P.O. Box 7465
Pine Bluff, AR 71611

Precision Shooting Equipment, Inc.
P.O. Box 5487
Tucson, AZ 85703

Premier Archery Corp.
P.O. Box 132
Ocono Falls, WI 54154

Pro Line Co.
1675 Gun Lake Rd.
Hastings, MI 49058

Quillian's Archery Traditions
483 W. Cloverhurst Ave.
Athens, GA 30606

Rancho Safari
P.O. Box 691
Ramona, CA 92065

Robin Hood Archery
P.O. Box 806
Fort Smith, AR 72902

Sierra/SeaStar International
P.O. Box 806
Fort Smith, AR 72902

Suretrak
P.O. Box 336
Rexburg, ID 83440

Total Shooting Systems, Inc.
390 W. Rolling Meadows Dr.
Fon Du Lac, WI 54935

York Archery
P.O. Box 110
Independence, MO 64051

ARROW AND ARROW SUPPLIES

Acme Wood Products
P.O. Box 636
Myrtle Point, OR 97458

Aero Trak
P.O. Box 82158
Portland, OR 97202

AFC, Inc.
Hwy. 52 S.
Chatfield, MN 55923

Anderson Archery
P.O. Box 130
Grand Ledge, MI 48837

Archers-Ammo, Inc.
P.O. Box 821
Issaquah, WA 98027

Archery Center International (ACI)
15610 S. Telegraph Rd.
P.O. Box A
Monroe, MI 48161

Arizona Archery
P.O. Box 25387
2781 N. Valley View Dr.
Prescott Valley, AZ 86312

Arrow Tech, Inc.
8905 Glen Lake Dr.
Austin, TX 78730

Aviatube-Pechinez
500 Plaza Dr.
Secaucus, NJ 07096

Barrie Archery
2 Knoll Drive
Waseca, MN 56093

Beman Archery Corp.
3065 North Rockwell St.
Chicago, IL 60618

Bi-Delta Archery
25 Dempster
Buffalo, NY 14206

Bohning Col Ltd.
7361 N. Seven Mile Rd.
Lake City, MI 49651

Custom Archery Equipment, Inc.
21529 Menlo Ave.
Torrance, CA 90502

Jim Dougherty Archery
4418 S. Mingo Rd.
Tulsa, OK 74146

Easton Aluminum, Inc.
5040 W. Harold Gatty Dr.
Salt Lake City, UT 84116

Forestline International Corp.
775 Rt. 82
Hopewell Junction, NY 12533

F/S Discount Arrows
P.O. Box 8094
Fountain Valley, CA 92708

Godfrey Enterprises
1000 Goodlander Circle
Selah, WA 98942

Magnus Archery
P.O. Box 144
Otis, KS 67565

Mar-Den Co.
RR 1, Box 744A
Willcox, AZ 85643

O.H. Mullen Sales
Rt. 2
Oakwood, OH 45873

Muzzy Products Corp.
3705 S.W. 42nd Pl.
Gainesville, FL 32608

Nirk Archery Col
Rt. 1, Box 80
Potlatch, ID 83855

North Star Archery Products, Inc.
527 Elizabeth Ave.
Grand Rapids, MN 55744

Satellite Archery
1111 Corporate Dr.
Farmington, NY 14425

True Flight Arrow Co., Inc.
RR 5, Box 746
Monticello, IN 47960

WASP Archery Prod., Inc.
9 W. Main St.
Plymouth, CT 06782

L.C. Whiffen
923 S. 16th St.
Milwaukee, WI 53204

Whitetail Disguise
P.O. Box 22187
Chattanooga, TN 37421

Zwickey Archery, Inc.
2571 E. 12th Ave.
St. Paul, MN 55109

ARCHERY ACCESSORIES

Accra 300
805 S. 11th Ave.
Broken Arrow, OK 74012

Chuck Adams Bowhunting Co.
Box 228
Stevensville, MT 59870

Adventures in the Wild
3168 S. 108th E. Ave.
Tulsa, OK 74146

Aimpoint
203 Elder St.
Herndon, VA 22070

Allen Co., Inc.
525 Burbank St.
Broomfield, CO 80020

Bob Allen Co.
Box 477
Des Moines, IA 50302

All Rite Products, Inc.
1001 W. Cedar Knolls S.
Cedar City, UT 84720

Americase
Box 271
Waxahachie, TX 75165

Ames Industries
3631 Interlake Ave. N.
Seattle, WA 98103

AMS, Inc.
411 W. Highway 29
Abbotsford, WI 54405

Archer's Advantage, Inc.
Box 7134
Marietta, GA 30065

Archery Center International (ACI)
15610 S. Telegraph Rd.
P.O. Box A
Monroe, MI 48161

Arizona Optical Case Co.
1015 S. 23rd St.
Phoenix, AZ 85034

Arizona Rim Country Products, Inc.
1035 S. Vineyard
Mesa, AZ 85210

Arrowzona Products Mfg., Inc.
P.O. Box 50551
Tucson, AZ 85703

Autumn Tracker Design, Inc.
Box 658
Floodwood, MN 55736

Bagmaster Mfg., Inc.
3014 N. Lindbergh St.
St. Louis, MO 63074

E.W. Bateman & Co.
Box 751
Fischer, TX 78623

Benders No-Glov
Rt. 2, Box 609
Stoddard, WI 54658

B-K Archery Products, Inc.
P.O. Box 531
Mason, WV 25260

Black Sheep Brand
#220 W. Gentry Parkway
Tyler, TX 75702

Bowhunters Discount Wrhse, Inc.
Box 158, Zeigler Rd.
Wellsville, PA 17365

Bowhunters Supply, Inc.
1158 46th St.
P.O. Box 5010
Vienna, WV 26105-0010

Boyt Sporting Goods, Inc.
P.O. Drawer 668
Iowa Falls, IA 50126

BPE, Inc.
Rt. 3, Box 92
Emporia, KS 66801

Brauer Brothers Mfg. Co.
2020 Delmar Blvd.
St. Louis, MO 63103

Brownell & Company
P.O. Box 362
Moodus, CT 06469

Brunsport, Inc.
Box 65
Aurora, IL 60507

BSI
Box 5010
Vienna, WV 26105

B-Square Co.
Box 11281
Fort Worth, TX 76110

Buckey Sports Supply
2655 Harrison Ave. S.W
Canton, OH 44706

Bushmaster Cases
451 Alliance Ave.
Toronto, Ontario M6N 2J1
CANADA

Chek-it Products
Onalaska, WI 54650

Corbra Mfg. Co., Inc.
P.O. Box 667
Bixby, OK 74008

Custom Chrono
5305 Reese Hill Rd.
Sumas, WA 98295

Deerslayer Gloves
Box 260
Chillicothe, MO 64601

Delta Industries, Inc.
117 E. Kenwood St.
Reinbeck, IA 50069

Desert Archery
1437 W. Hilton Ave.
Phoenix, AZ 85007

Diamond Machining Technology
85 Hayes Memorial Dr.
Marlborough, MA 01752

Doskocil Mfg. Co.
P.O. Box 1246
Arlington, TX 76010

Jim Dougherty Archery, Inc.
4418 S. Mingo Rd.
Tulsa, OK 74146

Emerging Technologies, Inc.
Box 581
Little Rock, AR 72203

C.W. Erickson's Mfg.
Rt. 6, Box 202
Buffalo, MN 55313

Fast Fletch Archery
#92 Rt. 6
Columbia, CT 06237

Ferguson Adventure Archery
Hwy. 36 W.
Hartselle, AL 35640

Fieldline
533 S. Los Angeles St.
Los Angeles, CA 90013

Fine-Line, Inc.
11220 164th St. E.
Puyallup, WA 98374

Flex-Fetch Products
1840 Chandler Ave.
St. Paul, MN 55113

Foam Design
444 Transport Ct.
Lexington, KY 40581

Freeman's Animal Targets
111 S. Griswold Rd.
Indianapolis, IN 46234

Full Adjust Archery
2195A Old Philadelphia Pike
Lancaster, PA 17602

Game Tracker, Inc.
3476 Eastman Dr.
Flushing, MI 48433

Golden Key-Futura
14090-6100 Rd.
Montrose, CO 81401

Gordon Plastics, Inc.
2872 S. Santa Fe Ave.
San Marcos, CA 92069

Gorman's Design
P.O. Box 21102
Minneapolis, MN 55421

Granpa Specialty Co.
3304 Woodson Rd.
St. Louis, MO 63114

Grayling Outdoor Products, Inc.
P.O. Box 192
Grayling, MI 49738

Gun-Ho Sports Cases
110 E. 10th St.
St. Paul, MN 55101

Hasmer Sales Co.
24550 Rosewood
Oak Park, MI 48237

Hawkeye Distributor
822 First Ave.
North Escanaba, MI 49829

HHA Sports, Inc.
6210 Wintergreen Dr.
White Rapids, WI 54494

Hilsport by Hilco, Inc.
2102 Fair Park Blvd.
Harlingen, TX 78550

Stanley Hips Targets
17585 Blanco Rd.
San Antonio, TX 78232

Hoppe's
Airport Industrial Mall
Coatesville, PA 19320

Horne Archery Mfg.
P.O. Box 1616
Pascagoola, MS 39567

Impact Industries, Inc.
333 Plumer St.
Wausau, WI 54401

Inventive Technology
120 W. 330 S.
American Fork, UT 84003

Kalispel Case Line
P.O. Box 267
Cusick, WA 99119

Kapul, Inc.
P.O. Box 9018
Trenton, NJ 08650

Keller Mfg.
5628 Wrightsboro Rd.
Grovetown, GA 30813

King Archer Archery Products
Rt. 1, Box 895
North Wilkesboro, NC 28659

Kinsey's Archery Products, Inc.
1660 Steel Way Dr.
Mount Joy, PA 17552

Klasic Kase Products
9727-D Business Park Dr.
Sacramento, CA 95827

KLP Mfg.
278 Calvin Ave.
Holland, MI 49423

Kolpin Mfg., Inc.
123 S. Pearl St.
Berlin, WI 54923

Kwikee Kwiver
P.O. Box 130
Acme, MI 49610

Lakewood Products, Inc.
627 Coon St.
Rhinelander, WI 54501

Leals' Archery Sights
62 Liberty St.
E. Taunton, MA 02718

Lewis & Lewis Corp.
1013 Co. Hwy. AA
Nekoosa, WI 54457

L.W. Lyons
1122 De Witt Ave.
Niles, MI 49120

Maple Leaf Press
1215 Beach Tree St.
Grand Haven, MI 49417

Mason Mfg. Co.
4115 Silverleaf Cove
Memphis, TN 38115

McKenzie Supply
P.O. Box 480
Granite Quarry, NC 28072

MTM Molded Products
3370 Obco Ct.
Dayton, OH 45414

Neet Products, Inc.
Rt. 2
Sedalia, MO 65301

New Archery Products Corp.
6415 Stanley Ave.
Berwyn, IL 60402

Norman Archery Wholesale
132 N. Santa Fe
Norman, OK 73069

Northeast Products
3 Thompson St.
P.O. Box 8
Methuen, MA 01844

Okie Mfg., Inc.
Rt. 1, Box 155
Hendrix, OK 74741

"Ole" Norms
P.O. Box 966
Clemson, SC 29631

Ole Whiskers, Inc.
43 Rd. 3523
Flora Vista, NM 87415

Original Brite-Site
34 Kentwood Rd.
Succasunna, NJ 07876

Pape's Archery, Inc.
9115 Minors Lane
Louisville, KY 40219

Penguin Industries
Airport Industrial Mall
Coatesville, PA 19320

Pilgrim Archery Products
3706 Clear Falls Dr.
Kingwood, TX 77339

Potawatomi Products
16931 W. 6th Rd.
Plymouth, IN 46563

PP&S Archery Targets
P.O. Box 375
Raceland, LA 70394

Pride Plastics
575 Glaspie
Oxford, MI 48051

Pro Release
P.O. Box 609
Utica, MI 48087

Quality Shop
Box 291
Dana Point, CA 92629

Quillian's Archery Traditions
Outdoor Edge Cutlery
2888 Bluff St., Ste. 130
Boulder, CO 80301

Range-O-Matic Archery
35572 Strathcona Dr.
Mt. Clemens, MI 48043

Ranging, Inc.
Rtes. 5 & 20
East Bloomfield, NY 14443

Razor Edge Systems, Inc.
P.O. Box 150
Ely, MN 55731

Ridgewood Group
8909 19th St. W.
Rock Island, IL 61201

Sagittarius
9030 Carroll Way #5
San Diego, CA 92121

Sapona Archery Supply, Inc.
Rt. 2, Box 481
N. Wilkesboro, SC 28659

Saunders Archery Co.
Box 476
Columbus, NE 68601

Sight Master Bowsight
293 Hwy 12 East
Townsend MT 59644

Smith Whetstone Company
1500 Sleepy Valley Rd.
Hot Springs, AR 71901

Southern Archery
P.O. Box 204
Louisville, MS 39339

Stuart Products, Inc.
P.O. Box 1587
Easley, SC 29641

Suretrak
P.O. Box 336
Rexburg, ID 83440

Target Systems
315 W. Sherman St.
Lebanon, OR 97355

Timberline Archery Products
P.O. Box 333
Lewiston, ID 83501

Timberline Targets
P.O. Box 667
Williston, ND 58802

Tink's Safariland Corp.
Box 244
Madison, GA 30650

Toxonics
796 Hoff Rd.
O'Fallon, MO 63366

Trautman's Outdoor Creations
2082 S. First
Hamilton, MT 59840

Trophy Glove Co.
Box 668
Albia, IA 52531

Tru-Fire Corp.
7355 State St.
N. Fond du Lac, WI 54935

Tundra Targets
Box 683
Brandon, Manitoba R7A 5Z7
CANADA

Western Recreation, Inc.
3505 E. 39th Ave.
Denver, CO 80205

Whitewater Glove Co.
216 Main St.
Hingham, WI 53031

Winn Archery
13757 64th St.
South Haven, MI 49090

Wyandotte Leather
1811 6th St.
Wyandotte, MI 48192

Ziegal Engineering
2108 Lomina Ave.
Long Beach, CA 90815

TREE STANDS AND BLINDS

Action Products Co.
Box 100
Odessa, MO 64076

A&J Products
3560 Karen Ct.
Hart, MI 49420

Amacker Tree Stands
1212 Main St.
Delhi, LA 71232

Apache Products
2208 Mallory Pl.
Monroe, LA 71201

A.P.I. Outdoors, Inc.
602 Kimbrough Dr.
Tallulah, LA 71282

Basse Deer Blynds
3410 Belgium Ln.
San Antonio, TX 78219

Brell Mar Products
5701 Hwy 80 W.
Jackson, MS 39209

Camouflage Systems, Inc.
Box 1133
Thermopolis, WY 82443

Centaur Archery, Inc.
45 Hollinger Crescent, Unit 1
Kitchener, Ontario N2K 2Z1
CANADA

Deer Me Products
1208 Park St.
Anoka, MN 55303

Deerhunter Tree Stands
Box 1397D
Hickory, NC 28602

East Enterprises, Inc.
2208 Mallory Pl.
Monroe, LA 71201

Evans Sports
Hwy. 63 & B
Houston, MO 65483

Forrester Outdoor Products
3495 Marion Ct.
Buford, GA 30518

LOC-ON Company
1510 Holbrook St.
Greensboro, NC 27403

Loggy Bayou, Inc.
1615 Barton Dr.
Shreveport, LA 71107

Lone Wolf, Inc.
3314 E. Grange Ave.
Cudahy, WI 53110

Ocmulgee Sales
Box 127
Eastman, GA 31023

Pack-A-Stand Mfg.
14920 Butternut St. N.W.
Anoka, MN 55304

Seat-A-Tree, Inc.
25450 Ryan Rd.
Warren, MI 48091

Silent Stalker, Inc.
RR 5, 4500 Rt. E.
Columbia, MO 65202

Sport Climbers, Inc.
2926 75th St.
Kenosha, WI 53140

Summit Specialties, Inc.
P.O. Box 786
Decatur, AL 35602

Thomas Tree Stand Co.
905 East St.
Texarkana, AR 75502

Trailhawk Treestands
108 Clinton St.
La Crosse, WI 54603

Warren & Sweat Mfg. Co., Inc.
P.O. Box 440
Grand Island, FL 32735

SCENTS AND LURES

Advanced Hunting Products
Box 9335
Spokane, WA 99206

Buck Stop Lure Co., Inc.
3600 Grow Rd. N.W.
Stanton, MI 48888

Cover Up Products, Inc.
RR 1, Box 66
Hill City, KS 67642

Cross River
W2649 Hillcrest Ave.
Nekoosa, WI 54457

Deer Run Products, Inc.
261 Ridgeview Terrace
Goshen, NY 10924

D&H Products, Inc.
465 Denny Rd.
Valencia, PA 16059

Dr. O's Products, Ltd.
Box 111
Niverville, NY 12130

Foggy Mountain
Box 2009
Bangor, ME 04401

Glacier Valley Sporting Scents
210 W. Liberty St.
Evansville, WI 53536

Hunter's Specialties, Inc.
5285 Rockwell Dr. N.E.
Cedar Rapids, IA 52402

Johnson Labs, Inc.
Box 381
Troy, AL 36081

Milligan Brand
Rt. 14, Box 202E
Santa Fe, NM 87505

Outdoor Technologies
23179 Bear Run Rd.
Danville, OH 43014

Pete Rickard, Inc.
Rt. 1
Cobleskill, NY 12043

Robbins Scent, Inc.
Box 779
Connellsville, PA 15425

Robinson Laboratories
2833 15th Ave. S.
St. Paul, MN 55407

Tele Mark, Inc.
4020 Will Rogers Pkwy.
Suite 600
Oklahoma City, OK 73108

Tri-Lakes Outdoor Products
Box 1561
Kerrville, TX 78029

Ultimate Lures
Rt. 2, 9506 Hwy Y
Sauk City, WI 53583

Wildlife Research Center, Inc.
4345 157th Ave. N.W.
Anoka, MN 55304

Woodstream Corporation
Box 327
Lititz, PA 17543

HUNTING FOOTWEAR AND APPAREL

Ace Sprtswear, Inc.
700 Quality Rd.
Fayetteville, NC 28306

All Weather Outerwear Co., Inc.
1270 Broadway
New York, NY 10001

Avid Outdoor
1120 W. 149th St.
Olathe, KS 66061

B.C.B. International, Ltd.
Clydesmuir Rd.
Cardiff, CF2 2QS
GREAT BRITAIN

Bell Fatigue Co.
Box 14307
Augusta, GA 30919

Brigade Quartermasters, Ltd.
1025 Cobb International Blvd.
Kennesaw, GA 30144

Broner, Inc.
359 Robbins Dr.
Troy, MI 48083

Browning
Rt. 1
Morgan, UT 84050

Chippewa Shoe Co.
610 W. Daggett
Fort Worth, TX 76113

Clarkfield Enterprises, Inc.
1032 10th Ave.
Clarkfield, MN 56223

Classic Designs, Ltd.
Box 1064
Rockwall, TX 75087

Codet, Inc.
Box 440
Newport, VT 05855

Columbia Sportswear
6600 N. Baltimore St.
Portland, OR 97203

Commander Garment Co.
Box 659
Cambridge, MD 21613

Danner Shoe Co.
12722 N.E. Airport Way
Portland, OR 97230

Dunham Boot Co.
P.O. Box 813
Brattleboro, VT 05301

Duofold, Inc.
120 W. 45th St.
New York, NY 10036

Duxbak, Inc.
903 Woods Rd.
Cambridge, MD 21613

Empire Insulated Wear
114-120 Forrest St.
Brooklyn, NY 11206

Fabric Distributers, Inc.
1207 Boston Rd.
Greensboro, NC 27407

Famous Trails, Inc.
3804 Main St., Suite 1
Chula Vista, CA 92011

Fieldline
533 S. Los Angeles St.
Los Angeles, CA 90013

C.C. Filson Co.
Box 34020
Seattle, WA 98124

Bob Fratzke Winona Camo
625 Clarks Lane
Winona, MN 55987

Haas Outdoors, Inc.
200 E. Main
West Point, MS 39773

Herman Shoe Co.
1 Sound Shore Dr.
Greenwich, CT 06830

I.S.W.
Box 5492
Chico, CA 95927

Kamik Footwear
554 Montee de Liesse
Montreal, Quebec H4T 1P1
CANADA

Kaufman Footwear
410 King St. W.
Kitchener, Ontario N2G 4J8
CANADA

LaCrosse Footwear, Inc.
P.O. Box 1328
La Crosse, WI 54602

Melton Shirt Co., Inc.
56 Harvester Ave.
Batavia, NY 14020

National Dye Works
Rt. 1, Box 3
Lynchburg, SC 29080

Pendleton Woolen Mills
218 S.W. Jefferson St.
Portland, OR 97201

Predator Marketing, Inc.
Box 727
Sergeant Bluff, IA 51054

Quiet Wear
Box 563
Milwaukee, WI 53201

Ranger Mfg. Co., Inc.
P.O. Box 14069
Augusta, GA 30919-0069

Red Ball, Inc.
100 Factory Ct.
Nashua, NH 03060

Red Head Corp.
P.O. Box 7100
Springfield, MO 65801

Red Wing Shoe Co.
314 Main St.
Red Wing, MN 55066

Rocky Boots
45 Canal St.
Nelsonville, OH 45764

Skyline Camo
184 Ellicott Rd.
West Falls, NY 14170

Spartan-RealTree
1390 Box Circle
Columbus, GA 31907

10X
2915 LBJ Freeway, Ste. 133
Dallas, TX 75234

Tempo Glove Mfg.
3820 W. Wisconsin Ave.
Milwaukee, WI 53208

Timberland Co.
Box 5050
Hampton, NH 03842

Trebark Camouflage
3434 Buck Mountain Rd.
Roanoke, VA 24014

Vasque Hiking Boots
314 Main St.
Red Wing, MN 55066

Walls Industries
P.O. Box 98
Cleburne, TX 76033

Woolverine Boots
Courtland Dr.
Rockford, MI 49351

Woolrich
Mill St.
Woolrich, PA 17779

HUNTING KNIVES AND ACCESSORIES

Adventure Supply
1227 N. 2nd St.
El Cajon, CA 92021

Al Mar Knives
P.O. Box 1626
5755 S.W. Jean Rd.
Suite 101
Lake Oswego, OR 97034

Anza Knives
P.O. Box 710806
Santee, CA 92072-0806

Atlanta Cutlery Corp.
Box 839
Conyers, GA 30207

Ballard Cutlery
1495 Brummel Ave.
Elk Grove, IL 60007

Benchmade Knives
15875-G S.E. 114th St.
Clackamas, OR 97015

Beretta USA
17601 Indian Head Hwy.
Accokeek, MD 20607

Bianchi International
100 Calle Cortez
Temecula, CA 92390

Blackjack Knives, Catoctin
P.O. Box 188
Smithsburg, MD 21783

Boker USA
14818 W. 6th Ave., No. 17A
Golden, CO 80401-5045

Browning
Rt. 1
Morgan, UT 84050

Brunton/Lakota
620 E. Monroe
Riverton, WY 82501

Buck Knives
Box 1267
El Cajon, CA 92022

Camillus Cutlery
54 Main St.
Camillus, NY 13031

W.R. Case & Sons
P.O. Box 22668
Knoville, TN 37422-2668

U.S. Cavalry
2855 Centennial Ave.
Radcliff, KY 40160-9000

Charter Arms Corp.
430 Sniffens Ln.
Stratford, CT 06497

Cold Steel, Inc.
2128 Knoll Dr., Unit D
Ventura, CA 93003

Cole Consumer Products
5777 Grant Ave.
Cleveland, OH 44105

Colonial Knife Co.
P.O. Box 3327
Providence, RI 02909-0327

Colorado Ceramic Abrasives
1988 Fallen Rock Rd.
Conifer, CO 80433

Damascus USA
Rt. 3, Box 39A, Wildcat Rd.
Edenton, NC 27932

Degen Knives
1830 S. Robertson Blvd.
Los Angeles, CA 90035

DMT
Hayes Memorial Dr.
Marlborough, MA 01752-1892

Ek Commando Knife Co.
Box 6454
Richmond, VA 23230

Eze-Lap Diamond Sharpeners
Box 2229
Westminster, CA 92683

Fine-Line
11220 164th St. N.E.
Puyallup, WA 98374

Fiskars
P.O. Box 8027
Wausau, WI 54402-9027

Frsot Cutlery
P.O. Box 21353
Chattanooga, TN 37421

Fulcraft Knives
P.O. Box 177
Memphis, TN 38101

Gerber Legendary Blades
P.O. Box 8027
Wausau, WI 54402-8027

Grayling Outdoor Products
P.O. Box 192
Grayling, MI 49738

Gutmann Cutlery
120 S. Columbus Ave.
Mt. Vernon, NY 10553

Hansen & Co.
244-246 Old Post Rd.
Southport, CT 06490

House of Muzzleloading
1019 E. Palmer
Glendale, CA 91205

Imperial Knife Co.
1776 Broadway
New York, NY 10019

Iron Mountain
P.O. Box 2146
Sparks, NV 89423

Ka-Bar Cutlery
5777 Grant Ave.
Cleveland, OH 44105

Ken's Finn Knives
P.O. Box 126
Republic, MI 49879

Kershaw Knives
25300 S.W. Parkway
Wilsonville, OR 97070

Lansky Sharpeners
The Lansky Protection Co, Inc.
P.O. Box 800
Buffalo, NY 14221

Loray, Inc.
16740 Indian Hollow
Grafton, OH 44044

Marksman Products
5622 Engineer Dr.
Huntington Beach, CA 92649

Matthews Co.
4401 Sentry Dr.
Tucker, GA 30084

Mountain Forge Corp.
P.O. Box 1354
Cleveland, GA 30528

The Muller Co.
12460 E. Los Reales Rd.
Tucson, AZ 85747

Normark Corp.
1710 E. 78th St.
Minneapolis, MN 55423

Norton Co.
Worcester, MA 01616-2698

Olsen Knife Co.
Howard City, MI 49329

Outdoor Edge
2888 Bluff St.
Boulder, CO 80301

Precise International
3 Chestnut St.
Suffern, NY 10901

Precision Sports
P.O. Box 30-06
Ithaca, NY 14850

Queen Cutlery Co.
P.O. Box 367
Titusville, PA 16354

Chris Reeve
6147 Corporal Ln.
Boise, ID 83704

Remington Arms
1007 Market St.
Wilmington, DE 19898

A.G. Russell Co.
1705 Highway 71 N.
Springdale, AR 72764

Schrade Cutlery
99 Madison Ave.
New York, NY 10016

Bob Schrimsher's Knifemakers Supply
P.O. Box 308
Emory, TX 75440

Smith Whetstone
1500 Sleepy Valley Rd.
Hot Springs, AR 71901

SOG Specialties
P.O. Box 1024
Edmonds, WA 98020

Sport Blades
447 E. Gardena Blvd.
Gardena, CA 90248

Spyderco
P.O. Box 800
Golden, CO 80402

Taylor Cutlery
P.O. Box 1638
Kingsport, TN 37662

Timberwolf Cutlery
P.O. Box 757
Clenton, AL 35045

Tru-Balance Knife Co.
2155 Tremont Blvd. N.W.
Grand Rapids, MI 49504

United States Cutlery
P.O. Box 846
Shelton, CT 06484-0913

Victorinox
P.O. Box 846
Shelton, CT 06484-0913

Wenoka Cutlery
P.O. Box 8238
West Plam Beach, FL 33407

Westbury Sales Co.
373 Maple Ave
Westbury, NY 11590

Western Cutlery Corp.
1800 Pike Rd.
Longmont, CO 80501

Wyoming Knife Corp.
209-2 Commerce Dr.
Fort Collins, CO 80524

BINOCULARS AND SPOTTING SCOPES

Brunton USA
620 E. Monroe
Riverton, WY 82501

Bushnell
300 N. Lone Hill Ave.
San Dimas, CA 91773

Celestron International
2835 Columbia St.
Torrance, CA 90503

Jason Empire
9200 Cody
Overland Park, KS 66214

Leica USA, Inc.
156 Ludlow Ave.
Northvale, NJ 07647

Leupold & Stevens, Inc.
Box 688
Beaverton, OR 97005

Minolta Corp.
101 Williams Dr.
Ramsey, NJ 07446

Nikon, Inc.
623 Stewart Ave.
Garden City, NY 11530

Pentax Corp.
35 Inverness Dr. E.
Englewood, CO 80112

Redfield
5800 E. Jewell Ave.
Denver, CO 80224

Simmons Outdoor Corp.
14530 S.W. 119th Ave.
Miami, FL 33186

Steiner Binoculars
216 Haddon Ave.
Westmart, NJ 08108

Swarovski Optik
2 Slater Rd.
Cranston, RI 02920

Swift Instruments, Inc.
952 Dorchester Ave.
Boston, MA 02125

Tasco Sales, Inc.
7600 N.W. 26th St.
Miami, FL 33122